I0024279

GLOBAL PENTECOSTALISM IN THE 21ST CENTURY

GLOBAL
PENTECOSTALISM
in the 21st Century

Edited by Robert W. Hefner
Afterword by Peter L. Berger

Indiana University Press
Bloomington and Indianapolis

This book is a publication of

Indiana University Press
Office of Scholarly Publishing
Herman B Wells Library 350
1320 East 10th Street
Bloomington, Indiana 47405 USA

iupress.indiana.edu

Telephone orders   800-842-6796
Fax orders   812-855-7931

© 2013 by Indiana University Press

All rights reserved

No part of this book may be reproduced or utilized in any form or by any means, electronic or mechanical, including photocopying and recording, or by any information storage and retrieval system, without permission in writing from the publisher. The Association of American University Presses' Resolution on Permissions constitutes the only exception to this prohibition.

♾ The paper used in this publication meets the minimum requirements of the American National Standard for Information Sciences—Permanence of Paper for Printed Library Materials, ANSI Z39.48-1992.

Manufactured in the United States of America

Library of Congress Cataloging-in-Publication Data

Global Pentecostalism in the 21st century / edited by Robert W. Hefner; afterword by Peter L. Berger.
      pages   cm
   Includes bibliographical references and index.
   ISBN 978-0-253-01081-0 (cloth : alk. paper) — ISBN 978-0-253-01086-5 (pbk. : alk. paper) — ISBN 978-0-253-01094-0 (ebook) 1. Pentecostalism—History—21st century. 2. Christianity and culture—History—21st century. I. Hefner, Robert W., date, editor of compilation.
   BR1644.G56   2013
   270.8'3—dc23
                                         2013021517

1 2 3 4 5   18 17 16 15 14 13

CONTENTS

PREFACE

After its establishment by Peter L. Berger in 1985, one of the first research projects to which the Institute on Culture, Religion, and World Affairs (CURA) at Boston University turned was on the rise of Evangelical and Pentecostal Christianity in Latin America. The project was directed by one of CURA's earliest international partners, David Martin, a sociologist of religion at the London School of Economics and a leading scholar of modern religion and comparative Christianity. At the time, the secularization thesis reigned supreme in the social sciences, and many researchers were convinced that Evangelicalism and Pentecostalism were antimodern throwbacks destined to decline as societies became "modern." David Martin and Peter Berger were convinced that something more complex was afoot, and that, rather than being antimodern, Pentecostalism might yet prove itself an alternative avenue to modernity. Their views were to prove prescient.

Fresh from almost a decade of anthropological research on religious change in Indonesia, I joined CURA in 1986, the first year of the Martin project and four years after finishing my Ph.D. Anthropology was the one among the social sciences in which secularization theory had never been securely hegemonic. Nonetheless, many of my friends in the discipline looked with a mixture of skepticism and bewilderment at the CURA project, not because they thought Pentecostalism antimodern, but because in those years (quite unlike today, see chapter 1) most anthropologists found global Christianity inauthentic and uninteresting. Complicating matters further, some of my colleagues thought that, to the degree that Pentecostal and Evangelical varieties of Christianities were taking hold in the global south, it was primarily as a result of an unholy alliance between fundamentalist Christians and the United States government.

Although at first projects like the one David Martin conducted for CURA inspired collegial doubts, then, CURA continued over the years to sponsor projects on Evangelical and Pentecostal Christianity. In the mid-1980s, in the course of carrying out research on Islamization in East Java, Indonesia, I stumbled onto and studied a small network of Christian converts. Most were self-consciously Evangelical; in the 1990s, many split off to become Pentecostal, joining a wave of Pentecostal conversion sweeping across the minority margins of this Muslim-majority society, as well as portions of its Singaporean, Malaysian, and Philippine neighbors. CURA fellows continued their involvement with charismatic Christianity in other fields as well. In the late 1990s and early 2000s, CURA launched another project collaboration with Bernice and David Martin, who had now established themselves as pre-eminent figures in the sociology of Pentecostalism and Evangelicalism. In the 2000s, we worked with Ann Bernstein and the Centre for Development and Enterprise in Johannesburg to conduct two projects on Pentecostalism and socioeconomic change in West and southern Africa. From 2008 to 2012, and under the direction of Timothy Shah and James Wallace (both at the time Research Fellows at CURA), we sponsored a United States–based project, "The Emergence of a New Evangelical American Intelligentsia." From 2009–2012, Robert P. Weller, a senior CURA fellow and anthropologist at Boston University, organized a team of Chinese researchers to examine religious change in the lower Yangtze region, in which Pentecostalism figured centrally.

In the meantime and well beyond CURA's seminar rooms, interest in the growth of Pentecostalism across the global south soared from the mid-1990s onward. Once diffident toward the topic, anthropology developed a new and remarkable subfield known as the anthropology of Christianity, in which Pentecostalism figured prominently. Sociologists, students of comparative Christianity, and finally political scientists caught wind of the phenomenon as well, not least because its implications for global Christianity and demo-cratic citizenship remained largely unknown.

It was against this background that in November 2009 Peter Berger and I thought it might be intellectually interesting to bring together a few scholars with experience in Pentecostal studies as well as an interest in the broader question of religion and globalization, to stand back and assess the state of the field, from a slightly different perspective than that common in many studies. Our aim was not to add to the impressive body of literature on the causes of Pentecostal conversion, but to look more closely at what happens to Pentecostals once their numbers have grown and their commu-nities are sufficiently secure that they begin to confidently engage the insti-tutions and cultures of the larger society. In other words, we were interested in what happens as Pentecostals move from their earlier habits of protective "rupture" and moral separation toward engagement and civic integration. We were also interested in exploring the "developmental tensions" resulting from Pentecostal efforts to come to terms with three realities that, whether welcome or not, affect all religions and public ethical traditions in our late-modern age: capitalist markets; the state and its associated practices of citi-zenship; and the challenge of modern multicultural diversity (see chapter 1 for discussion of moral separation and developmental tensions). In short, our aim was to explore the Pentecostal experience of today and the near future.

With these ends in mind, we invited the scholars who went on to contribute to this book to a workshop at Boston University in June 2010. At the meeting, we discussed and refined our ideas on the project's aims and methods. After the conference, and with a set of shared concerns in mind, the participants headed off for different parts of the world, to conduct additional research and, after that, prepare a project report. The reports were presented at a conference at the CURA offices at Boston University in April 2011. In the months that followed the conference, we continued our discussion by email; we revised our papers in light of these discussions, ultimately creating the present book.

I want to take this opportunity to thank the participants in the project, and especially Peter L. Berger, David Martin, and Bernice Martin. A little known fact from his remarkable biography, Peter conducted research among immigrant Pentecostals in New York City in the 1950s. David and Bernice played pivotal roles in the shaping of the post-1960s sociology of religion and the 1980s creation of the sociology of global Christianity. Although the contributors to this volume come from a variety of disciplinary backgrounds and work in different world areas, all of us came to the project in inspired dialogue with Peter, David, and Bernice. This book is dedicated to the three of them.

ROBERT W. HEFNER
Director, Institute on Culture, Religion,
and World Affairs, Boston University

GLOBAL PENTECOSTALISM IN THE 21ST CENTURY

The Unexpected Modern—Gender, Piety, and Politics in the Global Pentecostal Surge

ROBERT W. HEFNER

It is by now a commonplace in sociology, anthropology, and comparative religious studies to observe that Pentecostalism is the fastest growing religious movement in the contemporary world. Over the past several years, demographers of religion have refined their estimates and concluded that the worldwide communion of Pentecostals and charismatic Christians may include as many as 500 or even 600 million people.[1] Even if only approximate, this figure bespeaks an extraordinary change in global Christianity. It means that more than one-fourth of the world's Christians are Pentecostal or charismatic;[2] among Christian denominations, Pentecostalism is second only to Roman Catholicism in its demographic girth; and Pentecostalism is the majority variant of Protestant Christianity professed in the global south. Confounding those who saw it as an antimodern throwback destined for the dustbin of history, Pentecostal Christianity has turned out to be one of the great religious globalizations of our age. Just why this is so, the changes Pentecostalism has undergone in the course of its worldwide expansion, and what further refiguring this faith tradition may experience as it steadies itself in the twenty-first century are the questions at the heart of this book.

The speed of Pentecostalism's spread appears all the more remarkable when one recalls in how short a period of time this Christian movement has achieved its global scale. Although the scholarly consensus today sees Pentecostalism and its charismatic cousins as having had multiple births rather than just one (at Los Angeles's Azusa Street revival in 1906, see below), the North American variety of Pentecostalism goes back no further than the first decade of the twentieth century. No less striking, the spike in Pentecostal numbers across the global south is even more recent: since the 1970s in Latin America, the 1980s in Africa, and the 1990s in China and Southeast Asia.

Of course demography can be an unsubtle measure of religious change, and its gauge is especially imprecise when the phenomenon in question is as theologically and sociologically multifarious as Pentecostalism. Should our estimates of Pentecostal growth include the illiterate women healers in rural China today who draw on indigenous traditions of spirit medium-ship as well as early twentieth-century Chinese Pentecostalism?[3] Should our 500 to 600 million include the African-Independent Churches (AICs) that, several generations back, declared their organizational independence from European overseers?[4] Or, to cite one last example, does Pentecostalism include the tens of millions of charismatic Catholics and Protestants, as well as a smaller number of Christian Orthodox, who otherwise identify with a mainline congregation (and are thus not "Pentecostal" in a denominational sense) but observe a faith marked by gifts of the Holy Spirit, including proph-ecy, spiritual healing, and speaking in tongues?[5]

There is as yet no scholarly consensus on just where to draw Pentecost-alism's borders, and there probably does not need to be, in any too-tidy sense. As observers as varied as Allan Anderson and Harvey Cox in Church studies, David and Bernice Martin in sociology, and Birgit Meyer and Joel Robbins in anthropology have all emphasized, it is more realistic to speak not of one but many Pentecostalisms. Because they are concerned primarily with the sociology and ideals of Pentecostalism's contemporary globalization rather than demarcating theological borders, the contributors to this volume iden-tify Pentecostalism in inclusive terms, ones closer to and revelatory of, we hope, the varied understandings and practices of local religious practitioners.

With this working ambition in mind, our characterization of Pentecost-alism begins broadly, with three of the faith movement's most conspicuous experiential characteristics. These are, first, an emphasis on the achieve-ment of a personalized and self-transforming relationship with Jesus Christ (being "born-again," an experience that Pentecostals share with many among their Evangelical cousins); second, ritual performance that highlights the ever-present power of the Holy Spirit ("baptism in the Holy Spirit," a practice given far greater emphasis in Pentecostalism and charismatic Christianity than in most other modern varieties of Christianity); and, third, religious enthusiasm centered on the experience of charismata ("gifts of the Holy Spirit"), including prophecy, exorcism, miraculous healing, and speaking in tongues (glossolalia). Put simply, Pentecostalism is an affectively expressive, effervescent Christianity that takes literally the wondrous miracles described in the New Testament's Acts of the Apostles (2:1–4), and proclaims their availability and importance for believers today.

Just what role these experiential characteristics have played in Pentecost-alism's global diffusion is, of course, another question, one that lies at the heart of the chapters in this book. Our primary concern in the essays that follow is with the recent growth of Pentecostalism, especially in the global south, where two-thirds of the world's Pentecostals now live. What qualities of religious organization and cultural idealization have facilitated this powerful religious globalization? What developmental tensions have marked its ascent or might curb its long-term growth?[6] Although dedicating some attention to the varied genealogies of Pentecostal conversion, the project at the core of this volume differs from previous studies in that it looks forward from initial conversion processes to today's world and Pentecostalism's future. In particular, we aim to examine what happens to Pentecostal idealism and social relations as the community grows, its members feel more secure, and they move from what Joel Robbins has vividly described as "rituals of rupture" and protective separation toward engagement with the institutions and values of the broader world. In the twenty-first century, as Pentecostal communities consolidate their numbers and integrate into surrounding societies, one especially important question will move to the fore: In what ways are Pentecostals engaging the three behemoth realities that so mark our age and so challenge all public religious traditions? The realities in question are late-modern capitalism; the modern state and citizenship; and the media, mobility, and postmodern plurality of our age. As the case studies in this book demonstrate, the Pentecostal engagement with these forces and circumstances provides insight into this Christian movement's remarkable past and its likely social futures.

North American Antecedents

North American histories of this Christian movement typically trace its roots back to the Azusa Street revival, which took place in south Los Angeles between 1906 and 1909. The revival was led by an African American minister by the name of William Joseph Seymour (1870–1922). Seymour's biography exemplifies the peripatetic restlessness and cultural hybridity still characteristic of much Pentecostalism, particularly that of the poor and uprooted in the global south.

A son of slave parents, Seymour spent 1905 in Topeka, Kansas, with a Euro-American Evangelical minister named Charles Fox Parham (1873–1929). A former Methodist pastor active in the Holiness movement,[7] Parham is credited with having formulated the basic tenets if not the full menu of ritual practices of what has come to be known as the first-wave or classical variant of North American Pentecostalism. Parham's theology linked an Evangelical emphasis on scriptural literalism and personal conversion with gifts of the Holy Spirit as evidenced in miraculous signs and wonders, including faith-healing and, most crucially for Parham, speaking in tongues.[8] After his brief sojourn with Parham, Seymour headed west to Los Angeles, where in April 1906 he opened his revival center on Azusa Street. There he not only put Parham's theological tenets into practice, but spiced his worship service with styles of healing, dancing, and ecstatic weeping borrowed from the African American wing of the Holiness movement.[9] Emotional performance and universal access to gifts of the Holy Spirit would henceforth distinguish Pentecostalism from its Evangelical cousin. But there was one more distinction. In contrast to the strict segregation that characterized most U.S. congregations at the time, "One of the miracles of the Azusa Street meetings was the free and relaxed mixing of the races."[10]

In the years that followed, the movement spread to cities and towns across the United States and Canada. From the very first Pentecostalism showed a strong missionizing impulse, one given theological urgency by the premillennialist conviction that the end times might be near. What was and is still today so distinctive about Pentecostal outreach, however, was the way in which it prompted not just credentialed pastors but people of humble means to set out to spread the Word. "The Pentecostal revival resulted in a category of ordinary but 'called' people called 'missionaries' spreading out to every corner of the globe within a remarkably short space of time."[11] By 1910, some 185 Azusa-inspired missionaries had set out from North America for other mission fields.[12] Churches were up and running in Norway, England, India, China, and Chile by 1907; South Africa by 1908; Brazil by 1910; Russia by 1911–1914; Mexico by 1914; the Netherlands East Indies (today's Indonesia) by 1921; and the Philippines by 1926.

Early North American Pentecostalism's relaxation of racial, class, and gender hierarchies no doubt explains part of its populist appeal, much as variations on these same traits resonate with believers in assembly halls and chapels across Latin America, Africa, and Asia today (see below). Although during these early years some churches barred women from formal leadership roles, most parted ways with their mainline counterparts by allowing women to serve as preachers, teachers, and healers. Pentecostalism's emphasis on universal access to gifts of the Holy Spirit provided a religious rationale for women's participation, as well as that of racial and ethnic minorities. In this and later periods, however, whether this egalitarian promise was realized in church practice depended on a more complex set of social and religious concerns.

Indeed, and not surprisingly, the soft inclusivity of the early movement soon ran up against the hard American realities of race, class, and gender. Here was a developmental tension in the North American scene that in decades to come was to reappear regularly on the global Pentecostal stage. The tension weighed most heavily on congregations further along in the long march from peripheral sects of the hopeful poor to institutionalized churches with fash-ionably clad claimants to middle-class standing. In the latter settings, it was not uncommon for church leaders to signal their aspiration to respectability by conforming to mainstream models of dress, hierarchy, and social exclu-sion. And so it was that in the United States in the 1910s and 1920s, "one by one most of the Pentecostal denominations separated on the basis of race."[13] One of the largest of North America's Pentecostal denominations today, the Assemblies of God (AOG), was during its first decades segregated along racial lines. Although some among its founders had first-hand experience of the racial pluralism of the Azusa Revival, AOG leaders quietly ushered African Americans drawn to the church's egalitarian message outside to the predom-inantly African American Church of God in Christ, today America's largest Pentecostal denomination.[14] A similar controversy arose around the question of women pastors, with some early congregations seeking to circumscribe women's ministry by subsuming female leadership under the role of the pas-tor's wife.[15] Never fully removed from the hierarchies many believers had no doubt hoped to escape, Pentecostalism was to experience developmental ten-sions of a similar nature decades later as it pressed into the global south.

As in the biography of all religions, there was much that was unique and even accidental to the early genesis of North American Pentecostalism. There were, among other things, the clear liturgical imprint of American Methodism; an emphasis on affective ("heartfelt") conviction rather than strict doctrinal drills;[16] the ready adoption of African American Holiness worship styles by believers from diverse ethno-racial backgrounds; and the seemingly unstoppable reimposition of American racial, class, and gender hierarchies in disregard of the revivalist promise of gifts-of-the-Spirit-for-all. It goes without saying that many of these characteristics would not have been associated with movements of charismatic renewal in, say, Wales or south-ern India around this same time (see below). However, what insured that the North American movement had transnational potential was that many among its core features emerged as religious adaptations to a sociological and public-ethical environment not at all unique to the early twentieth-century United States. The confluence of peripatetic mobility, radical insecurity, and dreams of spiritual birth so apparent in the first wave of North American Pentecostalism, was, so to speak, about to go global.

Genealogical Parallels

In historical retrospect, five parallels stand out between the social gene-alogy of early Pentecostalism in North America and Pentecostalism in the global south today; together they take us some of the way toward understanding the circumstances and powers conducive to Pentecostal growth in both times and places. The first and most mundane condition is that, where the Pentecostal message resonates with local hearts and minds, it does so in part because the restless wayfarers attracted to its appeals are religion-minded rather than secularist in world view. This cultural precondition may at first seem trivially self-evident. However, the public pervasiveness of a secularist social imaginary provides part of the explanation as to why Pentecostalism, while blossoming across the United States and (today) the global south, never made much headway among the indigenous laboring and middle classes of twentieth-century Europe, or among those few pockets of high secularity in the global south, like Uruguay, the most secularized nation in continental Latin America.[17] In these latter settings, there may well be no shortage of marginalized-but-mobile citizens aspiring to new experiences of existential power and born-again dignity. Rather than to gifts of the Holy Spirit, however, these latter wayfarers look to some mix of secular liberalism, socialism, ethno-nationalism, consumerism, or expressive individualism to provide the terms for participation in a brave but disenchanted new world.[18]

The second condition many early North American Pentecostals shared with their cousins in the global south today follows from this first. That is, although religious-minded and desiring a small island of ethical fellowship in a turbulent social sea, many among the spiritual wayfarers found themselves marginalized from established religious institutions, the leadership of which lay in the hands of religious luminaries with cozy ties to established political and economic elites. Finding oneself at the margins of a cronyist establishment is, of course, the default condition for the great mass of people in the state-based societies that first appeared on the global scene several thousand years ago; with that in mind, marginalization is itself insufficient to bring a movement for new religious fellowship into existence.[19]

But there is something additionally distinctive to southern Los Angeles in 1906 or São Paolo in 2006, a circumstance guaranteeing that social marginalization may result not in dispirited alienation but in social rupture and religious renewal of the self. In the United States of the early twentieth century, as in urban Brazil or Nigeria today, migration, urbanization, and cultural dislocation weakened the hold of once-secure elites on political, economic, and religious affairs. For some among the dislocated, the loosening of social bonds may lead to the shapeless anomie described a century ago by the French sociologist Émile Durkheim. Worse yet, as Ruth Marshall has observed in a subtle analysis of Pentecostalism in urban Nigeria today, the change may lead to the "extreme instrumentalisation of social relations" and "a kind of Hobbesian sense of 'all against all,'" as "the old forms of community . . . have proved unreliable sources of support."[20] However, for other moderns, the collapse of the old ways prompts a hopeful search for new religious fellowship and inspirited techniques for subjective reformation. Whether on Azusa Street or the global south today, some individuals come forth to declare their independence and affirm their dignity and power through the adoption of a more emotive, participatory, and personally accessible variety of Christianity.

It is under these same circumstances of heightened insecurity, growing detraditionalization, forced or self-initiated migration, and an explosion of new aspirational imaginaries that the peculiar organizational characteristics of popular Pentecostalism achieve additional resonance, in a way that illustrates a third genealogical parallel between Pentecostalism in early twentieth-century North America and today's global south. Although in some mission fields, North American, European, or (as in large parts of Asia and even some parts of Latin America today) Korean missionaries serve as midwives to new Pentecostal churches,[21] most small congregations quickly become localized and self-organizing—"postmissionary" to borrow a phrase from the anthropologist Brian M. Howell.[22] Particularly in their early years and with as yet nondenominationalized churches, successful churches strike a balance between organizational flexibility and pastoral authority. The churches' mobilizational genius lies "in their ability to channel the wave of enthusiasm within a supple yet powerful structure, which harnessed the informal, democratic force behind the wave of conversions, giving opportunities to individuals who had heard the personal 'call' to express their evangelical zeal within a network of institutionalized support."[23] In at least these respects, these young churches look like prototypical examples of "civil society" organizations; however, as we shall see, Pentecostal churches show a rather untidy variety of attitudes toward the state and citizen politics.

As in the Zimbabwean, Ukrainian, south Indian, and Chinese cases discussed in this volume, larger and more "denominationalized" churches—particularly those promoting some variety of the prosperity theologies that burst onto the global scene in the 1980s and 1990s (see below)—may also make a point of highlighting their ties to a transnational communion, one that today not uncommonly shows North American influences. Notwithstanding this global gaze, the leadership of most Pentecostal movements localizes, in part as a result of the faith's most striking organizational characteristics: open access to the ministry and the low start-up costs for worship facilities. Unlike the Roman Catholics and mainline Protestants with whom they often compete, Pentecostals (or, again, the most populist among Pentecostalism's diverse currents) believe that the primary qualification for founding a little church or Bible-study circle is not years of seminary study but gifts of the Holy Spirit. "The vast majority of the preachers were 'of the people,' not separated from their congregations by ethnic or class barriers."[24] The resources required are modest and readily at hand: a simple room, some chairs, an open Bible, perhaps a microphone if the congregation has grown, and, above all else, the boundless energy that divine gifts inspire.

Not surprisingly, this is a point on which there is some variation, even in the early stages of a Pentecostal movement's development. As was already the case among North American Pentecostals in the 1920s and 1930s, some among the better-organized churches may move early on to displace the free-flowing-gifts-of-the-Spirit for a more restrictive pastoral structure. This is, of course, a Pentecostal variation on the familiar theme of the routinization of charisma, a process identified by Max Weber as an aspect of most religious traditions' development. Margaret M. Poloma's study of North America's Assemblies of God revealed just such a pattern to that church's growth during its first seven decades.[25] So too did Andrew Chesnut in his study of Brazil's Assemblies of God, the largest of that country's Pentecostal churches; as did David Maxwell, in his study of the Zimbabwe Assemblies of God Africa (ZAOGA), that country's largest Pentecostal church.[26] In chapter 5 in this volume, Nanlai Cao reminds us that, dominated two decades ago by "illiterate or semi-illiterate, experientially inclined lay women," Pentecostalism in China is today undergoing a transition toward male pastors with "textually based theological education." In her discussion of Catholic charismatics in the Philippines (chapter 8), Katharine Wiegele reveals that the El Shaddai movement is undergoing a similar routinization of a once free-flowing faith. As Marsh and Tonoyan show in their overview of the Ukraine and Russia (chapter 6), the routinization process among Pentecostals in these countries is compounded by the generational tension between old-school "Russians" and new-school "cosmopolitans." Finally, as Rebecca and Timothy Shah highlight in their essay on south India (chapter 7), the tension between charismatic independence and routinized respectability there overlaps with stark hierarchies of caste, class, and gender.

In these and other examples, where pastors and congregants strive to be more respectably established, church organization tends to become less charismatic, more hierarchical, and more masculine. Some among these churches may begin to require that pastors show not only proof of gifts of the Holy Spirit, but seminary credentials. Similarly, and as has been widely reported from contemporary West Africa and Latin America, what was at first a non- or interdenominational movement with multiple authority figures (pastors, preachers, prophets, healers, Bible-study teachers) may give way to a clear denominational pattern of exclusive affiliation and strict or even authoritarian pastoral control.[27]

Notwithstanding this pattern, even in established churches like the AOG or the ZOAGA rates of lay participation remain high, not least by comparison with their Catholic and mainline Protestant counterparts. Equally revealing, a developmental tension often simmers just below the smooth surface of congregational life. As some among the faithful opt to settle in neat church pews, others read the Acts of the Apostles and, flush with the faith of the Holy Spirit, set out to establish their own house-church or assembly hall. "Faith gives divine permission to speak without certification through the authoritative offer of new names and re-formed identities."[28] Again and again, it seems, Pentecostalism's energies are not easily contained. Its fissiparous dynamism also helps to explain why Pentecostals, though scriptural literalists, are not properly termed "fundamentalist." Contrary to the pattern of doctrinal drilling and ideological inflexibility seen in fundamentalist faiths, Pentecostal churches show wide variation on matters of theology, doctrine, and belief. Especially when a church is just getting started, congregants seem more interested in the direct experience of gifts of the Holy Spirit than in theological indoctrination.

There is a fourth and equally important parallel to Pentecostalism's genealogy in North America and today's global south, and it has to do with the structure of resocialization set in motion by conversion. For most believers, the central aim of Pentecostalism has little if anything to do with state-centered politics or macrosociological questions of economic policy or social justice. In this regard Pentecostalism differs from Catholic liberation theology, the Evangelical Moral Majority in the 1980s United States, and most contemporary varieties of political Islamism or Hindu nationalism. For those drawn to the faith, Pentecostalism is first and foremost a matter of individual and local rebirth—ethical subject formation, not structural reform. For this reason, too, the social processes that accompany being born-again have a distinctive directionality: they proceed from the individual to the family, the family to the congregation, and only then, and most uncertainly in terms of constancy of program or vision, outward into the broader society. "Once born again, the Pentecostal convert is brought into a 'community of the saved' . . . where he or she strives to maintain a state of inner purity necessary to receive empowerment from the Holy Spirit."[29]

However subjective and individualizing, Pentecostalism does not produce the atomized individualism associated with some varieties of spirituality and "lifestyle coaching" in the postmodern West.[30] The Pentecostal search for inner purity prompts two trademark modes of relational sociability: heightened participation in the social and religious activities of one's church or assembly hall; and withdrawal from an array of preconversion rituals and commensalities. The latter are now seen as moral dangers, threatening to drag the born-again believer back down into preconversion sin. As Birgit Meyer, Matthew Engelke, and Joel Robbins have all emphasized, converts may seek to minimize such threats by engaging in "deliverance rituals" or "rituals of rupture" that stigmatize preconversion relationships and erect high moral walls between believers and unbelievers.[31] Secular entertainments such as dance halls, bars, and movie houses are proscribed for both sexes. Some but not all Pentecostals may also forbid secular forms of learning, not least in the humanities and social sciences (although among the new generation of college-educated, middle-class Pentecostals, this latter prohibition is fading).

Some of the most subjectively demanding prohibitions take aim at men. Their preconversion privileges are re-presented as sins and misdeeds indulged at the expense of their female partner and children. Drinking, smoking, fighting, and sexual carousing—the staples of masculinist diet in so much of the world—are the focus of special moral disciplining, not just by a man's wife or partner but also by his pastor and church fellows. A stream of positive injunctions accompanies the negative proscriptions, as men are enjoined to shift their social energies and their pocket monies back to the family and conjugality.

The combination of heightened religious participation and diminished interaction with old fellows may serve, then, to redirect the convert's energies away from his or her extended family and back to the nuclear group. Although the attachments that emerge vary from one church and country to another, the result is less commonly atomizing than relationally re-embedding, as the believer and his or her family are drawn into a voluntary community of church sisters and brothers. But the process often shows a gendered dimension, as illustrated in a report from a Pentecostal slum in Mozambique: "The emphasis on mutual aid and social support . . . attracts many women. . . . One woman explained that she joined the church 'to have family in the church or brotherhood in the church. For example, when you get sick you have someone who can help you. . . . When someone is suffering, they come to help with whatever, it could be money.'"[32] Many men find the prospect of church propriety and monogamous bliss a price too high to pay. So in Mozambique, as in many other parts of the global south, many born-again women find themselves alone with children in the pews, dreaming of ways "to bring errant husbands into their churches."[33]

As this discussion illustrates, Pentecostal rebirth has powerful gender effects. This points to a fifth genealogical parallel between the first stages of Pentecostal growth in the early twentieth-century United States and the global south today. In some congregations in North America, and in much of the global south, women make up the majority in the assembly hall or the Bible study group. In male-dominated Latin America, two-thirds of the Pentecostal congregation may be female.[34] In China up through the 1980s, Christianity was "largely a rural indigenous Pentecostal phenomenon and an overwhelmingly female institution," as Nanlai Cao notes in his chapter in this volume. In south India, as Rebecca and Timothy Shah show, Dalit ("untouchable")-oriented congregations are also predominantly poor and female. In these and many other cases, Pentecostal services involve a more diverse array of ritual roles than Catholic or mainline Protestant services, and women are especially active in prophecy, healing, and Bible study, even if the roles of pastoring and preaching remain disproportionately male.

This division of religious labors indexes a developmental tension long pervasive in Pentecostal circles. As Allan Anderson has observed, many among the earliest pastors, preachers, and prophets in North America were women.[35] As Bernice Martin also notes in her chapter in this volume, at the time of its founding in 1914, a full third of the North American Assemblies of God's ministers and two-thirds of its missionaries were women. But high rates of female participation were no guarantee of congregational equality. The church's general council did not give women a right to vote in church affairs. When, in 1935, the church officially gave women the right to be ordained as elders (pastors), the restrictions it imposed made "apparent that the ethic of domesticity thrived in the Assemblies of God."[36]

But Pentecostalism's gender effects reach deeper than official ritual roles and church hierarchy. As Elizabeth Brusco, Salvatore Cucchiari, John Burdick, and Bernice Martin first observed two decades ago, "Above all, women have used the Pentecostal religious discourse to rewrite the moral mandate on which sexual relations and the family rest"; they have done so by instituting a "family discipline . . . which puts the collective needs of the household unit above the freedom and pleasures of men and which has called an end to the long-tolerated double standard of sexual morality."[37] It is this process that Brusco, in her now classic ethnography of Colombian Pentecostals, has described as "the reformation of machismo."[38]

The tension between women's public witness and formal male leadership has been a recurring feature of Pentecostal growth in North America and today's global south. However, as Brusco argues in a more recent article, "concentration on church hierarchy, which privileges the voices of those in formal leadership roles, camouflages the importance of women in Pentecostal churches,"[39] as evidenced in women's prophecy, healing, teaching, and Bible study. But the cultural ambivalence surrounding women's roles is real, and it underscores a gender paradox at the heart of Pentecostal sociability:

> An unresolved tension remains between the *de jure* system of patri-archal authority in church and home and the *de facto* establishment of a way of life which decisively shifts the domestic and religious pri-orities in a direction that benefits women and children while mor-ally restraining the traditional autonomy of the male and the self-ish or irresponsible exercise of masculine power. The implicit deal seems to be that a substantive shift toward greater gender equality will be tolerated so long as women are not seen to be publicly exer-cising formal authority over men.[40]

This pattern is widespread and important. However, as one would expect with a phenomenon as foundational of social life as gender, the pattern also shows great regional variation. Among recent middle-class converts to charismatic Protestantism in parts of China, the highly sexualized models of femininity associated with the new capitalism combine with local gender ideologies, which emphasize the "emotionality" of women and the "rationality" of men; the result is to greatly compromise the egalitarian impact of the Pentecostal message.[41] In East and Southeast Asia, Pentecostal women have benefited greatly from new educational opportunities, and are also active in teaching, preaching, mission, and administration. However, in most denominations the ordination of women is not permitted and "almost all leadership positions are taken by men."[42] The situation in Africa is even more complex. In West Africa, there has been an increase in female-founded Pentecostal churches since the 1970s, but both here and in southern Africa pastoral roles are overwhelm-ingly male. Nonetheless, women and youth are drawn to Pentecostal revival because "members . . . put aside the usually pronounced respect for social status found in Nigerian culture." No less important, "Although in doctrine the woman was presented as subordinate to the authority of her husband in the home . . . husbands were enjoined to treat their wives like partners, involving them in daily decisions, and helping to take responsibility for child rearing."[43] In sum, Pentecostalism's gender paradoxes are pervasive, and con-tingencies and contradictions abound. But there is a general and important trend nonetheless. It centers on the refiguration and conjugalization of family relations, but typically stops short of the gender-equalization of family or church leadership.

A final genealogical commonality across the Pentecostal world, whether in its early North American variety or in the global south today, is modern Pentecostalism's antecedents in Western Christianity. Pentecostalism has roots in the German pietistic movements that originated in the early phases of the Protestant Reformation. However, its more immediate precedent is the Anglo-American Methodism of the late eighteenth and nineteenth centuries. Both of these popularly based Christianities "traveled in the ambit of a mobile society, a global movement prior to globalization," where "the ancient territorial emplacements of religion begin to dissolve into fraternal associations."[44] However specific these circumstances may at first have been to North America and Britain, the juggernaut of colonialism, capitalism, and migration was soon to make them global.

Although the North American variety has played a central role in the global diffusion of Pentecostalism, Christianities of an inclusive and effervescent sort emerged more or less independently in other parts of the world both prior to and after the North American movement's appearance. In 1860, almost a half century before the Azusa revival, a Tamil evangelist named Aroolappen set a proto-Pentecostal revival in motion in Tamil Nadu, India.[45] In 1907, a North American Methodist revivalist working in Valparaiso, Chile, read a mission pamphlet describing revivalist activities in the Mukti region of India, and drew on this (after his expulsion from the Methodist Church in 1910) to form the Methodist Pentecostal Church. Today Chile's Pentecostal Church remains different from North American prototypes and is that country's largest non-Catholic denomination.[46]

These examples remind us that Pentecostalism—or, to be more awkwardly precise, proto-Pentecostal charismatic Christianity—had not one but several birthplaces. The multiplicity of locales shows that the late nineteenth and early twentieth centuries gave rise to a widened circulation of affectively effervescent and subjectivity-remaking modes of Christian profession. The "Korean Pentecost" in 1903, "which began among missionaries in Pyongyang in 1903, and soon spread to thousands of Korean people,"[47] got under way independently of any direct Azusa influence. The same was true of Welsh Revival of 1904, among others.[48]

Citing these and other examples, Alan Anderson has lamented what he describes as "a fundamental misconception in the writing of Pentecostal history that needs correcting, a bias interpreting that history from western, and predominantly North American, perspectives."[49] From a comparative sociological perspective, and from the perspective of the studies in this book, Anderson's reminder is timely and important. It underscores the need to balance a recognition of transnational flows and North American influences

with an appreciation of the irreducible agency of the "thousands of indigenous workers in the early Pentecostal movement,"[50] as well as the millions in
Asia, Latin America, and Africa today. Certainly, the founders of the North
American variety of Pentecostalism played a disproportionate role in the first
phase of Pentecostalism's global dissemination from the 1900s to the 1920s.
Their successors also played a pivotal role in the 1980s and 1990s, as a new
wave of Pentecostalism surged across the global south and brought with it
a U.S.-inspired "prosperity gospel." Nonetheless, these globalizing influences
would have amounted to nothing had it not been for the efforts and imag-
inations of ordinary people determined to devise religious means for fore-
stalling the insecurities and seizing the promise of their fast-changing worlds.
In other words, Pentecostalism's globalization was irreducibly dependent on
the agency of those hoping to be born-again, which is to say, those intent on
refiguring their selves through a new vision of ultimate destiny and through
the miraculous immediacy of the Holy Spirit.

This later wave of Pentecostal growth, particularly that which began in
the 1980s, showed other influences besides Pentecostalism's trademark theology, associational fissiparousness, and gender paradoxes. Between the first
decade of the1900s and the 1980s, the whole world changed. The new world
order forced Pentecostals to more directly engage macrorealities of marginal
interest to the movement's first wave: state politics and late-modern capitalism. These otherwise secular forces were to leave an imprint of their own on
global Pentecostalism's practices and ethical imaginaries.

From Moral Rafts to Megachurches

Politics did not receive much attention in the first studies of
Pentecostalism, which appeared on the academic scene in significant numbers
only in the 1970s.[51] The omission in part resulted from the fact that social scientists were late to turn to the study of Pentecostalism, and most of the early
studies were carried out by theologians and historians of world Christianity.
Understandably enough, the primary concern of these latter scholars was
descriptive and typological, aiming to disentangle Pentecostalism from its
diverse contexts and explore its theological relationship to other forms of
modern Christianity.

The relative lack of attention to macropolitics also reflected the realities of Pentecostalism during the period immediately prior to the movement's global surge.[52] One of the earliest social scientists to conduct in-depth
research on Pentecostalism is a contributor to this volume, the British sociologist of religion David Martin. When in the mid-1980s he began his studies in

Latin America, Martin observed that in several countries Pentecostalism had spread so widely that the movement had "clear political potential." However, Martin went on to observe that the high costs of oppositional politics in Latin America during the 1970s and early 1980s were such that Pentecostals had "little hope of power through politics"; they dedicated themselves instead to "creating their own free space," a project that was "predicated on the avoidance of secular entanglements, among which politics are included."[53]

Although he recognized that it had some middle-class adherents, in his early studies Martin described Pentecostalism as a "religion of the poor"[54] and likened it to a life raft, on which "men and women lash themselves for safety": "Initially most of their energy is expended on constructing the raft, devising fraternities and sororities of mutual aid, of communication, and useful connection. Those who guide the raft may well be politically very cautious and conservative, anxious to avoid the destructive turbulence of political contention and polarization."[55] Martin noted that an additional reason for Pentecostalism's political timidity had to do with its normative emphasis on the proximate and personal rather than the distant and structural. Pentecostalism, he wrote, sustains a "primary experience of unique personhood or of personalized interactions in the small voluntary group"; its adherents have difficulty with "large-scale social mechanisms . . . which resist individual moral action"; this in turn results in "a truncated understanding of the social world."[56]

In both Roman Catholic and academic circles, social critics of Pentecostalism reached conclusions similar to those of Martin but often presented them in blunter terms. Many decried what they regarded as Pentecostals' failure to address the "real" causes of poverty and social marginalization. Writing in 1991, Paul Gifford, a leading historian of West African Christianity, observed, "With its emphasis on personal healing, it [born-again Christianity] diverts attention from social ills that are crying out for remedy. . . . By emphasizing personal morality so exclusively, it all but eliminates any interest in systemic or institutionalized injustice."[57] Influenced by a modified variety of liberation theology, the supporters of Catholic base communities in Latin America and the Philippines agreed with their Pentecostal brethren that social change must begin with the reformation of individual subjectivities. But they lamented the fact that Pentecostals failed to understand that the ultimate goal of Christian renewal must also be structural, ending in "the transformation of society."[58]

Although observers judged their political impact differently, these assessments showed that in the first generation there was broad agreement in academic circles on Pentecostal politics: Pentecostalism was a rickety raft in a turbulent sea, and the raft's occupants saw little benefit in, or showed a willful disregard for, throwing themselves into raging political torrents. The problem with this view is not that it was wrong, but that it was soon to become anachronistic. Just as had happened with Pentecostalism in North America a few decades earlier, some rafts in the global southern seas were growing rapidly. Indeed, some turned into megachurches and became the focus of political bosses' attention. Although the Zimbabwe Assemblies of God Africa had begun as a small sectarian movement in the late 1950s and 1960s, it "mushroomed on a transnational scale" after Zimbabwe's independence in 1980, sending missions to neighboring African countries and even the United Kingdom, and claiming a million and one half members by 1995.[59] As the church's numbers grew, so too did its leadership's interest in cultivating ties with national politicians, although the interest waned when Zimbabwean politics turned severe. Protestant growth in the most heavily Pentecostal of Latin American countries, Guatemala, showed a similar politicization, albeit with a less consistently corporatist outcome. First appearing on the scene in the 1980s, neo-Pentecostal megachurches boomed after the signing of the 1996 Peace Accords, which ended that country's bloody civil war. The churches "placed themselves at the very heart of Guatemalan democratization in ways that go well beyond electoral politics." The churches promoted a Christian citizenship centered not on conventional party politics (although some faithful engaged in that too), but on "spiritual warfare," the favored methods of which included fasting, prayer, and speaking in tongues, all deployed to combat crime and save the nation.[60]

Its protean variation demonstrates that Pentecostal politics today is the result of the contingencies of social context more than it is any unchanging theological disposition. But one context appears to generate a family-resemblant political response in many national settings: where churches are big and politics patronal and competitive, there often emerges an "ecclesiastical corporatism which seeks to enlist state resources for church aggrandisement."[61] Researchers have documented this trend in Latin America as well as West and south-central Africa.[62] Megachurches and religious movements mean followers, and their numbers tempt politicians and pastors to dream of power-bloc deals.

It was just this type of process into which the largest of the Philippines' Catholic charismatic movements, the El Shaddai, was swept, a group that is the focus of Katharine Wiegele's chapter in this volume. As movement ranks swelled to some six to eight million people (the largest charismatic Catholic movement in the world), populist politicians made regular appearances at movement rallies, which could assemble half a million people, all so as "to court favor with the faithful who gather there," as Wiegele notes in her chapter. When in 2000 President Estrada became the target of corruption allegations that eventually led to his ouster, the movement's founder, Brother Mike Velarde, mobilized his congregation in support of the imperiled president. As Pentecostalism or its charismatic counterpart surged across the global south, then, some among its social carriers remained tiny rafts in a turbulent sea. But others became powerful vessels of their own, their captains sailing forth to "explore ways of making political capital out of their enormous membership."[63]

Latin America saw the earliest surge in Pentecostal numbers in the global south, and the process broadly coincided with a slow but steady transition to electoral democracy. The confluence of events revealed more quickly than in other regions the developmental tensions arising from the drawing of a movement for subjective piety into mass-based politics. Today, some 12 percent of Latin America's population is Protestant, and two-thirds of this group are Pentecostal.[64] In the 1970s and early 1980s, most Pentecostals steered clear of active party politics, although, as in the generals' Argentina and Pinochet's Chile, some were occasionally pressed into regime service.[65] Certainly, most Pentecostals were conservative on matters of abortion, homosexuality, and communism, but otherwise they did not fit neatly along any portion of the left-right spectrum.[66]

Over the next twenty years, however, the combination of church growth and democratic transition transformed the Latin American landscape, and there followed an unexpected boom in Pentecostal politics. True to that politics' shape-shifting form, the varieties of activism were many. As in postwar Guatemala, some megachurches dabbled in electoral politics, but they husbanded their greatest resources for a Christian citizenship centered on fasting, prayers, and spiritual warfare. "Christian citizens in Guatemala . . . are more likely to pray for Guatemala than pay their taxes; they tend to speak in tongues for the soul of the nation rather than vote in general elections; and they more often than not organize prayer campaigns to fight crime rather than organize their communities against the same threat."[67]

But not all electoral politics in transitioning Latin America was as corrupt and inconsistent as Guatemala in the 1990s and 2000s. Where national politics had gotten beyond such danger zones Pentecostals often moved boldly into the electoral and citizen arena. Indeed, whereas in the 1970s there had been almost no Protestant political parties, by the 1990s there were many. However, the parties' success at carving out an electoral niche varied by country, in a manner that depended in part on the type of electoral system used (proportionalism vs. winner-take-all), as well as the strength of existing parties.

There was an additional, epistemological quality to this new political turn. Where Pentecostal or Evangelical-Pentecostal parties formed,[68] they "usually emerged without any previous reflection on political theology,"[69] and thus without an agreed or well-formulated program for sociopolitical reform. Their animating conviction was that the time had come for Protestants to take their rightful political place, and that believers' powers of religious discernment were sufficient to make corrupted politics good. Although the electoral context was different (marked by the growing severity of Christian–Muslim competition), Ruth Marshall reports a similar epistemological dimension to Pentecostal politics in Nigeria. "[T]he rules and values the believer's conduct is supposed to express . . . are . . . relatively simple and not the fruit of a complex theological elaboration." As a consequence, "With its emphasis on individual salvation, interiority, and affectivity, coupled with its incipient messianism, [Pentecostalism] has great difficulty . . . creating the foundations of political community."[70]

Interestingly, most of the Protestant-based parties established in Latin America were founded by leaders of smaller Protestant congregations. The parties were not supported by mainstream Evangelical or Pentecostal politicians, because the latter were busy with political wheeling and dealing of their own. The assumption on the part of Protestant-party founders was that Evangelicals and Pentecostals would vote as a bloc. As it has turned out, however, "neither of these assumptions are ever correct."[71] Paul Freston thus concludes a broad survey of Pentecostal politics with the pessimistic prognosis, "It is unlikely that any of the existing Protestant Latin American parties will evolve into cohesive and competitive political actors. They are too personalistic and/or naïve, being largely vehicles for personal ambitions or for theocratic projects, which in any case founder on the reality of evangelical division."[72]

Notwithstanding the limited success of these efforts at forging faith-based parties, the broader impact of Pentecostal participation on this continent has been profound. In Brazil, the capital of Pentecostalism in the global south (as Freston puts it in his chapter in this volume), "All the major parties are quite happy to have Protestant candidates on their lists."[73] Equally important, and again testifying to the protean nature of their politics, in 2002 Pentecostal and Evangelical voters were more favorable to candidates of the two major left-of-center parties than was the Brazilian electorate as a whole.[74] Moreover, the tactical alliance spurred a startling discursive shift. It led to a "growing trend to an 'evangelical social discourse,' with an emphasis on justice that would have been unthinkable a few years earlier."[75] Having once demonized the Workers' Party, some of the leadership of Brazil's Universal Church of the Kingdom of God have embraced a center-left populism critical of neoliberal globalization. In sum, notwithstanding a tendency to retreat from structural engagements where these carry high social costs, the Pentecostal experience in Latin America hints at a remarkable global possibility. It suggests that the Pentecostal preoccupation with ethical-subject reformation need not end in an antipolitics or quietist retreat from the public sphere. The ethical self may extend its gaze to structural and social justice concerns, not least of all where politics is no longer an elite-dominated, zero-sum game.

It would be a mistake, of course, to make too much of the Brazilian or Latin American examples. Pentecostal and, especially, Evangelical churches in Latin America have on occasion made common cause with politicians of the far right—indeed, in Efraín Ríos Montt's Guatemala after 1982, a genocidal far right.[76] But the point is that Pentecostalism's success at winning converts has opened it to a plurality of interests and ideologies. The faith tradition's "continuing attraction as a religion of personal salvation brings in new types of people who end up changing that profile, showing it to have been merely contingent and not, as some analyses would have it, an essential part of evangelical identity."[77] The very qualities of social dispersion and fissiparous leadership that have facilitated rapid Pentecostal growth in the religious sphere hamper well-coordinated campaigns with regard to the state. However, rather than always being bad for participatory politics, in some settings, the competitive plurality may enhance the prospects for a sustainable citizen politics—and for a more sociologically articulate Pentecostal ethics.

It goes without saying that this conclusion need not apply to all of the global south. The events that pushed Brazilian Pentecostals away from political timidity and utopian exclusivism to pluralist engagement were facilitated by the fact that in the 1990s that country's electoral system had experienced a genuine opening. Had the political system remained violent, patronal, or closed, the outcome might have looked less democratic and more like Zimbabwe as described by David Maxwell, Ghana as described by Paul Gifford, or Nigeria as analyzed by Ruth Marshall. In all three countries, the born-again movement remains "animated by a dialectic between primitive egalitarian ideals on the one hand and hierarchy and authoritarianism on the other."[78] The contrast again underscores that Pentecostal politics is not governed by some finite set of unchanging doctrinal principles, but is perpetually reshaped by believers' efforts to respond to their world's radical insecurities and dreamed-of opportunities.

From Pious Poor to Gospel Prosperous

Just as church growth and structural shifts have ushered in unexpected political developments, Pentecostal engagements with global capitalism have changed since the 1980s. Pentecostalism's practical theology has much to say on matters of the self, family, and sociability, but few in its first generations presented extended reflections on markets, capitalism, and professional advance. Indeed, to the degree they said anything, church leaders tended to warn of the corrupting temptations of this world and to direct their congregants' attention to the rewards of the next. But this antimaterialist mien was to change in the final decades of the twentieth century. The change had more to do with shifts in the nature of capitalism and international economic governance than it did any long-standing feature of Pentecostal theology.

Seeing a parallel between nineteenth-century Methodism and late twentieth-century Pentecostalism, David Martin in 1990 had argued that Pentecostalism provided subjective habits useful for adapting to the disciplines and opportunities of the capitalist market, a point that had been made years earlier in studies on Protestantism in Africa.[79] Martin found, for example, that Pentecostals clustered together to offer each other mutual assistance;[80] this finding has been widely confirmed by researchers working among Pentecostals in other parts of Latin America, Asia, and in Africa. Martin also observed that, again as with English Methodists, Pentecostalism fostered habits of "orderliness in the sphere of work" that seemed well suited to the "rhythm of the factory."[81] In the sphere of consumption he also saw an important change: many Pentecostals broke with the fiesta celebration of the saints once so widespread in Latin America, which Martin portrayed as "the symbolic core of the old order" and prone to drain family resources into "wasteful ceremonial obligations."[82] In these and other regards, Martin concluded that Pentecostalism brought believers "into touch with the modern market."[83]

Some readers of the 1990 book saw Martin as suggesting that Pentecostalism was always the carrier of a Weberian Protestant ethic. In fact, however, Martin stopped well short of any such claim. Martin cited Lalive D'Épinay's Chilean study at great length, with its rejection of "any Weberian connection of the classical type between Pentecostalism and the growth of large-scale activity. . . . In Lalive D'Épinay's view, moral regeneration takes clear precedence over material advance," and it does not even "necessarily lead to increased savings."[84]

Martin's reluctance to endorse any simple conclusion as regards Pentecostalism's economic ethic became all the more pronounced in his 2002 work, *Pentecostalism: The World Their Parish*. Martin begins the economic discussion in this book with the important but familiar observation that the "pivotal transformation wrought by conversion" is the "restoration of the family" through the curtailment of masculinist prestige behaviors of "the street, bar, brothel, football stadium, and drug culture."[85] Drawing on Bernice Martin's insights on Pentecostalism, subjectivity, and postmodernity,[86] he then goes on to make another observation, one also heard in studies from contemporary Africa, as well as a newer body of research on religion and capitalism in the Muslim world.[87] These studies highlight two basic differences between late-modern capitalism and that of Weber's classic Protestant ethic. The first is that today's capitalism has a more powerful transnational and consumerist dynamic than that of old. Nations across the global north and south have today been drawn "into a single cultural and economic system," whose "cultural representations are consumed globally, so that the culture industries . . . increasingly play a key role in economic life."[88] A key feature of the new consumerist capitalism is that its taste-shaping industries bear the imprint of "the post-modern West, particularly the individualistic capitalism of . . . the USA."[89] So too, many researchers argue, does the newer variety of Pentecostalism. The carefully controlled borders that once guaranteed that national markets and economic moralities overlapped have given way to capital flows and consumer cultures in which unrestricted gratification seems the norm, even where the great mass of consumers lack the resources to fulfill these desires. Weber's Protestants faced no such ethical schizophrenia.

The second major difference between today's capitalism and that of yesteryear has to do with the shift to a more global, deregulated, and flexible system of neoliberal labor markets, in which postindustrial service industries and knowledge sectors play a far larger role than before. "In such a world the ability to be punctual, regimented, and obedient, so crucial in the (Fordist) factory system, is less relevant than the capacity to be self-motivating, to control the work process without direct supervision"; "Pentecostalism supplies just these personal qualities."[90] In economic life as in politics, of course, Pentecostalism is nothing if not variable, in a manner that reflects the complex contingencies of believers' life worlds. At the very least, however, it does appear that in certain settings "neo-Pentecostal Christianity provides a cultural register for the kind of individual responsibility that structural adjustment seems to demand."[91]

However indirect their influence, these features of late-modern capitalism have all contributed to what is arguably the most significant rupture in global Pentecostalism to this day: the rise of a third-wave Pentecostalism associated with the so-called prosperity gospel. The anthropologists Simon Coleman, Ruth Marshall, and Birgit Meyer, along with the historian of African religions Rosalind I. J. Hackett,[92] were among the first to draw attention to the global spread of the gospel of prosperity. Demonstrating that we are in the presence of a global structural change rather than one peculiar to any single faith tradition, researchers working on other religions, including Islam and Buddhism, have observed that a similar prosperity ethic has emerged in those faith traditions as well.[93]

Coleman rightly traces the theological roots of the Christian variant of the prosperity ethic back to the biblical idea of the Abrahamic covenant, and "the idea of blessing coming to those who are faithful to God."[94] The link between grace and prosperity is also found in classical Calvinism, of course, but, as Coleman observes, the new theology differs from Calvinism in having a more Methodist-like emphasis on the benefits of grace being available to all. More generally, "the tendency of indigenous religions to treat the material and the spiritual as inextricable and to expect the indigenous spirits to enter into 'contracts' to deliver worldly 'goods,' creates very fertile ground for a prosperity gospel, whatever its proximate Christian source."[95] The same openness to indigenous concerns helps to explain why in recent years a similar prosperity ethic has taken hold in many other world religions.

Whatever its theological genealogy, the prosperity gospel displaces first-wave Pentecostalism's antimaterialist injunctions against the sinful pleasures of the world for the message that God wants his followers to be healthy and get rich. However, here again the variety of capitalist economies, and the various ways in which contemporary Pentecostals relate to them, make it impossible to speak of any universal relation between the economy and a religious work ethic.[96] As Marshall has also observed,[97] and as David Maxwell notes in his chapter in this volume, the consumerist ethic may encourage public corruptions, occult mystifications, and dissolute gratifications that are anything but conducive to a Weberian economic discipline.

Indeed, in settings as varied as São Paulo and Lagos, the pastoral proponents of the more ostentatious varieties of prosperity theology sometimes make much of their Italian suits, luxury watches, and European sedans. In East Asia, overseas Chinese converts to Pentecostalism use their religious contacts to expand their business ties in a manner that, as Nanlai Cao shows in his chapter in this volume, sometimes results in a stark segregation of Christian values from business dealings. Indeed, it was in East and Southeast Asia that the prosperity gospel achieved some of its greatest success in winning middle-class converts to the faith. The message resonated, for example, among the well-heeled Chinese Christians with whom I interacted in Indonesia, Malaysia, and Singapore in the 1980s and 1990s.[98] Although Pentecostalism in mainland China assumes a dizzying variety of forms, the prosperity gospel variant has played a role in recruiting at least a portion of the tens of millions of believers won to the faith since the 1990s.[99]

In her *Investing in Miracles* (2005) and in her chapter in this volume, Katharine Wiegele has provided us with a subtle account of a Filipino variety of prosperity gospel, in this instance associated with a charismatic Catholic group. Wiegele's focus is the El Shaddai movement, which first appeared on the Philippine scene in 1981 but which today has six to eight million followers, most of them recruited from the ranks of the urban poor.[100] El Shaddai is grudgingly tolerated by the church hierarchy, but many clergy and progressive Catholics see it as little more than a lightly Christianized cargo cult, promising wealth in magical exchange for tithing donations to the "treasure boxes" so prominently displayed at El Shaddai's prayer rallies.

Wiegele rejects the cargo cult characterization, but concedes that El Shaddai members conceive their interaction with God along the lines of a spiritualized patron-clientism: through donations and prayer one seeks to "obligate God" into delivering miraculous favors. Wiegele also agrees that, as Paul Freston has observed in Latin America and Paul Gifford in Africa, the prosperity theology deflects any desire to problematize "structural, societal, or historical understandings of inequality."[101] The message is clear: If you've fallen on hard economic times, don't feel sorry for yourself; and don't get distracted with dreams of structural reforms or social justice. If you get right with God, however, you can expect miracles.

Social-psychologically, if not structurally, something miraculous may occur, especially when it comes to the poor.[102] As Wiegele explains, the El Shaddai brings "ritual space into the home and self." This spiritual empowerment of home and self allows "ordinary people to heal and to mediate with God"; it "rejects determining notions of poverty and seeks to retell life histories and futures in narratives of transformative miracles."[103] This self-empowering spirit is captured vividly in the slogan chanted by hundreds of thousands of mostly poor people at El Shaddai rallies: "I am rich! I am strong! Something good is going to happen to me!"[104]

However, just as with Pentecostal politics, the impact of prosperity theology is nothing if not varied. As in Central Java, Indonesia, in the 1990s, where a brash version of the doctrine at first held sway, many Pentecostals (most of whom are ethnically Javanese or Chinese Indonesians) today temper its promise of affluence with sober injunctions to work hard, spend carefully, and educate one's children. In Maxwell's Zimbabwe and Marshall's Nigeria, "the opposition between [anti-materialist] holiness and prosperity, so sharp in the early 1990s, has gradually decreased."[105] Indeed, whereas critics once regarded the prosperity gospel as "simply a spectral parallel of the market" or, worse yet, occulted consumerist fantasies, recent studies confirm that the shape-shifting of which Pentecostalism is capable in the political realm also applies to the marketplace. In a careful study of Botswana Pentecostals, Rijk van Dijk speaks of Pentecostal churches as "catapulting migrants toward a modern engagement with the market on its own terms."[106] In an important study of Pentecostalism and economic morality in the Zambian Copperbelt, Naomi Haynes writes that, contrary to those who claim that Pentecostalism is "relationally corrosive" and atomizing, Pentecostalism has encouraged the well-off to use their wealth in ways that "reached across economic rank to form relationships that promote others' well-being."[107]

The spread of the prosperity gospel coincided with another important change: a dramatic upward shift in the class profile and international orientation of some converts to Pentecostalism. Whereas the older Pentecostal churches in Latin America and Africa had emphasized "a doctrine of 'holiness' and anti-materialism, expressed in the eschewal of fancy clothes, expensive commodities, [and] modern media like television," many among this new-wave Pentecostalism are "young, upwardly mobile, [and] relatively well-educated."[108] This neo-Pentecostalism also brought with it megachurches offering diverse life-style services "as a literally concrete demonstration of what can happen if an initiative is taken 'in faith.'"[109] In a manner similar to the "market Islam" that gained force in the Muslim Middle East and Southeast Asia in the 1990s and 2000s, this neo-Pentecostalism also linked its appeals for piety to self-help discourses and therapies. It is telling that both prosperity Pentecostals and "market Muslims" imported many of the latter self-help techniques from North America's managerial and life-coaching industries.[110]

Neo-Pentecostal churches, particularly of the megachurch variety, also differed from their first-wave counterparts in their skilled use of modern electronic media, both to accompany religious services and to disseminate worship events through live or recorded broadcasts.[111] To cite a Guatemalan example: The church's audiovisual team "duplicates each sermon hundreds of times only moments after each sermon has been delivered. Their rush provides excited churchgoers with the opportunity to purchase a cassette copy of the day's talk."[112] The use of cassettes, videos, print publications, and the internet also helps the larger churches to strengthen their identification with a globalized communion, which may include a North American or Korean patron or a locally sponsored mission church in some distant land.

In sum, the social and economic ethic of today's Pentecostalism is, to say the least, greatly varied, and not reducible to any single and market-functional Protestant-ethic prototype. Not all of the main denominations have embraced prosperity theology, and even among those that have, the doctrine is interpreted in ways that result in differing moralities of wealth and consumption. Meanwhile, and as David Martin, David Maxwell, and Rebecca and Timothy Shah observe in their chapters, the majority of Pentecostals look to their faith for security and self-discipline more than they do for flashy prosperity. For these believers, the first-wave Pentecostal habits of cleanliness, self-discipline, and, most of all, antimachismo conjugality are still import-ant and real. These simple habits of the economic heart may well improve the life chances of some poor people. Paul Freston's observations on Latin America thus ring true for large swaths of the global south: "Latin American Pentecostalism does not have the classic Protestant work ethic, and operates in a different economic context. Evidence for mobility is scarce, and for a macro effect on economies even scarcer. But at the individual level, the trans-formative effect on the disorganized lives of many poor (and not so poor) people is evident."[113]

From Past to Future

Social scientists are taught not to make forecasts as to the future of the phenomena they study, save in a few narrow-gauge fields like market analy-sis and political polling. But the scale and speed of the Pentecostal surge in the global south invite two questions: Will the expansion be sustained? And two or three generations on, what type of faith are the converts' descendants likely to profess? To put the matter in theoretical terms, "Is the success of Pentecostalism tied to a phase of social development, which may eventually curtail or alter it?"[114] There are at least tentative answers to these questions in the chapters that follow.

One social fact provides us with a point of entry to thinking about the way in which Pentecostalism changes as it moves from society's margins to more centrally located neighborhoods. Pentecostals in the first generation steady their course by erecting a high moral wall between the world of the born-again and their preconversion fellows. The rituals of rupture may be accompanied by fierce denunciations of the old ways, and even "a power-fully destructive urge to smash all human traditions in order to return to a first-century world where the Holy Spirit reigned supreme."[115] As Maxwell's Zimbabwe study illustrates, and as Frederick Klaits has shown in a study of Pentecostals' response to the HIV/AIDs pandemic in Botswana, however, "Flight into the sanctuary of the Pentecostal community is often just the first stage of the conversion story."[116] As with the poor and abused Dalit women portrayed in Rebecca and Timothy Shah's chapter in this volume, converts from deprived circumstances may enter the faith with low self-esteem or suffering from debilitating illnesses. But slowly they "learn that they are not a 'nobody but a somebody'. . . . [T]hey have new *royal* identity as members of the Kingdom of God."[117] Once healed or otherwise renewed, a sense of being apart may continue, but now charged with a less oppositional sensibility: "With a new identity and authority Pentecostals are encouraged back into the world to lead victorious lives."[118] Social ruptures and born-again enclaves may give way to a concern for the common good—and even a "new face of Christian social engagement" that regards ministry for the sick, the poor, and the homeless as an integral part of evangelism.[119]

But engagements with mainstream society have risks of their own. In the 1900s, the movement of Pentecostalism into the American mainstream led this simple and egalitarian Christian movement to accept racial segregation and gender discrimination. In the 1980s and 1990s, some in the Pentecostal community responded to consumerist shifts in global capitalism by embracing a variety of prosperity theology that other Christians, even conservative Pentecostals, regarded as contrary to Jesus' message. In Brazil in the 1990s, the surge in Pentecostal and Evangelical ranks encouraged some leaders to depart from their political modesty and not merely join the political fray but succumb to its pomp and corruption. Most sobering of all, in Uganda in the 2000s, some Pentecostal and Evangelical believers came to subscribe to dominionist dreams of establishing an absolutist and coercive Christian state.[120]

Several conclusions follow from these examples, and from those presented in the chapters in this book. First, however effective its role in the microsocialization of individuals, Pentecostalism's move out into the macrostructures of state and market is often less steady. By comparison with long-established denominations like Calvinism or Lutheranism, Pentecostalism lacks a comprehensive political and public theology. As Freston observes, Pentecostalism "has little tradition of teasing out socio-political implications from the Christian scriptures, and may even lack the resources to go far with it." Absent such a theology and a religious intelligentsia to learn from history, Pentecostals may be tempted to fall back on scriptural quick fixes that draw on Old Testament or Hebrew law to address new world problems, and do so in an arbitrary and inconsistent manner. The parallels between this tendency and the habit of radical Islamists (but *not* mainstream Muslims) of turning the shari'a into what it never was—a blueprint for a political order—are obvious.[121]

However, and second, Pentecostalism's structural myopia often diminishes over time, sometimes quite quickly. Pentecostals in the United States, Brazil, and East Asia are today building impressive theological institutes in which public ethical and political issues are the subject of sophisticated reflection. Others are involved in ministering to orphans, the poor, and victims of HIV/AIDS. However, for some "sophisticated dissenters" (to borrow Maxwell's phrase), the effort may be too late, as some among the faithful have moved on to non-Pentecostal churches or study groups dedicated to a different form of public engagement.

In fact, Pentecostalism in some parts of the world, especially Latin America, may already be in the first stages of experiencing serious defections from its ranks. In his chapter in this volume, Freston comments that "a frontier of Pentecostal research today is . . . what one might call the historicization of Pentecostalism, that is, the move toward non-Pentecostal (although usually Evangelical) Protestant forms." This may prove to be an important horizon of research because, if the Latin American example proves general, significant numbers of Pentecostals are going to exit from their faith tradition for other varieties of Protestantism as they ascend the social and educational ladder.

Third, the restlessness caused by an inability to resolve vexing personal and social problems may lead some offspring of believers to give up a Christian faith entirely. As Freston and David Martin observe, upwards of 50 percent of Pentecostal offspring leave the faith, some for other religions, but a growing number away from all intensely professed religion (though these are not in the majority). Secularism and anticlericalism have stronger roots in Latin America than they do in most of Africa and much of Asia (the People's Republic of China being a notable exception), and it would be premature to suggest that the secularist trends Freston observes in Brazil are likely to gain momentum any time soon in Africa or Asia. However, in the late modern West, consumerism and higher education have proved to be powerful carriers of secularism in their own right; some second- and third-generation Pentecostals have been attracted to both. So we should not be surprised to see that, as Pentecostals move into the upper reaches of the new middle class, some among their offspring opt to ground their identities on something other than a born-again faith.

What all of these examples suggest is that, as late-modern religious movements go, Pentecostalism has the distinction of being both enormously successful but also, sociologically speaking, protean and unstable. Pentecostalism is a religion on the move for people on the go. But the religion's success at stabilizing families and facilitating social mobility may eventually turn it into a vehicle capable of traveling to other, non-Pentecostal destinations. For many born-again believers the latter will be some variety of Evangelical Christianity, a global movement that has now evolved its own impressive array of intellectuals, institutions, and polities.[122] But for other

Pentecostals the revolving door may lead to different social options: a more indifferent profession of Christianity; for young men, alcohol, football, and sexual predation; higher education and secularity; or a different religious or ethical tradition entirely.

But to say that Pentecostalism is energetic and unstable is not to say that its global horizons are likely to shrink any time soon. The dislocations and reorientations that facilitated Pentecostalism's growth in the global south during the late twentieth century may be steadying in parts of Latin America, but their force is still strong across much of Africa, Asia, and the Pacific. India and China may yet give rise to spectacular Pentecostal surges.

So what can we expect? All evidence suggests that we are in the midst of a great pluralization of Pentecostal horizons. The eager fascination with a Christian message that is personally powerful, gender gentle, and socially egalitarian may decline in some second- or third-generation circles. Among other believers, however, the decline may be forestalled by the emergence of a new class of Pentecostal cosmopolitans giving voice to a more intellectualized and socially accommodating version of the faith. More generally, however, the message shows no sign of losing its global appeal any time soon; indeed, today it is being reinterpreted to support more varied forms of evangelical witness and social engagement. Certainly, the harsh realities of our age, including the misadventures of church elders, have a habit of making short shrift of sweet religious idealisms. But that very harshness, and the distressing pervasiveness of threats to hope and human dignity, are part of the reason that some variety of inspirited Christianity will continue to resonate with global moderns for many years to come.

NOTES

1. Todd M. Johnson and Kenneth R. Ross, *Atlas of Global Christianity* (Edinburgh: Edinburgh University Press, 2009), 102–103. It is important to add that estimates still vary widely, from as low as two hundred million to six hundred million or more. As David Martin notes in his chapter in this volume, much of the variation turns on the extent to which one narrows or broadens one's categories to include all varieties of renewal or charismatic Christianity.

2. Both Pentecostals and charismatic Christians can be distinguished from other modern varieties of Christianity by their theological and performative emphasis on spiritual renewal (being "born-again") through the power and gifts (*charismata*) of the Holy Spirit. What distinguishes charismatics from Pentecostals is that, though both groups emphasize charismata, the former retain a formal affiliation with the historic churches, especially the Catholic, Anglican, and Protestant churches, as well as (in lesser numbers) the Orthodox churches. The Catholic charismatic movement is the largest among charismatics, and is today accepted by the church hierarchy, and

even seen as an important instrument of evangelization in the global south. The first generation of North American Pentecostals regarded their movement as a direct heir to a tradition of prophecy, healing, glossolalia, and other gifts of the Holy Spirit that had declined after the first century CE until its revival in Topeka and on Azusa Street in the first years of the twentieth century. But the movement's emphasis on spiritual renewal and "being born-again" has antecedents in ancient and medieval currents of Christianity as well as, most importantly, several varieties of nineteenth-century Evangelical revivalism. See discussion below, and Stanley M. Burgess, "Antecedents of Pentecostalism," in *Encyclopedia of Pentecostal and Charismatic Christianity,* ed. Stanley M. Burgess (New York: Routledge 2006), 30–34.

3. See Nanlai Cao's chapter in this volume, and D. Bays, "Chinese Protestant Christianity Today," in *Religion in China Today,* ed. Daniel L. Overmyer. *The China Quarterly,* special issue no. 3 (Cambridge: Cambridge University Press, 2003), 182–198.

4. A debate vividly analyzed from distinct disciplinary perspectives in three recent works: Ogbu Kalu, *African Pentecostalism: An Introduction* (Oxford: Oxford University Press, 2008), 65–82; Birgit Meyer, "Christianity in Africa: From African Independent Churches to Pentecostal-Charismatic Churches," *Annual Review of Anthropology* 33 (2004): 447–474; and J. D. Y. Peel, *Religious Encounter and the Making of the Yoruba* (Bloomington: Indiana University Press, 2000).

5. On Christian Orthodox and charismatic renewal in the countries of the former Soviet Union, see Christopher Marsh and Artyom Tonoyan, this volume; for an overview of the still-fledgling anthropology of Eastern Christianity, see Chris Hann and Hermann Golts, eds., *Eastern Christians in Anthropological Perspective* (Berkeley: University of California Press, 2010).

6. This book's highlighting of "developmental tensions" draws on David Maxwell's discussion of the same concept in his *African Gifts of the Spirit: Pentecostalism and the Rise of a Zimbabwean Transnational Religious Movement* (Oxford: James Currey, 2006), 213.

7. Especially influential in the latter half of the nineteenth century, the Holiness movement was a Methodist-inspired current that emphasized the importance of believers experiencing an "entire sanctification" through a second and instantaneous "work of grace" that replaced the inclination to sin with perfect love. The force of the experience was thought to reflect the work of the Holy Spirit, and was accompanied by expressive performance and boisterous emotion. See Paul M. Basset, "Holiness Movement," in *Encyclopedia of Christianity,* ed. John Bowden (Oxford: Oxford University Press, 2005), 575–578; Edith L. Blumhofer, *Restoring the Faith: The Assemblies of God, Pentecostalism, and American Culture* (Urbana: University of Illinois Press, 1993), esp. 26–30.

8. See J. R. Goff Jr., "Parham, Charles Fox," in *New International Dictionary of the Pentecostal and Charismatic Movements,* ed. S. M. Burgess, 955–957 (Grand Rapids, MI: Zondervan, 2002); and Vinson Synan, "America, North" in *Encyclopedia of Pentecostal and Charismatic Christianity,* 21–26.

9. See I. MacRobert, *The Black Roots and White Racism of Early Pentecostalism in the USA* (Basingstoke: MacMillan, 1988). Ann Taves's *Fits, Trances, and Visions: Experiencing Religion and Explaining Religion from Wesley to James* (Princeton: Princeton University Press, 1999), esp. 328–337, discusses the controversy caused by this borrowing of African American religious expressivity.

10. Synan, "America, North," 23.

11. Allan Anderson, "Revising Pentecostal History in Global Perspective," in *Asian and Pentecostal: The Charismatic Face of Christianity in Asia,* ed. Allan Anderson and Edmond Tang, 2nd ed. (Eugene, OR: WIPF and Stock, 2011), 22–29; citation from 25.

12. G. B. McGee, "Missions, Overseas," in *Dictionary of Pentecostal and Charismatic Movements,* ed. Stanley M. Burgess and Gary B. McGee (Grand Rapids, MI: Zondervan, 1988), 610–625; citation from 612.

13. Synan, "America, North," 23; cf. Estrelda Y. Alexander, "Race Relations," in Burgess, *Encyclopedia of Pentecostal and Charismatic Christianity,* 401–404; and Margaret M. Poloma and John C. Green, *The Assemblies of God: Godly Love and the Revitalization of American Pentecostalism* (New York: New York University Press, 2010), 6.

14. Poloma and Green, *The Assemblies,* 8.

15. Ibid., 159–161.

16. In discussing legacies bequeathed by European missionaries to West African Pentecostals today, both J. D. Y. Peel and Ruth Marshall point out that Protestant missionaries played a role in Africa not unlike that I am describing here for Methodists in the nineteenth-century United States. Both traditions emphasized what Peel calls a "religion of the heart, a state of living with a continuous sense of the saving presence of Jesus Christ and of the enthusing power of the Holy spirit. . . . [R]eligion was thus validated as much in psychological as in doctrinal terms." See Peel, *Religious Encounter,* 250; and Ruth Marshall, *Political Spiritualities: The Pentecostal Revolution in Nigeria* (Chicago: University of Chicago Press, 2009), 54–68.

17. See Paul Freston, "Introduction: The Many Faces of Evangelical Politics in Latin America." In *Evangelical Christianity and Democracy in Latin America,* ed. Paul Freston (Oxford: Oxford University Press, 2008), 3–36, esp. 13.

18. On the distinctiveness of Western European secularity, see José Casanova, "The Secular, Secularizations, Secularisms," in *Rethinking Secularism,* ed. Craig Calhoun, Mark Juergensmeyer, and Jonathan Van Antwerpen (Oxford: Oxford University Press, 2011), 54–74; Grace Davie, *Europe: The Exceptional Case: Parameters of Faith in the Modern World* (London: Dartman, Longman, and Todd, 2002); and *The Decline of Christendom in Western Europe, 1750–2000,* ed. Hugh McLeod and Werner Ustorf (Cambridge: Cambridge University Press, 2003).

19. Political subordination within a socially mobile and multiethnic empire in which rulers do not enjoy effective control over popular moral imaginaries, however, was one of the conditions facilitating the emergence of some among the "historic" or "world" religions. See my "World Building and the Rationality of Conversion," in *Conversion to Christianity: Historical and Anthropological Perspectives on a Great Transformation,* ed. Robert W. Hefner (Berkeley: University of California Press, 1993), 3–44.

20. See Ruth Marshall-Fratani, "Mediating the Global and Local in Nigerian Pentecostalism," in *Journal of Religion in Africa* 28:3 (1998), 278–315; citation is from 284.

21. See Timothy S. Lee, "Beleaguered Success: Korean Evangelicalism in the Last Decade of the Twentieth Century," in *Christianity in Korea,* ed. Robert W. Buswell and Timothy S. Lee (Honolulu: University of Hawaii Press, 2006), 330–350, esp. 341.

22. See Brian M. Howell, *Christianity in the Local Context: Southern Baptists in the Philippines* (New York: Palgrave Macmillan, 2008), 23. Howell's study of Southern

Baptists in the Northern Philippines offers richly generalizable insights into the tension between the local and the transcendent/universal in non-Western Christianities.

23. Marshall, *Political Spiritualities,* 75–76.

24. Maxwell, *African Gifts of the Spirit,* 187; the passage is referring to preachers in the Zimbabwe Assemblies of God Africa.

25. Margaret M. Poloma, *The Assemblies of God at the Crossroads: Charisma and Institutional Dilemmas* (Knoxville: University of Tennessee Press, 1989).

26. See R. Andrew Chesnut, *Born Again in Brazil: The Pentecostal Boom and the Pathogens of Poverty* (New Brunswick, N.J.: Rutgers University Press, 1997), 135; David Maxwell, this volume, and *African Gifts of the Spirit.*

27. See, for example, Maxwell in this volume; and Marshall, *Political Spiritualities,* 77. For a bracing example of a developmental process different from that of denominationalism, see Matthew Engelke, *A Problem of Presence: Beyond Scripture in an African Church* (Berkeley: University of California Press, 2007). The Zimbabwe-based "Friday apostolics" who are the focus of Engelke's study take the logic of universal gifts of the Holy Spirit to an extreme. Members insist that "In place of Scripture . . . they receive the Word of God live and direct from the Holy Spirit" (p. 3). Not surprisingly, then, "The sense of immediacy that stands at the heart of [the Friday apostolics'] . . . message militates against enduring forms" (p. 135).

28. David Martin, *Pentecostalism: The World Their Parish* (Oxford: Blackwell, 2002), 6.

29. David Maxwell, "'Delivered from the Spirit of Poverty?' Pentecostalism, Prosperity and Modernity in Zimbabwe," *Journal of Religion in Africa* 28:3, 350–373.

30. See Nigel Thrift, *Knowing Capitalism* (London: Sage, 2005), and "The Rise of Soft Capitalism," in *An Unruly World? Globalisation, Governance and Geography,* ed. Andrew Herod, Gearoid O'Tuathail, and Susan Roberts, 57–71 (London: Sage, 1998).

31. Joel Robbins, "The Globalization of Pentecostal and Charismatic Christianity," *Annual Review of Anthropology* 33 (2004), 117–143, esp. 128. Cf. Birgit Meyer, "'Make a Complete Break with the Past': Memory and Post-Colonial Modernity in Ghanaian Pentecostalist Discourse," *Journal of Religion in Africa* 28:3 (1995), 316–349; and Matthew Engelke, "Past Pentecostalism: Notes on Rupture, Realignment, and Everyday Life in Pentecostal and African Independent Churches," *Africa* 80:2 (2010), 177–199.

32. James Pfeiffer, Kenneth Gimbel-Sherr, and Orvalho Joaquim Augusto, "The Holy Spirit in the Household: Pentecostalism, Gender, and Neoliberalism in Mozambique," *American Anthropologist* 88:4 (2007), 688–700; citation from 697.

33. Ibid., 696.

34. See Chesnut, *Born Again in Brazil;* and André Corten, *Pentecostalism in Brazil: Emotion of the Poor and Theological Romanticism* (New York: St. Martin's Press, 1999), 27.

35. Allan Anderson, *Spreading Fires: The Missionary Nature of Early Pentecostalism* (London: SCM, 2007).

36. Edith L. Blumhofer, *Restoring the Faith,* 175.

37. Bernice Martin, "The Pentecostal Gender Paradox: A Cautionary Tale for the Sociology of Religion," in *The Blackwell Companion to Sociology of Religion,* ed. Richard K. Fenn (Oxford: Blackwell Publishers, 2001), 52–66; citation from 54. See also Salvatore Cucchiari, "Between Shame and Sanctification: Patriarchy and Its Transformation in Sicilian Pentecostalism," *American Ethnologist* 17:4 (1990),

687–707; and John Burdick, *Blessed Anastácia: Women, Race, and Popular Christianity in Brazil* (New York: Routledge, 1998).

38. Elizabeth E. Brusco, *The Reformation of Machismo: Evangelical Conversion and Gender in Colombia* (Austin: University of Texas Press, 1995).

39. Elizabeth Brusco, "Gender and Power," in *Studying Global Pentecostalism: Theories + Methods,* ed. Allan Anderson, Michael Bergunder, André Droogers, and Cornelis van der Laan (Berkeley: University of California Press, 2010), 80.

40. Ibid.

41. See Nanlai Cao's contribution to this volume, as well as his *Constructing China's Jerusalem: Christians, Power, and Place in Contemporary Wenzhou* (Stanford: Stanford University Press, 2011), 113–115.

42. See Julie C. Ma, "Asian Women and Pentecostal Ministry," in Anderson and Tang, *Asian and Pentecostal,* 116.

43. Marshall, *Political Spiritualities,* 113–114.

44. David Martin, *Pentecostalism: The World Their Parish* (Oxford: Blackwell, 2002), 7.

45. See Rebecca and Timothy Shah, this volume, and Michael Bergunder, "Constructing Indian Pentecostalism: On Issues of Methodology and Representation," in Anderson and Tang, *Asian and Pentecostal,* 143–173; and Gary McGee, "'Latter Rain' Falling in the East: Early-Twentieth Century Pentecostalism in India and the Debate over Speaking in Tongues," in *Church History* 69 (September 1999), 648–665; citation from 650.

46. Allan Anderson, "Revising Pentecostal History in Global Perspective," in Anderson and Tang, *Asian and Pentecostal,* 129.

47. Anderson, "Revising," 127. See also Daniel H. Bays, *A New History of Christianity in China* (Malden, MA: Wiley-Blackwell, 2012), 105.

48. On the debate over Pentecostalism as made-in-the-U.S.A. vs. having multiple origins, see Darrin J. Rodgers, "Pentecostalism, Classical," in Burgess, *Encyclopedia of Pentecostal and Charismatic Christianity,* 359–363; for an analysis of the debate in light of Africa's Christian history, see Obgu Kalu, *African Pentecostalism,* 11–22.

49. Anderson, "Revising Pentecostal History," 118.

50. Ibid., 121.

51. The pioneering study remains Walter J. Hollenweger's *The Pentecostals* (London: SCM Publishers, 1971); Hollenweger updated his analysis in his *Pentecostalism: Origins and Developments Worldwide* (Peabody, MA: Hendrickson, 1997). A notable exception to the lack of social scientific study of Pentecostalism is Christian Lalive D'Épinay's *Haven of the Masses: A Study of the Pentecostal Movement in Chile* (London: Lutterworth, 1969), which combined class analysis with deprivation theory to argue that Pentecostalism was a largely irrational response to political and economic marginalization.

52. An important exception to the nonpolitical focus of most research in this period is David Stoll's *Is Latin America Turning Protestant? The Politics of Evangelical Growth* (Berkeley: University of California Press, 1990). Stoll dedicated more of his attention to Evangelicalism than he did Pentecostalism, and much of his account portrays the sadly polarized nature of Protestant politics in Latin America and the United States at the time. However, his book's final pages include a short section titled "Pentecostalism as a Basis for Social Reformation" (314–321). Today this section's

insights into Pentecostalism's social vitality, gender impact, and capacity for broader public engagements seem prescient.

53. David Martin, *Tongues of Fire: The Explosion of Protestantism in Latin America* (Oxford: Basil Blackwell, 1990), 66.

54. Ibid., 108.

55. Ibid., 6.

56. Ibid., 266.

57. Paul Gifford, *The New Crusaders: Christianity and the New Right in Southern Africa* (London: Pluto, 1991), 65–66. Revisiting the same topic after more than a decade of change across Africa, Gifford reached a more nuanced conclusion. He noted that, on matters of structural reform, "the role of these churches since the 1980s has been mixed," with some churches addressing structural challenges while others tend "to divert attention away from them." See Paul Gifford, *Ghana's New Christianity: Pentecostalism in a Globalizing African Economy* (Bloomington: Indiana University Press, 2004), 197.

58. See Katharine L. Wiegele, *Investing in Miracles: El Shaddai and the Transformation of Popular Catholicism in the Philippines* (Honolulu: University of Hawaii Press, 2005), 89.

59. David Maxwell, "'Delivered from the Spirit of Poverty?,'" 352, and *African Gifts of the Spirit*, 88–106.

60. Kevin Lewis O'Neill, *City of God: Christian Citizenship in Postwar Guatemala* (Berkeley: University of California Press, 2010), 3.

61. Paul Freston, *Evangelicals and Politics in Asia, Africa, and Latin America* (Cambridge: Cambridge University Press, 2001), 305.

62. Based on his Ghanaian study, Gifford's conclusion is particularly severe. "The claim that charismatic churches of themselves or as such must be fostering socio-political reform has not been proved. Nearly all operate on neo-patrimonial or patronage rather than accountable bureaucratic lines, encouraging the emergence of the 'Big Man' rather than empowering the ranks." Gifford, *Ghana's New Christianity,* 197.

63. Maxwell, "'Delivered from the Spirit of Poverty?,'" 352. Cf. Marshall's analysis of the role of Pentecostals in Nigerian politics, in her *Political Spiritualities,* esp. 204–238.

64. Paul Freston, "Introduction: The Many Faces of Evangelical Politics in Latin America," in Freston, *Evangelical Christianity and Democracy in Latin America,* 3–36.

65. Stoll, *Is Latin America Turning Protestant?,* 316.

66. Martin, *Tongues of Fire,* 27.

67. See O'Neill, *City of God,* xvi.

68. As Elizabeth Brusco has observed, the boundaries between Evangelical and Pentecostal Protestants, fuzzy in many contexts, is particularly blurry in Latin America. See Brusco, *The Reformation of Machismo,* 14–22. Although the two varieties are easier to distinguish in Brazil, many of the countries' larger parties make their appeals as though the two communities overlapped.

69. Freston, "Introduction," 26.

70. Marshall, *Political Spiritualities,* 132–133, 165.

71. Freston, "Introduction," 27.

72. Ibid.

73. Freston, "Introduction," 28.

74. Ibid., 31.

75. Ibid., 32–33.

76. The role of Pentecostals and Evangelicals in today's postwar Guatemala is more complex, with high rates of Pentecostal electoral participation, but also distinctively Christian practices of citizenship. See O'Neill, *City of God.*

77. Freston, "Introduction," 33.

78. Maxwell, *African Gifts of the Spirit,* 3.

79. See Jean Comaroff, *Body of Power, Spirit of Resistance: The Culture and History of a South African People* (Chicago: University of Chicago Press, 1985); Terence O. Ranger, "The Local and the Global in Southern African Religious History," in *Conversion to Christianity: Historical and Anthropological Perspectives on a Great Transformation,* ed. Robert W. Hefner (Berkeley: University of California Press, 1993), 65–98.

80. Martin, *Tongues of Fire,* 33.

81. Ibid., 34.

82. Ibid., 96, 103.

83. Ibid., 105.

84. Ibid., 228–229.

85. D. Martin, *Pentecostalism: The World Their Parish,* 75.

86. See Bernice Martin, this volume and, especially, two earlier essays: "New Mutations of the Protestant Ethic among Latin American Pentecostals," *Religion* 25 (1995), 101–117; and "From Pre- to Postmodernity in Latin America: The Case of Pentecostalism," in *Religion, Modernity, and Postmodernity,* ed. Paul Heelas (Oxford: Blackwell, 1998), 102–146.

87. See, for example, Patrick Haenni, *L'Islam de marché: l'autre revolution conservatrice* (Paris: Seuil, 2005); James B. Hoesterey, "Sufis and Self-Help Gurus: Islamic Psychology, Religious Authority, and Muslim Subjectivity in Contemporary Indonesia" (Ph.D. dissertation, University of Wisconsin–Madison, 2009); and Daromir Rudnyckyj, *Spiritual Economies: Islam, Globalization, and the Afterlife of Development* (Ithaca: Cornell University Press, 2010).

88. D. Martin, *Pentecostalism,* 71.

89. Ibid., 77.

90. Ibid., 79.

91. O'Neill, *City of God,* xxiv.

92. See Simon M. Coleman, *The Globalisation of Charismatic Christianity: Spreading the Gospel of Prosperity* (Cambridge: Cambridge University Press, 2000); and Rosalind I. J. Hackett, "The Gospel of Prosperity in West Africa," in *Religions and the Transformations of Capitalism: Comparative Approaches,* ed. Richard H. Roberts (London: Routledge, 1995), 199–124.

93. On the rise of a new prosperity ethic in contemporary Islam, see Haenni, *L'Islam de Marché,* and Rudnyckyj, *Spiritual Economies;* on Theravada Buddhism, Rachelle M. Scott, *Nirvana for Sale? Buddhism, Wealth, and the Dhammakâya Temple in Contemporary Thailand* (Albany: State University of New York Press, 2009); on Asian faith traditions generally, see my "Religious Resurgence in Contemporary Asia: Southeast Asian Perspectives on Capitalism, the State, and the New Piety," *Journal of Asian Studies* 69:4 (2010), 1031–1047.

94. Simon M. Coleman, "America Loves Sweden: Prosperity Theology and the Cultures of Capitalism," in *Religions and the Transformations of Capitalism:*

Comparative Approaches, ed. Richard H. Roberts (London: Routledge, 1995), 161–179; citation from 167.

95. The quote is from Bernice Martin, personal communication, May 3, 2012.

96. Birgit Meyer, "Pentecostalism and Globalization," in Anderson, Bergunder, Droogers, and van der Laan, *Studying Global Pentecostalism,* 113–130; citation is from 115.

97. Marshall, *Political Spiritualities,* 177.

98. See also Mark Andrew Robinson, "Pentecostalism in Urban Java: A Study of Religious Change, 1980–2006" (Ph.D. dissertation, University of Queensland, 2008); and Jan Sihgar Aritonang and Karel Steenbrink, "The Spectacular Growth of the Third Stream: The Evangelicals and Pentecostals," in *A History of Christianity in Indonesia,* ed. Jan Sihgar Aritonang and Karel Steenbrink (Leiden: Brill, 2008), 867–902.

99. See Nanlai Cao, this volume; Bays, "Chinese Protestant Christianity," 195; and D. Martin, *Pentecostalism,* 155–157.

100. Wiegele, *Investing in Miracles,* 3.

101. Wiegele, *Investing in Miracles,* 103; Freston, "Introduction," 26.

102. Although not specifically focused on prosperity optimism, T. M. Luhrmann offers rich psychocultural insights into a related phenomenon: the intensely personal and transformative nature of charismatic prayer. See her *When God Talks Back: Understanding the American Evangelical Relationship with God* (New York: Alfred A. Knopf, 2012).

103. Wiegele, *Investing,* 171.

104. Ibid., 173.

105. Marshall, *Political Spiritualities,* 85.

106. Rijk van Dijk, "Social Catapulting and the Spirit of Entrepreneurialism: Migrants, Private Initiative, and the Pentecostal Ethic in Botswana," in *Traveling Spirits: Migrants, Markets and Mobilities,* ed. G. Hüwelmeier and K. Krause (New York: Routledge, 2009), 101–117; citation from 111.

107. Naomi Haynes, "Pentecostalism and the Morality of Money: Prosperity, Inequality, and Religious Sociality on the Zambian Copperbelt," *Journal of the Royal Anthropological Institute* (N.S.) 18 (2012), 123–139; citation from 136.

108. Marshall-Fratani, "Mediating the Global and Local," 282.

109. Ibid., 170.

110. See references in endnote 90.

111. See for example, Birgit Meyer, "Impossible Representations: Pentecostalism, Vision, and Video Technology in Ghana," in Religion, Media, and the Public Sphere, ed. Birgit Meyer and Annelies Moors (Bloomington: Indiana University Press, 2006), 290–312.

112. O'Neill, City of God, xx–xxi.

113. Freston, "Introduction," 16.

114. David Martin, "Issues Affecting the Study of Pentecostalism in Asia," in Anderson and Tang, *Asian and Pentecostal,* 22–29; quote is from 25.

115. Maxwell, *African Gifts,* 14.

116. Ibid., 192. See also Frederick Klaits, *Death in a Church of Life: Moral Passion During Botswana's Time of AIDs* (Berkeley: University of California Press, 2010).

117. Maxwell, *African Gifts,* 193.

118. Ibid., 194.

119. See Donald E. Miller and Tetsunao Yamamori, *Global Pentecostalism: The New Face of Christian Social Engagement* (Berkeley: University of California Press, 2007). While recognizing that it is just one current among Pentecostalism's many streams, Miller and Yamamori provide a panoramic survey of socially engaged Pentecostalism around the world, demonstrating that its presence is anything but marginal. For an ethnographic portrait of a related shift from separation and estrangement to faith-based outreach in a North American Evangelical context, see Omri Elish's *Moral Ambition: Mobilization and Social Outreach in Evangelical Megachurches* (Berkeley: University of California Press, 2011).

120. See Seth Dowland, "The New Dominionist Politics," *Religion in the News* 14:1 (spring 2012), 15–17.

121. The point here is that, contrary to portrayals by Western pundits and some Islamist militants today, Islamic jurisprudence historically provided no unchanging and comprehensive blueprint for state organization, but left most of the details of governance (Ar., *siyasa*) to rulers. However, an important difference between main-stream Pentecostal and Muslim viewpoints on politics remains apparent still today. Pentecostalism's initial emphasis on personal security and subjectivity-making has ensured that believers typically show an interest in developing a broader social theology only after securing themselves and their families and beginning to reengage the surrounding society. By contrast, the centrality of jurisprudence (*fiqh*) and legal education in some among the Muslim world's main public-ethical streams guarantees that, even if divine law lacks a blueprint for state-building, the mainstream Muslim imaginary more readily assumes God's law must somehow relate to the structural. Even here, however, there is enormous variation: not all streams in Islamic civilization place equal emphasis on religious law and legal education; popular piety and Sufi movements may deal lightly with jurisprudential concerns and direct the believer's primary gaze toward the refiguring of the subjective; and reform-minded propo-nents of the shari'a today may place greater emphasis on the "higher aims of the law" (maqasid as-shari'a) than on unchanging and specific injunctions or stipulations. See Sami Zubaida, *Law and Power in the Islamic World* (London: I. B. Tauris, 2003); Tariq Ramadan, *Radical Reform: Islamic Ethics and Liberation* (Oxford: Oxford University Press, 2009), 59–83; and my "Introduction: Shari'a Politics—Law and Society in the Modern Muslim World," in Robert W. Hefner, *Shari'a Politics: Islamic Law and Society in the Modern World* (Bloomington: Indiana University Press, 2011), 1–54.

122. See Timothy S. Shah and James C. Wallace, *Smarter Than You Think: The Surprising Emergence of an Evangelical Intelligentsia in America* (New York: Oxford University Press, forthcoming 2014).

ONE

Pentecostalism: An Alternative Form of Modernity and Modernization?

DAVID MARTIN

The religious origins of Pentecostalism lie in different strains of Christianity, but especially in the Methodist Holiness tradition. Likewise the social and geographical origins of Pentecostalism lie in locations as far apart as India and Wales, even though Pentecostals attach special importance to the explosion of fervor among a global concourse of people led by a black preacher in Los Angeles in 1906. After this paradigmatic event, white and black traditions of revival fused in a potent amalgam capable of crossing any number of cultural species barriers. A global starburst of missionary activity followed, often traveling along tracks pioneered by missionaries in the Holiness and Evangelical traditions.

Pentecostals take their cue from the New Testament and retrieve those aspects of the pristine gospel they believe to be lost in a mainstream rationalized Christianity, above all the gifts of Pentecost. Pentecostals recreate the New Testament, especially Luke–Acts, and their account of their origins echoes the time in Jerusalem when the disciples "received the Holy Ghost" during the post-Resurrection period of Pentecost. In Acts chapter 2 we are told that people were present from all over the Roman Empire and all heard the message "as it were in their own tongue." Missionaries spread out all round the Roman world, often following tracks laid down by Jewish proselytes. There is a parallel between global mobility in the late twentieth century, as that accelerated from the 1960s on, and the expanding network of communications in the Roman Empire. The empire was knit together by road, sea, and Greek and Latin, and the contemporary global reality is knit together by air travel, television, and the Internet, as well as English, Spanish, and other metropolitan languages.

We have in the early years, then, a fusion of white and black revivalist traditions, modern communications, and a metalanguage symbolically crossing ethnic and cultural barriers. Pentecostalism celebrates the gifts promised to everyone "baptized in the Spirit": tongues, healing, exorcism, and prophecy. Spiritual and physical healing are crucial to the witness of

Pentecostals, especially where secular provision is scanty. Women exercise the gift of prophecy, while men more often exercise the gifts of preaching and exposition.

Pentecostalism is a narrative and oral faith, preached in homely language with homely examples by homely people to homely people. Believers exercise their gifts by immediate experience on the job, not lengthy instruction in theological colleges, though further training may be offered by biblical institutes. The message is urgent because expecting the end-time can stimulate remarkable bursts of energy in the meantime. Conversion represents an emotional upheaval whereby people discover new energies and fresh agency to overcome whatever may befall, confident that they are in the hands of providence. They are empowered through faith to do "all things."

Pentecostal teaching exhorts worshippers to a better life in this world in every sense of what the Victorians called betterment. They believe in self-help, and their religion is one of self-control and self-fashioning in everyday life fueled by self-expression in worship, Bible reading, and constant prayer. They want to be victors, not victims, and they change their circumstances rather than expecting others to right their wrongs for them. They know how to organize and they offer believers roles with opportunities to learn skills of leadership and organization. Perhaps the church helps its members acquire useful crafts like house-building or gives them scope to improve their musical gifts through playing an instrument or conducting a choir. The Victorian ideal of improvement complements self-help and betterment.

Betterment and prosperity here and now have deep roots in the Old Testament, whereas the powers of the Spirit revive the promises of the New. Pentecostals are most successful where the local gods are associated with the everyday goods of this life and Pentecostals promote a good God, the moral good, and the goods. Martin Lindhardt describes them as seeking to moralize money rather than view it as a donation of Fortune.[1] Classical Pentecostals in the Holiness tradition are more alert to the dangers of possessions, whereas Neo-Pentecostals are more conscious of the constrictions of poverty and the benefits of consumerism. Neo-Pentecostals question whether anyone *wants* to be poor. The Pentecostal ethos is shown by texts that speak of "the day of small things," or propose advancement "not by might or power but by my Spirit,"[2] or warn believers not to "put money in a bag full of holes," or claim the righteous shall not "want for bread."

Pentecostal worship is participatory, with much body movement, free use of space, and rhythmic singing, so a service may last several hours at any time and often seems like a rock concert. Pentecostals have revived spontaneity in liturgy, though that requires greater control by pastors than fixed liturgies. The same style has been adopted by Catholic charismatics, for example in the Philippines, where the mass movement known as El Shaddai mobilizes populist religious sentiment (see Katherine Wiegele's chapter in this volume). Participation and spontaneity are associated with charismatic authority rather than with a priesthood mediating the divine through settled rituals. Moreover, the power of the divine sensed in major Pentecostal and charismatic events creates a sense of collective presence among participants.

The Development of a Transnational Voluntary Association

Pentecostalism spearheads the modern efflorescence of the transnational voluntary group, depending on protective borders around the believers rather than on territorial borders. It often lacks a sense of locality and place, and lies at the other end of the spectrum from territorial churches conferring membership by ethnic birthright. Voluntarism distinguishes Pentecostalism from the historic world faiths, all of which have major territorial emplacements. However, transnational voluntarism does not prevent Pentecostalism from sometimes appealing to ethnic minorities or bidding for political influence and local power.

Inevitably the historical roots of Pentecostalism lie within territorial churches. They reach back to Germany, where devotional and Pietist groups with missionary aspirations proliferated within Lutheranism, for example in Halle and Hernnhut, and more immediately to England, where groups influenced by German developments emerged within the Church of England. In England these devotional cells, preaching the need for an experience of conversion, broke away into voluntary groups to form a large voluntary sector. Meanwhile in North America various migrant groups, many of them closely linked to the voluntary sector and to revivalism in the British Isles, constituted the dominant form of religion. They created the first pluralistic society and the seedbed within which white and black revivalism might fuse in Pentecostalism.

Fusion and fission go together, and Pentecostalism has constantly broken up into groups started by rival religious entrepreneurs and adjusting to varied clienteles. As often happens with religious enthusiasm, men and women, white and black, may be fused together in the initial period of effervescence by a common purpose. Momentarily they enjoy a unity across barriers of gender and race. But as with previous movements, Methodism included, these barriers return as time goes on. Some churches, like the Four Square Gospel Church founded by Aimee MacPherson, accept female pastors, while others stress male headship although women play major roles in leadership.[3] Some churches are racially mixed and others not.

The missionary drive of Pentecostalism paralleled the missionary drive within the mainstream churches, notably the expectations voiced at the Edinburgh Missionary conference of 1910. Pentecostalism is the populist alternative to the mainstream churches, and is more aligned to inspirited religiosity in the majority world. It plans to "preach the gospel to every creature" and fulfill the "Great Commission" at the conclusion of Matthew's Gospel. Pentecostalism is the successor, as well as a rival, to Methodism, a mainstream church that used to play the social role now played by Pentecostalism. As Methodism was to the Church of England, so the Holiness branch of Methodism was to the more staid forms of Methodism, and so Pentecostalism was to the Holiness movement. Moreover, what Élie Halévy argued about the role of Methodism in preventing a French-style revolution in England can also be argued about Pentecostalism in the two-thirds world.[4] As Methodism mobilized subordinate groups and gave voice to their aspirations, especially in singing, so today Pentecostalism mobilizes newly emerging groups around the globe, giving voice to their hopes, especially in ecstatic utterance. Pentecostalism emulates *and* competes with groups, for example in Africa, that have already partly achieved those hopes and aspirations. It is the noisy ecstasy of the poor who are not so poor they cannot hope to be better off.

Wanting to Matter, to Be Mobile and Educated

Aspiring groups that eventually find a voice, or an ecstatic tongue, seek recognition; and they begin by asserting they are recognized by a God who overlooks the contemptuous hierarchies of men. As large assemblies of hitherto unnoticed and excluded people look around them, and as politicians learn their language to seek their support, the once-excluded realize they quite literally count for something. They cite inflated statistics of their success, congratulating themselves on the disciplines and experiences of responsibility that have assisted their social mobility thus far.

In time, the experience of social mobility may motivate some members to identify once more with a mainstream church, just as some Methodists have once more identified with the Anglican Church. In some places, for example in parts of Latin America, there is a complete alternative hierarchy of denominations, and religious mobility through this hierarchy mirrors social mobility. People may begin in a highly ascetic and humble group and graduate to a group with a more relaxed atmosphere, and one serving the social constituency to which they aspire rather than the one to which they currently belong. Members of groups that have already achieved success seek an atmosphere that speaks to their moral problems and existential anxieties. In Latin America, charismatic Anglicans or Baptists "in renewal" may meet their concerns more directly than the Catholic Church.[5]

Alternatively members of one generation may pass through the Pentecostal experience and achieve what they aspire to, only to find the Pentecostal environment too restrictive or culturally too limited and slip into a merely nominal Christianity. Some may leave the Assemblies of God and join a businessmen's fellowship or a house church. For others the Pentecostal experience is just a phase in the life-cycle, though one that probably leaves its mark before they depart. Plausible estimates suggest that roughly half of Pentecostal converts fall away, and male adolescents are particularly at risk, suborned by the adolescent life-style and football, sex, and alcohol at the weekend. All this makes it very difficult to identify the impact on social mobility of Pentecostal personal and familial discipline. Obviously, if you give up alcohol, tobacco, and philandering, replace the street with the domestic table, and rope yourselves together with others of like mind, your life chances are likely to improve. Mobility probably occurs over generations, but there are no longitudinal studies to document this.

The complexity of any estimate of what Pentecostalism contributes to social mobility becomes clear once you take into account people who are *already* mobile and who find the Pentecostal or charismatic ethos an attractive reinforcement of the discipline that has helped them advance hitherto. There are various patterns here. One or two Pentecostal churches, like the Redeemed Christian Church of God in Nigeria, seek out members of the elite. The RCCG offers a particularly exuberant example of the church as an international business corporation, and it appeals to people at ease in that environment.[6] Some entrepreneurs in the Chinese diaspora of Southeast Asia gravitate to a charismatic church partly on account of elective affinity but also because such a church offers a haven for an ethnic minority under pressure.

Given the variety of Pentecostal manifestations and the overlap with other forms of charismatic and Evangelical Christianity, particularly higher up the social scale, the attitudes of Pentecostals to education and their experience of it are difficult to summarize. Initially the main imperative for converts is enhanced survival within the secure boundaries of the church, dramatized by the all-embracing promise of transformation and shared *metanoia*. Survival is reinforced not only by mutual assistance but by the everyday skills converts can pick up in speaking, reading, and organizing. Pentecostals are also interested in those forms of education that lift you above the precarious zone of immediate needs: technical skills, and media, management, and business savvy. Humanistic education and the arts of self-cultivation, or theology embedded in the humanities, have no practical application and may involve disciplines that corrode faith, commitment, and confidence in the Bible. For example, some social science disciplines are imbued with postcolonial theories and ideas of indigenous cultural authenticity that may even induce contempt for the Pentecostal culture that initially put such disciplines within reach. Perhaps mathematics and music are relatively safe. A church that sings and plays instruments will induct you into musical skills that can eventually reach a genuinely serious level.

The education of the pastorate is based on apprenticeship and biblical institutes, and though it puts you somewhat above the people you serve, it does not equip you by way of a long formation with discourses alien to your origins. It remains, and needs to remain, demotic. Megachurches such as one finds in Nigeria and Brazil are likely to provide their own educational facilities, from Sunday schools to institutions imparting useful knowledge and even "universities." Over time educated Pentecostals emerge who believe their faith involves social outreach. Of course, other churches seek to appropriate the appeal of Pentecostalism. Mainstream churches, like the Catholic Church in Brazil, the Anglican Church in West Africa, and the Coptic and Lutheran Churches in East Africa, seek to preempt the unique selling points of Pentecostalism or pick up a charismatic atmosphere by contagion, recognizing its appeal to their membership.

Deregulated Religious Markets

Pentecostalism is a natural denizen of deregulated religious markets; its expansion benefits from, and reinforces, whatever pressure may already exist for deregulation. Thus it arose "naturally" in the unregulated religious market of the United States but exported the pluralistic and competitive model to a Latin America where the Catholic monopoly subsumed all kinds of inspirited religious activity. Spirit cults hitherto active within a Catholic ambience acquired a more autonomous religious profile at the same time as Pentecostalism provided the most dramatic instance of autonomy. Initially there was tension all round, from Catholics, historic Protestants, cultural nationalists, and spirit cultists alike, but Pentecostals very quickly assimilated "inspirited" aspects of local culture and became part of a variegated scene in spite of the sharp edge they presented to "the world."

The large-scale expansion of Pentecostalism to Africa from the 1970s on was easier, partly because Pentecostals had made a modest entry into the semi-Christianized and pluralist religious economy of sub-Saharan Africa much earlier in the century. Initially Catholic countries in Francophone and Portuguese-speaking Africa were more resistant than Protestant ones, but eventually their religious markets also opened up to competition and Pentecostalism thrived on the new opportunities.

The expansion of Pentecostalism in Latin America and then in Africa, and globally, has been interpreted as the simple consequence of exporting American religious styles to the rest of the world and therefore as an aspect of the global power of American culture. That interpretation can be combined with another approach based on the idea that Pentecostalism is the latest expression of classic Protestant ethic of Max Weber, though there is no necessary connection between the two approaches. I do not combine them myself, and my own variant of the Weberian approach suggests we are mainly dealing with the emotional, though disciplined, Protestantism of the "small sects" also discussed by Weber. Perhaps it is worth remembering that all branches of Protestantism, Calvinism included, have from time to time broken out in ecstatic manifestations.

Other observers, like Jean-Pierre Bastian, reject the Weberian hypothesis and regard Pentecostalism as a recrudescence of a global layer of inspired religiosity in Christian guise.[7] They argue that it lacks the rational articulation of Calvinism as well as the social conscience that powered the Protestant critique of physical and industrial slavery. However, it really is not necessary to treat the putative role of Calvinism in ushering in capitalist modernity as the only proper road for social development. Pentecostalism combines the technical modes of modernity with a freedom of the spirit capable of entering into the varied inspired cultures of the two-thirds world and reassembling them under the Christian aegis of the one Holy Spirit. Because Pentecostals revive apostolic gifts on the New Testament model, they name and claim powers much mainline Protestantism has abjured, and are therefore able to absorb indigenous forms and powers in the very act of defining them as potent and demonic.[8] Like the writers of the New Testament and the practitioners of inspired religion the world over, Pentecostals believe in demons and in exorcism.

Of course, this ability to straddle different worlds, including those ultimately deriving from Africa itself through slavery, may mean that versions of Pentecostalism emerge that some mainstream Christians regard as deviating seriously from historic Christian norms. The Universal Church of the Kingdom of God in Brazil was one of the first to arouse suspicions. It expanded rapidly and in a rather threatening manner in the 1980s by combining inspired black religion with a shockingly direct espousal of health and wealth and what looked like miraculous cures available without initial moral reformation. What the UCKG offered the poor by way of "liberation" could be contrasted unfavorably with the option for the poor of liberation theology, whether Catholic or Protestant. The same contrast existed between the "syncretistic" practices of some highly successful Pentecostal churches in Korea, and the Minjung branch of liberation theology. The Friday Apostolics in southern Africa studied by Matthew Engelke exemplify another deviant mode by consuming the letter of scripture in the spiritual fire of prophecy,[9] thereby enabling older "prophetic" styles to persist.

Europe is still a regulated market. It resists Pentecostal penetration and retains a model of territorial religion in a secularized or religiously passive form. European Pentecostalism has remained marginal within the Protestant "voluntary sector" or else has emerged in interstitial areas between major confessional blocs, such as Transylvania, or in interstitial groups like the Roma. Islam also resists by strongly defending its borders with communal and familial sanctions. In Islam Pentecostalism finds some modest scope available where religion is disorganized, as in parts of Central Asia, or at confessional and ethnic borders where Islam cannot entirely dictate the terms of engagement, as in parts of northern Nigeria. The situation in Asia is different because its historic non-monotheistic religions either allow Pentecostalism to flourish alongside a shared inspirited world, or resist it on nationalist grounds.

The Pastorate: Rupture and Continuity

Pentecostal pastors are religious entrepreneurs running enterprises from local house groups and store-front churches to massive transnational voluntary associations. One may look at them as a buried intelligentsia of energetic and highly intelligent entrepreneurs who find scope for their energy and talents running the religious version of a large-scale business. The pastorate provides the most obvious avenues of rapid social mobility, though not all can win and have prizes. There are thousands of small and medium-sized enterprises for every impressive and transnational megachurch. The pastorate focuses a persistent debate about how far Pentecostalism, particularly in its Neo-Pentecostal form, represents a radical break with the past and its network of relationships, and a process of increasing individualization. Birgit Meyer has given a nuanced account of the break, while some other observers of Ghana, like Karen Lauterbach,[10] have stressed continuity. Certainly "born-again" believers throughout West Africa stress the importance of a rupture with the past and with a corrupt present. Perhaps there may be a difference here between the megachurches of the mega-city, constituting complete alternative societies with health and financial facilities, and middle-sized enterprises where relationships are more locally embedded. Lauterbach shows how a career in the pastorate mirrors the figure of the "Big Man" in the wider society—except that the power of the chief is embedded in historic institutions, whereas the pastor has to build up a comparable nexus of power, wealth, and recognized status through charisma and access to spiritual power and authority. Once a pastor has built up a power base there is inevitably a temptation to engage in predatory behavior, and even to create family fortunes. Yet there are limits, given that members can move their custom elsewhere.

Pastors are a self-made men and women who draw on a repertoire embedded in local politics and culture as they begin an apprenticeship with an established pastor. Then they can branch out as independent religious entrepreneurs. Once established, their power and influence straddles and unites different platforms, political, economic, and religious, and the Big Man and the Big Woman feel confident of their ability to negotiate with major figures in other social spheres. They are serious power brokers. Moreover, the models of apprenticeship and entrepreneurship they provide are emulated by the membership and contribute to individual and collective mobility. Whole churches move up the social scale.

Global Mobilization From Below and Imagined Communities

The fact that Pentecostals have from the beginning propagated their faith through journals and biblical institutes at least suggests literacy and a Protestant literacy powers advancement as much as a Protestant work ethic. Pentecostals have always utilized advanced forms of modern communication, and they seek avidly for technical expertise and useful knowledge. Grant Wacker has characterized them as "seeking for Eden with a satellite dish"; they share the North American capacity to combine a mundane interest in effective techniques with images drawn from the further shores of the religious imagination.[11] Sometimes the mere presence of a technical artifact, even if broken or unnecessary, signifies access to power.

Not only does intense inward piety increasingly break out of the church-state framework, but it mobilizes groups further and further down the social scale, bringing them to religious self-consciousness. What began with the Magisterial Reformation and the Anabaptist Radical Reformation, in such free cities of Europe as Geneva and Münster, spread through the initial agency of the Methodist Holy Club to the artisanate and the aspiring classes of the English agricultural and industrial revolutions before "moving mightily" in the uproarious world of Methodists and Baptists on the American frontier. A collective mutuality that fosters individual self-help is now at work globally, with some minor retroactive impact on its countries of origin.

Pentecostals are not strictly "the damned of the earth," but those at a margin who stand on tiptoe to descry a redemption that includes redemption from social chaos, or—less often—those who fear for their fragile stake and seek firmer footing. People lash themselves together on rafts to ride treacherous seas with songs and exhortations of mutual encouragement. They entertain a prior aspiration to betterment and await only an explicit call to seek out others of like mind.

The horizons of hope include images of what life can be like elsewhere, including life in North America. In West Africa, for example, Pentecostals are themselves prolific makers of images and narratives through their own powerful religious media. These media transcend political frontiers and dramatize omnipresent demonic dangers in society and state to be overcome in the power of the Spirit and new birth. The imagined community of the faith can be as strong as the imagined community of the nation. Beyond that lies the imagined community of the modern world where images of the United States are particularly potent and where the stars of the megachurch world and transnational televangelists take the stage. Some observers have stressed the coercive power of American culture, others its genuine attractions.

National Patrimony against Transnational Association

Pentecostals occupy contested terrain. They are opposed by those who promote a national religious patrimony such as Catholicism provides in Latin America, or by those in African postcolonial elites who seek to reconstruct an indigenous religious ethos. Many Pentecostals leap over the boundaries of the local dominant culture to embrace an international modernity. That embrace may include simultaneously using a postcolonial rhetoric, for example the rhetoric of black power, and exploiting whatever American munificence and opportunities provided by trips to the United States have to offer. For that matter, the rhetoric of black power can be imported from the United States just as the rhetoric of authentic local religiosity can be imported directly from European sources, including anthropology, or acquired indirectly though local elites educated in the West. Culture, like agency, is never pure.

Much depends on local circumstances, and local circumstances in China and India are particularly interesting. China represents neither the monotheism of the Abrahamic traditions nor the absorbent polytheistic religion of South Asia, and Pentecostalism has to find niches in a highly regulated market resisting all outside cultural influences. This resistance reaches back to the implication of Christianity in the Taiping Rebellion and the subsequent branding of Christianity as a fifth column promoted by foreign devils. Of course, nationalism and the Marxist Cultural Revolution were themselves imported from the West, but the Marxists in particular adopted a scorched earth policy toward religion, above all toward Christianity as associated with U.S. as well as British missions. All external contacts were cut off and a clandestine expansion occurred, especially among lower-class women. These women were beneath the radar of government regulation and their underground faith was undeniably Chinese. Christianity, including Pentecostalism, also accompanied the long march to the mega-city in China and the ethos of the new professionals.

India is the other potential superpower of the twenty-first century, and the progress of Pentecostalism has gone relatively unremarked in spite of the pioneering work of Michael Bergunder.[12] Once again conversion is opposed by the political guardians of national patrimony—in the case of India, the Hindu nationalists. Pentecostal manifestations in India preceded Azusa Street and, as Timothy and Rebecca Shah show in their chapter in this volume, there has been a constant dialectic between virtually independent Indian initiatives, such as the Ceylon Pentecostal Mission, and initiatives from elsewhere, notably from Britain and the United States. Whether in Kerala, Tamil Nadu, or Andra Pradesh, the emergence of independent churches and constant fragmentation characterized Pentecostalism. Timothy and Rebecca Shah refer to indigenous churches, paradoxically controlled by elite castes, as well as to megachurches catering to the middle class and upwardly mobile. But they focus on the contemporary dynamism of independent churches spreading in poor areas, for example among Dalits and especially Dalit women, granting them self-definition, self-respect, and well-being, and enabling them to achieve some social and economic freedom. These people become "intentional Weberians," and they discipline their immediate needs to claim the future they believe God has in store.

New Arrivals and the Protestant Mainstream

Pentecostalism provides an alternative to whatever is the adjacent and relatively stabilized socioreligious hierarchy, and an alternative path to modernity. In Nigeria this is reinforced by the way the moral consensus associated with mainstream and independent churches has been undermined by the predatory activities of the state and the elite.[13] In sub-Saharan Africa, mainstream Protestants constitute a relatively stabilized hierarchy, one associated with the work of transnational NGOs as well as increasingly sympathetic with religious forms claiming African credentials through the usual conduits, including their own local intelligentsias. Tensions emerge between Pentecostals and mainline Protestants, especially when Pentecostalism attracts the young in mainstream Protestant churches.

In Latin America these mainstream churches are not the established echelons of Protestant power found in Africa but historical minorities who initially adopted Protestantism as a path to modernity on the North Atlantic model. Alternatively they were Protestant migrants encouraged to settle in Latin America by radical and anticlerical elites anxious to have the benefits of North Atlantic modernity without the faith. "Historical" Protestants initially disliked charismatic movements, despising them for their supernaturalism and fearful of their success, though competition soon stimulated many of them to become churches "in renewal."

Way Stations and Cross Border Migrations

Pentecostal mobilization is best understood through the idea of a movement rather than a church, because Pentecostals are people moved in their hearts to move across social and geographical borders in protective convoy, above all to the contemporary mega-city, and especially to its peripheries where they can number up to 30 percent compared (say) to 5 percent in the city centers. They are literally people on the move ready by faith to move mountains. As people on the move their tracks run parallel to the penetration of global communications, rather as Methodist chapels in Mexico ran parallel to the railway lines. Pentecostal churches are way stations punctuating the routes of contemporary migration. The chapels and churches of the Mexican para-Pentecostal church La Luz del Mundo provide way stations for believers moving back and forth in a perpetual pilgrimage between the headquarters in Guadalajara and church plants in various parts of the United States. The Pentecostals of the Dominican Republic set up their churches in New York, and Brazilian Pentecostals relocate themselves in the suburbs of Boston just as Irish and Italian Catholics did before them. Sometimes migration makes conversion more likely than it would be in the original cultural context, so that the rather Quaker-like Pentecostals in the Brazilian Congregation of Christ initially had a mostly Italian membership.[14]

Migration is no longer to permanent domicile elsewhere, but rather a continuous circulation, as for example when Filipinos pick up the faith in California (say) and carry it back to their homeland. Korean Pentecostals and Evangelicals are more likely than their immediate peers to migrate to the United States, and once established they attract other Koreans to their churches as familiar repositories of Korean culture. Korean missionaries migrate all over Asia, but particularly to the Philippines. Missionaries from Brazil go out to Portuguese-speaking Africa, while white South Africans itinerate between Johannesburg and Kazakhstan. Amsterdam and London are cities with large West African churches that service migration between the homeland and the European metropolis. New York is like Amsterdam and London in being a great city of capital, and religious flows from West Africa can be seen as following the money. The members of West African churches, whether explicitly Pentecostal or attracted by a charismatic contagion, move to and fro between Monrovia or Accra or Lagos and their adoptive newfound land and recreate the sacred locales of their countries of origin along the subways of the Big Apple, or even, in the case of the Redeemed Christian Church of God International Chapel, take over Madison Square Garden to celebrate and announce a transnational presence.[15]

The Social Niches of Pentecostalism

I have already canvassed a major mode of Pentecostal insertion manifest in the long march to the contemporary mega-city. Of course, this may take many forms. La Luz del Mundo is a megachurch of millions occupying and virtually running a sector of Guadalajara. Seoul is host to some of the largest megachurches anywhere, and one of them, pastored by Paul Yonggi-Cho, boasts some three-quarters of a million members arranged in a pyramid of cell-like structures widely copied elsewhere. The Rhema Church in the black township of Soweto is, with the hospital, the largest local organization; it provides a total environment for its members, once mainly white and now mainly black. It also hosts gatherings of the ruling ANC party.

Elsewhere there are different patterns. In Santiago de Chile, Pentecostal churches are concentrated in poor favelas visited from outside only by pastors, priests, and social workers. Here they compete with the bars for custom. Some streets are honeycombed with tiny house churches or small chapels with colorful names, while others lie in the proximity of a more imposing church belonging to the Methodist Pentecostal Church of Chile with extensive facilities. Then there will be the Catholic church, centrally placed, offering an impressive range of social services and perhaps a hub for Catholic charismatic churches appealing to social sectors somewhat above the social provenance of the Pentecostals. Further competition may come from the Kingdom Hall of the Jehovah's Witnesses or the Mormons, both of which have major constituencies in Chile, and indeed throughout Latin America.

But Pentecostalism not only mobilizes sectors of the aspiring among depressed classes; it also appeals to new middle classes in expanding economies like Nigeria and Brazil, China and Singapore. Just as the small

Pentecostal chapels are shadowed by small groups of Catholic charismatics, so the Pentecostal churches of the new middle classes compete with more affluent Catholic and Evangelical charismatics, the latter perhaps associated with mainstream Protestant churches "in renewal." There is a visible tension between classical Pentecostals wary of the perils of riches, and Neo-Pentecostal churches unafraid to promise health and wealth if you make the appropriate religious investment. Inevitably a gospel of success generates theodicies to explain why some people make the right investments without the promised rewards.

The churches of the affluent may offer havens where "executives may cry" and can release pent-up emotional energies. They also provide venues where people of like mind and status cope with problems of stress or corruption in their professional lives. Corruption in developing societies is ubiquitous, and there are many who need moral support in a religious community. Some believers will run businesses with a religious ethos and cooperate with other business people attached to the same church. Nigeria and Ghana are exceptional because a substantial sector of the university community is associated with Pentecostal and charismatic churches. Some Pentecostal churches promote an ethos of success in business and professional life indicated by a name like Winners Chapel. One really does not know whether people in such churches were successful before joining and found the ethos congenial, or whether the ethos propelled them forward.

A remarkable example is provided by so-called "boss Christians" in Wenzhou, a coastal city in southeastern China, discussed by Nanlai Cao.[16] Wenzhou has historically been a linguistic and geographical enclave with distinct local traditions at some distance from the centers of state power but with cosmopolitan trading connections. It is now home to an upwardly mobile business elite sometimes referred to as "the Jews of China" who exercise considerable local power and cooperate with the modernizing capitalist agenda of the Communist Party cadres. Protestant Christians make up about 15 percent of the city population of some six million and take for granted the link between Protestantism and economic expansion. Protestantism is a religion of lay leadership compared to Catholicism, while by comparison with folk "superstition" it is associated with modernity. Boss Christians comprise a male elite of entrepreneurs and white collar workers, very different from the largely female and often illiterate Christians of the rural areas. They have abandoned the division such people make between Christian and worldly concerns, and the male elite is not immune to accepted dubious practices outside the enclave of the church, though they also believe there is a Christian way of doing things that is more efficient and morally superior to the Communist way. They see themselves as modern people, prospering under God's care for his own, and they resemble American white Evangelical Christians or the Neo-Pentecostals of Brazil and Nigeria. For them, English is the language of modernity, and they promote a conservative sexual ethic with some gender separation. Christianity is a "religion of music" with many pianos and youth choirs and even recordings of Handel's *Messiah* played during the large-scale banquets that are held for business and friendship networks. It is all a long way from the time of the Cultural Revolution when Wenzhou was selected, like Nova Huta in Poland, as a showcase for atheism.

Marginal Peoples and Minorities

Wenzhou is a linguistic niche, and Pentecostals worldwide find a receptive niche among ethnic minorities at the margin either socially or geographically. Examples are provided by the Mapuche in southern Chile, the Aymara in the Andes, and the Maya in Central America. Sometimes these peoples have already been evangelized by other Evangelicals or Adventists and the result may be increased religious pluralism and some fragmentation. A marginal segment of the people may hive off through Pentecostal or other Evangelical conversion, while another segment may adopt a form of Catholic renewal or liberation.

For centuries South and Central American peoples have smoldered or revolted under the impact of Hispanic dominance; today, through Pentecostalism, they can reverse negative stereotypes that paint them as drunk and work-shy, or at best colorful objects for the gaze of tourists. Ceremonies requiring the competitive ritual consumption of alcohol may turn into competitions between singers and choirs. Believers find in Pentecostalism an opportunity to leap over boundaries and settled local hierarchies to international contacts and modernity. In both Bolivia and Mexico the proportion of Pentecostals among indigenes is above the national average. Believers will set out in convoy to capitals like La Paz, Santiago, Mexico City, or Guatemala City to form ethnically and linguistically homogeneous churches and keep something of the original culture alive.

Such changes can occur anywhere. In Nepal and China, for example, minority peoples may adopt different forms of Evangelical Protestantism, including Pentecostalism, just as minorities on the geographical margins of India and Burma earlier embraced some version of Evangelical Christianity. In Africa the expansion some decades ago of African Independent (or African initiated) churches, often with a strong base in a local ethnic group, may be supplemented and in some cases supplanted by the emergence of

African initiated Pentecostal churches. The Mossi people of Burkina Faso take their faith with them on their numerous trading expeditions in neighboring countries, and the Zimbabwe Assemblies of God Africa extends its activities among Zimbabweans who have migrated (say) to South Africa and to parts of neighboring Mozambique.[17]

The varying success of Evangelical and Pentecostal penetration in the Pacific Rim from Korea to Southeast Asia illustrates how the ethnic factor may assist or impede progress. Korea has proved most hospitable to Christianity because Christianity provided national definition over against both China and Japan and became involved in the early stages of Korean nationalism. Pentecostalism has sailed in on this favorable tide and has also picked some elements of Korean spiritism. The economic and educational ethos introduced by Christianity, particularly by the Presbyterians, took root in Korea, and Christianity was later reinforced by the hostility of Communist North Korea and the migration of Christians to the south.

Japan was far less hospitable, given that Christianity had for centuries been defined as a threatening intrusion by foreign cultural power, and this perception was reinforced by American occupation in 1945. Cultural nationalism in Japan finds expression in neo-Buddhist movements, as it also does to varying degrees in Korea, Taiwan, Singapore, and China. As already suggested, Evangelical Christianity has an elective affinity with the business ethos of Chinese culture and is regarded as a modern religion appropriate to modern and forward looking people. Given the strong identification of Malaysian nationalism with Islam and a similar if more relaxed identification in Indonesia, many in the successful Chinese diaspora in Southeast Asia have adopted charismatic or Pentecostal Christianity.[18]

Earlier I referred to the indifference of people in a secularized Europe still influenced by the territorial religious principles of the Westphalian settlement, suggesting that Pentecostalism might expand in interstitial areas such as Transylvania and Western Ukraine. One of the most successful megachurches is run by a Nigerian migrant in Kiev, though it has recently run into trouble through engagement with the corrupt politics of Ukraine.[19] There is also a significant Pentecostal movement on the margins of Europe in Sicily. And there are versions of the so-called Faith movement that stress this-worldly advantages offered by faith; these have a largely middle-class constituency in such unlikely places as Kaunas, Budapest, and Uppsala.[20] Such movements are very different from the initial early twentieth-century incursions of Pentecostalism along the margins of the Free Church sectors of Protestant Europe.

There is, however, one ethnic group in Europe that illustrates the appeal of Pentecostalism to a marginal and despised ethnicity: the Roma. As in Latin

America, the Roma who adopt Pentecostalism represent particular social sectors rather than the whole group, and there is consequently some tension between those who still find satisfaction in the old ways and those adopting the new. Nevertheless, the autonomous energies of Pentecostalism are more effective agents of social change than attempts at legislative reform. Old stereotypes of gypsies as work-shy and prone to theft are reversed, just as similar stereotypes have been in the Andes and elsewhere.[21] Australia offers the example of the Aborigines. Australia is a quite secular society on the British model. The aborigines belong to a category of "first peoples" believed resistant to Christian missions. Yet once the welfare activities of mainstream churches were curtailed, Pentecostalism made significant advances.[22]

There is just one more way in which Pentecostalism as an expression of the transnational voluntary principle concedes something to the ancient union of people, territory, and faith. Perhaps this manifests an inherent tendency for religion to gravitate toward such a union, but it also arises because Pentecostalism grounds itself in the whole of scripture and therefore reproduces the Hebrew longing for an earthly Zion. Most Pentecostals are well disposed to Israel, and many make a pilgrimage to the Temple Mount, perhaps inspired by some notion of the role reserved for Israel in the end-time. Some groups go further; the Olive Tree church in South Africa, for example, adopts some Jewish practices and fosters direct links with Israel.[23] Pentecostalism is a recent expression of a Christian Zionism that predates the emergence of a secular Jewish Zionism.

Politics and Civility

In his major study of the global role of Evangelicals in politics, Paul Freston rebuts any idea that Pentecostals reproduce the politics of the Evangelical Right in the United States, though clearly white Pentecostals in the United States are inclined to the Republicans.[24] One can see Pentecostalism as continuous with American and other populist traditions, in particular because it mobilizes newly emerging groups against whatever is the local configuration of power. Classical Pentecostals in the Holiness tradition used to be criticized as apolitical but many contemporary Pentecostals are active in civil society, sometimes, as Ben Jones indicates in Uganda, virtually constituting its local fabric. Pentecostals (and especially Neo-Pentecostals) are engaged across the political spectrum, Marxist parties excepted, though there was an initial bias to the center and the center-right. On issues relating to the family, abortion, and homosexuality, their position is not so very different from that of the Catholic Church.

I now select examples from Latin America, Africa, and Asia. I first indicate the style of Pentecostal politics in Brazil, an emerging power engaged in democratic consolidation. I then contrast Nigeria and Ghana with Zimbabwe, an increasingly impoverished and authoritarian state, before looking finally at the role of the Catholic charismatic movement El Shaddai in the Philippines.

Paul Freston, writing of Brazil, notes that numbers of Pentecostals continue to grow, if at a decreasing rate, and they now comprise perhaps some twenty-five million, thus constituting the largest concentration of Pentecostals anywhere.[25] Given that they are below average in education and status and include quite diverse groups, it is not surprising they lack a formal political theology. Although the interventions of the Universal Church of the Kingdom of God and its media empire have been controversial in the past, the overall Pentecostal representation after the 2010 elections rebounded from a reduction in 2006, illustrating a model of official denominational candidates mostly reliant on the church vote. Moreover, Evangelical (and largely Pentecostal) involvement in the presidential elections was also enhanced, partly because this election was characterized by an increase in voting influenced by values, such as abortion, rather than bread and butter issues, and partly because of the impressive showing of nearly 20 percent achieved by Marina Silva, the well-known Pentecostal politician, earlier associated with the Workers' Party, standing for the Greens. Freston points out that Marina Silva did not make overt use of her religious affiliation, and that Evangelical voters divided their support between Silva, the opposition candidate, and Lula's chosen successor as leader of the Workers' Party, Dilma Rousseff. The statements of Evangelical leaders were not conspicuously reflected in voting at Evangelical grassroots, so we are not dealing with an integrated religious bloc. Interestingly, the Universal Church in Brazil eventually threw its weight behind Lula through the Liberal Party. The UCKG has substantial assets in the media, and Pentecostals in Latin America, as elsewhere, can often exercise political influence through their media holdings and expertise.

In his survey of the influence of Evangelicals and Pentecostals on Latin American politics generally, Paul Freston comments on their contribution to democracy and civil society in the third wave of democratization late in the twentieth century.[26] Pentecostals create social capital and assist local empowerment among the underprivileged, as well as among indigenous peoples, and they provide avenues of political advancement to people who could not otherwise ascend into the political class. Politically they are fissiparous and decentralized, and lack coherent political theologies. They stress personal understandings of politics at the expense of proper experience of the political process. Naive hopes of cleaning up corrupt polities are rapidly dashed and disillusion easily follows. For example, the association of some Pentecostals/ Evangelicals with what looked like the reforming program initiated by Fujimori in Peru eventually mired them in a very dubious regime. Freston comments in the context of the clash between the Catholic Church and the military states in the 1970s that the Catholic Church is better at dealing with state violence and the Pentecostals at dealing with private (and, I would add, urban) violence. He also notes how effective they were in resisting the terrorist depredations of the Shining Path guerrillas.

Turning to Africa, I first use John Peel to indicate contrasts between the Islamic and the Evangelical/Pentecostal modes of insertion in Nigerian politics, more particularly in Yorubaland, where they are similarly placed in their influence and numbers.[27] Peel argues that the two religions, especially when it comes to Evangelical/Pentecostal Christianity, draw on different historical repertoires and cannot be treated as homologous in their contemporary Yoruba/Nigerian incarnations. Initially Christian missionaries sought the acculturation and Africanization of their supposedly alien faith (or else they defined "cults" as merely culture), while Reformist Muslims sought to deny their genuine long-term implication in local practices and modes of access to spiritual power. From the 1980s on, as political and economic crises deepened, the Evangelical/Pentecostal response became primarily pragmatic: from inward ethical renewal pursued in egalitarian prayer groups, Evangelicals and Pentecostals shifted to the creation of complete alternative societies, based on "divine" wealth creation and on deliverance from the demons of corruption, disease, and poverty. Having only a negative political theology, they had no preexisting frame of reference for political action. By contrast, Reformist Muslims could appeal to the shari'a as providing a platform for holding their elites to account and for the promotion of justice. Both Pentecostals and Reformist Muslims rejected the cultivation of African practices by nationalist elites as idolatrous.

I now contrast Pentecostal political stances in Zimbabwe with the cultural politics pursued in Ghana. David Maxwell charts the transition of the Zimbabwe Assemblies of God Africa (ZAOGA) from a sectarian enclave to a major church under successful leaders seeking respectability, recognition, and advantageous arrangements for the pursuit of organizational ends.[28] As elsewhere in Africa this may well mean some assimilation to a neopatrimonial style of favors exchanged between political and religious elites and based on clientelism, nepotism, corporatism, and tribalism. In practice that means avoiding conflict with incumbent powers by intermittently legitimating ZANU/PF, especially when the mainstream churches are critical, while keeping lines of communication open with the Movement for Democratic

Change (MDC). Overall, as in Nigeria, the state is not the critical referent and Pentecostals mainly engage in politics by criticizing those who promote secular agendas or immorality. ZAOGA benefits from the demand of ZANU/PF for indigenous religious leadership, though that also means it lacks the international profile enjoyed by the mainstream churches. ZAOGA has to meet the aspirations of its emerging middle class in a commercialized environment and also retain an original township base more interested in minimum security than in prosperity. Maxwell concludes that internal contradictions grow as ZAOGA comes closer to the powers that be, and he contrasts its incoherent opportunist style with the emphasis on education, critique, and responsibility associated with Mensa Otabil and the International Central Gospel Church of Ghana.

In Ghana, Birgit Meyer and Rijk van Dijk have analyzed the cultural politics of Pentecostals.[29] They stress the tension between the transnational culture represented by Pentecostalism (more particularly the large middle-class churches under charismatic pastors), "traditionalists" promoting a nationalist agenda, and the postcolonial politics of cultural heritage, often in implicit association with chiefly ethnic power, the state and the National Democratic Party. At the same time, Pentecostals position themselves against the more established denominations, regarding the latter's emphasis on "inculturation" as colluding with backwardness and with a demonic resistance to Christianity. Pentecostals engage in dramatic rituals of deliverance from the curses of the past, thus seeking to drive out African fire with African fire. Rijk van Dijk shows how in Ghana and the Ghanaian Dutch diaspora alike Pentecostals with a major stake in the media and the music industry embrace a transnational musical style, including African American elements, and find themselves at odds with the agenda of cultural nationalism to the point where Pentecostal instruments and "noisy" music-making have become sites of national political dispute.

We come finally to the politics of El Shaddai as the main Catholic charismatic body in the Philippines, as analyzed by Katherine Wiegele. She refers to the increasing popularity of Evangelical and renewal groups in the post-authoritarian era, including Pentecostals.[30] Though there is little distinctive about these groups taken as a whole, El Shaddai represents the mobilization of lower class people, whereas Couples for Christ and Loved Flock are more middle-class. Like the Pentecostals, for example the Jesus is Lord movement, El Shaddai holds mass outdoor rallies and builds up neighborhood cells and associations, as well as a media presence. In its neighborhood chapters El Shaddai promotes a semi-independent Catholic lay movement, and its healers merge shamanistic practices with prosperity teachings. These teachings reflect a major global shift from the Pietist view of the world as a vale of tears to an optimistic appraisal of possibilities to be seized by those with a positive outlook, as well as through the embrace of self-determination and transformation, and hopeful aspiration fired by charismatic inspiration. This is people power on the part of those hitherto ignored by the political class and participating in civil society by way of collective action manifested in performative displays. It is a vision of the new in the wake of the role of the Catholic Church in building democracy, though not always in agreement with official Catholic policies. It is aligned with development efforts but also expresses disappointment with post-Marcos failures to deal with corruption and poverty. In 2007 El Shaddai was represented in congress by the pro-life Buhay party.

A Major Niche: Women

One further niche favorable to Pentecostalism is found among the women of the two-thirds world, though I shall not attempt to summarize the account given by Bernice Martin in this volume. There are many contexts where Pentecostalism acts as a trade union for women, enabling them to organize for their own cultural defense. As ever, just how that defense is realized depends on local context. In Latin America it may take the form of a restoration of respect, given the treatment of women under the colonial and postcolonial gender regimes; in the West Indies respect is restored given the long-term effects of slavery; in southern Africa both young women and young men may seek to leave behind the control of traditional tribal elders; in West Africa it is often young women (along with young men and the lower class) who become "born again" after suffering from a predatory state and economic disaster; in China the women could embrace the new faith in the safety of the home, whereas the men were exposed to the rigors of the cultural revolution. Women are head pastors in only a minority of Pentecostal churches, and female status usually derives from prestigious male partners. At the same time in West Africa there are many examples of the "Big Woman" in the pastorate complementing the "Big Man." Women are also adept at prophecy, and they are often the main actors in programs of social amelioration.

Women find the "feminized man" of Pentecostalism an attractive proposition compared to the aggressive and irresponsible macho man. For that matter, Pentecostalism offers an alternative to the macho personality that many men are relieved to adopt and that their male peers often recognize. David Smilde, in his study of Pentecostal men in Caracas, Venezuela, recounts how the "new man" negotiates macho challenges and threats with the strategies of nonviolence.[31]

Instances of the appeal of Pentecostalism for women are provided from Colombia, where Pentecostal women hitherto at the mercy of the macho life-style find in their faith a spiritual source of confidence, agency, and gender equality. In Colombia, as in many parts of Africa, thousands have been displaced from the countryside to shantytowns by civil war between violent left- and violent right-wing antagonists. Half of displaced families are headed by women, and in small store front churches and megachurches alike people can protest and express their pain. They can create social service networks for the destitute and recreate the family and domestic order with new and more responsible male partners.

Alternative Modernities?

Much of the discussion so far has focused on the geographical mobility of a transnational movement and the social mobility of an autonomous movement of personal and group transformation. I turn finally to what might be thought of as the conceptual mobility involved in modernity as a condition and as a process. Modernization is one of those great nouns of process, like individualization, privatization, rationalization, and secularization, and it is often bound up in the same bundle. It is also seen as part and parcel of those large-scale historical changes, such as the industrial and scientific revolutions, as well as *the* Enlightenment, that the historian Jonathan Clark suspects of being reified and simplified in misleading "terms of art" for easy intellectual consumption as well as for rhetorical purposes.[32]

Much depends on whether modernization is regarded as a unilinear process presaged in Europe and moving toward a common destination that includes secularization, or as various changes that lead to "alternative" modes of modernity that may or may not include secularization. In this second reading, secularization is not necessarily implicated in modernization either conceptually or empirically. Perhaps those who focus on social differentiation as crucial to modernization are more open to the possibility of multiple modernities, while those who regard all the nouns of process as mutually supportive are more inclined to posit a common modern condition characterized by secularization in the sense of the purely private rather than the public importance of religion. Thus for the latter, Pentecostalism is likely to be cast as part of a transition to modernity rather than a mode of modernity in its own right. Just as Protestantism was present as a midwife at the birth of European modernity and was then sloughed off as rationalization accelerated, so Pentecostalism is today accompanying the transition to modernity in the two-thirds world.

Ruth Marshall, in her *Political Spiritualities*, argues for the irreducibility of Pentecostalism and draws attention to the dubious character of our cultural translations, as well as the political uses and misuses of the notion of religious "authenticity." For her, the discourse of secularization, the advance of rationality, and the confinement of religion to its proper sphere, all of which are encapsulated in the master narrative of modernity, are not only part of a specific Western social scientific project but also part of a political critique that is itself rooted in a utopian and salvific vision. She writes,

> To say that religion and witchcraft speak about material processes is one thing . . . to assert that religion and other forms of spirituality have these processes for their *object* . . . is to assert something altogether different for which the evidence is invariably lacking. . . . The argument that sees religious and spiritual practices principally as local interpretations or resistances to destabilizing global forces operates on tacit assumptions that still consider religion as performing a second-order process of adjustment. In the absence of the knowledge required for mastery . . . Africans make do with religion.[33]

One way to conceive of Pentecostalism as a variant of modernity is to ask how far its advance takes place in the context of the partial failure, or patchy implementation, of the liberal development narrative, and the evident failure of the Marxist narrative. With regard to the former, Ben Jones has shown in his account of Pentecostalism in Uganda how limited is the impact of development even though Uganda is often held up as a success story.[34] Jones describes how Pentecostalism has taken up the space of civil society in some areas, particularly in the wake of civil war. Indeed there are several countries where the traumas of civil war find some therapeutic release in Pentecostal practices.

Our criteria of modernity can look surprisingly ethnocentric and normative, so that even Russia and China, with their more collective models, fail to qualify in spite of being subjected to very violent modernization projects. In his discussion of modernity Joel Robbins cites criteria relating to individualization, democratization, free markets, pluralism, patriarchy, and supernaturalism.[35] Pentecostalism performs well by most of these criteria, even though the evidence is inconclusive with regard to democratization and there is what Bernice Martin has called "the Pentecostal gender paradox" with regard to patriarchy.[36] When it comes to pluralism and social differentiation, Pentecostalism scores very highly.

Robbins makes the interesting point that in its prosperity guise Pentecostalism founds bounded communities based on gift exchange that run counter to market norms. It would be really odd if gift exchange were to count against modernity. If this-worldliness and nonviolence are modern, then so is Pentecostalism. What really counts against it is supernaturalism, which suggests that modernity is established by definitional and philosophical fiat. Perhaps modernity is our fuzzy way of talking about Us and the Rest, as discussed in Peter Berger's edited volume *The Desecularisation of the World.*[37]

With regard to the failure of Marxism, and maybe of the promise of secular politics more generally, both Pentecostalism and Islam have moved in their different ways into the vacant space, though Christian and Islamic revivals alike try to remedy the major gaps in the provision of welfare in the two-thirds world. The biggest difference lies in their approach to politics, which in turn reflects the difference between a transnational voluntary association seeking a revolution in the sphere of culture and an organic faith seeking a revolution at the political and the legal level; though there are parts of the world, for example Nigeria and Brazil, where the more "worldly" forms of Neo-Pentecostalism seek political as well as cultural empowerment. Perhaps the contrast between Islam and Christianity reflects a difference in the initial repertoire of the two largest religions in the modern world. Islam was a faith forged from the beginning as a close union of the religious and the political. Christianity began as a voluntary group initially facing problems of its own regulation rather then the regulation of whole societies, with all that implies for the legitimation of violence. Both a revived Islam and a revived Christianity in its Pentecostal form represent, with Catholicism and Buddhism, major alternatives among the "multiple modernities" of the contemporary world.

NOTES

1. Martin Lindhardt, "More than Just Money: The Faith Gospel and Occult Economy in Contemporary Tanzania," *Nova Religio* 13:1 (2009): 41–67.

2. John D. Y. Peel, "'For Who Hath Despised the Day of Small Things': Missionary Narratives and Historical Anthropology," *Comparative Studies in Society and History* 37 (1995): 581–607.

3. Edith L. Blumhofer, *Aimee Semple MacPherson: Everybody's Sister* Grand Rapids MI: Eerdmans, 1993).

4. Élie Halévy, *The History of England in 1815* 3:1 (Harmondsworth: Penguin, 1938).

5. For a discussion of Pentecostalism in relation to social outreach, as well as to democracy and social mobility, see Donald Miller and Tetsunao Yamamori, *Global Pentecostalism: The New Face of Christian Social Engagement* (Berkeley: University of California Press, 2007), esp. chapter 6. Miller and Yamamori make a case for regarding Pentecostalism as postmodern.

6. Azonseh Ukah, *A New Paradigm of Pentecostal Power: A Study of the Redeemed Christian Church of God in Nigeria* (Trenton, NJ: Africa World Press, 2008).

7. Jean-Pierre Bastian, *La Mutación Religiosa de América Latina* (Mexico City: Fonda de Cultura Económica, 2003).

8. Birgit Meyer, *Translating the Devil: Religion and Modernity among the Ewe in Ghana* (Edinburgh: Edinburgh University press, 1999).

9. Matthew Engelke, *A Problem of Presence: Beyond Scripture in an African Church* (Berkeley: University of California Press, 2007).

10. Karen Lauterbach, "The Craft of Pastorship in Ghana and Beyond" (Ph.D. thesis, Roskilde University, Denmark, 2008); Birgit Meyer, "Mediating Tradition; Pentecostal Pastors, African Priests as Chiefs in Ghanaian Popular Films," in *Christianity and Social Change in Africa,* ed. Toyin Falola (Durham, NC: Carolina Academic Press, 2005), 275–306.

11. Grant Wacker, "Searching for Eden with a Satellite Dish," in *The Primitive Church in the Modern World,* ed. Richard Hughes (Urbana: University of Illinois Press, 1995), 139–160.

12. Michael Bergunder, *The South Indian Pentecostal Movement in the Twentieth Century* (Grand Rapids, MI: Eerdmans, 2008).

13. Ruth Marshall, *Political Spiritualities: The Pentecostal Revolution in Nigeria* (Chicago: University of Chicago Press, 2009), 109.

14. George St.Clair: unpublished paper on the Brazilian *Christian Congregation* for an anthropology seminar at the London School of Economics, 2010.

15. Mark Gornik, *Word Made Global: Stories of African Christianity in New York City* (Grand Rapids, MI: Eerdmans, 2011).

16. See Nanlai Cao's chapter in this volume, and *Constructing China's Jerusalem: Christians, Power, and Place in Contemporary Wenzhou* (Stanford: Stanford University Press, 2010).

17. David Maxwell, *African Gifts of the Spirit: Pentecostalism and the Rise of a Zimbabwean Transnational Religious Movement* (Oxford: James Currey, 2006).

18. Juliettte Koning and Heidi Dahles, "Spiritual Power: Chinese Managers and the Rise of Charismatic Christianity in Southeast Asia," *Copenhagen Journal of Asian Studies* 27:1 (2009): 5–37.

19. Catherine Wanner, *Communities of the Converted: Ukrainians and Global Evangelism* (Ithaca: Cornell University Press, 2007).

20. Simon Coleman, *The Globalization of Charismatic Christianity: Spreading the Gospel of Prosperity* (Cambridge: Cambridge University Press, 2000).

21. Paloma Gay y Blasco, "The Politics of Evangelism: Hierarchy, Masculinity and Religious Conversion among Gitanos," *Romani Studies* 5:10, issue 1 (2000): 1–22.

22. Peggy Brock, ed., *Indigenous Peoples and Religious Change* (Leiden: Brill, 2005).

23. Kristina Helgesson, *"Walking in the Spirit": The Complexity of Belonging in Two Pentecostal Churches in Durban, South Africa* (Uppsala: Elanders, 2006).

24. Paul Freston, *Evangelicals and Politics in Asia, Africa and Latin America* (Cambridge: Cambridge University Press, 2001).

25. Paul Freston, ed., *Evangelical Christianity and Democracy in Latin America* (Oxford: Oxford University Press, 2008).

26. Paul Freston, *Evangelical Christianity and Democracy in Latin America.*

27. John Peel, "Nigerian Religious Movements and the Anthropology of World Religions," unpublished, Bapsybanoo Marchioness of Winchester Lecture in the Religions of the World, Oxford, May 11, 2011

28. Maxwell, *African Gifts of the Spirit.*

29. Rijk van Dijk, "Silence: The Ban on Drumming and the Musical Politics of Pentecostalism in Ghana," in *Ghana Studies* 4 (2001): 31–64; Birgit Meyer, "The Power of Money: Politics, Occult Forces and Pentecostalism in Ghana," *African Studies Review* 41:3 (1998): 15–37.

30. Katherine Wiegele, *Investing in Miracles: El Shaddai and the Transformation of Popular Catholicism in the Philippines* (Honolulu: University of Hawaii Press, 2005).

31. David Smilde, *Reason to Believe: Cultural Agency in Latin American Evangelicalism* (Berkeley: University of California Press, 2007).

32. Jonathan Clark, "The Eighteenth Century Context," in *The Oxford Handbook of Methodist Studies,* ed. William Abrahams and James Kirby (Oxford: Oxford University Press, 2008), 1–29.

33. Marshall, *Political Spiritualities,* 29.

34. Ben Jones, *Beyond the State in Rural Uganda* (Edinburgh: Edinburgh University Press, 2008).

35. Joel Robbins, "The Anthropology of Religion," in *Studying Global Pentecostalism,* ed. Alan Anderson, Michael Bergunder, and Cornelis Van Der Laan (Berkeley: University of California Press, 2010), 171–173.

36. Bernice Martin, "The Pentecostal Gender Paradox," in *The Blackwell Companion to the Sociology of Religion,* ed. Richard K. Fenn (Oxford: Blackwell, 2001), 52–66.

37. Peter Berger, ed., *The Desecularization of the World* (Grand Rapids, MI: Eerdmans, 1999).

TWO

The Future of Pentecostalism in Brazil: The Limits to Growth

PAUL FRESTON

Developmental Tensions, Transitions, and Historicization

Brazil can claim to be the world capital of Pentecostalism. It has about 25 million members, nearly one in seven of the population, comprising numerous small denominations but also some huge and highly influential ones. It has high-profile Pentecostal televangelists and members of congress; indeed, the third-placed candidate in the 2010 presidential election, with almost 20 percent of the vote, is Pentecostal. Its missionaries are in over a hundred countries, evangelizing the native populations. In the period between the censuses of 1991 and 2000, Brazilian Pentecostals more than doubled in number. Brazil would seem, therefore, to be at the forefront of the global Pentecostal advance that has attracted so much recent academic and journalistic attention.

Yet there are reasons for doubting Brazilian Pentecostalism's ability to continue its headlong growth, or even perhaps, in a while, to continue growing at all; and also grounds for wondering whether it will ever be able to achieve the sort of social and political influence that its size might lead us to expect, let alone that which it fondly imagines for itself. There are even signs that it might not only be losing numerical steam but also floundering in its attempts to transition to new ways of being in Brazilian society.

Ecclesiastical institutions, like all others, are subject to what might be called developmental tensions. The largest Brazilian Pentecostal denominations date from 1910 (the Congregação Cristã) and 1911 (the Assembleia de Deus), with Italian and Swedish founders respectively. There are, of course, other large denominations (nearly all founded by Brazilians) with shorter histories and at different stages in their development; but there is also such a thing as an established "Pentecostal field" into which they have to insert themselves. The century of history is not irrelevant, therefore, even for understanding a more recent denomination such as (to mention the best-known) the Igreja Universal do Reino de Deus. But we should not think of Brazilian Pentecostalism only in terms of developmental tensions (emphasizing internal factors); rather, it is approaching a fundamental transition, where the emphasis is on external factors deriving from society and the broader religious field. Its future, therefore, depends largely on the interplay of this transition with the developmental tensions and even, I would suggest, developmental limitations. The latter threaten to make the former more dramatic than it might otherwise be. Whether Brazilian Pentecostalism can successfully navigate the simultaneous approach of numerical stabilization, the entry into its second century of history, the social and educational changes within its constituency, and the country's rise to economic respectability—this is an open question. Will it manage to learn how to behave in a context where there is no longer the same possibility of rapid numerical growth? Some of its wounds (the scandals, authoritarian leadership, and poor political performance that have severely affected its public image) are self-inflicted, and there may be time to heal them sufficiently before irreparable damage is done. But other problems may actually (as some internal critics are starting to say) lie deeper, representing fundamental limitations that, in the long run, will lead either to decline or to a personal or institutional mutation into something that is not really, any more, Pentecostalism. For all these reasons, it seems appropriate, on the fortieth anniversary of the Club of Rome's report, to apply to Pentecostalism the title it used for the global economic predicament: "the limits to growth."

All this is not to swell the chorus of those who see Pentecostalism fundamentally in terms of benightedness, authoritarianism, and unscrupulousness. Yet, in all the efforts to explain Pentecostalism's success in very varied contexts, it is easy to forget the holes on its global map and its limitations even where it has done well numerically. Indeed, a frontier of Pentecostal research today is precisely about what one might call the historicization of Pentecostalism, that is, the move toward non-Pentecostal (though usually Evangelical) Protestant forms. (I use the term historicization because the Portuguese-language academic literature usually divides up the Brazilian Protestant world, known generically as *evangélicos,* into *pentecostais* and *históricos.*) Historicization is therefore one form of de-Pentecostalization. The latter, of course, could take many forms, including a (re)turn to Catholicism, or to other religions on the Brazilian landscape such as Umbanda, or a drift into the amorphous census category of "no religion." All these do happen, but (as yet?) less frequently than does historicization.

If we think of Pentecostal and historical not as separate compartments but as ideal–typical polarities on a continuum along which people and institutions are distributed, and in relation to which people and institutions can be in movement, then clearly that movement can be either toward greater Pentecostalization or toward greater historicization. The former process was for many decades the more common, so much so that at one stage it was often asked whether the *históricos* had any future in Brazil. If any movement from Pentecostalism was deemed probable in the future, it was toward "no religion." In other words, if socially embedded Catholicism had given way to volatile pluralistic Pentecostalism, the latter in turn would surely, one day, cede to outright secularity; far from being an alternative way of being modern, Pentecostalism would be merely a transitional stage in the grand narrative of secularization. Now, it starts to look as if one has to interpose another possibility, historicization, although that also will presumably be regarded as merely one more "transitional stage" by true believers in the grand narrative.

Historicization can take various forms. It can imply total abandonment of Pentecostal practices, beliefs, or self-labeling, or just partial abandonment. It can mean a conscious adoption of historical Protestant thinking in a particular area for which Pentecostal thought is regarded as nonexistent, inadequate, or plain wrong. Historicization can apply to institutions or individuals. Both people and institutions age; in the case of people, the important thing is not just physical aging (though that is also important, especially in the sense of the average age of members of a church), but also length of time "in the faith" (since conversion or since birth). And both families and institutions go through generational shifts. The existence or absence of rapid numerical success not only affects the composition of church membership and expectations, but also tends toward different types of "elitization" of the clergy (roughly corresponding to leadership based on personal charisma versus leadership based on rational or traditional forms). Laypeople, on the other hand, are related more to other types of elitization: either through generational rise of families reaping the benefits (which do often exist, though perhaps not as frequently or dramatically as many "testimonies" make out) of decades of Pentecostal adherence; or through Pentecostalism as such rising up the social scale and developing an appeal to people who are already at higher social levels.

To all these factors from within the Pentecostal field, one should add factors from the broader religious field (leading to approaching Pentecostal numerical stagnation, as explained below) and society (general trends toward institutional decommitment, and the socioeconomic and educational transformations in this "emerging economy" and "emerging power").

The Global Success of Pentecostalism

Most work about Pentecostalism around the world, even that by authors who portray it in essentially negative terms, seems impressed by its growth and prospects and eager to explain its success. Pentecostalism, it is predicted, is likely to become the predominant global form of Christianity.[1] It has dominated the emergence of an "anthropology of Christianity,"[2] which has suggested reasons for its global success. Robbins sees it as "one of the great success stories of the current era of cultural globalization,"[3] combining indigenizing differentiation with globalizing homogenization in a cultural hybridization in the form of a "culture 'against culture.'" Or, in an alternative formulation, Robbins adopts Coleman's idea of Pentecostalism as a "part-culture." Since a part-culture cannot be lived wholly on its own, Pentecostals "will have to negotiate with a past that rhetorically they often insist they have simply left behind."[4] That negotiation commonly takes the form of "spiritual warfare" against local spiritual phenomena. Indeed, Pentecostalism is characterized by "anti-ritual ritual"; it nominally rejects ritual but is replete with "affectively-charged interactions."[5]

Two further ideas relate to Pentecostalism's capacity to become the form in which Protestantism achieves universality. Robbins echoes Appadurai's distinction between hard and soft cultural forms. While soft forms are easily adopted piecemeal, hard forms have links between value, meaning, and embodied practice that are difficult to break.[6] Pentecostalism's location toward the hard end of this continuum helps its globalization as a distinctive religious phenomenon. Olivier Roy stresses deculturation as vital for globalization; but, says Roy, some religions are better placed than others to become deculturated. Pentecostalism's emphasis on emotion, healing, and tongues, and its dissociation from the Word, place the Holy Spirit beyond culture.[7] Roy's implicit contrast seems to be with Evangelicalism. We can say that, whereas Evangelicalism is formed around the Word (in the sense both of the incarnate Christ and the also incarnate Bible), which needs to be understood in its original context and applied to other contexts, Pentecostalism is formed around the unincarnate Spirit, obviating the need for translation and cultural adaptation.

In reaction to all this, I would say Pentecostalism's prospects are less rosy than might be imagined, not because these explanations are wrong, but because the characteristics that represent assets today can become liabilities tomorrow, and because the comparative advantage of Pentecostalism today can be eaten away by creative adaptation on the part of religious rivals tomorrow.

Two Looming Transitions in Latin American Religion[8]

It is important to put Brazilian Pentecostalism in the context of what is happening in the Brazilian and Latin American religious field. The religious field of Latin America is changing rapidly, with both Protestantism and (to a lesser extent) "no religion" growing at the expense of Catholicism. This Protestant growth is from within (not significantly stimulated by missionaries or immigrants) and from the bottom up (not by top-down national reformations). Thus, Latin American religious change is due to conversion, differing greatly from change in Europe, where the new religious pluralism results more from immigration and secularization. In terms of cultural and political implications, there is a fundamental difference between diasporic globalization and conversionist globalization. In this regard, Pentecostalism is vital, as the engine of religious and religio-political change. It structures the emerging model of the religious field, a model that includes other actors but whose main creators are the Pentecostals, in various ways. First, by their very numerical success: All over the region, Pentecostalism is now the second religious force (except in Uruguay, where it loses to the "nonreligious");[9] second, by "Pentecostalizing" other sectors (through imitation, as in the Catholic Charismatic Renewal, or through hostile reactions that lead to changes in competing religions). Even the growing internal pluralism of the Catholic field is related to this, since Pentecostal expansion obliges people to justify remaining Catholic, much more than mere secularism does.

And finally, Pentecostalism not only changes religious percentages but also effectively introduces a new model of the religious field. In relation to Brazil, Velho talks of the hegemonic national ideology (both popular and erudite) that considers "mixture" as typically Brazilian.[10] But the growth of Pentecostalism, he adds, has had some success in denaturalizing Catholicism and the religious complex that it benevolently headed. I have called this model hierarchical syncretism (because it combines nonexclusiveness with acceptance of Catholic institutional hegemony); and Pentecostalism is the first major grassroots religion to reject this hegemony and propose an alternative, which we can call competitive pluralism.

Pluralism is advantageous for Pentecostalism, since it does best in a world that is tranquilly religious, rather than in a defensively religious one (where conversion is socially or legally difficult) or else in a secularized world. The religious tranquility of Latin America comes out in Ronald Inglehart's analysis of the World Values Survey. The region is characterized by strong emphasis on traditional values such as religion, but also on the free choice and self-expression, which are more common in wealthy countries. Thus,

Latin America rivals the Islamic world in the importance given to religion (even if the level of practice is only moderate in global terms.)[11] But in subjective well-being and sense of being in control of one's life, the region rivals the Nordic countries![12] In Brazil, conversion (from one religion to another, or to "no religion") is now similar to the United States: 26 percent compared to 29 percent.[13]

Relations between religion, society, and politics in Latin America have changed dramatically in recent decades, with the Catholic Church facing various dilemmas, and with Protestants growing numerically and attempting to transfer their tradition of activism to the field of formal politics. But even greater changes seem in store in coming decades, mainly due to the cumulative effect of the transformations that stem from the 1950s in Chile and Brazil, and from the 1970s and 1980s in the rest of the region. We are not far from a tipping point in which old patterns of relationship between religion, state, and society will not only be questioned but may be entirely changed. Multidimensional pluralism, numerical decline, relative institutional weakness, and the effects of democracy and the fragmenting of civil society will lead to Catholic loss of "churchly" status. I call this critical moment the Catholic transition. It may not happen in all countries of the region, but it is likely in at least a significant number. A symbolically important moment, in any country, would of course be when the percentage of the population that declares itself Catholic falls below one-half. But there is nothing magical in this, since it depends also on other factors such as level of practice and the historic strength of Catholic institutions in each country. In any case, the Catholic transition is when the old sociopolitical roles become unsustainable.

However, besides the Catholic transition, there will also be a Protestant transition. The latter may come after the former in some countries, but not in all. Where it happens first, it may make the Catholic transition unnecessary . . . but not inevitably, because the latter may happen because of the sum total of other circumstances. In any case, the Protestant transition refers to the fact that there will be a ceiling on Protestant growth and therefore on Protestant political aspirations. This ceiling will not be uniform throughout the region; there will probably be significant variations in the "final" percentage of Protestants in each country. But everywhere, the ceiling will radically change the nature of Latin American Protestantism and its relationship to society, politics, and other religions.

The moment of Protestant levelling off is probably not very distant in some countries, and may even be followed by a numerical fall. My concept of levelling off is not based on previous predictions, such as Lalive D'Epinay's idea of a social class limitation (which may apply to Chile but not to most countries),[14] or Cleary's notion of the incapacity of Pentecostalism to become a religion of the masses because it is too demanding (every day in Brazil morally and socially more flexible churches are created!).[15] Even so, the Protestant ceiling in Brazil will probably be reached within two or three decades. There are two factors in this. First, Catholic decline (currently at almost 1 percent per year) will reach a limit; there is a solid nucleus of about 25–30 percent of the population that will not disappear. Second, Protestantism currently receives only about one of every two people who abandon Catholicism. No less important, the Catholic Church is learning (albeit slowly) to compete better and diversify its appeal. For these reasons, it is hard to imagine that the Catholic population will fall below about 40 percent, a figure that will put a ceiling of about 35 percent on Protestant aspirations. But another possibility is that the Protestant ceiling will be lower than that, being determined not merely by the Catholic reaction but also by damage to the image of Protestantism caused by scandals, authoritarian leadership, unfulfilled promises, a negative political image, and limited ability to produce social transformation (unlike individual transformation, at which Pentecostalism is very successful). We would have, in that case, a Protestant ceiling somewhere between its current level of about 20 percent and 35 percent. We can thus foresee a Brazilian religious future comprising a Catholicism that is slimmer (perhaps a little above or below half of the population) but revitalized, more practicing, and committed; followed by a large but stable (and highly fragmented) Protestantism; and finally a considerable sector of non-Christian religions and of nonreligious.

In this highly pluralist future, Catholicism would maintain its position as the largest religious confession, with residual social and political privileges, especially as Protestantism would be unable to create solid representative institutions, and no denomination alone would be able to rival the Catholic institution. The distance from Latin Europe would increase, since apart from the mass Protestantism there would also be a large nonreligious sector but with little European-style secularism.

With numerical stabilization, everything will change for Brazilian and Latin American Protestantism. There will be an increasing percentage of birth members and older converts, and this will produce more demand for teaching and for different types of church leaders. There will be less triumphalism and greater expectations in the field of social action, and interaction with other religions will change radically. There will also be other ways of relating to politics. All this will constitute the Protestant transition.

Religion in a BRIC

Within Latin America, Brazil occupies a central place, having by far the largest community of Pentecostals (probably half of all those in the region). Indeed, in global terms Brazil stands out: it has probably the second-largest number of practicing Protestants in the world, nearly two-thirds of whom are in Pentecostal churches. But Brazil is not only an ebullient religious world; it is also a member of the "BRIC" countries (Brazil, Russia, India, China), which will transform the economic map of the globe in the next generation. Brazil is both rising world power and world capital of Pentecostalism.

Nevertheless, generalizations about the rest of the region, let alone about Pentecostalism in the global south, must be made with great caution; one reason for this is that differences in the availability and prestige of historical Protestantism in each country will affect the evolution of Pentecostalism.

Pentecostalism in Trouble? Recent Data from Brazil

Brazilian Protestantism, buoyed by a Pentecostal wave, did extremely well in the second half of the twentieth century, and especially in its final years. On census evidence, the growth rate for Protestants as a percentage of the population was between 20 percent and 33 percent per decade until 1990. This already healthy rate was far surpassed in the 1990s, when Protestantism grew by 75 percent. In the 2000 census 15.5 percent of Brazilians (some 26 million people) proclaimed themselves Protestant; 18 million of those were in Pentecostal churches (10.4 percent of the population). Not only had the denominations imported from abroad become thoroughly nationalized, but the Protestant field was starting to be dominated by an autochthonous process of ecclesiogenesis: a survey of greater Rio de Janeiro in the early 1990s found that 37 of the 52 largest denominations were of Brazilian origin.[16] Most of these were Pentecostal.

In the absence of the religious results of the 2010 census,[17] we shall use other data released by the census-gathering agency during the first decade of the twenty-first century. A 2009 survey produced the following figures: Catholics 68.4 percent, Protestants 20.2 percent (of which Pentecostals were 12.7 percent and other Protestants 7.5 percent), and nonreligious 6.7 percent.[18] Two states already have Catholic minorities: the Amazonian state of Rondonia (46.8 percent) and the third most populous state of Rio de Janeiro (49.8 percent); the same states also have the highest percentages of nonreligious (19.4 percent and 15.9 percent). But Piauí, in the Northeast Region, is still 87.9 percent Catholic.

The same 2009 data also show considerable variation in the percentage of Protestants. Piauí has only 8.2 percent, whereas the Amazonian state of Acre has four and a half times as many (36.6 percent). The state of Rio de Janeiro has 24.8 percent, while the most populous state of São Paulo is just above the national average, at 21.7 percent. In overall terms, Protestantism is stronger in the newly developing regions of Amazonia and the "cerrado," which roughly correspond to the official regions known as the North (26.1 percent) and the Center-west (24.6 percent). In the more traditional Northeast Region, it has only 15.0 percent. The remaining regions, the Southeast and the South, which constitute the most developed areas, come in between, at 21.9 percent and 20.1 percent. But there are differences in the geography of Pentecostals and of historical Protestants. Pentecostalism has starker regional variations, from 18.3 percent in the North to 9.4 percent in the Northeast. The historicals vary only between 8.6 percent in the South and 5.6 percent in the Northeast; their national spread is somewhat more even.

Another difference emerges along the rural-urban spectrum. Protestants as a whole are disproportionately urban (being only 14.2 percent of the rural population). In state capitals, they are more than half as much again (21.7 percent), but even higher in the (mostly poor) metropolitan areas around the capital cities: 25.4 percent. However, while Pentecostals are especially strong in metropolitan areas and in smaller cities, the historicals are especially strong in the (generally more prosperous) capital cities themselves.

A third difference has to do with gender: Pentecostalism is more accentuatedly female (14.2 percent of the female population versus only 11.3 percent of the male population) than is historical Protestantism (7.9 percent versus 7.0 percent).

Comparing this 2009 survey with a similar one from 2003, we see that in that six-year period Pentecostalism grew by only 0.27 percent, whereas other Protestants grew by 2.08 percent. Most of this is due to changes in the Southeast Region (which includes the three largest cities of São Paulo, Rio de Janeiro, and Belo Horizonte), where Pentecostals fell from 15.09 percent to 13.81 percent, while historicals grew from 6.03 percent to 8.08 percent. If we give credence to these figures (which do not have the same reliability as the census), then for the first time in at least seventy years historicals are growing faster than Pentecostals. On the basis of these surveys, the proportion of Protestants who identify as members of Pentecostal churches fell from 67.0 percent to 63.7 percent. The overall Protestant growth rate in the 2000s seems similar to that which characterized the 1950s to the 1980s (i.e., much slower than the 1990s but still fairly impressive); but with the important difference that this growth is now more historical and less Pentecostal. In addition, the Catholic decline, between the two surveys, was more than double the Protestant rise.

Another significant change between the 2003 and 2009 surveys is in the categories labeled "Protestants without institutional link" and "Pentecostals without institutional link."[19] While the sum of these in 2003 came to a mere 0.7 percent of the population, by 2009 they had quadrupled, thanks almost exclusively to the "Protestants without institutional link" category. When these results were published in 2011, much was made in Brazilian media reports about the rise of "nonchurchgoing Protestants," a phenomenon previously rare in Brazil. But that is not the necessary implication of the finding. Rather, these seem largely to be people happy to identify as Protestants (*evangélicos*, in Portuguese), but not as belonging to this or that denomination. Most are probably not nonpracticing, but people who may even regularly attend several churches, or transfer between denominations quite frequently. All this, of course, fits phenomena of decommitment familiar from elsewhere, and possibly the increasing influence of Protestant options available on the internet; but in Brazil it may also represent a trauma or weariness with ecclesiastical fads and excesses.

At least these Protestants without institutional links are still self-identifying as Protestants, and sometimes explicitly as Pentecostals. However, much has been made recently of the fact that Pentecostalism is no longer almost exclusively the beneficiary of religious switching, but also a loser from it.[20] While large-scale surveys on this are lacking, smaller studies have pointed to an increase in such switching from Pentecostalism to a variety of alternatives—for example, to Umbanda, although this seems usually to be by people in some sense returning, as in the case of a *pai-de-santo* (priest) who was an Umbandista as a teenager, then converted to Pentecostalism and became a pastor before reverting to Umbanda. "These [Pentecostal] churches commercialize the figure of Christ and I did not feel happy in my faith," he says.[21] A more common trajectory is to historical Protestant churches, as in the case of a locksmith, an elder in the Assemblies of God, who became a Methodist. The alleged motives concerned liturgy and lifestyle. In the Methodist Church, "worship is offered to God and not to the congregation"; and, questioning the behavioral taboos in his former denomination, "In the Methodist Church I found a God who forgives, not a vigilante."[22] The researcher attributes this sort of switch to the good economic times in Brazil, which reduce the need for material blessing and "awaken to ethical values."[23] But transferring to a historical church can result from varied social and religious motives.

The members of newer Pentecostal churches, often referred to as neo-Pentecostal, which are especially given to prosperity teachings, are reputed to be exceptionally prone to switching within the Protestant sphere and seem to represent a diminishing portion of it (although their beliefs and practices have penetrated deep into the older Pentecostal and charismatic denominations). In fact, neo-Pentecostal success in the 1980s and 1990s forced the older Pentecostal churches into a double reaction: on the one hand, imitation of the neo-Pentecostals, and on the other, a critical distancing that valued greater contacts with the historical Protestant world. Perhaps a "turn" to the historical world is less likely for neo-Pentecostals themselves; the exception would be the more middle-class independent charismatic groups founded from the late 1970s, some of whose leaders came from Presbyterian backgrounds.

Neo-Pentecostalism is usually portrayed very negatively by the secular media and historical Protestants, and sometimes by older Pentecostals as well. The Igreja Universal do Reino de Deus (IURD) has been the central figure in painting a garish canvas of absurdities, financial scandals, ludicrous promises, manipulation of the vulnerable, and political ambition. But the neo-Pentecostal phenomenon has also meant innovative initiatives, greater penetration of segments of society and a new relationship with the culture; in short, a more creative and less timid way of being in the Brazilian context. For these reasons, neo-Pentecostals have been on the frontline of Protestant advance in the last twenty-five years, and not only numerically. If the neo-Pentecostal wave is in fact receding (the 2009 survey detected a significant diminution in the IURD, only partly compensated by the growth of the dissident Igreja Mundial do Poder de Deus), it will bring benefits to the broader Protestant world (not least, fewer scandals and motives for ridicule)—but at the cost of a loss of dynamism.

We have talked of Pentecostal switching to historical Protestantism and other minority religions. But are Pentecostals converting to the other major categories of "no religion" and Catholicism? The category of nonreligious (few of whom are atheists) was a mere 1 percent in 1980, and has grown in tandem with the Pentecostal explosion. Its geographical distribution is remarkably similar to that of Pentecostalism. The main difference is that it includes a well-off and highly educated segment lacking in Pentecostalism. Yet overall, the nonreligious are concentrated in the same urban peripheries and rural frontiers as the Pentecostals, among the young and darker-skinned. However, they are overwhelmingly male, whereas Pentecostals are disproportionately female. It might therefore be a temporary option, a luxury of young unattached and underemployed males that is later replaced by Pentecostal domesticity, rather than a new tendency that will work its way through the age cohorts. The best statistical evidence we have is already rather old: a survey of the city of São Paulo in 1995 suggests that the number of people going from "no religion" to "Pentecostalism" (about 1.5 percent of the population) is three times greater than the number going in the opposite direction.[24]

With regard to gender, a recent interpretation of religious change in Brazil calls attention to the parallel curves of conversion (especially to Pentecostalism) and increasing female participation in the labor market.[25] The author talks of "elective affinities" between religious choices and the economic changes affecting women. While men have either remained Catholic or joined the nonreligious, women have migrated disproportionately to other religions. He attributes this to the Catholic Church's difficulty in regard to questions of female emancipation such as contraception, divorce, and professional success. In the mid-1990s, a survey in greater Rio de Janeiro found that Protestant affiliation made a greater difference in reproductive behavior (fewer children), the lower the social class involved.

At lower social levels, Pentecostalism's advantages for women seem clear: despite its patriarchal discourse, it is practically efficacious in restoring the dignity of women and often also in domesticating their menfolk. (See the chapters by Bernice Martin and Rebecca and Timothy Shah in this volume). In any case, other discourses of female empowerment are inaudible in that social context, or virtually impossible to appropriate. But at the middle-class level in Brazil, the situation is different. The middle-class is very Western and is capable not only of hearing but of appropriating such alternative discourses. If Pentecostal growth is slowing in Brazil, it may be partly because it is less attractive to women who are moving into the lower middle class and accessing higher levels of education.

What about Catholicism? Several factors might favor stronger Catholic resistance to Pentecostal advance than in the past. One is demography. Catholic clericalism and "heavy" territorial structure struggled in eras characterized by demographic mobility. But now, population growth is slowing, internal migrations are diminishing, and urban growth is going more to medium-sized cities, all of which should favor Catholicism's capacity to react. A second factor is Catholic adaptation. It was almost inevitable that Catholicism would suffer heavy losses once real religious competition began in Brazil. But that is only a first moment. As Froehle and Gautier say: "In countries [such as the United States] where the Church has long existed side by side with Evangelical Protestants in an open, pluralist setting, Catholics have developed particularly strong forms of local parish life, commitment to practice and participation, and a sense of stewardship and relatively high church giving. In other words, the Church has learned from the strengths characteristic of these other Christian traditions."[26] It is probably not coincidental that the most vibrant Catholic movement in Brazil today, the Charismatic

Renewal, began in the United States and fits well with the Brazilian church's need to reinvent itself in a more "denominational" context. Finally, a third factor is socioeconomic change and government policies. The social programs of the Lula government (2003–2009), such as the *bolsa-família,* created a larger state presence among the most underprivileged sectors, reducing somewhat the need for economic "crisis management," to which Pentecostal churches cater in so many ways.

All the above factors, however, refer to the possibility of greater Catholic resistance to erosion by Pentecostalism, notwithstanding the continued Catholic decline detected in recent surveys. But evidence of actual transfer from Pentecostalism to Catholicism, whether by former Catholics returning or by first-time converts, is still minimal.

Historicization and the "Reformed Turn"

On current data, therefore, Pentecostalism in Brazil is "in trouble" if compared to the 1990s, although not yet in overall terms; but there are reasons for expecting such a crisis to appear fairly soon. However, one must already take into account the effect of a growing perception of slower Brazilian Pentecostal growth on a community with grossly exaggerated expectations. One reaction is to deny the validity of the data, preferring in-house estimates that predict a Protestant majority by 2020. But some of my recent interviews with leading Pentecostals suggest another reaction, a sense of crisis that transcends numerical concerns. In some cases, this is even traced back to the movement's origins. "The Pentecostal movement has aged very badly," says the head of one medium-sized Pentecostal denomination, "because there were already seeds of death in its origins." What the speaker means is that early Pentecostalism hoped to be a revival movement, but because it was expelled from the existing churches it "created a church without a tradition," one that, moreover, "despised traditions." As a result, "they had to bring themselves up, and people who have to bring themselves up are badly brought up! The list of scandals began very early." Pentecostalism "became a populist and anti-intellectual movement . . . led by people who were charismatic but not necessarily ethical."

Not all internal dissidents go as far as this historically rooted critique, but an increasingly common trend is to see the solution for Pentecostalism's malaise in a turn to historical Protestantism, and often specifically to its Reformed (Calvinist) branch. The Reformed presence in Brazil is over 150 years old, but the doctrinally Calvinist elements have often been downplayed in Brazilian Presbyterianism. But today the attraction is a local refraction of an international trend, which sees charismatic churches in Singapore, Hong Kong, and Kuala Lumpur adopt the (nineteenth-century neo-Calvinist) language of "cultural mandate"[27] and the head pastor of the Elim Pentecostal church in El Salvador say "don't call me Pentecostal, call me Calvinist."[28] In a similar manner, *Time* magazine includes Calvinism in its list of "Ten Ideas Changing the World": "The energy and the passion in the [American] evangelical world" are with those who believe (as *Time* puts it unsympathetically) in "an utterly sovereign and micromanaging deity, sinful and puny humanity, and predestination." The newsmagazine's explanation for this in the American context is twofold: first, that young people who have grown up "in a culture of brokenness, divorce, drugs or sexual temptation . . . have plenty of friends [but] what they need is a God"; and second, that in hard economic times more Christians are searching for security.[29]

In Brazil, the "culture of brokenness" is certainly present although the hard economic times are definitely not. But there are other reasons for Calvinism's attraction for Brazilian Pentecostals, depending perhaps on the aspect of that tradition being emphasized: whether the "cultural mandate" side, or the "utterly sovereign deity and predestination" side. Let us look at three examples.

First, from a leading member of the Assemblies of God, whose concern is more with the dimensions of Christian existence which, he feels, Pentecostalism is unable to speak to. There is, he says, "no Pentecostal political project for society," as opposed to the many Pentecostal political projects in Brazil that contemplate merely the strengthening of the church, or a very limited agenda of "moral questions," or the conquest of power by "the *evangélicos.*" What is the solution? "The idea would be, like Abraham Kuyper, to have a worldview, to redeem the sociopolitical role of the church." I am intrigued by this unexpected reference to Kuyper, the late nineteenth- and early twentieth-century neo-Calvinist theologian, party leader and, finally, prime minister of the Netherlands. Does this reference to the Reformed tradition, I ask, imply that Pentecostalism does not have the necessary elements from within its own tradition? His reply, although indirect, seems indeed to imply a Pentecostal lack:

> The Pentecostal tradition has worked hard to 'win souls for Christ.' And [it has had] an urgent eschatology. . . . But today . . . also because of the rise of neo-Pentecostalism, there are many Pentecostals who are very close to the Reformed. There is a symbiosis. Nowadays I consider myself Reformed. As a reaction against neo-Pentecostalism, and also as a reaction to the old Pentecostal vision that you have heaven waiting so don't worry about anything.

I comment that he seems to be implying that the neo-Pentecostals show a certain audaciousness in occupying spaces in society, but without an adequate Christian content in their efforts. Yes, he replies, "the neo-Pentecostals have a project of power, strictly denominational." And what about the older Pentecostal denominations, like his own? "The leaders of the classical Pentecostals are too compromised, too concerned with their empires."

From this example of a "Reformed turn" motivated seemingly by a presumed Pentecostal incapacity to think Christianly about society, we move to our second example, that of the aforementioned head of a medium-sized Pentecostal denomination. After his damning critique of Pentecostal origins, I ask him why the need to look outside the Pentecostal tradition should lead him specifically to the Reformed option. His reply does not go in the direction of Dutch neo-Calvinism, and the sociopolitical equipping that its worldview makes possible; rather, he is concerned with the sixteenth- and seventeenth-century debates over free will and predestination. His reply starts with the assertion that Pentecostalism is "a predominantly Arminian tradition" (i.e., opposed to Calvinist ideas of predestination). And "one of the great frustrations of the Pentecostal movement is the feeling of responsibility, and also of failure, for not converting everybody. Which leads to the question Calvin himself asked: why doesn't everybody convert? Of course, Calvinism doesn't resonate well with the spirit of our times, the self-determination and individualism." But it offers a "density of thought . . . something more robust and vigorous" than is found in the Pentecostal world, which is "based a lot on experience, on testimonies, on a few verses from here and there." But are there not obstacles in adopting Calvinism, such as its opposition to Pentecostal beliefs in present-day miraculous gifts of the Holy Spirit and its weaker evangelistic thrust? No, he affirms. "Calvinism does not eliminate the continued miraculous working of God in the world"; and "the Calvinist tradition is a great evangelistic motivator. . . . Any Calvinist who does not have a broken heart for the lost of this world is not a good Calvinist."

So we have seen the Reformed tradition adopted as worldview and sociopolitical resource, and now also as a theodicy that makes sense of unsuccessful evangelism. Finally, we meet a broader synthesis of the existential, the ecclesiastical, and the liturgical, in a pastor who has broken with the Assemblies of God and founded his own church, which he has officially registered as Pentecostal-Reformed. This man was among the first generation of Assemblies members to gain a university education. He is an engineer and (without being involved in party politics) has held positions, including that of secretary of the environment, in the municipal government of his city (population of over 300,000). As a child in the Assemblies of God, he spoke in tongues and prophesied, and later became a youth leader. At university, he had contact with other denominations. Although he later studied at the Assemblies' seminary and became a pastor (alongside his professional activities), he did not abandon his interdenominational links. Participation in pan-Evangelical conferences enabled him to "consolidate a more Reformed view, but without losing my Pentecostal characteristics." He even managed to bring prominent non-Pentecostal speakers to the church where he was assistant pastor.

In the end, however, he left the Assemblies to start his own Pentecostal-Reformed church. How does he integrate these very diverse traditions? "There is respect for Pentecostal manifestations at the end of the service or in a prayer meeting. But on the other hand, we are very zealous in listening to and discussing the Word." In other words, a church that synthesizes his own trajectory, in which people brought up in Pentecostalism conclude that their tradition does not have the resources to meet certain expectations or answer certain questions, but do not wish to reject that tradition wholesale. But, once again, why turn specifically to the Reformed tradition? His reply deepens the "theodicy" line of reasoning: Our duty is to preach and pray for people, but we do not know whom God will save or cure. "In the Pentecostal church, there is little knowledge of grace." The implication seems to be, I put to him, that a real belief in the sovereignty of God frees the preacher from thinking that everything depends on him and that therefore he has to be always up to date with the latest methodologies or gimmicks for disseminating the message, and also the latest technologies, which are usually expensive and lead to adopting theologies that justify endless fundraising. Precisely, he agrees. When in the Assemblies of God, "I felt a weight, and this weight led me to activism. [Today, I have] an unhurried vision, without the constant concern over numbers." Or the constant concern with "fads and pragmatism, with immediate returns."

This pastor is convinced he is not atypical. "For a high percentage of people in Pentecostal churches, the Pentecostal experience by itself no longer satisfies. Just listening to a message which leads to a catharsis isn't fulfilling any more." Why not, I ask, if it satisfied in the past? "Because the old-style Pentecostal leaders reined in anyone who wanted more knowledge." He compares them to the *coronéis,* the caudillo-like local bosses from the more traditional regions of Brazil. But now, that leadership style is less effective, and more Pentecostals have the chance to hear voices from the broader Protestant world.

This pastor does not explicitly make the connection, but one can presumably relate this broadening of theological horizons to a general rise in educational levels among Pentecostals, thanks both to general social processes and to the way Pentecostalism specifically promotes investment in education. This results in more Pentecostals moving into a larger cultural world. But then, as I put it to him, the question is whether these people think they can find resources within Pentecostalism for their new concerns, or feel they have to look elsewhere. His reaction is indicative: "To break with one's own tradition is the most difficult thing to do, because it means leaving one's comfort zone . . . and if you're not careful, it can result in losing the simplicity of the gospel." But to this heartfelt reflection on experience, he adds another observation. "Pentecostals who move toward historical Protestantism are more tolerant than the historicals who move toward Pentecostalism." If true, I believe this is due not only to the former process being rather of addition and continuity than a radical break; there is also a class dimension. Generally occupying a higher social and cultural level, the historical will only listen to the "little Pentecostal brother" when in a severe crisis. But the reverse is not the case. Although some Pentecostals still have a traditional rejection of "knowledge that doesn't save" and that "goes to your head," once that has disappeared there are no class barriers to learning from the historicals.

These cases illustrate some motives for historicization, to which one can add others: the growing trend for Pentecostal pastors to study in government-recognized "Sciences of Religion" master's and doctoral courses, most of which are in universities of historical Protestant or Catholic origin; the effect of increasing Pentecostal experience in missionary work abroad; and difficulties faced by young Pentecostals in institutions of higher education where the image of Pentecostalism is poor. With regard to the specific attraction of Calvinism, apart from its solid identity and strong international networks, one should not minimize the other concern expressed by my interlocutors: the search for relief from the overriding concern with the religious market and resulting slavishness to the latest fads. The idea that Calvinism can provide a safe haven from this is in fact corroborated by the experience of the oldest (and second-largest) Pentecostal denomination in Brazil. The Congregação Cristã rejects all mass propaganda methods.[30] Proselytism occurs exclusively inside the church or by personal contact. A strong belief in predestination (probably acquired by the Italian founder in his passage through Presbyterianism in the United States) helps to maintain this pattern. The conviction that God will bring into their midst the people he desires to save frees this church from the pressure to adapt methods constantly, in the name of evangelistic efficacy, to social change and technological advance. Rejection of the mass media, so readily associated with politics in Brazil, helps to maintain its apolitical ideal. And the operational cost of the church is low, diminishing the need for political contacts. As a result, it is far removed from the current mercantilist image of Pentecostals in Brazil. Although its other (highly sectarian) characteristics mean it is not an attractive refuge for dissident Pentecostals, it does demonstrate the effects of theological differences on church practices and relations with society.

If historicization becomes widespread in Brazil, it will invite the question whether a repeat of the Western trajectory toward theological liberalism is only a matter of time. But in the Brazilian context, still far more religious, it may be more reasonable to expect a transition not so much to liberalism as to various types of Evangelicalism, whether Reformed or not.

Class and Education Level

How does (or will) all this play out in the spheres of education and political participation? First, in terms of class and educational level. The 2009 survey revealed that only 11.3 percent of Brazilian employers are Protestant, scarcely more than half the Protestant rate in the population as a whole (20.2 percent). This difference is largely due to the Pentecostals. In terms of income (using the Brazilian descending classification in "classes" from A to E), Pentecostals are only 6.3 percent of classes A–B (i.e., upper and middle), but reach their strongest level of 15.3 percent in (the lowest-but-one) class D. Historical Protestants, on the other hand, are 8.4 percent in A–B and 8.7 percent in C (lower-middle-class), declining to only 4.7 percent in the lowest class, E. Within this general tendency for Pentecostalism to be overrepresented near the bottom end of the income scale, it is perhaps significant that the category of "Pentecostals without institutional links" is an accentuatedly class C phenomenon.

Data on color (traditionally linked to class) reveal a similar pattern. The most "Pentecostal" color is black (16.5 percent), followed by browns (14.1 percent), indigenous (13.0 percent), whites (11.0 percent), and yellows (10.5 percent). If we leave out the indigenous (less than 1 percent of the Brazilian population), we see that the Pentecostal presence declines as the average socioeconomic level improves.

In terms of education, Brazilian Pentecostalism is still heavily skewed, but there are signs of change. At the lowest educational level (3 years or fewer of schooling), Pentecostals are 13.6 percent, a rate which changes little at the next two levels: from 4 to 7 years, 13.6 percent; from 8 to 11 years, 13.0 percent. However, among those with 12 years or more of schooling, Pentecostals are still only 6.7 percent. This profile contrasts with that of historical Protestants: in the four ascending levels, they represent 6.2 percent, 7.3, 8.7 percent and 8.6 percent respectively. However, historicals are overrepresented among university graduates (9.6 percent) but underrepresented among people with masters and doctoral degrees (5.6 percent). They are not one of the truly intellectual religious minorities, which in Brazil are supremely the spiritists and to a lesser extent the nonreligious. If we look in a similarly detailed way at the Pentecostal educational profile, we see that they are overrepresented (14.8 percent) among the *pré-vestibular* category, i.e., those taking preparatory courses for the competitive university entrance exams. This suggests a repressed demand for higher education, and means that a large-scale Pentecostal arrival in the universities might be about to take place.

We can consider the potential implications of this by looking at Chile through the work of sociologist Cristián Parker. He emphasizes that the expansion of higher education has resulted in a high number of "Catholics in my own way." In Chile, education generates distrust in religious institutions and dogmas but not in religion as such. But Protestantism is also affected. Parker discovers that Protestants are greatly influenced by educational level, and that its rise seems to put a ceiling on Protestant growth.[31]

This raises the question whether Chile, in many ways the most socio-economically advanced country in Latin America, is the future of the region in religious terms, or whether it has unique cultural and religious characteristics. Chile has the oldest mass Protestantism in Latin America. Its Protestantism is highly Pentecostalized, and its Pentecostalism is even more concentrated at the lower end of the social scale than in Brazil and faces a virtually impenetrable social ceiling. Other characteristics result from this: the high percentage of nonpracticing Pentecostals; the relative difficulty in finding Protestant ecclesiastical alternatives suitable to upward social mobility. So, does the expansion of higher education have a very negative effect on Protestant prospects in Chile precisely because of the social characteristics of the country and the Protestant community, whereas in other countries different consequences might ensue? Where the social ceiling is less impenetrable, the expansion of education might simply generate new forms of Protestantism, rather than an abandonment of it or a turn to nonpractice. We shall see. But, interestingly, this was the spontaneous conclusion drawn in one of my interviews, by a female Pentecostal pastor in Brazil. When she was growing up in a backwater of the impoverished Northeast, "The church taught us to read because we had to read the Bible and the Sunday school magazine. We were taught to take care of our parents, and for that we had to have jobs, which meant we were encouraged to study." But in the past, I interject, it was said that Pentecostals were indifferent or resistant to education, even demonizing it as bad for faith. "That's definitely not what I experienced! Pentecostal young people spend a lot of time together, and one pulls the other along. If one gets into university, the others want to go too. In church we learned we had to go to school and respect the teacher and get the best grades, without cheating! So the Pentecostal church did not reach the school through a miracle. It sought out the school!" That may be, I say, but (mentioning the Chilean data on education and Protestant growth) won't that very thing be the kiss of death? Not at all, she replies. "It just leads to creating more open denominations!"

Pentecostalism and Politics: Learning Curve or Inherent Limitation?

In marginal areas in Brazilian cities, virtually untouched by other sectors of civil society or indeed the state,[32] the Pentecostal presence is generally perceived as vital. It is said that only two institutions really function in the shantytowns: organized crime and Pentecostal churches. Other forms of organized religion are generally absent or weak, and so is the state. This is Pentecostalism's "civilizing" mission, providing people with ways of escape from criminality, prostitution, and drug addiction.

Against this backdrop, there is a widespread perception in academia and the Brazilian media that Pentecostalism is very good at personal transformation and has a largely positive role in poor and peripheral sectors of society, but that in formal politics its performance has been very poor and even risible. To what should we attribute this gap between microlevel competence and macrolevel incompetence?

First, it should be pointed out that Pentecostalism in Brazil has achieved a level of political visibility rivaled in very few countries (one thinks, perhaps, of Guatemala and Zambia).[33] Pentecostalism in the developed West, of course, has never achieved this sort of numerical strength in a democratic context. The Pentecostal entry into Brazilian politics since the mid-1980s has provided political mobility for some individuals who would normally stand very little chance of occupying such positions.

In addition, Pentecostalism ("arguably the largest self-organized movement of urban poor people on the planet")[34] is nothing if not optimistic. Its discourse is one of victory, not of victimhood (as characterizes some dynamic religious movements in today's global context). It is therefore almost never given to political violence. It is, however, prone to a self-regarding triumphalism, based on the mystique of a Puritan-like "rule of the saints" ("we are the answer to Brazil's problems"; but the answer is never spelled out), and ultimately on the dream of electing a "godly ruler" whose mere presence in government would unleash a cascade of divine blessings. The flip side of this triumphalism is the tendency to demonize not only other religions and certain lifestyles (especially related to sexuality), but also certain political tendencies. Even though Robbins, in his work on global Pentecostalism, talks of "spiritual warfare" as "locally meaningful idioms for talking about social problems,"[35] this has severe limits in Brazil, which is far more Western than Africa and Asia and where there is more and more need to dialogue meaningfully with secular ideologies.

Even though theocracy is out of reach for Brazilian Pentecostals, the tendency to messianism remains. If Islamist currents in the Middle East such as the Muslim Brotherhood go through internal debates between short-term strategies focused on taking the reins of power and long-term plans focused on the recruitment of students and professionals and a painstaking infiltration of strategic positions in society, Brazilian Pentecostalism has no such debates. It has no "infiltration" strategy; instead, it has the recurrent hope of electing a *presidente evangélico,* an illusory shortcut to influence for groups that are still not really all that influential.

The messianism of taking over from the top down is shared with Pentecostals in some other Latin American countries.[36] But since 1986 Brazilian Pentecostalism has also developed a unique form of political representation based on top-down initiatives by the major denominations. Denominational leaders select a candidate for federal deputy, or state deputy, or municipal councilor. Often, the person chosen is a relative of the head pastor, or perhaps a businessman affiliated to the church, or a singer or preacher well-known through the church's electronic media. Very occasionally, the candidate is the head pastor himself. Then, all the denomination's churches in the relevant electoral district (the municipality in local elections; the state in federal and state elections) are instructed to allow space for the candidate to present himself (or, in a few cases, herself) from the pulpit, and all church members are instructed to vote accordingly. Members are never totally faithful in this respect, and sometimes resoundingly refuse to cooperate, but in a considerable number of cases enough votes are obtained to elect the "official" candidate.

This corporatist model depends not only on large denominations with considerable cohesion and sufficiently pliant membership, but also on a diffuse party system (Brazil currently has twenty-two parties with representation in congress) and an electoral system based on large state-wide electoral districts and proportional representation with open party lists. In this system, virtually all parties are interested in having Pentecostal candidates to increase their overall percentage of the vote. And the open list system means party hierarchs do not decide in advance which of their candidates will have preference for the seats obtained, but such preference will be decided by the popular vote received by each candidate.

So successful has this model been, that "official" Pentecostal candidates have made up the majority of Protestants in congress since the return of democracy in the mid-1980s. In the congress elected in 2010, there are nearly 70 Protestant members (over 13 percent) of the lower house. But the model has also been disproportionately connected to corporatist politics, frequent party switching, and corruption. Involvement in financial corruption scandals began already in the late 1980s and reached a peak in the mid-2000s. In fact, in the elections of 2006, so notorious was Pentecostal involvement in scandals that only about a quarter of Protestant federal deputies managed to win reelection. It seemed as though Brazilian Pentecostalism might be about to enter a post-corporatist and post-triumphalist phase . . . until the corporatist model returned with a vengeance in 2010.

What can we conclude from this, in relation to the future of Pentecostalism in Brazil? Pentecostal corruption, well-publicized and related to other characteristics such as the general lack of transparency in the internal dealings of the large churches, starts to have a negative influence on its public image and on its capacity to continue reproducing itself numerically. While the self-image talks of a messianic role in cleansing the country of all sorts of evils, the reality is a disproportionate susceptibility to the worst elements in Brazilian political culture. It is true that such susceptibility may not be due to Pentecostalism as such, but rather to the "official candidate" model. But might there be other reasons why Pentecostalism as such has difficulty learning certain lessons at the societal and political levels? Might the pneumatic be an obstacle to sociopolitical maturation?

It is true that new political actors, especially those from disadvantaged sectors traditionally distant from politics, need time to go through a steep learning curve. It is also true that no religious movement is frozen in time, and certainly not the ebullient world of Pentecostalism. But, after twenty-five years, it is time to ask whether the learning curve of Pentecostal politics is actually going anywhere, and whether there might be structural reasons why not. Might it be the case that Pentecostal virtues at one level are vices at another, and therefore being good at personal transformation and poor at societal transformation are merely two sides of the same coin?

At the ecclesiastical level globally, the Pentecostal doctrine regarding the gifts of the Holy Spirit has been the way of making the Protestant doctrine of the priesthood of all believers effective. Pentecostals rarely use the language of "empowerment," but with great frequency use the terminology of "power." Empowerment is from without, whereas power is from within; or, if one prefers, empowerment is through other human beings whereas power comes unmediated from "on high." The latter is very effective for personal transformation but runs into evident limits for social transformation; with the former, the opposite is the case.

Is Pentecostal social and political engagement hamstrung by central elements of Pentecostalism's own self-conception? The problem is not the possibility of Pentecostal social or political engagement (they have both existed now for some time), but the quality of such engagement. Pentecostalism's intense self-belief and its pragmatism discourage a humble and teachable attitude and perseverance through long and slow learning processes.

In the history of Pentecostalism, these characteristics did not at first appear as great disadvantages. In the very early days, the attitude was usually that there was no need to think of any level higher than that of personal transformation, since the end-times were at hand. Later, this transmuted into the facile belief that the growing number of transformed individuals would automatically transform society. Still later, some sectors adopted a sort of intuitive holism modeled on gospel descriptions of the ministry of Jesus. This sort of imitation of Christ, with little reflection on efficacy or implications, can lead to considerable social activism. But eventually, for some, this activism leads to reflection on how to relate the social to the political, and to a perception that ignoring the political hampers the social impact. However, it is at this point that the "virtues-into-vices" syndrome comes into play, in which the humility and teachability necessary for undertaking long apprenticeships in social and political activism tend to be swamped by the self-belief and pragmatism that function so effectively at the personal and ecclesiastical levels.

One can make a comparison here with the sphere of transcultural missions, where Pentecostal enthusiasm, conviction of calling, and charismatic gifting all may have a role but cannot substitute for a long and painful process of learning the other language and culture, and learning from the positive and negative experiences of previous missionaries. The current difficulties of Brazilian Pentecostals in this sphere (the subject of my current research) seem almost to have been foreshadowed in the very origins of Pentecostalism itself. To a considerable extent, Pentecostalism began as a missionary movement based on the idea that "tongues-speaking" was not so much glossolalia (praising God in unintelligible sounds) but xenolalia (the miraculous ability to speak a foreign language that one had never learned). Pentecostal missionaries embarked for places such as China with the pious belief that they would be given the ability to speak the native language once they arrived. The xenolalia illusion was abandoned long ago, but is emblematic of a broader Pentecostal problem: the ultimate desire for a short-circuiting, a quick fix that would eliminate all need to study and learn and understand others (whether those others happen to be natives of foreign societies or political actors in one's own society).

There may also be broader political implications that affect not only Pentecostalism but all forms of "primitivist" Christianity. Each religion has certain political dilemmas that stem from its tradition and not just from its current context. The political dilemmas of Islam have been widely debated in recent decades, but those of Christianity are also relevant, especially with the global spread of Pentecostalism. Christianity's problems include how to incorporate the Hebrew Scriptures, with their notions of holy war and holy commonwealth; different approaches to the relationship between the two Testaments suggest different political postures. But it is always hard to develop Christian justifications using only the Old Testament. However, if Christian politics relies purely on the New Testament, it falls under Tocqueville's strictures about the lack of a civic ethic. Primitive Christian thought, said Tocqueville, lacked the idea of moral citizenship and created a dangerous political void.[37] Primitive Christianity alone is deficient for a democratic age, which needs active citizens and not passive subjects. Catholics, of course, have an ongoing magisterium, and the Reformed tradition (at times) has used a concept of "unfolding." But many Protestants, especially Pentecostals, are bound to primitivist concepts of a return to original purity, which in the Christian case was distant from the state, leading to the default danger of apolitical conformism; and this can be exploited by authoritarian regimes.

Pentecostalism has little tradition of teasing out sociopolitical implications from the Christian scriptures, and may even lack the resources to go far with it. If that is so, the only solution would be a return to seeing itself (as some of our informants hint at) not as a separate segment of the faith but as exclusively a renewal movement within existing currents, which therefore has a specialized function and does not have to supply a complete theology and social ethics. In addition, rapid growth in the global south places market pressures on church leaders that are unfavorable to ethical reflection. And, since Christian origins were times of powerlessness, the search for scriptural purity does not produce clear-cut political proposals or the consensus for effective action.

Tocqueville also stressed the importance of Christianity to democracy, but only in the right relationship (separate from the state and partisanship, keeping clergy out of electoral disputes, yet undergirding politics) and only if performing some necessary tasks. Envy and difference are the perils facing democracy. Christianity can redress the first by averting the soul's gaze toward heaven, and the second by insisting upon an underlying unity. Democracies need long-term thinking to balance the democratic impulse toward the short-term; and that can best be provided by religion. But Brazilian Pentecostalism has not done well in maintaining distance from the vicissitudes of party politics, or in averting people's gaze from materialistic envy, or in balancing democratic impulsiveness with long-term thinking. The Pentecostal self-belief that assists personal transformation is a liability in politics. And the charismatic ritualism that can produce results at the micro level (by expelling the "demons" of fear or promiscuity, for example) does not function at the macro level (e.g., in attempts to expel the "demon of corruption" from the national congress).

The Future of Pentecostalism

Caution is necessary in extrapolating from Brazil to the rest of Latin America, let alone to other parts of the global south where Pentecostalism has grown. For one thing, an important factor in differential evolution of Pentecostalism may be the relative strength or weakness of the historical Protestant tradition in each country. Both Chile and Central America have far weaker historical Protestant fields than Brazil, and thus offer fewer options to Pentecostals for personal and ecclesiastical experimentation or for ecclesiastical transfer. Other factors, such as the degree to which Protestantism runs up against a social ceiling, or the degree to which its public image has been eroded by negative perceptions of its electoral and parliamentary involvement, or the extent to which Protestant growth is connected to indigenous ethnic identity, will also play a role.

Pentecostalism does seem to have many advantages in an era of globalization; but maybe these are only temporary (until rivals learn to imitate them), and then the disadvantages become more obvious. Pentecostalism will probably reveal itself to have been the main means of accession to Christianity in some parts of the world, and of accession to Protestantism in other parts. But it is unlikely to become dominant numerically or in other senses in world Christianity, because of the inherent limitations that begin to show themselves even in its "world capital" of Brazil. None of this, of course, means that Pentecostalism will disappear. Much of it will feed into new Christian syntheses, both in the sense of new denominations and of influencing existing non-Pentecostal denominations, as well as a profound reshaping of (at least portions of) existing Pentecostal denominations.

The Protestant doctrine of universal priesthood is made more effective by the Pentecostal doctrine of the gifts of the Holy Spirit. This accounts for many of its characteristics and for much of its cultural adaptability and numerical success. But Pentecostalism does not implement the ecclesiology of the relevant New Testament texts regarding the democratic implications of the manner in which the Christian God distributes spiritual gifts. A grasp of this would take effective implementation of the universal priesthood even further; but without it, Pentecostalism has run into the limits of its genuine theological innovativeness, and not merely the limits of its pragmatic fads.

In addition, Pentecostalism, as an extreme form of voluntarism, is very much a prisoner of the religious market. But religious markets, like all others, are socially produced and changeable. In Brazil, the demand for some of Pentecostalism's most common products is slowing, either because those needs are being met in other ways through economic growth or better state provision, or because Pentecostalism's ability to truly meet them is being more and more cast in doubt. In addition, the growth of a new middle class is leading to a lower tolerance for corruption in public life, and this may in time be reflected in lower tolerance for corruption in church life.

Since some time in the 1980s, Pentecostals have been the majority in the Brazilian Protestant world; but their numerical advantage may not out-last, say, the 2030s. Some twenty years ago, David Martin commented that historical Protestantism in Latin America had been "a vehicle of autonomy and advancement for some sectors of the middle class," but since it had come wrapped in "the worldview, ethos and ideology of the prosperous cap-italist countries . . . the whole Protestant style had remained distant from the masses."[38] But it may end up being attractive for many of those leaving Pentecostalism.

NOTES

The author wishes to thank Boston University's Institute on Culture, Religion, and World Affairs (CURA) and the University of Southern California's Pentecostal and Charismatic Research Initiative (PCRI) for the funding that made possible the research for this article carried out in 2010 and 2011.

1. José Casanova, quoted in Simon Coleman, "An Anthropological Apologetics," *South Atlantic Quarterly* 109:4 (fall 2010): 791–810; quote from 800.

2. Coleman, *Apologetics,* 799; cf. Birgit Meyer, "Aesthetics of Persuasion: Global Christianity and Pentecostalism's Sensational Forms," *South Atlantic Quarterly* 109:4 (fall 2010): 741–763; citation on 741.

3. Joel Robbins, "The Globalization of Pentecostal and Charismatic Christianity," *Annual Review of Anthropology* 33 (2004): 117–143; citation on 117.

4. Joel Robbins, "Anthropology, Pentecostalism, and the New Paul: Conversion, Event, and Social Transformation," *South Atlantic Quarterly* 109:4 (fall 2010): 633–652; citation on 649.

5. Jon Bialecki, "Angels and Grass: Church, Revival, and the Neo-Pauline Turn," *South Atlantic Quarterly* 109:4 (fall 2010): 695–717; citation on 699.

6. Joel Robbins, "On the Paradoxes of Global Pentecostalism and the Perils of Continuity Thinking," *Religion* 33:3 (2003): 221–231; citation on 224.

7. Olivier Roy, *Holy Ignorance* (New York: Columbia University Press, 2010), 182–183.

8. The following section is adapted from my keynote address in Spanish at the XV Jornadas sobre Alternativas Religiosas en América Latina, organized by the Asociación de Cientistas Sociales de la Religión del Mercosur, in Santiago de Chile, November 2009, and subsequently published in Portuguese as "As Duas Transições Futuras: Católicos, Protestantes e Sociedade na América Latina," *Ciencias Sociales y Religión / Ciências Sociais e Religião*, 12:12 (Oct. 2010): 13–30; and forthcoming in Spanish as "Las Dos Transiciones Futuras: Católicos, Protestantes y Sociedad en América Latina," in *Religión, Cultura y Política en América Latina: Nuevas Miradas*, ed. Cristián Parker, Santiago de Chile, Ed., Instituto de Estudios Avanzados USACH-Ariadna Ediciones, 10–38.

9. Instituto Nacional de Estadística (Uruguay), *Encuesta Nacional de Hogares Ampliada, 2006* (www.ine.gub.uy/enha2006).

10. Otávio Velho, "An Assessment of the Interreligious Situation in Brazil," World Council of Churches (www.wcc-coe.org/wcc/what/interreligious/cd36-03.html).

11. In attendance at religious services, Latin American countries range from fairly high (Colombia, Peru, just above the United States), through moderate (Brazil, Argentina, Chile), to low (Uruguay, just below Britain). See Pippa Norris and Ronald Inglehart, *Sacred and Secular: Religion and Politics Worldwide* (New York: Cambridge University Press, 2004), 101.

12. Ronald Inglehart, "Cultural Change, Religion, Subjective Well-Being, and Democracy in Latin America," in *Religious Pluralism, Democracy, and the Catholic Church in Latin America*, ed. Frances Hagopian (South Bend, IN: University of Notre Dame Press, 2009), 67–95; citation on 87.

13. *Spirit and Power* (Washington, DC: The Pew Forum on Religion and Public Life, 2006), 125.

14. Christian Lalive D'Epinay, *O Refúgio das Massas* (Rio de Janeiro: Paz e Terra, 1970), 76.

15. Edward Cleary, "Shopping Around: Questions about Latin American Conversions," *International Bulletin of Missionary Research* 28:2 (2004): 50–55.

16. Rubem César Fernandes, *Censo Institucional Evangélico CIN 1992* (Rio de Janeiro: ISER, 1992).

17. The 2010 census results were only released while this chapter was being proofread, and basically confirm the analysis presented here. In the census figures, Catholics were 64.6 percent of the population and Protestants were 22.2 percent. Pentecostals were three-fifths of those Protestants (that is, 13.3 percent of the total population).

18. Pesquisa de Orçamento Familiar (POF), carried out by the Instituto Brasileiro de Geografia e Estatística (IBGE). Figures presented here are taken from the analysis of the 2003 and 2009 POFs, in Marcelo Côrtes Neri (coord.) *Novo Mapa das Religiões* (Rio de Janeiro: FGV/CPS, 2011).

19. It should be noted that a Pentecostal who had no institutional link would not necessarily choose the "Pentecostal without institutional link" category, since the alternative of "Protestant [i.e. *evangélico*] without . . ." would also be acceptable. "I am *evangélico*" is a perfectly normal self-identification for a Pentecostal in Brazil.

20. The following cases are cited from Rodrigo Cardoso, "O Novo Retrato da Fé," *Isto É*, 35, 2180, 24 August 2011.

21. Cited in *Isto É*, from a study by Lídia Maria de Lima. It is interesting to note the *ethical* emphasis in this critique of a branch of Christianity by a leader in an Afro-Brazilian religion, despite the fact that the latter are usually regarded as having less of an ethical emphasis than the former.

22. Cited in *Isto É*, from Patrícia Cristina da Silva Souza Alves, "Todos os caminhos levam a Deus: Uma análise das motivações de Gênero no trânsito religioso de pentecostais para a Igreja Metodista na região do ABCD paulista" (master's thesis, Universidade Metodista de São Paulo).

23. Patrícia Alves, cited in *Isto É*.

24. Reginaldo Prandi, "Religião Paga, Conversão e Serviço," in Antônio Flávio Pierucci and Reginaldo Prandi, *A Realidade Social das Religiões no Brasil* (São Paulo: Hucitec, 1996), 257–273.

25. Marcelo Neri, "A Ética Pentecostal e o Declínio Católico," Rio de Janeiro, FGV (www.fgv.br/cps/artigos/conjuntura/2005/a%20ética%20Pentecostal%20e%200%20 declínio%20católico_mai2005.pdf).

26. Bryan Froehle and Mary Gautier, *Global Catholicism* (Maryknoll: Orbis, 2003), 132.

27. William Kay, personal communication, 6 August 2012.

28. Timothy Wadkins, personal communication, 12 May 2011.

29. "Ten Ideas Changing the World Right Now: The New Calvinism," *Time*, 12 March 2009 (http://www.time.com/time/specials/packages/article/0,28804, 1884779_1884782_1884760,00.html).

30. See Paul Freston, "Pentecostalism in Brazil: A Brief History," *Religion*, 25 (1995), 119–133.

31. Cristián Parker Gumucio, "Education and Increasing Religious Pluralism in Latin America: The Case of Chile," in Hagopian, *Religious Pluralism*, 131–181; citation on 162.

32. A situation that *may* be changing now, as the Brazilian state tries to regain control of such areas in advance of the country's global "coming-of-age" through its hosting of the 2014 World Cup and the 2016 Olympic Games.

33. See the chapters on Guatemala and Zambia in the following works: Paul Freston, *Evangelicals and Politics in Asia, Africa and Latin America* (Cambridge: Cambridge University Press, 2001); and Paul Freston, *Protestant Political Parties: A Global Survey* (Aldershot: Ashgate, 2004).

34. Mike Davis, "Planet of Slums," *New Left Review* 26 (March–April, 2004): 5–34; citation on 32.

35. Robbins, "The Globalization," 124.

36. See, for example, on Guatemala and Nicaragua, in Freston, *Evangelicals and Politics*, 250–280; Freston, *Protestant Political Parties*, 108–118, 132–134; Roberto Zub, "The Evolution of Protestant Participation in Nicaraguan Politics and the Rise of Evangelical Parties," in *Evangelical Christianity and Democracy in Latin America*, ed. Paul Freston (New York: Oxford University Press, 2008), 97–130.

37. Larry Siedentop, *Tocqueville* (Oxford University Press, 1994), 134.

38. David Martin, *Tongues of Fire* (Oxford: Blackwell, 1990), 230.

THREE

Social Mobility and Politics in African Pentecostal Modernity

DAVID MAXWELL

The coincidence of Africa's born-again takeoff with the end of the Cold War and the dawn of the neoliberal era raises a host of questions about the movement's relation to social, economic, and political change. Peter Berger contends that Evangelicalism is "the most modern religious community in the contemporary world" because it is a movement constituted by choice: "The voluntary association is its natural social expression, engendered from within by its religious self-understanding."[1] Students of development grow increasingly interested in forms of Protestantism that can motivate large numbers of adherents to donate scarce resources to charity and church growth, and whose leaders inspire far greater levels of trust than politicians.[2] As David Martin has recently observed, "Economists are also realists and may well be interested in people who refuse to be victims, organize for mutual assistance, and foster aspirations as a battalion of irregulars in the war on poverty."[3] Martin has also argued that Pentecostalism, Evangelicalism's most vital strand, acts as a "school for democracy." The results might be visible only in the *longue durée,* but by creating voluntary popular institutions, Pentecostal religion contributes to the formation of civil society and a broader culture of self-determination that provide the necessary ecology of democracy.[4]

My own research on African Pentecostalism confirms many of these tendencies. There are ethics, ascetic codes, and rituals of rupture that enhance social mobility, and there are practices that underpin a democratic political culture. However, contemporary African Pentecostalism is a broad river with currents flowing in different directions, creating contradictions that are continually being worked out. Pentecostal religion's sectarian sources do create enclaves in which social relations can be reconstructed.[5] However, the believer's consequent drive for respectability leads increasingly to a world-embracing culture. The populist voluntarist origins of the movement are in tension with a tendency toward hierarchy and authoritarianism in Pentecostal leadership. Given its protean quality, Pentecostalism is as much transformed as socially transforming. As chapters in this volume by Bernice Martin and Tim and Rebecca Samuel Shah illustrate, patriarchy can reimpose itself upon egalitarian gender relations and Pentecostal communities can become riven by the politics of caste. Moreover, as Paul Freston has shown, successful born-again leaders can lose touch with the egalitarian tendencies that initially animated their movements. In search of recognition, they get drawn into the clientalism and corporatism of modern African politics and practice nepotism and tribalism as they seek to pass on the fruits of their labors to their kin. Their leadership becomes characterized by a lack of accountability and transparency.[6] Such corruption stymies free enterprise, removing ladders to social mobility from those who lack connections.

Drawing upon historical and ethnographic data, this chapter explores the tensions inherent in Pentecostalism in order to offer an assessment of its significance in social, economic, and political realms. It will also describe modernity in an African Pentecostal setting.

Zimbabwe Assemblies of God Africa (ZAOGA) and African Pentecostalism

After a century of growth there is enormous variety within African Pentecostalism, reflecting its different traditions and the range of contexts in which it exists. The new South African movements such as Mosa Sono's Grace Bible Church and Tshabi Mogale's Divine Hope Bible Centre remain close in doctrine and organization to the classic Pentecostal missionary denominations from which their leaders emerged. In Ghana, Pentecostal leaders such as Lawrence Tetteh now place more emphasis on prosperity and success than upon personal moral reformation, and the born-again label appears to be little more than a token. At the other end of the Ghanaian spectrum, Mensa Otabil refutes much of the Faith/Prosperity Gospel and encourages his followers to take responsibility for their actions.[7] The older Brazilian-derived Universal Church of the Kingdom of God, now active in Mozambique, Angola, and South Africa, grows ever more bureaucratic and clerical in order to manage its enormous operation. In part it resembles the historic denominations, and yet it shares some ritual practices with Christian independency.[8] A complication is whether one places the white-robe-wearing Aladura, Apostolic, and Zionist churches of Christian Independency, with their strong emphasis on exorcism and healing, within the Pentecostal category. Many of these movements certainly have Pentecostal missionary antecedents.[9] Moreover, some have "Pentecostalized" though close proximity to Pentecostal media, Bible schools, and assemblies.[10] In often-ignored rural areas some Pentecostal movements resemble Independency in their mission to protect adherents from sickness, witchcraft, and spirit possession.[11]

My own research has focused on many of these expressions of Pentecostalism: Christian Independency, classical missionary Pentecostalism, and African-led Pentecostal movements, in Zimbabwe and more recently Democratic Republic of Congo.[12] In particular, I have made an in-depth historical and ethnographic examination of a major transnational Pentecostal movement, the Zimbabwe Assemblies of God Africa (ZAOGA).[13] ZAOGA provides a good case study. It has expanded from its township base into neighboring African states, America, Europe, and of late, into Australasia, claiming over 1.5 million members. Having evolved considerably since its founding moment in the mid-1960s, it embodies in its vast transnational reach many of the tensions inherent within Pentecostalism.

Since 2000, Zimbabweans have experienced severe decline in their livelihoods marked by hyperinflation, unemployment, famine, and pestilences such as cholera and the continuing AIDS pandemic. This social and economic malaise has been accompanied by widespread political violence as the ruling party, ZANU/PF (Zimbabwe African Union/Patriotic Front), clings to power in the face of an assertive opposition led by the Movement for Democratic Change (MDC).[14] The Zimbabwean example also prompts the pressing question of what becomes of Pentecostal promises of health, wealth, and prosperity in times of extreme crisis.

• • •

ZAOGA took root during the era of Zimbabwean open mass nationalism in the 1960s. Its pioneers offered an alternative model of liberation to African nationalism through a strategy of economic uplift centered upon the family. The chances of social reproduction were maximized through sobriety, industry, self-discipline, the avoidance of waste, and the virtues of Christian motherhood. There was an emphasis on small-scale enterprise or "penny capitalism" following the teaching of former South African communist turned Pentecostal evangelist Nicholas Bhengu. Like U.S. African Methodists, adherents were encouraged to live lives of Christian respectability and racial vindication.[15] The movement was small and highly sectarian, espousing a holiness Pentecostal theology and a highly realized eschatology in which adherents believed that they lived in end times.[16] In its early phase of growth, ZAOGA was world retreating or countercultural, "its rigors too drastic to appeal to any but a small minority."[17] At this stage it most resembled Puritanism. In spite of its exacting demands on believers, the movement gradually expanded during the 1960s and 1970s.[18]

Mirroring the Pentecostal takeoff elsewhere in Africa, ZAOGA's expansion in the late 1980s coincided with the continent's democratization and embrace of neoliberal capitalism. Democratization, liberalization, and the commercialization of the media brought about the remaking of postcolonial states and emergence of new public spheres in which religion could thrive.[19] ZAOGA's teaching shifted to reflect the culture of the new era. Its new prosperity gospel emphasized consumption, health, and worldly success. It Christianized popular culture, particularly film and music. The movement was no longer world-retreating but world-embracing, its millennial emphasis declining. As its members became more socially mobile and it attracted new middle-class converts, it changed the rules of engagement with the world, presenting success as the reward of those who led exemplary born-again lives. The prosperity gospel legitimated the aspirations of Zimbabwe's growing middle class.[20] Prominent members of the movement began to espouse what they called a Theology of Entitlement. Born-again Christians were Sons and Daughters of the King, a Royal Priesthood, and a Chosen People who should expect riches.[21]

Discussing the trajectory of American Pentecostalism, J. D. Y Peel observes how it quickly started to move up in the world, so that by 1950 it was no longer solely a religion of the poor and marginal.[22] Little historical research has been done on African Pentecostalism, but ZAOGA's trajectory from a small Holiness sect to a prosperity church is replicated elsewhere, particularly by the influential Redeemed Christian Church of God in Nigeria, which has been analyzed in a similar manner by Ruth Marshall.[23]

ZAOGA's relentless growth has not been retarded by Zimbabwe's crisis. It has been business as usual. The personal advance of the movement's leader, Archbishop Ezekiel Guti, has not diminished, and the movement's future is increasingly entwined with that of his family. Previously titled "Dr.," Guti is now "Professor," while his nephew, wife, daughter and son-in-law have been awarded doctorates courtesy of the North American Friends Christian University. With an eye to succession, Guti's wife, Eunor, is now also an "apostle" and "prophetess" who increasingly speaks for her husband in media interviews and at public events. Like the archbishop, she is now the subject of her own published tracts in the movement's propaganda. The movement continued its remarkable expansion overseas following the Zimbabwean diaspora into new locations such as Australia and New Zealand, and from there into India, Bangladesh, Singapore, Malaysia, Indonesia, and Thailand.[24] When not visiting these new transnational church plants, Ezekiel and Eunor Guti spend much time in the United States, where one of their daughters is married into the leadership of an Illinois-based African American church. The

Gutis' image is managed on ZAOGA's impressive new website, www.fifmi.org. ZAOGA has made great progress with the electronic media, having its own television channel, Ezekiel T.V., which mostly streams the Gutis' sermons into ZAOGA members' homes. International connections have also intensified. Henry Madava, a leading pastor from the famous Victory Church in Ukraine, was an invited speaker at the movement's recent 50th Jubilee celebrations.[25]

Like other Zimbabwean churches during the crisis, ZAOGA members received aid from their brethren in churches abroad, particularly from Botswana. Within Zimbabwe the annual working of Talents—an institutionalized scheme of female entrepreneurship for church funds—continued unabated, even during Operation Murambatsvina, the state-sponsored demolition of thousands of dwelling places in townships. There was also a series of new publications on the Prosperity Gospel by the Gutis and their acolytes.

By the 2000s ZAOGA had become a victim of its own success. It had engendered social mobility, creating and attracting a small middle-class membership while retaining its original township base and expanding into the rural areas. It had become a microcosm of the wider society, embodying its social stresses. Analyzing the expansion of Pentecostal movements, David Martin observes: "Much depends on the balance, which Pentecostalism maintains between its ability to expand among the masses, by remaining of the masses, and its ability to advance their condition. If the former remains powerful the latter must operate at the margin."[26] Martin's observation is an apt description of ZAOGA's predicament.

A small middle class within ZAOGA has become socially mobile by combining what Peter Berger describes as the "ingredients of the Protestant ethic": "A rational attitude to the world, a systematic approach to economic activity, individual agency seen as a religious mandate ('vocation'), a sober lifestyle implying delayed gratification and saving (Weber's inner worldly asceticism), a foregoing of wider kinship ties in favor of the nuclear family, and last but not least a high regard for education."[27] However, the comparison of modern Pentecostals with Puritans breaks down when it comes to "sober lifestyle implying delayed gratification" and "inner worldly asceticism" because of the former's strong emphasis on "pleasure and consumption."[28] Wealth is an *intended consequence* of the Prosperity Gospel. The message is explicitly advanced in sermons and self-help manuals. The recent book by ZAOGA member Cathrine Marurama clearly conveys this message. It is titled *Giving: Change your Measure*. The words of the title are emboldened in gold print and amplified by the scripture: "For with the measure you use, it will be measured back to you" (Luke 6:38). On the front cover is a photo of Pastor Cathrine dressed in a gold jacket, gold blouse, and gold skirt, adorned with chunky gold rings, necklace, and earrings. Superimposed into the background are bank notes and coins, euros and U.S. dollars, the signs of prestigious transnational connections, rather than worthless local billion-dollar Zimbabwean bills. Not to judge the book by its cover, one reads inside:

> Sometimes I sow [give away] clothes for a particular miracle in my life, I get the miracle, but still I have discovered I still reap clothes. Clothes keep coming to me. Sometimes in my wardrobe I have three or four new outfits waiting to be worn. . . .
>
> The desire that I have for my pastor, the man of God, and woman of God [Ezekiel and Eunor Guti], is that they must not ever think of clothes or worry about clothes; they should just do the work of God while we take care of that .. . . . I don't like to see them putting on a suit that they were putting on last year or the year before; I believe that they have passed that stage. They must preach in new clothes every time, I don't want to see them on Ezekiel T.V. with the same clothes a number of times.[29]

The reader is struck by excess rather that Marurama's desired message of success. However, while her message is shared by some ZAOGA members in suburban churches and in particular by her mentor, Mrs. Guti, the vast majority of the movement who reside in townships and rural areas seek basic security rather than prosperity. Their prayers are not for luxurious German motor cars, large houses, or fine clothes, but for the avoidance of disease and other trauma associated with poverty. A man of humble origins, Ezekiel Guti remains more aware of where his real constituency lies: "Financial blessing is when you have enough money to give to God through your church and enough to have your needs met not with a credit card. True prosperity is not money all the time. True blessing is to have enough to eat. The key is peace of mind, peace in the heart, peace in the family and good health."[30] This text comes from one of his own recent publications, *Prosperity That Comes Through Obedience*. In this self-help manual wealth is generated through the shrewd marshaling of limited resources rather than miraculous multiplication. The book's title is amplified by the aphorism: "To be a millionaire starts with you spending less than you earn." Such advice is reminiscent of the respectability on a shoestring that characterized the movement's first generation of adherents.

Guti's expanded definition of prosperity to encompass personal security means that it no longer represents "uniform success" but rather "staggered advancement" within a hierarchy of inequality. However, his retooling of prosperity is not necessarily at odds with Pastor Cathrine's definition.

Fellowship among believers within and between assemblies amounts to series of relationships that "span a graded continuum of progress." Relations between higher- and lower-status believers facilitate the fulfillment of social obligation through creation of opportunity and the fulfillment of material needs, and enable social mobility.[31]

Nevertheless it is personal security, rather than prosperity, that defines movements such as ZAOGA. In a recent press interview Guti acknowledged that healing remained central to the church's appeal.[32] Interestingly, ZAOGA's new high-tech medical center is situated on the south side of the railway tracks in Harare, among the poorer township dwellers, rather than in the plush northern suburbs where much of the medical infrastructure is located. While some adherents are drawn into the church to get rich rather than to find forgiveness, the archbishop retains a relentless proselytism. He seizes every opportunity to call people to repentance, even at high-profile public events that are attended by visiting politicians.

The intensification and evolution of prosperity theology as a response to Zimbabwe's crisis extends beyond ZAOGA into other Pentecostal movements. Of particular note is recent schism within the Apostolic Faith Mission (AFM) led by Emmanuel Makandiwa, whose Sunday services at the Harare City Sports Centre draw thousands of people. Makandiwa critiques traditional AFM classical Holiness theology, observing that adherents are full of the Holy Spirit but materially poor. He argues that poverty does not necessarily draw believers to God but causes them to question His goodness. Makandiwa believes that he has a calling to help Pentecostals live in the "realm of plenty."[33] There are similar tendencies toward prosperity theology in Zimbabwe's Elim Church, another classic Pentecostal movement.[34]

All of these movements draw the same mix of adherents: the poor in search of personal security, the aspirational, and the pious rich who desire a moral map to help them navigate the lures and pitfalls of modernity. With regard to the latter, it should be noted that some have prospered directly from Zimbabwe's crisis: from access to redistributed farm land, privileged access to foreign exchange, from state contracts and occupying gate-keeping jobs in customs and excise, and immigration. Others have prospered through a growing private sector.

Redemptive Uplift: Processes of Social Mobility

ZAOGA presents itself as a church that creates social mobility. Its canonical history, recited annually at the movement's anniversary, tells a story of redemptive uplift. There are themes of material expansion: a movement that progressed from mud huts and classrooms to a cathedral that can seat over a thousand people; a movement founded on the poor southern side of Harare's railway tracks that has expanded into the plush northern suburbs previously inhabited by whites; a movement that has spread from Southern Africa into the rest of the world. In parallel runs the story of the transformation of its leader from a humble carpenter into a globetrotting evangelist who rubs shoulders with politicians and is saluted by other born-again luminaries.[35] During the anniversary celebrations ordinary members testify to the material blessings God has bestowed upon them, and some of their accounts have been published.[36] Interviews with ordinary adherents give a similar picture of changed circumstances.

It is worth examining in more detail the processes that engender social mobility, because alongside the thesis that born-again religion represents a revised Protestant ethic there is a counterinterpretation. In his early work Paul Gifford argued that the Prosperity Gospel and rituals of rupture are no more than a mystification of the harsh realities of neo-liberal Africa.[37] Criticizing David Martin's argument about the long-term effects of cultural reformation he concluded: "Even someone with a high estimate of the power of culture might feel that the current plight of Africa demands something structural and something immediate."[38]

ZAOGA's primary means to social mobility is its fostering of "penny capitalism" through what is known as Talents.[39] This is the vending of cheap foodstuffs and clothes to finance the expansion of the church. It is predominantly based upon female labor; women instruct each other on production and marketing though testifying and instruction in church services. Some women sew and crochet. Others make use of the relaxation of customs and currency restrictions to buy and resell at a profit. ZAOGA members are well known at borders, which they cross regularly to buy bales of clothes, blankets, and electrical goods. Many women cook peanuts, chips, and cakes, sell sweets, and sew cushion covers in keeping with the initial conception of the teaching. But others, aided by chip-fryers, popcorn-makers, sewing and knitting machines, and a small work force, have launched themselves as successful "indigenous businesswomen." In general the levels of production are small scale; or, as one informant put it, ZAOGA members are "little moving shops who sell everything . . . we do not have very rich people in ZAOGA. Everyone is involved in selling small things."[40] Significantly, once the period of Talents is over, the women are encouraged to continue their production and make money for themselves. The working of Talents resembles the microfinance initiatives adopted by poor Dalit women in Bangalore, India, who are the subject of Tim and Rebecca Samuel Shah's chapter in this volume.

Members are also given a good deal of instruction on social reproduction and how to progress in the modern world. Some of this education comes from basic self-help manuals written by Ezekiel Guti, which focus upon issues of diet and hygiene, manners and mores.[41] Believers also have to change their attitudes toward work. Husbands need to work hard for their families, but also for their companies. If a believer is promoted to foreman, he should go home later than his team. And work is to be done to a high standard.[42] Guti preaches things missionaries would love to say but no longer dare: "Some black people today complain. They have got black children and they only earn $100. They complain 'I have got many children. My money is little.' Who bore the children?"[43]

Guti's instruction on modernity is compelling because his writings and teachings are patterned on his accessible and widely circulated autobiography-cum-canonical history, *The Sacred History.* His early life is noteworthy for its representativeness. He was the archetypal modern Zimbabwean man. From a humble background he came to the city and struggled to find permanent work and residence, education and respectability. He struggled against racism, not just at work but also in the church. He was successful and built a life of dignity and prosperity. His followers are called to emulate him. Young pastors who are the object of a good deal of his instruction are encouraged to imitate his smart attire by using their first "love-offerings" to buy a suit. Sometimes other favored members of the movement are allowed to publish manuals, such as Pastor Bright Samundombe's *Youth Survival.* The manual instructs young men on the virtues of self-improvement and how to avoid being sucked back into the chaos of machismo:

> Lack of money is not a sign of holiness, don't be lazy, do something, don't just sit and speak in tongues, after tongues you need to dress, eat, travel. . . .
>
> Dressing: do not buy cheap, buy the best, look at quality not just wear for the sake of it, some clothes are what I call (Mudohlo) poor quality, ask around, be conscious, don't dress like an old man when you are not one. . . . The moment you cease to have a desire of improving yourself that is the commencing of your death.[44]

Church members also receive instruction on propriety and domesticity through "ministries," where they dine, study the Bible, and listen to visiting speakers. These associations act as finishing schools for aspirants to the middle classes who did not gain social polish with their basic secondary education.[45] Moreover, new Pentecostals also benefit from the material support of the church community. The believer is immediately supported by a system of informal fraternal networks: small-scale welfare systems found within and between local assemblies and fellowship groups. Richer Pentecostals will often engage poorer church members in their homes, garages, shops, and sewing and knitting businesses. Those offering employment or searching for it will make their needs known to the assembly. Finally, Pentecostal culture domesticates the wayward violent male, socializing him back into peaceful manners and mores. The creation of a peaceful psyche provides another key to Pentecostal growth in the 1980s, in that Pentecostalism offered a powerful alternative to the violence of decolonization in southern Africa. The born-again experience advances a type of personhood—nonviolent, trustworthy, and incorruptible —that challenged the destructive practices of the liberation movements. A similar picture emerges from northern Uganda, where Pentecostal exorcism reintegrated those involved in torture and the spilling of blood.[46]

Exorcism is but one of the rituals of rupture that mark out new believers; others are full immersion baptism and the destruction of polluted objects associated with witchcraft and traditional religious practice. But the most prominent means of marking discontinuity with the past is deliverance from the Spirit of Poverty. The teaching can be summarized as follows: Africans remain poor because of a Spirit of Poverty; even though they are born again, only their soul has been redeemed. The pernicious influence of ancestral spirits remains in the blood. These ancestors were social and economic failures during their own lifetimes. They led lives of violence, indolence, drunkenness, polygamy, ancestor veneration, and witchcraft: lives of waste and poverty rather than accumulation. Their legacy, transmitted through their bloodline, accounts for the precarious existence of Zimbabweans during the age of liberal economic structural adjustment programs in the 1980s and 1990s, and now at the time of Zimbabwe's crisis. Spirits of Poverty accounted for the experience of never being able to accumulate: the new shirts burnt by the iron; the car that always breaks down; the money "vanishing" from a person's pockets with little trace of where it goes. In sum, misfortune is passed from generation to generation via demonic ancestral spirits.

This doctrine of deliverance from the Spirit of Poverty could be interpreted as the magical religion of a cargo-cult, yet it is efficacious. Rupture separates the believer from kin and associated demands of commensality enabling him or her to refocus energies on the nuclear family. The teaching also encourages rigorous self-examination with regard to habits and mentalities that undermine social mobility. However, the believer is supposed to demonstrate his or her new state of deliverance by generous giving, and this is where the some of the more outlandish claims of the prosperity gospel are made. Believers are told that they remain poor because they have not given enough.[47] Close analysis of Pastor Cathrine's manual, *Change Your Measure,* reveals that the highly public form of giving she advocates is often gift exchange within specific assemblies. Moreover, the supposed plush suburb that provides the Zimbabwean example in her book is located in the less salubrious margins of Harare.

Some of the outlandish claims about the prosperity gospel are matched by a paucity of teaching. University students and young professionals observe that the notion of post–born-again redemption from the ancestral curse in the blood line is not biblical. Others object to the poor grammar and argument in ZAOGA manuals, which often began life as rhetorically brilliant sermons by Ezekiel Guti, but which do not read well once printed in unedited form. Others complain about the rudimentary level of their pastors' training in the local Bible school. These sophisticated dissenters are the social category most likely to migrate to smaller middle-class charismatic bodies such as Faith Ministries or Glad Tidings. The leaders of these two churches, Ngwisa Mkandla and Richmond Chudidza, both well-educated graduates, represent the beginnings of a charismatic intellectual class. Their flocks include bankers, lawyers, and university lecturers, who have already achieved social success and now seek a less constricting atmosphere that engages with the demands of a middle-class existence.

Until recently African Pentecostals have had a rather ambivalent attitude toward education. ZAOGA's aspiring middle classes will do whatever possible to maximize their children's chances, including sending them to Catholic schools. A university degree from Cape Town, Britain, or the United States is highly valued. But when it comes to formal training of the pastorate, ZAOGA has elevated Bible knowledge over theology. In the 1990s there were few texts in the college's library save Guti's manuals and the works of a few external born-agains who met with the movement's approval. The emphasis was on indoctrination and policing ZAOGA's distinctive identity. ZAOGA also lagged behind other born-again trusts and ministries, which began to found Christian secondary schools from the late 1980s onward, though it did have informal evening schools based in its assemblies.

The initial reluctance to embrace formal education owes much to the Pentecostal missionary legacy, which, driven by a millennial fervour, placed great emphasis on proclamation. In 1916 Cecil Polhill, founder of the British Pentecostal Missionary Union, published his *Practical Points Concerning Missionary Work.* He instructed the prospective missionary: "To consider yourself an evangelist throughout your term of service. Let others educate, doctor, do philanthropy. . . . avoid the incubus to the evangelist of day schools, orphanages, and the 101 things which may be accumulated in station life. . . ."[48] It is not surprising that first- and second-generation Pentecostals used business as a social lever in the absence of educational opportunities. Nevertheless, one can detect a greater openness to education among the third generation. The trajectory is clearly illustrated in the Nigerian Pentecostal movement, the Christ Apostolic Church, which has origins in early 1920s and by the late 1990s had its seminary affiliated to the University of Ibadan.[49] More recently, in 2010, ZAOGA was granted leave by the Zimbabwean government to found a university in Bindura. In the first place its range of courses will be quite limited. It will offer degrees in areas related to Christian ministry and other vocational subjects such as media or business studies. As David Martin observes in his essay in this volume, this type of practical education appeals to sharp young Pentecostals with a desire to advance. Moreover, the urge to achieve technical modernization, or "upgrading" as Guti puts it, is almost a defining feature of African Pentecostalism.[50] It is difficult to see ZAOGA's Bindura University offering degrees in social science in the near future, and this lack of social scientific and theological sophistication in Pentecostal thinking shapes their engagement with politics.

Moving Close to the Flame of Power: Pentecostals and Politics

Many of the characterizations of Pentecostals' formal engagement with politics derive from the Latin American context, where they entered the political arena a decade or so before their African brethren.[51] In general, born-again Christians take their civic responsibilities seriously. They avoid conflict because it disrupts evangelism, and hence they tend to support incumbent authorities. But it is now difficult to predict who born-agains will vote for. In the post–Cold War era they no longer feel obliged to take anti-left positions and are biddable from the left and right. On the whole they tend to be socially conservative, although, as Bernice Martin reminds us in her chapter in this volume, they have a distinctive gender politics that advances female interests through the domestication of men and the pursuit of family stability.[52] They are most vocal concerning hot-button moral issues such as abortion and homosexuality, although in these matters their stance is often not at great variance from the mainstream of popular opinion. Political and church leaders who fall prey to sexual indiscretions or dabble in esoteric religions, as did Kenneth Kaunda, the former president of Zambia, quickly lose their support.[53] Pentecostals are intrigued by politics, but unlike Roman Catholics they have no coherent theology of the state and, at times, are quite confused. The closer they get to the flame of power the more internal divisions arise within their movements.

As Paul Gifford has shown, these characterisations also hold for much of Africa.[54] Gifford does make exception for Mensa Otabil, leader of the International Central Gospel Church. Otabil stands out as a Pentecostal for his insight into the structural, geopolitical causes of Africa's contemporary problems. Alongside his views on dependency and global inequality, he has more recently developed arguments about the threat to Ghana's modernization by prevailing cultural attitudes. These include a continued deference to the white man, a divisive tribalism, the elevation of culture and heritage over progress, a preference for magical and spiritual solutions over merit and hard work, and a tendency to elect leaders concerned with power and status rather than performance and responsibility. Against these "strongholds" of culture Otabil advocates the liberating power of education and personal responsibility.[55]

Otabil is immensely popular and influential in Ghana and beyond, and Gifford raises the possibility that he might reform the whole Pentecostal sector. At present there appears little chance of that. Guti has often shared a stage with Otabil and has cited some of his choicest ideas about dependency. But Guti's political thinking essentially lacks an ideological content that can be readily transformed into a political program. Guti's approach to politics finishes where it begins, with "spreading the gospel" for the salvation of individuals. Even his famous sermon to the nation of February 1988, "Lift up the Standard for the People" (cited in the movement's canonical history) finishes with an altar call. Ultimately it is "righteousness that exalts a nation," a righteousness that comes from "receiving Jesus Christ the son of the living God" by being "born again by the Spirit of God."[56] For Guti and many other Pentecostals, political engagement is the handmaid of evangelism. Citing 1 Timothy 2:1–2, he instructs church members to pray for leaders, because "good government allows the gospel to be preached freely."[57]

Although Guti's preaching lacks a theology of politics, he does engage in "politicking"—an activity highly conducive to the neopatrimonialism that so often characterizes the practice of African states. This political practice functions through personal ties between religious and political elites under the pretext of reforming the political process: "Our major thrust is to become a catalytic agent for unity among Christian leaders, statesmen, churches and Ministries who desire to share a common bond of commitment to the Kingdom of God."[58] It is a politics of influence that takes place at state banquets, presidential prayer breakfasts in international hotels, and high-profile Christian conventions.[59]

In essence, the state is not Pentecostalism's "critical referent."[60] Pentecostalism's fire is directed primarily at other elements within civil society, though not to the exclusion of the state's present regime. ZAOGA is critical of institutions fostering secular or liberal values, and of media agencies that encourage immorality and promiscuity. Pentecostals also criticize the historic mission churches for being "cold," "worldly," "unsaved," and "demon possessed." The historic mission churches are its major rivals, and it is mainly in this context that the state assumes importance. Members of ZAOGA's leadership are accomplished in what Paul Freston describes as "time serving," "the art of keeping oneself close to power, regardless of ideology or principle, in order to receive benefits."[61] The end is "ecclesiastical corporatism," the enlisting of state resources for church aggrandizement.[62] Favors with customs control, visas for foreign travel, planning permission for new buildings, and media contracts give them an important advantage over their competitors.

For a brief moment in the late 1990s, when the historic mission churches openly criticized the ruling party, ZAOGA did attempt to fill the legitimacy gap by working closely with ZANU/PF. But ZAOGA soon learned its lesson. As ZANU/PF's legitimacy grew ever more tenuous and it resorted to political violence to stave off the MDC, so ZAOGA's love affair with the government came to an end. Given that the bulk of its membership in the townships were terrorized by a coalition of war veterans, police, and the army, who saw them as potential MDC supporters, ZAOGA could not ignore their plight. Political violence and instability made the movement's primary goal of evangelism far more problematic, while inflation and the shortage of foreign currency hindered entrepreneurship. By 2010 politics was now a "no-go area" for ZAOGA, an arena in which one could be "led astray."[63] The movement now adopts a wait-and-see attitude to politics, restricting itself to joining broader ecumenical calls for national healing and reconciliation.[64]

To some extent ZAOGA's response to Zimbabwe's crisis has a generational explanation. In Uganda, the situation is rather different. Over the last decade, a Ugandan movement of young, urban, educated Pentecostals and charismatics has been campaigning for the moral renewal of the nation. Known as the Joseph Generation, its members present themselves as a revolutionary movement of youth working against a "corrupted" generation whom they blame for Uganda's social and political malaise, which is symbolized by the AIDs Pandemic. Their desire to associate themselves with the Hebrew figure Joseph is highly significant because, as they observe, he refuses the duplicitous courtship of his Egyptian master's wife: "He later becomes a leader in Egypt but the beginning of his journey is marked by the moral strength that allows him to resist sexual temptations." Thus Uganda's Joseph Generation embraces politics, seeking to "walk the careful line between contact and contamination."[65] Younger members of ZAOGA have expressed their disquiet about the connections their elders have made with the ruling party. But these young pastors and students are a long way from the seat of power and have little influence over the direction of their movement.[66]

But context is also crucial. ZAOGA's leadership is too shrewd to commit itself to one side or the other of the current political divide. Although Zimbabwe represents a failed state in that it cannot provide its citizens with social and economic security, it is not a weak state. It still retains a great capacity to coerce its citizens. Pentecostal leaders such as Guti have seen the ruthlessness with which the state has acted against the legitimate Bishop Gandiya and his wing of the Anglican Church, who have been barred from the cathedral and other prominent church buildings by the police and war veterans to the advantage of the ZANU/PF stalwart and apostate Anglican bishop, Nobert Kunonga. ZAOGA has seen the regime's cunning neutralization of the outspoken Catholic bishop Pius Ncube and has watched the decline of the Family of God Church, whose leader Andrew Wutuwanashe enjoyed too close a relationship with the Mugabe government. Guti is only too aware of his movement's vulnerability as an "indigenous church." The historic mission churches have formal external links to the Vatican, Lambeth Palace, and the World Council of Churches, providing a vital counterbalance to local state pressure and allowing the freedom to denounce dictatorial regimes and reconcile warring factions. Movements such as ZAOGA lack such "power to influence nations."[67]

But being an indigenous church does have advantages, especially in the current political climate. ZAOGA has allowed itself to be coopted into ZANU/PF's cultural agenda. In a recent article in *The Tablet* titled "Mugabe's act of Supremacy," Terence Ranger describes President Mugabe's attempts to rein in outspoken churches through the assertion of "indigenization." Ranger refers to a sermon delivered by Mugabe just before the March 2008 elections at the Apostolic Faith Church (which is Pentecostal) in Bulawayo, in which he called for every church in Zimbabwe to have Zimbabwean leadership. Foremost in Mugabe's mind was Anglicanism, where the excommunicated bishop, now self-styled Archbishop Kunonga—denounced to the United Nations by Archbishops Canterbury and York—presides over civic occasions such as his own inauguration as president in 2008.[68]

Ezekiel Guti embodies the kind of Zimbabwean "archbishop" the ruling party is looking for, and he has been heralded as such. Vice President Joyce Mujuru recently announced that she was pleased that the idea of a ZAOGA-founded university in Bindura came from an indigenous person.[69] Her fellow vice president, John Nkomo, went further in his praise. As a guest at ZAOGA's 50th Jubilee Celebrations in National Sports Stadium on 22 August 2010,

Nkomo told Guti: "We are proud of what you have done on this planet. We are proud that you have put Zimbabwe on the map . . . we are proud that you have been part of the harvest. . . . I am proud to say to you that the government of Zimbabwe stands by you. And the government of Zimbabwe will continue to create a conducive environment."[70]

Indigenization also shapes ZANU/PF's economic policy, in which it pursues affirmative action to deliver the economy from white and international interests into the hands of a prosperous indigenous middle class. Here ZAOGA also scores points. In the past Talents was "self-reliance," but now it is "indigenous business." ZAOGA's Businessmen's Fellowship has morphed into the Professional and Business Network backed by Kingdom Asset Management. The network's inaugural meeting on 16 November 2010 was attended by the minister for youth, indigenization, and empowerment, Savior Kasukuwere, who commented: "Apostle E. H. Guti, has ushered many to spiritual empowerment and now it is time to usher those same people to economic empowerment."[71] Nine days later at another meeting of the network Kasukuwere encouraged Christians to "emulate the Muslim world which has developed financial institutions to serve Muslims' particular needs."[72]

Although ZAOGA does have genuine ideological commitment to fostering entrepreneurship, there is a complication in taking up the mantle of "indigenous" with too much vigor. As Ranger observes, "every kind of [Zimbabwean] church is supranational," and it is through its transnational connections rather than local economic levers that ZAOGA has sustained itself through the decade of the crisis.[73] Nevertheless in the true spirit of time serving, the movement's leadership is happy to accept plaudits from the ruling party while inviting MDC dignitaries to other high profile meetings.[74]

African Pentecostal Modernity

David Martin observes in his chapter in this volume that while Pentecostalism's relation to democratization is inconclusive, it performs well by other criteria for modernity, such as individualization, free markets, and pluralism. As a practical matter, Pentecostals have come to live with "the technological gains and governing social arrangements of modernity—structural differentiation, procedural rationalism, and centralized management." However, although some observers assume that cultural modernism and social modernization come together in the same package, African Pentecostals have, like other conservative Christians, approached them selectively. They have generally preferred to borrow from modernity's tools, such as print and the electronic media or rational bureaucracies, rather than adopt its relativistic approach to truth.[75] Like other ardent believers within the global born-again movement and beyond, African Pentecostals sift Western modernity. ZAOGA has a strong critique of "backslidden" Western people for their liberal positions on gender, sexuality, and laxity in child rearing. ZAOGA's leadership views the West as a place where people simply have too many rights. Europe has become a mission field because its former churches are apostate; European Christians have "the Bible of God without the God of the Bible."[76] Significantly, ZAOGA's canonical history is a premodern narrative of the restoration of the Acts of the Apostles, when signs and wonders abounded and the authority of sacred texts went unquestioned.[77]

African Pentecostal modernity appears to be a coexistence of things that look modern and things that look premodern, but the mix makes sense on the ground. Leaders and members of ZAOGA, and movements like it, exhibit a self-conscious modernity. They have a strong discourse on building an efficient church bureaucracy and a perpetual focus on modernizing. These are prominent themes of ZAOGA's canonical history, which is itself continually updated.[78] Moreover, "personal choice" defines the Evangelical born-again experience. While the new Christian does join a social enclave in which there is strict control of his or her time, money, speech, and sexuality, as Bernice Martin observes, believers willingly embrace a conservative ascetic code, rigorously enforced by an authoritarian pastorate, because it offers the rewards of self-disciplined freedom and new sources of social capital.[79] The general direction of evolution of movements like ZAOGA has been that the strong sectarianism and authoritarianism that animated them has given way to greater freedoms as they have ushered believers toward modernity and greater social mobility.

In their desire to succeed in the modern world, Pentecostals have consistently fought against traditions, mentalities, and conglomerates, material and spiritual, that appeared to stand in their way. By the 1980s, movements such as ZAOGA were particularly well equipped to respond to modernity's latest neoliberal incarnation. With its capacity for individuation through enabling believers to rewrite their own personal narratives and break with the past, symbolized through violent exorcism, Pentecostalism has proved immensely significant. Although essentially a religious movement offering the path to salvation through healing and personal transformation, it creates a modern individual subject well suited to the demands of the post-industrial, post-Fordist economic culture. It engenders the flexibility, trust, and self-motivation required by the lightly supervised sectors of the service economy.[80] And Pentecostal virtue is both personally and socially beneficial, building up levels of trust that facilitate market-based economics.

However, individuation can be overemphasized.[81] Because the promises of modernity never fully materialize and neoliberal economics create
unprecedented levels of insecurity and volatility in Africa, Pentecostalism
rejects neoliberalism's cultural agenda of atomization that strips away old
networks of social support. Pentecostal assemblies create new solidarities
that mitigate neoliberalism's worst effects. The restored family is the first line
of defense against the ravages of poverty. Next, adherents find stability, security, and a new divinely ordained moral order within their assemblies.

Finally a much-overlooked manner in which Pentecostalism has come
to express the spirit of modernity is in what J. D. Y. Peel calls its "unmistak-
able unity in diversity" which is "realized through a dense, many stranded,
non-centered global network of exchanges, employing a distinct but ever
shifting stock of themes and motifs." This condition, which Peel compares to
the internet, "permits its participants both to feel their fellowship as part of a
movement across which there is much sharing and borrowing, and to draw
on this stock and to innovate as they respond to the demands being made
in their part of the network."[82] The capacity to be both global and local helps
explain Pentecostalism's success as a religious movement.

•   •   •

As with the claims of the prosperity preachers, there is a danger in
being misled by the hype surrounding the growth and influence of African
Pentecostalism. Referring to the "Irvingite" New Apostolic Church—Zambia's
third-largest denomination, which experienced an increase of 409 percent
in membership in fourteen years—Paul Gifford writes: "Sometimes the
impression is given that a 'Pentecostal explosion' is taking place in Africa.
This church proves that there is far more going on than that, for a church
less Pentecostal would be hard to imagine."[83] The reality is that most expressions of African Christianity are expanding. A visitor to Lubumbashi in
Democratic Republic of Congo would be struck by the newly constructed
buildings to house recently established born-again churches, or by the way
Pentecostals have bought up former cinemas and cafes for meeting places.
Yet they would also very quickly come to grasp that the Catholic Church,
Pentecostalism's most vital competitor, still dominates the city. It has its own
garage and gas station, it runs the best schools, and it has seminaries that
far exceed the state university in terms of resources and faculty. Catholic
dominance is symbolized by the cathedral in the center of town, which tow-
ers above all other buildings and on Sundays is filled to the brim in each of
its four consecutive services, attended by smartly clad elites in four-wheel-
drives.[84] A similar picture of Catholic influence emerges for Harare. While

both the ruling party and the MDC have feted Pentecostal churches, both parties are interested in multiple sources of legitimation and seek to address communities across the religious spectrum.[85]

Yet Pentecostalism is the most dynamic strand of African Christianity, and the majority of interchurch migration goes in the Pentecostal direction. In order to defend their flocks, the historic mission churches have adopted charismatic forms such as the gifts of the Spirit, gospel music, and Evangelical fellowships and ministries. Analysis of Pentecostalism's capacity to foster social mobility and create a democratic political culture depends on precisely which strand is selected. Karen Lauterbach's Ph.D. thesis, *The Craft of Pastorship in Ghana and Beyond,* is a salutary reminder that not all Pentecostal leaders make the big time. Rather than conduct another fashionable study of one of Africa's electronic megachurches, she has studied Ghanaian examples of the myriad lower-order Pentecostal churches found in the towns and cities. Ghanaian Pentecostalism *does* represent an avenue to advancement in a local political economy that has blocked so many other options, but some budding young pastors never manage to secure the material resources in the form of plastic chairs, banners, venues, and mobile phones; the support of kin; or the patronage of a Pentecostal big man to make their storefront church a going concern.[86]

But as Peter Berger observes, it is not essential that an entire population adopt a Protestant ethic for development to take place; a highly active minority or "vanguard" can be a vehicle for development. Small groups of prosperity-seeking Pentecostals such as those who compose ZAOGA's inner circle are enough to have the desired effect. Similar groups—the Huguenots in Prussia, Jews in Poland, Jains in India—have stimulated economic advance.[87] From an African perspective it would be worth researching from precisely where in the social hierarchy emerge the successful Pentecostals of the neoliberal era and what their preexisting connections of kin and tribe once were. ZAOGA's pioneering generation all came from families who held leadership positions, Christian or traditional, in rural society. Moreover, the Pentecostal scene is not exactly an open and free market. There is only so much space for successful movements, and once established, Pentecostal dynasties can block the advance of others as they secure the interests of kin and supporters.

The real significance of born-again religion lies in its provision of personal security rather than prosperity—a fact that has not escaped secular observers. In 2004, *New Left Review* published an article by Mike Davis titled "Planet of the Slums." This was a truly shocking piece about the growth of world poverty among an informal proletariat living on the margins of cities in the global south. The article had a startling conclusion. Davis contended that "for a moment at least, Marx has yielded the historical stage to Mohammed and the Holy Ghost. If God died in the cities of the industrial revolution, he has risen again in the post-industrial cities of the developing world." His point is that "the twenty-first century's surplus humanity" might find emancipation in Pentecostalism, which is becoming the "largest self-organized movement of urban poor on the planet."[88]

ZAOGA originated in the same area of Harare that gave birth to Zimbabwean nationalism, at more or less the same moment as the formation of nationalist parties, but there is little evidence of an evolution from religion to politics. Essentially Pentecostalism is a religious movement of cultural reformation that begins by remaking individuals and quickly progresses to the remaking of the family. While Pentecostal leaders and adherents have exhibited a quixotic response to formal politics, their commitment to maximizing the chances of social reproduction has been unwavering. Given the choice, they have consistently opted for making families rather than making revolutions. African Pentecostalism has evolved in relation to politics, shaped by shifts from anticolonial nationalism to one-partyism. And some movements have developed a critique of the dominant political culture, violence, authoritarianism, and clientalism, even if the leadership sometimes replicates some of these traits. However, given the *immorality* of the dominant political culture and the inability of the state to bring about political change that is both meaningful and lasting, Pentecostals have sought an alternative route to development through self-improvement.

The rhetoric has shifted from righteousness and respectability to deliverance from the spirit of poverty, but the focus on the well-being of the family has remained the same. As a female ZAOGA pastor at City 2 Assembly, Harare told her audience: "We are priests for our families, breaking the traditions of our forefathers, saving our families from calamities: daughters not marrying, sickness and poverty."[89]

NOTES

1. Peter Berger, "Born-again Modernity," *American Interest,* July–August 2009: 2 and 7.

2. Séverine Deneulin with Masooda Bano, *Religion in Development: Rewriting the Secular Script* (London: Zed Books, 2009), 43, 79–82. See also Roger Southall and S. Rule, eds., *Faith on the Move: Pentecostalism and Its Potential Contribution to Development* (Johannesburg: Centre for Development and Enterprise, 2008).

3. David Martin, "Another Kind of Cultural Revolution," in Southall and Rule, *Faith on the Move,* 12.

4. David Martin, *Forbidden Revolutions: Pentecostalism in Latin America and Catholicism in Eastern Europe* (London: SPCK, 1996), 11–16.

5. David Martin, *Tongues of Fire: The Explosion of Protestantism in Latin America* (Oxford: Blackwell, 1990), 287.

6. Paul Freston, *Evangelicals and Politics in Asia, Africa and Latin America* (Cambridge: Cambridge University Press, 2001).

7. Paul Gifford, *Ghana's New Christianity: Pentecostalism in a Globalising African Economy* (London: Hurst, 2004).

8. On the southern African movements, see "New Dimensions in the Study of Pentecostalism," special issue, *Journal of Religion in Africa* 35:1 (2005): 1–129.

9. David Maxwell, "Historicising Christian Independency: The Southern Africa Pentecostal Movement 1908–1950," *Journal of African History* 40 (1999): 243–264; and Birgit Meyer, "Christianity in Africa: From African Independent Churches to Pentecostal-Charismatic Churches," *Annual Review of Anthropology* 33 (2004): 447–474.

10. Diedre Crumbley, *Spirit, Structure and Flesh: Gendered Experiences in African Instituted Churches among the Yoruba of Nigeria* (Madison: University of Wisconsin Press, 2008).

11. Thomas Kirsh, *Spirits and Letters: Reading and Charisma in African Christianity* (New York: Berghan Books, 2008).

12. David Maxwell, *Christians and Chiefs in Zimbabwe: A Social History of the Hwesa People c.1870s–1990s* (Edinburgh: International African Library, 1999); David Maxwell, *African Gifts of the Spirit: Pentecostalism and the Rise of a Zimbabwean Transnational Religious Movement* (Oxford: James Currey, 2006); David Maxwell, "'The Soul of the Luba': W. F. P. Burton, Missionary Ethnography and Belgian Colonial Science," *History and Anthropology* 19:4 (2008): 321–351; "Photography and the Religious Encounter: Ambiguity and Aesthetics in Missionary Representations of the Luba of South East Belgian Congo," *Comparative Studies in Society and History* 53:1 (2011): 38–74.

13. Maxwell, *African Gifts.*

14. Amanda Hammar and Brian Raftopoulos, "Zimbabwe's Unfinished Business: Rethinking Land, State and Nation," in *Zimbabwe's Unfinished Business: Rethinking, Land, State and Nation in the Context of Crisis,* ed. Amanda Hammar, Brian Raftopoulos, and Stig Jensen (Harare: Weaver Press, 2004), 1–47.

15. James Campbell, *Songs of Zion: The African Methodist Episcopal Church in the United States and South Africa* (Oxford: Oxford University Press, 1995).

16. Adrian Hastings, *The Church in Africa 1450–1950* (Oxford: Clarendon Press, 1994), 502.

17. Philip Mayer, *Townsmen or Tribesmen: Conservatism and the Process of Urbanisation in a South African City* (Cape Town: Oxford University Press, 1961).

18. This section draws upon my *African Gifts.* The movement's evolution was reconstructed using a variety of data: executive minutes; a collection of publicity documents/canonical histories and life histories.

19. Birgit Meyer, "Religious Revelation, Secrecy and the Limits of Visual Representation," *Anthropological Theory* 64:4 (2006): 431–453.

20. These shifts in taste and expectation are powerfully illustrated in transcribed accounts of two separate question and answer sessions between a) Guti and

his pastors and b) Guti and pastors' children: Pastors Conference Discussions ca. 1992 and General Conference Questions ca. 1991, file, Sermons, ZAOGA Archives, Waterfalls, Harare (henceforth ZAW).

21. These were prominent themes of sermons in the 1990s. See *African Gifts,* chapter 8.

22. J. D. Y. Peel, "Post-Socialism, Post-Colonialism, Pentecostalism," in *Conversion after Socialism: Disruptions, Modernities and the Technologies of Faith,* ed., Mathijs Pelkmans (Oxford: Berghahn, 2009), 183–201.

23. Ruth Marshall, *Political Spiritualities: The Pentecostal Revolution in Nigeria* (Chicago: University of Chicago Press, 2009), 68–91.

24. Ezekiel Guti, *Believers Guide for Blessings* (Waterfalls: EGEA Publications, ND), 59.

25. Forward in Faith Ministries International, http://www.fifmi.org/Media/ NewsFIFMIZAOGA/tabid/8604/ctl/ArticleView/mid/15368/articleId/990/Default .aspx.

26. Martin, *Tongues,* 232.

27. Berger, "Born-again Modernity," 6.

28. Meyer, "Pentecostalism and Neo-Liberal Capitalism: Faith, Prosperity and Vision in African Pentecostal Charismatic Services," paper presented at WISER, University of Witwatersrand, South Africa, 14 April 2005, 5 and 7.

29. Cathrine Marurama, *Giving: Change your Measure* (Harare: EGEA Publications, 2010), 80–81.

30. Ezekiel Guti, *Prosperity That Comes through Obedience* (Waterfalls: EGEA Publications, ND), 13–14.

31. Naomi Haynes, "Pentecostalism and the Morality of Money: Prosperity, Inequality, and Religious Sociality on the Zambia Copperbelt," *Journal of the Royal Anthropological Institute* 18 (2012): 127–132.

32. Jennifer Dube, "The Man Behind ZAOGA," *The Standard,* 5 September 2010.

33. Pastor Charles Chipere, UK Overseer, AFM, personal communication. For the heated public debate on Makandiwa's movement see Rejoice Ngwenya, "Religious Entrepreneurship," *The Herald,* 29 March 2011; see also Jealousy Mawarire, "Ngwenya Needs Schooling, Spiritual Deliverance," *The Herald,* 1 April 2011.

34. Philip Chibisa, "A Response by an African Christian to the Nature, Role and Significance Attributed to the Ancestors in African Traditional Culture and Religion in Zimbabwe," M.Phil. thesis, University of Bangor (2009).

35. Ezekiel Guti, *The Sacred Book of ZAOGA Forward in Faith pt. 1 and pt. 2* (Waterfalls: ZAOGA, 1989 and 1995).

36. Anniversary Celebrations, City 1 Assembly, Baines Avenue, 9 May 1996 and University of Zimbabwe Humanities Theatre, 12 May 1996, fieldwork notes.

37. Paul Gifford, *The New Crusaders: Christianity and the New Right in Southern Africa* (London: Pluto, 1991); Paul Gifford, *African Christianity: Its Public Role* (London: Hurst, 1998).

38. Gifford, *African Christianity,* 348.

39. Martin, *Tongues,* 206.

40. Female ZAOGA member, interview by Samson Mudzudza, Gweru, 17 December 2010.

41. Ezekiel Guti, *What Makes Church to Grow* [*sic*] (Harare: EGEA Publications, 1995), 32; Ezekiel Guti, *Does Your Marriage Look Like This?* (Harare: EGEA

Publications, 1994), 67–76; Ezekiel Guti, *The Vision That Gives You Direction and Produces Faith* (Harare: EGEA Publications, 1995), 40–41.

42. Ezekiel Guti, Sermon to General Conference 1984, file, Sermons, ZAW.

43. Ezekiel Guti, "Third World Mentality," Mutare, 11 November 1989, file, Sermons, ZAW.

44. Bright Samundombe, *Youth Survival* (Harare: EGEA Publications, 2007), 9, 61, 62.

45. R. Mate, "'Wombs as God's Laboratories': Pentecostal Discourses of Femininity in Zimbabwe," *Africa* 72:4 (2002): 549–568.

46. Ben Jones, *Beyond the State in Rural Uganda* (Edinburgh: International African Library, 2008).

47. Jean Henderson, annotated notes, Pastors Conference, autumn 1996. Copies in possession of the author.

48. Cited in P. Kay, "Cecil Polhill, the Pentecostal Missionary Union, and the Fourfold Gospel with Healing and Speaking in Tongues: Signs of a New Movement in Missions," North Atlantic Missiology Project, Position Paper no. 20 (1996).

49. Crumbley, *Spirit, Structure and Flesh*, 39–41.

50. Maxwell, *African Gifts*, 1–3.

51. Paul Freston, "Popular Protestants in Brazilian Politics: A Novel Turn in Sect-State Relations," *Social Compass*. 41:4 (1994), pp. 537–70, and *Evangelicals and Politics*.

52. Bernice Martin, "The Pentecostal Gender Paradox," in *The Blackwell Companion to the Sociology of Religion*, ed. Richard K. Fenn (Oxford: Blackwell, 2001), 52–66.

53. Gifford, *African Christianity*.

54. Ibid.

55. Gifford, *Ghana's New Christianity*, pp. 113–39

56. Guti, *The Sacred Book*, pt1. 27.

57. Ezekiel Guti, *Guidance and Example of Praying Church* [*sic*] (Harare: EGEA Publications, 1995), 12–13.

58. "Introducing the Third World Leaders Association," n.d., file, International Third World Leaders Association 1993–1996, ZAW.

59. Martin, *Forbidden Revolutions*, 35.

60. Ruth Marshall, "'Power in the Name of Jesus': Social Transformation and Pentecostalism in Western Nigeria 'Revisited,'" in *Legitimacy and the State in 20th Century Africa*, ed. Terence Ranger and Olufemi Vaughan (Oxford: St Antony's Macmillan Series, 1993), 213–246, citation from 216.

61. Freston, "Popular Protestants," 563.

62. Freston, *Evangelicals and Politics*, 285.

63. Female ZAOGA member, interview by Samson Mudzudza, Gweru, 17 December 2010.

64. Churches of Zimbabwe, Press Statement, January 2011.

65. Alessandro Gusman, "HIV/AIDS, Pentecostal Churches, and the 'Joseph Generation' in Uganda," *Africa Today* 56:1 (2009): 67–86, citations from 75, 76.

66. Maxwell, *African Gifts*, 148.

67. Ezekiel Guti, *The Church and Political Responsibility* (Harare: EGEA Publications, 1994), 64.

68. Terence Ranger, "Mugabe's Act of Supremacy," *The Tablet*, 21 June 2008.

69. *The Herald* September 10, 2010.

70. Forward in Faith Ministries International, http://www.fifmi.org/Media/NewsFIFMIZAOGA/tabid/8604/ctl/ArticleView/mid/15368/articleId/990/Default.aspx.

71. Nigel Pfunde, *H-Metro,* 16 November 2010.

72. Zimbabwe Broadcasting Corporation, http://www.zbc.co.zw/news-categories/local-news/4505-benefit-from-indigenisation-churches-urged.html

73. Ranger, "Mugabe's Act of Supremacy."

74. Zimbabwe Broadcasting Corporation, http://www.zbc.co.zw/news-categories/local-news/577-church-commended-for-national-healing.html April 21, 2010.

75. Grant Wacker, "Searching for Eden with a Satellite Dish," in *The Primitive Church in the Modern World,* ed., R. T. Hughes (Urbana: University of Illinois Press, 1995), 139–166, citations from 142, 154–155.

76. Ezekiel Guti, Sermon, London, 13 August 1994, fieldwork notes.

77. Chris Bayly, *The Birth of the Modern World, 1780–1914* (Oxford: Blackwell, 1994), 11.

78. Guti, *The Sacred Book* 1989 and 1995.

79. B. Martin, "From Pre- to Post-Modernity in Latin America: The Case of Pentecostalism," in *Religion, Modernity and Post-Modernity,* ed. P. Heelas (Oxford: Blackwell, 1998), 102–146, citation from 137.

80. B. Martin, "From Pre- to Post-Modernity."

81. Harri Englund and James Leach, "Ethnography and Meta-Narratives of Modernity," *Current Anthropology* 41:2 (2000): 225–248, citation from 233–236.

82. Peel, "Post-Socialism," 193.

83. Gifford, *African Christianity,* pp. 184–186.

84. Fieldwork notes July 2006.

85. For instance, Mugabe and Tsvangirai and other cabinet members have also recently addressed large gatherings of white robe–wearing apostles, attending barefooted and robed out of respect. See article by Never Kadungure, 21 July 2010, Zimbabwe News and Internet Radio Station, http://nehandaradio.com/2010/07/21/mugabe-in-desperate-attempt-to-woo-apostolic-sect/.

86. Karen Lauterbach, "The Craft of Pastorship in Ghana and Beyond'" (Ph.D. thesis, Roskilde University, Denmark, 2008).

87. Peter Berger, "Max Weber Is Alive and Well and Living in Guatemala: The Protestant Ethic Today"; paper prepared for conference The Norms, Beliefs, and Institutions of 21st Century Capitalism: Celebrating Max Weber's *The Protestant Ethic and the Spirit of Capitalism,* Ithaca, NY, October 2004.

88. Mike Davis, "Planet of the Slums: Urban Involution and the Informal Proletariat," *New Left Review* 26 (2004): 5–34, citations from 30 and 32.

89. Fieldwork notes, David Livingstone Assembly, Harare, 5 May 1996.

FOUR

Tensions and Trends in Pentecostal Gender and Family Relations

BERNICE MARTIN

Interviewer: What's changed in your relationship since conversion?

C: Changes happened slowly because we didn't know how to live as a couple according to the plan of God. We used to live like partners in a business, nothing of that thing of wife and husband. . . .

I: What sort of teaching does the church give about this?

C: They support us a lot. Courses on the internal healing of the couple. A lot of things have changed between us, such as mutual respect, more awareness of the role each one has to have.

I: What do they teach about the role of the man and the woman?

C: What's in the Bible. That the man has to love his wife as Jesus loved the church, look after her as the weaker part. That the woman has to be submissive to her husband. That submission is not an inferior position but of helping the husband in the mission he has, being "under his mission." That there must be agreement between the couple, otherwise God cannot bless. That there must be prayer together, pardon, understanding of each other's defects. That children are an inheritance that God has given, and must be looked after with care. Knowing that in practice all this is very complicated, at least with us it is, because previously we used to quarrel so much, ugly quarrels and fights. God is restoring this but it's not by any means the ideal yet. I think it's been the hardest area for us to recover. To begin with we were totally against marriage. We only got married because [the pastor] said it was better because God would bless us more. That was four months after our conversion . . . but we did it out of obedience, not because we really believed it.

I: What about the upbringing of children?

C: It's changed a lot. Before, we used to think that [our son] had to learn everything for himself. We didn't teach him anything. We let him run loose, without limits. He even smoked marijuana with us. He asked and we gave him. Now there is more discipline, and Paulinho is the one who exercises more authority over him. But the one who looks after him more is me, as it always was: food, clothing, hygiene, schooling. But in the case of correction, beating him from time to time, Paulinho does it.

(Interview by Paul Freston with Claudia, a member for four years of Renascer um Cristo, in the Cambuci district of São Paulo, November 1991. She and her partner Paulinho had been drug-using, heavy-drinking members of a bohemian rock band and now played rock evangélico and what Paulinho described as "world music" in the church services and on the church's radio station, for which Claudia worked.)[1]

The upsurge of Pentecostalism since the mid-twentieth century has spawned a formidable body of research, but no systematic studies tracing the social, economic, and educational histories of successive generations. Nevertheless, a clear picture emerges of developments in the global movement since the mid-twentieth century and the tensions they manifest.[2]

Allan Anderson devised a widely accepted typology, based on theological and ecclesiological criteria, that also constitutes a rough chronology.[3] He distinguishes categories he titles the "Classical Pentecostalism" of the first decades of the twentieth century; the "Older Independent Spirit Churches" that mostly emerged in the 1920s and '30s, especially in China, India, and sub-Saharan Africa; "Older Church Charismatics," developing from the 1960s within the Catholic, Anglican, and mainstream Protestant churches; and "Neo-Pentecostal and Neo-Charismatic Churches," dating from the 1970s, associated with the spread of a prosperity gospel and the appearance of megachurches. The first two laid the foundation of the worldwide movement, but it is primarily the later stages of development we are concerned with, the growth where myriads of storefront churches grew alongside the longer established Pentecostal denominations, from the 1950s in Latin America; in Asia mainly from the 1970s (China largely from the 1990s); in Africa mainly from the 1980s, when the African Instituted churches faced competition from the neo-charismatic and neo-Pentecostal wave; and on a smaller but significant scale in Eastern Europe before, and at accelerated pace after, the fall of communism. In Western Europe the movement remains small except for an increasing presence among the Roma. In the United States it is a small sector of the Evangelical spectrum with both white and black membership. For most of its history Pentecostalism was the faith of the poor and only acquired a middle-class constituency from the 1970s and 1980s. It is not clear how far this middle-class growth involves mobility within Pentecostalism and how far it is made up of first generation converts. In Asia and parts of sub-Saharan Africa recent growth has included the young and the better educated, often university students, alongside continuing increases among the poor and marginalized. In Asia it has taken off among people with non-Christian backgrounds who associate Christianity with rationality and modernity, not least in the Chinese diaspora.

Before considering gender and family relations, two debates need clarification: the paradoxical nature of the Pentecostal movement; and Pentecostalism and "modernity."

Pentecostal Paradoxes

Birgit Meyer points to Pentecostalism's fluidity, its lack of a common set of fixed doctrines, creeds, or institutional forms beyond a small cluster of core elements, and believes this adaptability is the key to its global success.[4] Joel Robbins emphasizes the way Pentecostalism "encourages and feeds off" its constituent tensions rather than trying to reduce or reconcile them.[5]

Pentecostalism is a hybrid. It united the holiness strand of European Protestantism with African American revivalism in the case of Azusa Street, and elsewhere in the Christian mission field from India to Africa and China, with a wide variety of indigenous spiritual traditions.[6] It is generally accepted that there is an elective affinity between Pentecostal emphasis on *pneuma,* the gifts of the Spirit, and many indigenous practices of spirit possession and shamanism.[7] The world of the New Testament is readily experienced as continuous with the indigenous world of teeming spiritual forces. The morally ambiguous spirits of pre-Christian practices are absorbed into the Pentecostal system as the devil and his host of spiritual agents responsible for evils against which the Holy Spirit alone is powerful. The indigenous cosmos and spiritual sensibility are transmuted but kept alive within Christian belief and practice. This elective affinity is so marked that some early observers of the mid-twentieth-century growth of Pentecostalism saw it as indigenous "religion" under a thin Protestant veneer, indistinguishable from the old syncretism of New World Catholicism.[8] I turn first to the paradoxes this juxtaposition builds into the movement, creating a force field attractive to people already inhabiting an inspirited world, before taking up the issue of Pentecostal modernity.

The primary tension lies in the combination of biblical inerrancy and the gifts of the Spirit. The former asserts the primacy of God's Word in scripture, and the latter the primacy of kinetic ecstasy, prophetic inspiration, and supernatural healing through the Holy Spirit:[9] rational exposition and literacy against emotional expression not indebted to book-learning. This creates competing spiritual authorities: those, usually men and usually pastors, claiming special authority through the Word; and those, also pastors but often also women, young men or old, and illiterate believers, who manifest the gifts of the Spirit. This tension frequently involves a gender dimension, because women are acknowledged as especially receptive to the gifts of the Spirit, and the current focus of anthropology on bodily practices engaging the senses as a source of knowledge underlines both the crucial role of women and the tendency for male leaders to use their control of the biblical "words of power" (and the microphone) to reinforce (gendered) hierarchy.[10] It is tempting to see this as male "modernity" against female "tradition," but the reality is more ambiguous. The Bible is not just a source of (male dominated) exegesis but used performatively in Pentecostal rituals in conjunction with gifts of the spirit;[11] moreover, a division in which men cultivate a rational, instrumental self while women cultivate emotions and the senses mirrors the gendered distinction in the modern West between instrumental and expressive individualism, notably in post-Christian "new spiritualities."

A related tension arises between the asceticism and moral perfectionism of the holiness tradition and the ecstatic expressiveness of the gifts of the Spirit. The former results in a ban on idolatrous artistic representations, sometimes in sexually segregated seating, and often in strict dress codes; while the latter produces expressive excess involving glossolalia, popular and often very loud music, and uninhibited physical manifestations of spiritual ecstasy that constitute a colorful Pentecostal "aesthetic" and form an expressive counter-axis to the ascetic implications of the moral rules.[12] Thus, Pentecostalism both celebrates and moralizes the body. (The *rock evangélico* performed by Claudia and Paulinho in the services of the Renascer church was as sensual as their secular performances had been).[13] The perfectionism of the holiness strand also underpins the strict moral control of behavior and the focus on the world-to-come, while the emphasis on the gifts of the Spirit underlines the power of the Holy Spirit to heal not only the spiritual but the physical and material condition of believers; the self-denial and other-worldliness of the holiness tradition exists in tandem with world- and body-affirming practices consonant with indigenous traditions but also with the importance of this-worldly well-being in "modern" Western secular culture.

The emphasis on individual conversion and the openness of the Spirit to all believers carries an egalitarian logic that is partly contradicted by the claim of pastors to special authority. One consequence is the Pentecostal tendency to fission, and another is the ease with which the principle of hierarchy, including gendered differences of authority, reasserts itself when the surrounding culture is authoritarian and hierarchical. An emphasis on hard work in the service of God can breed mistrust of worldly success and riches; yet ascetic Pentecostalism, like the Protestantism of the early modern period, often demonstrates that self-denial can result in modest worldly prosperity, or at least better chances of survival, even in acute economic hardship. But as consumer affluence and material comfort spread (or are monopolized and flaunted by a small elite), the belief in God as all-powerful to bestow the literal riches of his kingdom can support the prosperity gospel that marks the latest wave of neo-Pentecostal development. Apocalyptic beliefs exist alongside the struggle to provide for the morrow. And what Peter Berger calls "robust supernaturalism" sits alongside enthusiastic deployment of modern science, modern business practice, and modern technology. Circumstances may shift any of these potentially unstable combinations toward one rather than the other axis, including in gender relations.

Pentecostalism and "Modernity"

Most observers initially saw the growth of mid-century Pentecostalism in Latin America through the dominant secularization paradigm and assumed it was a regressive, demodernizing movement.[14] It became clear by the 1990s that the movement was not only global but the most successful contemporary form of Christianity mobilizing the masses of the global south *for* the modern world, especially as part of the great trek to the megacities, and that it had parallels in Islam. By this time these paradigms of secularization and modernity themselves faced criticism from postcolonial and globalization perspectives.

I described Pentecostalism as a hybrid, a term used in globalization discourse to indicate the recombination of elements of central and peripheral, local and metropolitan cultures. Some versions of globalization theory are lightly reworded critiques of global capitalism, replacing Marxist terminology by a new vocabulary—globalism, localism, "glocalism," hybridity, and so on.[15] In this context hybridity can imply that the integrity of a local culture has been compromised by neoliberal capitalist and/or colonial globalization.[16] Anthropology has often colluded in this by defending the "integrity" or "authenticity" (non-hybridity) of the "premodern" communities that were its original subjects, and regarding the incursions of "modernity" both as deplorable and as disqualifying the groups concerned as proper subjects for anthropologists (as distinct from sociologists).[17] It is only in the last decade or so that most anthropologists have accepted the study of world religions among "premodern" peoples as legitimate subject matter for their discipline.[18] Postcolonial theory, globalization theory, and modernization theory have all shared anthropology's temptation to essentialism with regard to indigenous communities, now often termed "first nations" in an ideological move placing them under the ecological umbrella as a social "species" threatened with cultural extinction. The forces that "menace" them—colonialism, including its missionary adjuncts, capitalist globalization, or modernity—have often been reified, and sometimes demonized.

Yet postcolonial critiques and globalization theory have also unpicked those same essentializing assumptions in exposing the Eurocentric bias of theories of modernity and secularization. The peoples of the Majority World have agency; they should not be regarded as hapless victims, any more than Europe's development over the last five centuries should be taken as a universal blueprint. Hybridity, in this view, is the result of the selective, active appropriation by local cultures of what benefits them from among the cultural items brought by missionaries, colonial agents, or global commercial processes.[19] Studies of colonial encounters have become ever more subtle examinations of how each party changes the other.[20] Talal Asad's influential work shows how the very concepts of "religion," "the secular," and "modernity" emerge from the colonial encounter, reflecting but also inflecting the power imbalance between colonizers and colonized, expressed in the way "modernity's Other" is identified.[21] Modernity, like secularization, has to be treated as a contested, relational, and historically variable phenomenon.

Eisenstadt's concept of multiple modernities might have settled the matter, proposing a variety of ways to be modern, including religious ones, and showing how they interact with the modernity that originated in the West, changing it and changing with it.[22] Despite a degree of secularization in developed societies, globalization gives religion a new salience by transplanting religious and ethnic diasporas from one "civilizational complex" into others, making it necessary for international agencies and increasingly porous nation states to take account of them in national and geopolitical processes. Rather than religion fading away, religious competition goes global and intensifies contests both within and between religions.[23] A bracketed-out technical rationality can coexist with a variety of cosmological visions.[24] Charles Taylor came to a similar conclusion.[25]

For Eisenstadt the problem is the Jacobin or sectarian character of the new transnational fundamentalisms, among which he includes Pentecostalism.[26] His model allows for a modernity that accommodates the "robust supernaturalism" and "Christian patriarchy" of Pentecostalism, but twins Pentecostalism with the Iranian or Taliban version of Islam (rather than, say, early Methodism), and regards its modernity as radically different from that of Western Europe.[27]

Steve Bruce, champion of the secularization paradigm, rejects the notion of multiple modernities, arguing there must be some limit to the elasticity of the term "modernity" if is to have any coherent meaning.[28] Bruce accepts Western modernity as historically contingent, but sees the processes it set in train as irreversible. Beyond a high level of economic development, he specifies three core features of modernity: the emergence of autonomous social spheres; individualism; and pluralism. States that use coercion to exclude these developments cannot be considered modern. He defends the secularization paradigm with Peter Berger's (now repudiated) argument that the global juxtaposition of many supernatural belief systems weakens the plausibility of them all. Material well-being and globalized access to plural viewpoints stimulate the desire for individual autonomy, which erodes the ability of religious institutions and states to impose conformity. Thus, for Bruce, the core features of modernity are also the prerequisites of secularization. Religion survives only where it acts as cultural defense, as in the ethno-religious revivals of Eastern Europe, or where it is a transitional feature of modernization, providing the slipway but succumbing to secularization once the impact of pluralism and individualism is felt. For Bruce, Pentecostalism is merely a transitional phenomenon.

In reviews of the literature on global Pentecostalism, two leading anthropologists conclude that the modernity of the movement is ambiguous.[29] Joel Robbins believes the ethnographies of Pentecostalism in the non-Western world suggest it introduces a "rupture" with the past and displays features associated with what "in a rough-and-ready way" seem to be central to "modernity," notably "modern formations of individualism, gender, economy and politics." He is unsure whether the ambiguity and variability of these features allow firm judgments about how modern they really are, even though social scientific definitions of modernity are themselves "fuzzy, ever shifting and often only implicit."[30] Birgit Meyer stresses the symbiosis of "rupture" and "continuity." Rupture entails a break with the past but carries that past forward in the process of defining the future by reference to it. John Peel insists on the ambiguity of rupture and the importance of continuities but emphasizes the historical and contextual contingency of how the balance between them is struck.[31] Such ambiguities make the issue of Pentecostal modernity hard to resolve even though the claim to be modern is a prominent feature of Pentecostal discourse.

Ruth Marshall further muddies the water by rejecting dichotomous conceptualizations of tradition and modernity. She believes Asad and Meyer falsely reify these terms in lining up particular items on one side or the other—using Foucault's term, she characterizes this as "objectification." Objectifications are subject to contest and struggle "staged through the play of differences between relations of power and knowledge."[32] So-called traditional and modern forms should be recognized as "fully contempo-raneous and mutually constituted through the same historical events," as witchcraft and the born-again revival in Nigeria are. She rejects Eisenstadt's "multiple modernities" and Meyer's "domesticated modernity," because the born-again revival in Nigeria claims access not to a subaltern African modernity or African Christianity but to a "universal form" by reference to which it "critically engages with local cultural practices, moral codes, modes of sociability, rituals, forms of authority and techniques of power, subjecting them to a normative reevaluation, which renders possible and legitimates new practices."[33] John Peel sees this as a reaction against an earlier period of Africanization involving self-conscious reflection on Christian sources and traditions as well as responses to current social conditions.[34]

Pentecostalism's incomplete modernity may even be a judgment on modernity's undesirable aspects rather than evidence of Pentecostalism's transitional status. Birgit Meyer argues that Pentecostalism constructs a "space" in its "imaginary," most dramatically through its use of popular media, where believers weigh up the pitfalls as well as the benefits of modernity:[35] Pentecostalism's own discourse suggests as much.[36] Themes in the literature support this; for instance, research on new business and professional con-verts, especially in Asia, highlights the church's role as haven from the ruthless competition and atomistic individualism of the economic sphere. Much of the African ethnography suggests that the experience of neoliberal capitalism raises issues about good and evil routes to prosperity for Pentecostals, particu-larly if witchcraft is involved. The interview at the head of this chapter suggests another problem. Claudia and Paulinho were members of a Brazilian church attracting the business, media, and professional classes of São Paulo. They had been minor rock music celebrities, not over-disciplined bureaucrats or ruthless entrepreneurs trapped in Weber's iron cage. The church put bounds to their expressive hyper-individualism and put to Christian use a spiritualized version of their art. From Weber and Durkheim onward, individualism has been a problematic as well as crucial feature of the West's "modernity": the culture wars of the 1960s were fought over whether the "modern" individual was too untrammeled or too constrained.

"Modern" Gender Equality and Pentecostal "Patriarchy"

The feminist movement in the West and the rise of global Pentecostalism in the Majority World in the second half of the twentieth century occurred together, and their interaction is part of the movement's play of differences with Western modernity. There was a tension over gender in Pentecostalism from the beginning, and the importance of women in the inception of the movement is only now being restored to the record.[37]

In its initial effervescence Pentecostalism threw up many women pastors, preachers, and prophets and was spread by indigenous missionaries, most of them women.[38] In Allan Anderson's words, "Early Pentecostals declared that the same Spirit who anointed men also empowered women."[39] Women with charismatic gifts were welcomed and celebrated. Anderson believes the original predominance of women reflects their role as ritual practitioners among the indigenous peoples in the colonial mission field.[40] When the Assemblies of God, the earliest and largest Pentecostal church, was formed in 1914 in America, a third of its ministers and two-thirds of its missionaries were female, but its general council did not give women a vote, and even when it agreed to women's ordination in 1935, the limitations were so severe that even though women constituted the large majority of members and missionaries, few sought ordination.[41]

Early Pentecostalism swiftly adopted the gender and race divisions of the societies in which it existed. Racial segregation became formalized in the U.S. and South African movements, while caste strongly inflected the Indian movement.[42] A theology of gender and family emerged with clear general tendencies despite local variations. Women were largely squeezed out of the pastorate, and a dichotomous gender ideal was derived from a selection of New and Old Testament texts representing masculine leadership, strength, and superior rationality, and women's emotionality and weakness as requiring their subordination. The position is indicated by Claudia above. Sometimes the subordination of women to husbands and male pastors was justified by reference to Eve as the first sinner,[43] but more often it was a reflection of the Old Testament patriarchs (though without the polygamy and concubinage they so often practiced), plus the injunctions of St. Paul: the Gospels are more problematic and so less cited.[44] Thus, in spite of a fundamentally egalitarian doctrine of salvation, and though women were acknowledged as vessels of the Spirit, they were mostly forbidden to preach and teach except to women and children (who, of course, constitute the main body of the movement). Men were the guardians of the Word, the preachers, teachers, and leaders.

A dress code was widely introduced, designed to inhibit public expressions of sexuality while emphasizing the difference between men's and women's bodies, though rules varied according to local custom. In some churches seating was segregated to minimize the temptation to unchaste thoughts. A ban on alcohol and other stimulants was enforced, commercial entertainments such as cinema, theater, and dance halls, sometimes even football, were forbidden as sources of lasciviousness, drunkenness, and frivolity. A strict code of premarital chastity, sexual modesty, and marital faithfulness was imposed on both sexes, and homosexuality was denounced.

Allan Anderson believes the early experience of spiritual gender equality was snuffed out because Pentecostalism felt the need to conform to the prevailing norms of male domination, particularly because the movement was almost entirely confined to poor, low-status sectors for whom social respectability was simultaneously important and elusive: Chilean converts were doubly despised, first for their poverty and then for their Protestantism, and *dalit* converts in South India were similarly multiply marginalized.[45] Anderson sees the American fundamentalist/Evangelical example as influential in sustaining these gender rules while other mainstream churches gradually liberalized. When the movement entered its second phase of growth in the mid-twentieth century, its gender norms were widely perceived as regressive by "modern" standards.

Yet women still numerically dominated the movement in the second half of the twentieth century just as they had in its first decades, constituting over 60 percent of adherents in most places, sometimes considerably more, and they still supplied the lion's share of missionaries. If the movement was so explicitly patriarchal, why did it appeal so strongly to the women of the Majority World?

Charles Taylor shows how five hundred years of history in Western Christendom gave rise to the "modern identity" and the "modern moral system," the first characterized by individual autonomy and reflexivity, and the latter enshrined in the program of human rights. He stresses the historical specificity of these phenomena, and traces their hidden roots in Christianity, refracted through the Enlightenment, Romanticism, and various visions of Modernism.[46] He has, of course, been castigated for his Western-centric notion of modernity.[47] Nevertheless, the West clearly has institutionalized a modern moral program, the core of which, as Taylor claims, is the value of "human flourishing" and individual autonomy. Gender equality was added in the course of the 1980s in the wake of the renewed feminist movement of the 1970s.

The principle of gender equality was adopted by most legislative systems in the developed world and enshrined in the constitutions of the United Nations and its specialist agencies, the European Union, the European Court of Human Rights, international NGOs and aid agencies, and institutions such as the World Bank and the IMF. These institutions carry the principle to the Majority World, especially to the many places receiving Western development assistance or aid because of economic failure, crises of the state, natural disasters, humanitarian emergencies, civil wars, revolutions, and the AIDS epidemic.

Pentecostal diasporas from the Majority World living in the West encounter these principles daily in the culture and the laws of the host society.[48] Most mainstream churches now subscribe to programs of gender equality and the empowerment of women, even though the Catholic and Orthodox communions still restrict women's liturgical roles. Other, and possibly more powerful, sources of modern representations of gender are the Western mass media and their imitators. The women of the Majority World can hardly remain ignorant of the Western discourse of gender equality broadcast globally through megaphones of this kind.[49]

The Intersection of the Program of Gender Equality and Second Wave Pentecostalism

The rise of Pentecostalism in Latin America, mainly Chile and Brazil, from around the 1950s did not attract much attention from scholars outside Latin America until the 1980s, and it was then readily assimilated into the American culture wars as another example of regressive "fundamentalism" supposedly exported by the United States. Its gender beliefs and practices were pertinent to this perception, and the feminists of the period tended to condemn the development as another instance of women's oppression and the control by men of women's bodies. There are still traces of this assumption in the first volume of the *Fundamentalism Project* in 1991.[50] Research began to tell a different story. Studies at the end of the 1980s by Salvatore Cucchiari, on Sicilian Pentecostalism, and Roger Lancaster, on Pentecostals in Nicaragua under the Sandinistas, showed that Pentecostalism improved the lives of women, ameliorating the effects of male dominance in an "honor and shame" culture.[51] Cucchiari showed how the Pentecostal emphasis on equality of salvation replaced the gendered routes to salvation of folk Catholicism. Conversion cancelled the shame women, but not men, experienced over failed sexual relationships, and Cucchiari was perhaps the first to highlight the influence of modern ideas of romance and companionate marriage picked up from popular culture by women converts. Lancaster showed that Pentecostalism protected Nicaraguan women against customary abuse by men. He was one of the first to emphasize Pentecostalism's effectiveness in counteracting violence, particularly in the wake of the civil wars and revolutionary insurgencies that plagued the region.

In 1986, Elizabeth Brusco's doctoral thesis on Colombian Evangélicos was the first research to take the gender and family relationships of converts in Latin America as its primary focus. Brusco's research was not published as a book until 1995, though she summarized it in a feminist journal in 1986 and then in an influential volume on Latin American Pentecostalism in 1993, while David Martin drew attention to it in *Tongues of Fire* in 1990.[52] Her findings did not fit Western feminist perceptions of the family as the institution *par excellence* of women's oppression, and she hints in later essays that positioning her argument within the 1980s feminist paradigm caused some strain.[53] Brusco's *The Reformation of Machismo,* republished in 2010, became the classic text on Pentecostal gender and family.[54]

Brusco found that conversion improved the marital relationships of Colombian Evangelical converts and stabilized their families. Although moral restrictions fall heavily on women, those laid on their menfolk—giving up alcohol, tobacco, drugs, promiscuity, violence—compensate by drawing men out of the culture of *machismo* of the street and bar and returning them to the home. Money not wasted on male vices puts food on the table and sends the children to school. Men find a new dignity as head of the household and responsible providers, while marriage, though formally based on the superiority of the man and the submission of the woman, in practice becomes more companionate. This is often summarized as the domestication of the male. (Nancy Ammerman described a similar dynamic in American Evangelical families in her 1987 study).[55]

Brusco argues that conversion promotes individualism, though within limits because the nuclear family rather than the isolated individual constitutes the primary moral unit among Colombian Evangélicos. She also notes the networks of mutual aid the churches facilitate among women without male breadwinners or adequate state support. Not all of them could find new partners when around a third of Colombian women were lone mothers, a proportion common among the poor in Latin America at the time. The key element of her analysis is the transformation and pacification of domestic life, the arena most important to women.

Despite the empirical basis of Brusco's findings, the perception of the Pentecostal family could still be colored by the contest between "reactionary" defenders and "progressive" detractors of the ideal of the intact nuclear family in the West. In his study of Brazil in the mid-1990s, David Lehmann treated the accounts of Pentecostal women as a largely a fantasy of "petty bourgeois respectability."[56] Brusco recently remarked with some sharpness that the stabilization of the family is an achievement the West has found elusive and it ill becomes critics of Pentecostalism to discount it as less significant than women's public leadership.[57]

In a follow-up to his Nicaraguan study in 1992, Roger Lancaster contextualized Brusco's picture by examining machismo in the lives of the poor in Central America.[58] He describes an unstable system in which a man's honor is chronically challenged. Honor requires him to exercise total domination of his womenfolk for fear they shame him, but it also demands competitive drinking, fighting, whoring, and asserting aggressive masculinity in workplace, street, and bar. Any failure reduces him to the same low status as women and *cochónes* (*bichas* in Brazil), roughly translated as "queers" or "faggots," the contemptuous term for the submissive partner in a male-on-male sex act. The result is a way of life shot through with danger, anxiety, and insecurity for men and extensive abuse for women (and cochónes), including domestic violence, sexual exploitation, and abandonment by men who routinely form and fail to support secondary families.

This analysis explains why Pentecostal conversion holds any attraction for Latin American men. The moral requirements mean onerous curbs on their liberty, which perhaps accounts for men being a minority in the churches, and for their higher dropout rates.[59] But in exchange they gain the right to withdraw from the dangerous world of competitive machismo into the havens of home and church. They can exercise a dignified leadership as respected head of the family and organizer of any of a host of church activities. Elizabeth Brusco believes the churches offer a "self-confident *machismo*" instead of the customary "self-doubting *machismo*,"[60] enabling the Pentecostal to become a New Man, softer and more feminized, obliged to consult his wife and come to amicable agreement on matters that affect her, while still being regarded as more authoritative than women in some spheres.[61] David Smilde's research on Venezuelan male Pentecostals emphasizes the way Pentecostal men lay special claim to "reason," even in accounts of their conversions, reflecting a "patriarchy," constrained and pacified by the church but mirroring the gender culture of the wider society.[62] Among the Wenzhou "boss Christians," Nanlai Cao found an even stronger emphasis on male reason, consonant with traditional Chinese gender distinctions and associated with the economic rationality of capitalism.[63] This pattern is clearly widespread, and usually legitimated in Pentecostalism by the appeal to (selective) Biblical literalism. Some evidence suggests it is most emphasized in groups where the Evangelical element is more prominent than the charismatic;[64] certainly male boss Christians resemble Evangelicals, while charismatic practices are confined to women.

Research since the 1990s reinforces the findings for Latin America and the Caribbean and documents similar patterns in Africa and among the

Roma in Europe.[65] John Burdick even wondered whether Pentecostalism might have more impact than modern feminism in improving the lot of women in the popular classes.[66] Cecilia Mariz found the Brazilian Pentecostal churches more effective than other agencies in tackling the alcoholism that intensifies poverty and damages families. She also showed women creating roles for themselves in church and community, and publicly shaming men for breaking the moral rules.[67] Andrew Chesnut and Rowan Ireland paint similar pictures of Pentecostalism enabling women to improve their domestic circumstances.[68] Diane Austin-Broos analyzed the "moral order" of gender in Jamaican Pentecostalism. Having initially seen the ritual purification of women by male pastors as an example of blaming the victim in a culture with double standards of sexual morality, Austin-Broos' came to recognize the transformative power of such rituals for the whole community in symbolically cancelling the common shame of slavery.[69]

The Context of the Pentecostal Gender Bargain

It is not difficult to see why the Pentecostal bargain—complementary gender roles involving the formal "submission" of women to male authority in exchange for more stability in the nuclear family and a selectively "feminized" masculinity—was more relevant to the lives of the poor in Latin America than the Western discourse of strict gender equality. Fast economic development and urbanization increased women's dependence on a male breadwinner. Both sexes often had to move to the megacity or migrate to find work, and as the marriages of the poor were often informal, most Pentecostal churches operated a liberal regime allowing new, postconversion marriages in the church. The disorder and squalor in the slums of the megacities made the achievement of domestic order precious. Violence and insecurity at times of dictatorship and civil strife increased the number of families without a male protector and intensified the need for enclaves of safety.

The phenomenon of street children in the Latin American megacities caught the attention of the wider world, including United Nations agencies and international NGOs in the 1980s. Media commentary and academic responses tended to associate it with the debate about the decline of the Western family that was in contention in the American culture wars.[70] Evidence eventually showed that the numbers had been widely exaggerated and that the majority of the children living and working on the street were still attached to family, usually through mothers: the main problem was poverty, with absent fathers as a contributory cause.[71] The pattern among the street children of the African megacities today is probably similar,[72] and street children are a rich recruiting ground for contemporary neo-Pentecostal churches.

Complementary and unequal gender roles had long been established in Latin America, and even the risk of AIDS has been ineffective as a deterrent to male sexual license. In theory the moral rules of the Pentecostals were no different from the code of Catholic Church, although, as Cucchiari found in Sicily, Lancaster in Nicaragua, and Burdick in Brazil, the church connived at the unequal sanctions, especially for sexual sins. Pentecostal churches abolished that collusion with custom over sexual double standards and gave women the moral authority to protest.

In Latin America this gendering of moral rules had a long history. The initial European settlement after the conquest largely consisted of men without wives and families, and both conquest and slavery commonly meant the sexual expropriation of indigenous and black women by Iberian men. It is notorious that this led eventually to the enactment of legal fictions that, after a few generations, expunged the black or indigenous "pollution" in a wealthy family's genetic record.[73] A system of racial status differences evolved and, along with the Iberian culture of "honor and shame" out of which machismo developed, produced a custom for high-status men to form secondary liaisons and have children with women of lower status than their wives. This mark of prestige was copied by lower status men, so that it became common for them, too, to form secondary families, which they often could not or did not support. It also meant that the darker-skinned and more indigenous-appearing women had the worst chances of striking a good marital bargain. Matters were hardly better for lower-status men, who were subject to what postcolonial and feminist discourse calls "subordinated masculinities," deprived of legitimate sources of pride *as men,* apart from their sexual and reproductive prowess and their ability to survive the perpetual ordeals of machismo. Two Pentecostal theologians from Ecuador explicitly connect this history of exploitation with the Pentecostal project to reconstruct the Latin American family, restoring dignity to both partners in a marriage, and changing the image of the father, and with it the image of God the Father, from an arbitrary despot to a loving and considerate protector.[74] Women as well as men benefit from a Pentecostal model of gender and family that compensates men for the loss of face entailed in such a history and perpetuated by a culture of "insecure" machismo.

In Britain and America the feminist movement split over a cognate issue in the 1980s. Black feminists defended black men from "demonization" by white feminists for their sexist attitudes, blaming racist society for imposing subordinated masculinity on them. Another straw in the wind is Ann

Kubai's research among women in African diaspora churches in Sweden who choose not to challenge traditional African male superiority, even though Swedish law would support them, because so many African men are already humiliated by unemployment and loss of self-respect in a strange land.[75] Katharine Wiegele's study of El Shaddai is an arresting instance of Catholic charismatics among the poor of the Philippines inventing their own version of the Pentecostal gender bargain.[76] Filipino women often leave the family for years at a time to work abroad to finance the family, usually in domestic service and the lower reaches of the service sector in more affluent societies, leaving husbands to face the indignity, and temptations, of a role that offers them little traditional masculine prestige. It is women's duty to remain "womanly" and support the threatened masculinity of men in order to preserve the family. Frederick Klaits's study of a female-led African Initiated Church in Botswana also shows women refusing to blame men for the devastating effects of their long years of absence in the South African mines.[77]

Women in Leadership Roles?

A dimension of gender politics that emerged first in the Latin American research is the way Pentecostal women create roles for themselves in the church even though they have mostly been kept out of the pastorate, at least until the latest wave of middle-class Pentecostal growth. They become visitors, healers, and street preachers when the men are at work. They form women's organizations for prayer, healing, and mutual support. They teach children, read the Bible together, run or take part in the choirs and bands that are central to the church's worship. In this way they inflect the worship to express women's concerns and affect Pentecostal theology and images of God. Miller and Yamamori also show women in the forefront of the recent trend toward social outreach work, usually in hands-on roles and often among street children.[78] Elizabeth Brusco claims research has been too preoccupied with the scarcity of women in official leadership as an index of Pentecostal gender inequality. This fails to take account of these self-created roles, without which churches could not function; it undervalues the "domestic" work of women in the church, just as it undervalues the domestic sphere as a whole, reflecting a male-dominated value system in Western scholarly accounts.[79] Deirdre Crumbley makes similar observations about women's agency and effective leadership in two African Instituted churches, even though the gender practices they have to work around include menstruation taboos and a prohibition on ordination.[80] Mark Gornik also celebrates the prominent role of women as founders of congregations in AICs in Africa and America.[81]

Women and the Gifts of the Spirit

Women are major carriers of the charismatic elements of the movement, particularly through their powers of healing, prophecy, and "powerful prayer." The use of these gifts creates the aesthetic of the movement as well as the ritual healing of individuals and families. Martin Lindhardt argues that the spiritual and social potency of Pentecostalism, including its ability to foster new forms of subjectivity, comes directly from ritual activity centered on the body and the senses and carried over into the everyday practices of believers.[82] Catherine Wanner's account of the megachurch in Kiev, the Embassy of the Blessed Kingdom of God for all Nations, founded by the Nigerian evangelist, Sunday Adelaja, reveals that, although Adelaja is the head pastor and media star, two women senior pastors, both converted addicts, perform the day-to-day work of healing and outreach through the exercise of their spiritual gifts and are responsible for the church's astonishingly successful program for drug and alcohol addicts.[83] Mariz and Machado admire the boldness of Brazilian Pentecostal women who make their sufferings public in prayer and prophecy, not asking permission from men because their first obedience is to God.[84]

Regien Smit sounds a note of caution over the emancipatory potential in this. Among Brazilian Pentecostal congregations in the Netherlands and Brazil, women knew it was unsafe to bring certain things into the open.[85] Smit distinguishes "heroic suffering" women disclose in public testimonies from "secret suffering" never voiced in church, though she believes women often read its mute signs in others. The greater power and prestige of men are often at the root of these problems, though it is significant that the men would be shamed by public knowledge that they do not live up to the ideal of responsible and considerate behavior.

Women's spiritual gifts can shield them from the pervasive pollution of the conditions in which they live. Miriam Rabelo and her coauthors show how women from a slum in Salvador, Brazil, carry back into the degrading surroundings of their daily lives the protective blessing they receive when the Holy Spirit enters their bodies during worship.[86] Timothy and Rebecca Shah illustrate the same effect for a *dalit* Pentecostal woman suffering chronic misuse by her husband.[87]

Charismatic virtuosity among women Pentecostals echoes the role of women as healers and shamans, vessels of spirit possession and prophets in many traditional cultures. It is the primary source of women's spiritual power and a means through which they nudge toward the "modernization" of *de facto* gender roles. Yet it also represents a continuation of traditional spiritualities inside Pentecostalism and links women with emotion and the manipulation of premodern spiritual powers. Among the boss Christians of Wenzhou, male leaders privately solicit prayer and prophecy from older charismatic women but ruthlessly keep them out of the formal worship of the church.[88]

The Pentecostal Self:
Individuality and "Dividuality" in the AIDS Crisis

The Pentecostal self is less obviously "autonomous" than the modern self, which, in Charles Taylor's term, is "buffered" against the invasion of supernatural agencies.[89] Only the indwelling of the Holy Spirit secures a measure of (always threatened) autonomy. This has ambiguous implications for notions of personal responsibility in Pentecostalism. If an abusive, alcoholic, or drug-addicted man is liberated by the power of the Holy Spirit, he can blame his bad conduct on the powers of evil—sometimes summoned by the witchcraft or *macumba* of others—rather than on himself, even though he may constantly tell his fellow believers what a terrible sinner he was before his redemption. This is very different from modern ideas that see the past as never unequivocally discarded. On the other hand, emphasis on the rupture may make it easier for the Pentecostal to begin anew.

One problem with this argument is its assumption that we know what the modern self is. Arguably, the buffered self, the autonomous, reflexive self associated with modernity, is a fiction of Enlightenment discourse, just as the self in which the past is active in the subconscious is a Freudian construct, and the chimerical postmodern self, all masks and charades, is a fiction of postmodern theory. We should be wary of assumptions about selfhood and individualism that construct the "modern" individual in ways that do not even fit the modern Western reality. Humans are inescapably relational, not just Pentecostals who see themselves as one element in the family and the church to which they owe duties. We need to be more attuned to how Pentecostals understand their subjectivity and practice the moralization of the self, rather than assuming the nonmodernity of any deviation from a hypothetical autonomy.

Recent research on the Pentecostal response to the AIDS crisis, particularly in Africa, is pertinent here.[90] Rijk van Dijk and Richard Werbner argue that the African self is experienced as fundamentally relational, inextricably enmeshed in a field of influences and web of relations that include ancestors, living persons, and spiritual forces.[91] Something similar is found in all the "inspirited" cultures where Pentecostalism thrives. Van Dijk and Werbner believe the best conceptual tool for understanding this is the idea of "dividuality"—not a buffered self but a web of partly shared selfhood. The term was coined by McKim Marriott in an interpretation of Indian caste relations in 1976 and taken up in the late 1980s by Marilyn Strathern in her analysis of kin exchange in Papua New Guinea, but it has been deployed recently by anthropologists of African Christianity.[92] Werbner's "holy hustlers" of Gabarone experience the pain and suffering of others through a charismatic super-empathy on which their ability to diagnose and heal depends.[93]

In a moving account of a small AIC in Botswana at the height of the AIDS epidemic, Frederick Klaits makes a cognate argument.[94] Setswana experience the self as incorporating aspects of other bodies and spirits—for example, through the exchange of bodily fluids and emotional connection in sex or in childbirth. According to traditional beliefs, anything involving "dirty blood," which includes contact with women in early pregnancy or soon after giving birth, can cause illness. This indigenous discourse is disjunctive with the medical discourse of the campaign against AIDS. Multiple sexual partners, early and frequent childbirth, and long postponement of marriage are common survival strategies for men and women on the insecure margins of capitalist employment. Condoms are rejected as associated with the "promiscuity" of the one-night stand rather than relationships involving some mutual trust and benefit. Becoming "responsible" for one's own sexual health is seen as selfish. Klaits's study shows how the woman prophet of the Baitshepi church fostered a moral passion directed to holding families and the church community together. She refused to engage with the AIDS discourse and avoided attributing sexual blame, managing against the odds to maintain mutual obligations and familial duties toward the sick and bereaved. The moral responsibility that derived from the indigenous understanding of the dividual self precluded confronting the sexual behavior that spread the disease, but preserved a moral responsibility of mutual care that prevented communal breakdown.

These examples concern small African Instituted churches that incorporate more traditional spiritual practices and discourse than Pentecostalism proper. Moreover, although the AICs often revere the Christian ideal of monogamy, they are less than strict in their approach to sexual matters, and some accept traditional African polygamy. The assumptions of the dividual self remain strong in this branch of African Christianity.

Yet there are signs that the AIDS epidemic is changing discourse and behavior in some larger African neo-Pentecostal and charismatic churches in a more modern individualistic direction, and earlier attempts to shame the sexually blameworthy are being abandoned. Research in progress in Botswana, Zambia, and Zimbabwe suggests Pentecostal churches are actively collaborating with medical and state agencies, encouraging HIV testing and persuading people to take responsibility for their own and their partner's sexual health. Pentecostals are often involved in the counseling that accompanies the test and the distribution of antiretroviral therapies. A discourse has emerged in counseling sessions, which often take place on church premises, and even in sermons, stressing Christian monogamy and promoting the nuclear family as the unique locus of emotional, sexual, and moral satisfaction. Early marriage is strongly recommended, and techniques for sustaining sexual pleasure and variety with one lifelong partner are elaborated in startling biological and psychological detail.[95]

Spiritual Warfare

Richard Werbner's "holy hustlers" use their charismatic gifts to sniff out witchcraft causing AIDS and other misfortunes. This is "spiritual warfare." In Latin America spiritual warfare generally targets the evil in the obvious sinner, such as the unfaithful husband or the gang members terrorizing the *favela*. In other places, including Haiti and much of sub-Saharan Africa, the situation is more confused when occult practices become fused with Christian understandings. Evil forces may be located not in an obvious sinner but in the secret machinations of someone else—the jezebel who tempts him, or someone who has caused evil forces to harm him, his family, or his business. This would appear to limit the development of that individual moral responsibility we associate with Protestant individuation, particularly if it is embedded in a dividual construction of selfhood.

Ruth Marshall diagnoses a contradiction between two predominant practices characterizing the born-again revival in Nigeria.[96] The first is what she calls, following Foucault, "subjectivization," the ways in which the self works on the self to achieve the spiritual transformation. Marshall believes its effectiveness is undercut by the equal predominance of spiritual warfare, which represents the demonic as endemic in the surrounding world, encouraging a perpetual engagement with the demonic *in others*. The persons believed to be possessed by these forces are very often those closest to the believer, "in a continent where . . . intimate spaces are often the most dangerous."[97]

Marshall sees the predominance of spiritual warfare as a corollary of the mutual constitution of witchcraft and the born-again revival in Nigeria: most discourses on witchcraft are produced and distributed from born-again sources through popular videos and audiotapes. Asonzeh Ukah and Magnus Echtler describe "Born-Again witches" who switch their occult power to Christian uses.[98] Martin Lindhardt gives a similar analysis of the mutual constitution of charismatic Christianity and occult forces in urban Tanzania.[99]

Ruth Marshall believes spiritual warfare inhibits collective action to ameliorate "the ordeal of everyday life." The remarkable achievement of the woman prophet studied by Frederick Klaits was to prevent that breakdown of collective action, partly through refusing to countenance witchcraft accusations in the AIDS epidemic.[100] Ukah and Echtler remark that the recent appearance of "Born-Again witches-turned-pastors" in Nigeria may embody the power struggle between men and women, since most witches, including the born-again variety, are women.[101]

This kind of evidence suggests that there is no fixed relationship between "traditional" elements, such as occult practices, and Pentecostal practices, nor any predetermined effect on gender relations. The upsurge of witchcraft is recent, occurring alongside economic and political deterioration in Nigeria. In Latin America spiritual warfare has often played a role in the pacification of (predominantly male) violence and disorder, as with the conversions of violent gang members in some urban slums in Brazil. Christianity in rural China also involves spiritual warfare conducted by peasant women as a restorative measure. In common with much of China, the religious landscape of coastal area facing Taiwan studied by Chen-Yang Kao was razed by the Cultural Revolution. In the 1990s peasant women began to dig up buried Bibles from the disbanded Methodist mission, and reinvented a virtually all-female version of Christianity out of fractured memories of Methodism and the Dao/Confucian synthesis destroyed with the temples. Women had traditionally had dealings with the "small and dirty gods" concerned with women's matters, local problems, and "malevolences," while men were the religious bureaucrats dealing with the "clean, high gods" and in Christianity had become the pastors. The new "practice-led Pentecostalism" focuses on women's spiritual warfare to heal the human relationships broken in the Cultural Revolution.[102]

Many of these themes appear in Jane Soothill's *Gender, Social Change and Spiritual Power,* a study of three charismatic churches in Accra. Soothill's is one of very few pieces of research outside Latin America to focus on gender. She concentrates on the discourse of gender, drawn from the statements of congregational leaders and pastors, including some women pastors, so that her study does not replicate Brusco's account of what actually takes place in the home. Like Ruth Marshall, Soothill believes spiritual warfare inhibits collective action, particularly female solidarity, and that it undercuts the domestic stability it aims to protect, because the prime threat to a woman's nuclear family is normally seen as the occult machinations of another woman in or close to her family—malevolence in the intimate spaces.

Though women pastors are common in the African Born-again movement, they still reflect the unequal gender relations of the society. Their spiritual power is modeled on traditional forms and is subordinate to the power of men: They are "Big Women leading Small Girls," while male pastors are the equivalent of "Big Men." Most of the women pastors initially derive their charisma from the Big Men who are their husbands or fathers. Like male pastors they use it to dominate their followers, but temper autocracy with invocations of mothering and nurturing. They claim special charisma because female "emotionality" makes them especially receptive to divine blessing through the gifts of the Spirit.

Soothill discusses the Pentecostal discourse on the family in the context of wider debates in Ghana about the partial stalling of the expected "modernization" of the family. She underlines the Pentecostal appropriation of Western models of romance and companionate marriage. The dominant theme of public debate was that economic uncertainty and cultural change were undermining the stability of the marital bond and causing an increase in the numbers of women and children abandoned by men. Soothill shows the charismatic churches robustly addressing this with their own discourse associating autocratic male superiority over women with "African tradition" and contrasting it unfavorably with a Christian masculinity that promotes the loving and responsible husband and father. Soothill quotes hard-hitting sermons and pastoral opinions castigating promiscuous men, often through ridicule and broad humor. The charismatic discourse represents a strong marriage as the best defense against the devil, and every woman is encouraged to cultivate such a marriage, not by confronting a man with his delinquencies but by patient prayer. Pastors may be hard-hitting, but women are discouraged from the confrontation in public prayer that Mariz and Machado celebrate in their Brazilian study. Nevertheless, what Soothill describes has much in common with the Latin American gender bargain. Images of Western modernity are important in the struggle to define Christian modernity against a "traditional" past (and, as John Peel reminds us, an earlier Africanized Christianity) where gender inequalities were unambiguously endorsed. Similar findings come from other African case studies: Kristina Helgesson, for instance, analyzes the dualism of "hegemonic masculinity" and "emphasized femininity" in South African AOG churches, and describes recent efforts to curb the violence in South African ideals of masculinity through a new style of "servant leadership."[103]

Current Trends

Elizabeth Brusco thinks it unlikely that the gender dynamic of Pentecostalism is the same everywhere, even though conditions that fostered the Latin American pattern have been replicated in many other areas of Pentecostal growth.[104] Despite claims that "originally" women and men were equal[105] or that women once exercised matriarchal dominance in indigenous societies,[106] there is little evidence for anything but unequal/complementary gender roles and separation of spheres even before the colonial and missionary period. The Christian missions were more successful in imposing European norms of modesty and piety on women than on men, and they had difficulty introducing Christian monogamy into cultures where polygamy was common, at least for high-status men: Polygamy is still a problem even for the mainstream churches in parts of Africa. The sexual politics of conquest and slavery left a lasting mark. The pattern of multiple sexual liaisons as a mark of status for men, with or without a history of polygamy or the systematic humiliation of low-status men by powerful outsiders, is common over large parts of the non-Western world.

While most of Asia is experiencing the disruptions and new possibilities that accompany economic development and fast urbanization, as Latin America did in the 1970s, much of sub-Saharan Africa, with the exception of South Africa, remains economically precarious. This is particularly evident where corrupt elites dominate, despite agricultural, oil, and mineral wealth, burgeoning megacities, and a patchy but high growth rate. Nevertheless, alongside the older and still expanding constituency of the poor, African, like Asian, Pentecostalism has grown an educated middle-class constituency, and emerging business and professional strata make use of the global networks of Pentecostalism. Yet civil war, revolutionary incursions, failing states, recurrent famines, and humanitarian disasters remain commonplace in sub-Saharan Africa, while the AIDS epidemic devastated communities throughout the continent, most of all in southern Africa, until the mass availability of state- or charity-subsidized antiretroviral therapies began to control its impact in the early 2000s. These conditions have accompanied the fast growth of neo-Pentecostal and neo-Charismatic churches since the 1980s. As Ruth Marshall argues, these churches often initially saw their role as redeeming the failure of the postcolonial and postindependence political project, although as David Maxwell notes, they can find themselves in an ambivalent relation to the state, and try to make pragmatic accommodation with dictators like Mugabe in the face of persecution of their members.[107] In many parts of Africa churches provide a whole-life system for members in the absence of effective institutional provision of law and order, welfare support, or education. As John Peel argues, this is often a response to the failure of earlier revivals to redeem the state. Along with international NGOs, churches often stand in for an absent or inadequate state and civil society.

Ben Jones found the Pentecostal church in rural Uganda more effective than international development programs.[108]

The aftermath of war and civil war or state persecution in Liberia, Rwanda, Angola, Sudan, Uganda, Zimbabwe, or the Democratic Republic of the Congo presents women with problems as least as acute as those that faced Latin American women in the wake of dictatorship and civil war. Rape and kidnap as a tactic of warfare, the brutalization of soldiers, including kidnapped child soldiers and camp-followers, and the endemic violence inflicted on civilians leave a legacy of sexual violence. Ben Jones shows Pentecostal churches in rural Uganda having modest success in pacifying communities and converting returning fighters.[109] But the Pentecostal gender bargain may not be enough to heal such situations, particularly where men who have committed war crimes return, sometimes as pastors, to the community where the crimes occurred.[110] Regien Smit's study of a Pentecostal church in the Netherlands composed of Angolan asylum seekers suggests that normalization will be difficult. The need for secrecy about what cannot safely be brought into the open through prayer and testimony undermines the Pentecostal "break with the past" and leaves a legacy of contested memory, which the church handles by silence and a focus on becoming "winners" in the future.[111] The negotiation of gender roles in these circumstances is likely to be complex and full of conflict.[112]

While there is information about gender in the literature on Asian and African Pentecostalism, few studies have focused primarily on the issue. Nevertheless, there are indications that something like the Latin American gender bargain is occurring worldwide, among the new middle classes as much as the poor. Asian Pentecostalism tends to emphasize gender differences. The businesswomen in the Chinese diaspora in Malaysia and Singapore studied by Koning and Dahles were drawn to Evangelical Christianity by personal and family problems, where for the men it was business problems.[113] Nanlai Cao's study of the boss Christians of Wenzhou depicts a sharply gendered division of labor, with men as the active, rational sex, matching their entrepreneurial role in the new capitalism, and women as the emotional sex whose sphere is domestic and whose role is to support men. Even such traditional gender inequality shows hints of tension when the women's commitment to cultivating charismatic spiritual experience interferes with their domestic duties. Moreover, while the male boss Christians are prepared to be wily with scripture to justify morally dubious economic necessity, they distance themselves from traditional male sexual license even if, as yet, there is little sign of the softer New Man—although the advent of male missionaries from the Chinese diaspora may be about to change that.[114] On the other hand, as Kelly Chong's study of the vast and successful Yoido Full Gospel Church in South Korea shows, there are instances of Pentecostal practices that serve to resubjugate independent modern women within church and family.[115]

Pentecostalism in sub-Saharan Africa (with the partial exception of the AICs) and in Asia tends to cut or weaken ties with wider kin networks in favor of the nuclear family, as in Latin America. Obligations to kin and ancestors are deeply embedded in these societies and associated with dividual selfhood, so the weakening of these obligations constitutes an installment of individuation associated with mobility and the move to the city; and it is often actively promoted by pastors who represent the church as the "spiritual family" and the congregation, not the kin group, as the appropriate source of marriage partners for the young.[116] Active promotion of marital fidelity and the emotional and sexual enrichment of marriage is an increasingly common feature, particularly in middle-class urban megachurches.

There has been a considerable increase in the number of women pastors and preachers since the 1980s, most marked in the neo-Pentecostal, neo-Charismatic, and independent megachurches but also in older denominations. Many of these women pastors, especially in Asia and Africa, assist their husbands in man-and-wife teams. The dress codes associated with the classical Pentecostalism of the poor have not been transferred to the more recent churches, particularly those with a significant middle-class membership: the uniform of the classical Pentecostals marked them out as poor as well as pious. This change reflects partly a tendency to stress the spirit rather than the letter of the rules of modesty and chastity among better educated urban business and professional class Pentecostals, and partly their positive attitude to worldly success: The Wenzhou churches, for instance, use tall, glamorous, expensively dressed young women to greet the congregation at the church door.[117] Some older denominations have also relaxed these rules: traditional Pentecostal women in the Ukraine who began to wear their headscarves loose instead of tightly tied were influenced by the relaxed manners of coreligionists from the North America diaspora who visited the Ukraine after the fall of communism.[118] Regien Smit's study of Angolan and Brazilian diaspora congregations in Rotterdam also found that the rigorous patriarchy preaching there was undermined when ambitious Westernized young women evaded the rules about marital submission by not marrying their partners, and pastors were afraid of disciplining them in case they left the church.[119]

More startling is the emergence of a few "bicha" (third gender, or, in approximate Western parlance, "gay") Pentecostal congregations in Brazil who believe that homosexuals are created by God rather than possessed by the demon Pomba-Giras.[120] This hardly constitutes a general softening of the Pentecostal condemnation of homosexuality, which anyway reflects the surrounding culture in most of the Majority World, but even Roger Lancaster could not have predicted such a development in the heartland of machismo.

Sectors of the Pentecostal middle class and the growing Pentecostal intelligentsia are clearly moving in a liberalizing direction. The American Cheryl B. Johns, cited by Allan Anderson as critic of the movement's treatment of women and campaigner for women in leadership, is not alone in developing a more sophisticated Pentecostal theology of the family and gender.[121] Attempts to retrieve the buried history of the pioneer women of the movement are also part of this rethink.[122] The initiation of Pentecostal social action finds women prominent in the initiatives if not in the public leadership, and may also suggest the influence of Pentecostalism's liberation theology rival, probably via mainstream Protestant examples.[123] In the dialectic between Pentecostalism and Western modernity, recent decades have seen further appropriation of aspects of that modernity, including tentative nudges in the direction of softening gender divisions while supporting the integrity of the monogamous Pentecostal family.

Wherever it appears the Pentecostal movement places great spiritual value on the close nuclear family, with gendered role differences based on cooperation, peaceableness, mutuality, and responsible nurturing of children (although, as Claudia's interview illustrates, this does not preclude physical chastisement and a pattern of strict childrearing that might appall Western opinion but is consonant with the surrounding cultural norms).[124] This type of nuclear family is compatible with what is considered economic and social modernity. Yet we do not have evidence to show whether the (relative) stabilization of the Pentecostal family actually improves the chances of mobility for the next generation, though that seems likely on commonsense grounds (especially in economically successful societies like Brazil and China) and there are occasional nuggets of evidence for such a speculation.[125] Nor do we know how far the movement holds on to its second and third generations. It has clearly developed niches to suit every class, but we do not know whether there is a generational ladder linking them. We cannot say that gender divisions have been uniformly ameliorated: In some places they may be intensified. In the end we come back to the instability of those Pentecostal paradoxes and the need to contextualize every case.

NOTES

1. From research for David Martin, financed by the Pew Foundation through the Institute for the Study of Economic Culture of Boston University (interviewer, and translator from the Portuguese, Paul Freston).

2. The concept of developmental tensions is taken from David Maxwell, *African Gifts of the Spirit: The Rise of a Zimbabwean Religious Movement* (Oxford: James Currey, 2006).

3. Allan Anderson, *An Introduction to Pentecostalism: Global Charismatic Christianity* (Cambridge: Cambridge University Press, 2004).

4. Birgit Meyer, "Pentecostalism and Globalization," in *Studying Global Pentecostalism: Theories and Methods,* ed. Allan Anderson, et al. (Berkeley: University of California Press, 2010), 113–130.

5. Joel Robbins, "Anthropology of Religion," in Anderson et al., *Studying Global Pentecostalism,* 156–178; citation on 161.

6. Allan Anderson, *Spreading Fires: the Missionary Nature of Early Pentecostalism* (London: SCM, 2007); Michael Bergunder, *The South Indian Pentecostal Movement in the Twentieth Century* (Grand Rapids: Eerdmans, 2008); Randall J. Stephens, *The Fire Spreads: Holiness and Pentecostalism in the American South* (Cambridge: Harvard University Press, 2008).

7. David Westerlund, ed., *Global Pentecostalism: Encounters with Other Religious Traditions* (London: I. B. Tauris, 2009).

8. Jean-Pierre Bastian, *Protestantismo y Sociedad en Mexico* (Mexico City: Casa Unidad de Publicaciones, 1983).

9. The Friday Apostolics, who have abandoned the Bible entirely in favor of charismatic gifts, are described in Matthew Engelke, *A Problem of Presence: Beyond Scripture in an African Church* (Berkeley: University of California Press, 2007).

10. Miranda Klaver, *This Is My Desire: A Semiotic Perspective on Conversion in an Evangelical Seeker Church and a Pentecostal Church in the Netherlands* (Amsterdam: Pallas Press, 2011); Regien Smit, *More than Conquerors: Space, Time and Power in Two Lusophone Pentecostal Churches in Rotterdam* (Amsterdam: Pallas Press, 2012).

11. Paul Gifford, "The Ritual Use of the Bible in African Pentecostalism," in Martin Lindhardt, ed., *Practicing the Faith: The Ritual Life of Pentecostal-Charismatic Christians* (New York: Berghahn Books, 2012), 179–197; Simon Coleman "Voices: Presence and Prophecy in Charismatic Ritual," in Lindhardt, *Practicing the Faith,* 198–219.

12. Birgit Meyer, "Religious Sensations: Why Media, Aesthetics and Power Matter in the Study of Contemporary Religion," Inaugural Lecture, Vrij Universitiet Amsterdam, 2006, http://www.fsw.vu.nl/en/images/Text%20Inaugural%20Lecture%20prof%20Meyer_tcm31-42292.pdf; Bernice Martin, "Women and the Pentecostal Aesthetic," the Lucy F. Farrow International Lecture, Uppsala University, 2008, forthcoming in the *Journal of Contemporary Religion.* Martin Lindhardt and the contributors to his volume, including Joel Robbins, tend to subsume the aesthetic into ritual in their impressive argument about the efficacious nature of Pentecostal ritual; Lindhardt, *Practicing the Faith.*

13. On the ritual implications of loud music in the popular idiom, see also Martin Lindhardt, "Introduction," in Lindhardt, *Practicing the Faith,* 1–48.

14. Bernice Martin, "Latin American Pentecostalism: The Ideological Battleground," and "Interpretations of Latin American Pentecostalism: 1960s to the

Present," in *Pentecostal Power: Expressions, Impact and Faith,* ed. Calvin L. Smith (Leiden: Brill, 2011), 85–110 and 111–136.

15. Peter Beyer and Lori Beaman, eds., *Religion, Globalization and Culture* (Leiden: Brill, 2007).

16. George Ritzer, *The MacDonaldization of Society* (London: Sage, 2008).

17. John D. Y. Peel, "Not Really a View from Without: The Relations of Social Anthropology and Sociology," in *British Sociology Seen from Without and Within,* ed. Albert H. Halsey and W. Garrison Runciman (Oxford: Oxford University Press, 2009), 70–93.

18. Fenella Cannell, ed., *The Anthropology of Christianity* (Durham: Duke University Press, 2007); Joel Robbins, *Becoming Sinners: Christianity and Moral Torment in a Papua New Guinea Society* (Berkeley: University of California Press, 2004).

19. Susanna Rostas and André Droogers, eds., *The Popular Use of Popular Religion in Latin America* (Amsterdam: CEDLA, 1993), especially the introduction by Rostas and Droogers, 1–16.

20. John D. Y. Peel, *Religious Encounter and the Making of the Yoruba* (Bloomington: University of Indiana Press, 2000); Westerlund, *Global Pentecostalism.*

21. Talal Asad, *Genealogies of Religion: Discipline and Reasons of Power in Christianity and Islam* (Baltimore: Johns Hopkins University Press, 1992); Talal Asad, *Formations of the Secular: Christianity, Islam, Modernity* (Stanford, CA: Stanford University Press, 2003).

22. Shmuel N. Eisenstadt, "Multiple Modernities," *Daedalus* 129 (2000): 1–30.

23. Shmuel N. Eisenstadt, *Fundamentalism, Sectarianism and Revolutions: The Jacobin Dimension of Modernity* (Cambridge: Cambridge University Press, 1999).

24. Shmuel N. Eisenstadt, "New Religious Constellations in the Framework of Contemporary Globalization and Civilizational Transformation," in *World Religions and Multiculturalism: A Dialectical Relation,* ed. Eliezer Ben-Raphael and Yitzhak Sternberg (Leiden: Brill, 2010), 21–40. Toward the end of his life Eisenstadt was increasingly willing to reconsider his inclusion of Pentecostalism under the Jacobin category, as shown in discussions at the conference in Jerusalem that resulted in this volume dedicated to his memory, though in his essay he does not discuss particular movements, confining himself to general categories such as fundamentalism in updating the argument of his earlier book.

25. Charles Taylor, *A Secular Age* (Cambridge: Harvard University Press, 2007).

26. Eisenstadt, *Fundamentalism, Sectarianism and Revolutions.*

27. Bernice Martin, "Contrasting Modernities: 'Postsecular' Europe and Enspirited Latin America," in *Exploring the Postsecular: The Religious, the Political and the Urban,* ed. Justin Beaumont et al. (Leiden/Boston: Brill 2010), 63–90.

28. Steve Bruce, *Secularization: In Defence of an Unfashionable Theory* (Oxford: Oxford University Press, 2011).

29. Joel Robbins, "The Globalization of Charismatic and Pentecostal Christianity," *Annual Review of Anthropology* 33 (2004), 117–143; Birgit Meyer, "Christianity in Africa: From African-Independent to Pentecostal-Charismatic Churches," *Annual Review of Anthropology* 33 (2004): 447–474.

30. Robbins, "Anthropology of Religion," 172.

31. John D. Y. Peel, "Nigerian Religious Movements and the Anthropology of World Religions," the unpublished Bapsybanoo Marchioness of Winchester Lecture in the Religions of the World, Oxford, 19 May 2011.

32. Ruth Marshall, *Political Spiritualities: The Pentecostal Revolution in Nigeria* (Chicago: University of Chicago Press, 2009).

33. Marshall, *Political Spiritualities,* 26 and 6–7.

34. Peel, "Nigerian Religious Movements."

35. Birgit Meyer, *Translating the Devil: Religion and Modernity among the Ewe of Ghana* (Edinburgh: International African Library, 1999), 242.

36. Elizabeth Brusco, "Gender and Power," in Anderson et al., *Studying Global Pentecostalism,* 74–92.

37. Anderson, *Spreading Fires.*

38. Ibid.

39. Anderson, *An Introduction to Pentecostalism,* p. 273.

40. Anderson, *Spreading Fires;* Ogbu Kalu, *African Pentecostalism: An Introduction* (Oxford: Oxford University Press, 2008).

41. Anderson, *An Introduction to Pentecostalism,* 274.

42. Anderson, *Spreading Fires;* Stephens, *The Fire Spreads;* Kristina Helgesson "*Walking in the Spirit*": *The Complexity of Belonging to Two Pentecostal Churches in Durban, South Africa* (Uppsala: DICA, 2006); Bergunder, *The South Indian Pentecostal Movement.*

43. Jane Soothill cites Mensa Otabil, a prominent pastor in Ghana who used this story to criticize irresponsible men, reminding them that God held Adam responsible, and wondering where Adam was when the serpent came to tempt Eve; Jane E. Soothill, *Gender, Social Change and Spiritual Power: Charismatic Christianity in Ghana* (Leiden: Brill, 2007), 186–187.

44. Amos Yong, "Children of the Promise (Acts 2:39): Toward a Pentecostal Theology of the Family," plenary lecture, GloPent Conference on Pentecostalism and the Family, Uppsala, May 2011.

45. Anderson, *An Introduction to Pentecostalism,* 274–275; Edward L. Cleary and Juan Sepúlveda, "Chilean Pentecostalism: Coming of Age," in *Power, Politics and Pentecostalism in Latin America,* ed. Edward L. Cleary and Virginia Stewart-Gambino (Oxford: Oxford University Press, 1993), 97–121; Bergunder, *The South Indian Pentecostal Movement.*

46. Charles Taylor, *Sources of the Self: The Making of the Modern Identity* (Cambridge: Cambridge University Press, 1989).

47. See blogs on The Immanent Frame website of SSRC—eg., Tomoko Masuzawa, "A Secular Age: The Burden of the Great Divide," http://blogs.ssrc.org?tif/2008/01/30/the-burden-of-the-great-divide/.

48. Ann Kubai, "Being a 'Fulfilling Woman, Minister and Mother': Gender Relations in African Migrant Churches in Sweden," paper presented at the GloPent Conference on Pentecostalism and the Family, Uppsala, May 2011.

49. Kubai, "Being a 'Fulfilling Woman.'"

50. Pablo A. Deiros, "Protestant Fundamentalism in Latin America," in *Fundamentalisms Observed,* ed. Martin E. Marty and R. Scott Appleby (Chicago: University of Chicago Press, 1991), 142–196; Martin, "Interpretations of Latin American Pentecostalism."

51. Salvatore Cucchiari, "Adapted for Heaven: Conversion and Culture in Western Sicily," *American Ethnologist* 15 (1988): 417–441; Salvatore Cucchiari, "Between Shame and Sanctification: Patriarchy and its Transformation in Sicilian Pentecostalism," *American Ethnologist* 18 (1991): 687–707; Roger N. Lancaster, *Thanks to God and*

the Revolution: Popular Religion and Class Consciousness in the New Nicaragua (New York: Columbia University Press, 1988).

52. Elizabeth E. Brusco, "Colombian Evangelicalism as a Strategic Form of Women's Collective Action," *Gender Issues* 6:2 (1986): 3–13; Elizabeth E. Brusco, "The Reformation of Machismo: Asceticism and Masculinity among Colombian Evangelicals," in *Rethinking Protestantism in Latin America,* ed. Virginia Garrard-Burnett and David Stoll (Philadelphia: Temple University Press, 1993), 143–158.

53. Elizabeth E. Brusco, "Pentecostalism in Colombia as Fundamentalism and Feminism," in *Global Pentecostalism,* ed. David Westerlund (London: I. B. Tauris, 2009), 227–242; Brusco, "Gender and Power."

54. Elizabeth E. Brusco, *The Reformation of Machismo: Evangelical Conversion and Gender in Colombia* (Austin: University of Texas Press, 1995, repr. 2010).

55. Nancy Ammerman, *Bible Believers: Fundamentalists in the Modern World* (New Brunswick: Rutgers University Press, 1987).

56. David Lehmann, *Struggle for the Spirit: Religious Transformation and Popular Culture in Brazil and Latin America* (Cambridge: Polity Press, 1996). Lehmann focused on Pentecostal "discourse" and based his scepticism partly on the fact that so many Pentecostal women had no male partner.

57. Brusco, "Gender and Power," p. 80.

58. Roger N. Lancaster, *Life is Hard: Machismo, Danger and the Intimacy of Power in Nicaragua* (Berkeley: University of California Press, 1992).

59. Henri Goren, *Religious Disaffiliation and Conversion: Tracing Patterns of Change in Faith Practices* (New York: Palgrave/Macmillan, 2010).

60. Brusco, "Pentecostalism in Colombia as Fundamentalism and Feminism."

61. Michael Bergunder quotes a convert recalling how startled he had been when he first saw Pentecostal men "crying and weeping like a woman." Bergunder, *South Indian Pentecostalism,* 221; see also W. Bradford Wilcox, *Soft Patriarchs, New Men: How Christianity Shapes Fathers and Husbands* (Chicago: Chicago University Press, 2004), which analyzes modern evangelical gender practices in the United States through a study of the Promise Keepers. Wilcox does not deal with Pentecostals and the term New Man, though widely associated in the United States with Wilcox's analysis, is St. Paul's designation of Christians and has recurred in many progressive movements, including socialism and the counterculture of the 1960s and 1970s.

62. David A. Smilde, *Reason to Believe: Cultural Agency in Latin American Evangelicalism* (Berkeley: University of California Press, 2007).

63. Nanlai Cao, *Constructing China's Jerusalem: Christians, Power, and Place in Contemporary Wenzhou* (Stanford, CA: Stanford University Press, 2010).

64. Martin Riesebrod and Kelley H. Chong, "Fundamentalisms and Patriarchal Gender Politics," *Journal of Women's History* 10:4 (1999): 55–77.

65. Ruth Marshall, "'Power in the Name of Jesus': Social Transformation and Pentecostalism in Western Nigeria 'Revisited,'" in *Legitimacy and the State in Twentieth Century Africa,* ed. Terence Ranger and Olufemi Vaughan (Oxford: St Anthony's Series/Macmillan, 1993), 213–246; Maxwell, *African Gifts of the Spirit;* Paloma Gay y Blasco, "The Politics of Evangelism: Hierarchy, Masculinity and Religious Conversion among *Gitanos,*" *Romani Studies,* Series 5, 10:1 (2000): 1–22; David Thurfjell, "Pentecostalism and the Roma: Cultural Compatibility and Ethno-

Genesis," in *Global Pentecostalism: Encounters with Other Religious Traditions,* ed. David Westerlund (London: I. B. Tauris, 2000), 179–191.

66. John Burdick, *Looking for God in Brazil: The Progressive Catholic Church in Urban Brazil's Religious Arena* (Berkeley: University of California Press, 1993).

67. Cecilia Loreto Mariz, *Coping with Poverty: Pentecostals and Christian Base Communities in Brazil* (Philadelphia: Temple University Press, 1994).

68. R. Andrew Chesnut, *Born Again in Brazil: The Pentecostal Boom and the Pathogens of Poverty* (New Brunswick, NJ: Rutgers University Press, 1997); Rowan Ireland, *Kingdoms Come: Religion and Politics in Brazil* (Pittsburgh: University of Pittsburgh Press, 1991).

69. Diane J. Austin-Broos, *Jamaica Genesis: Religion and the Politics of Moral Orders* (Chicago: University of Chicago Press, 1997).

70. Rubén Katzman, "Why Are Men So Irresponsible?" *CEPAL Review* 26 (1992): 45–87.

71. Roslyn A. Mickelson, ed., *Children on the Streets of the Americas: Globalization, Homelessness and Education in the United States, Brazil and Cuba* (London: Routledge, 2000).

72. Richard Burgess, "Family Networks and Social Engagement," paper presented at the GloPent Conference on Pentecostalism and the Family, Uppsala, May 2011, and personal communication on work in progress on street children in Lagos.

73. Ann Twinam, *Public Lives, Private Secrets: Gender, Honor, Sexuality, and Illegitimacy in Colonial Spanish America* (Stanford, CA: Stanford University Press, 1999); Jorge Amado, *Tent of Miracles* (New York: Knopf, 1971).

74. Virginia Novilos and Eloy H. Novilos, "Pentecostalism's Theological Reconstruction of the Identity of the Latin American Family," in *Pentecostal Power,* ed. Calvin L. Smith (Leiden: Brill, 2011), 205–226.

75. Kubai, "Being a 'Fulfilling Woman.'"

76. Katharine L. Wiegele, *Investing in Miracles: El Shaddai and the Transformation of Popular Catholicism in the Philippines* (Honolulu: University of Hawai'i Press, 2005); Katharine L. Wiegele, this volume.

77. Frederick Klaits, *Death in a Church of Life: Moral Passion during Botswana's Time of AIDS* (Berkeley: University of California Press, 2009).

78. Donald E. Miller and Tetsunao Yamamori, *Global Pentecostalism: The New Face of Christian Social Engagement* (Berkeley: University of California Press, 2007).

79. Brusco, "Gender and Power."

80. Deirdre Helen Crumbley, *Spirit, Structure and Flesh: Gendered Experiences in African Instituted Churches among the Yoruba of Nigeria* (Madison: University of Wisconsin Press, 2008).

81. Mark R. Gornik, *World Made Global: Stories of African Christianity in New York City* (Grand Rapids, MI: Eerdmans, 2011).

82. Martin Lindhardt, *Power in Powerlessness: A Study of Pentecostal Life Worlds in Urban Chile* (Leiden: Brill, 2012); Lindhardt, *Practicing the Faith:* chapters by Joel Robbins, "The Obvious Aspects of Pentecostalism: Ritual and Pentecostal Globalization" (49–67), and Thomas Csordas, "Ritualization of Life" (129–151), make a strong case for regarding its ritual practices as the key to the potency of the charismatic movement.

83. Catherine Wanner, *Communities of the Converted: Ukrainians and Global Evangelism* (Ithaca: Cornell University Press, 2007).

84. Cecilia Loreto Mariz and Maria das Dores Campos Machado, "Pentecostalism and Women in Brazil," in *Power, Politics and Pentecostals in Latin America,* ed. Edward L. Cleary and Virginia Stewart-Gambino (Oxford: Oxford University Press, 1993), 41–54.

85. Regien Smit, "The Netherlands and Brazil: Twofold Mission, Threefold Suffering and a Distance-bridging Spirit," paper presented at the GloPent Conference on the Interdisciplinary Study of Global Pentecostalism, Amsterdam, 2007.

86. Miriam Rabelo et al., "Cultivating the Senses and Giving in to the Sacred: Notes on Body and Experience among Pentecostal Women in Brazil," *Journal of Contemporary Religion* 24:1 (2009): 1–18.

87. Rebecca Samuel Shah and Timothy Samuel Shah, this volume.

88. Cao, *Constructing China's Jerusalem.*

89. Taylor, *Sources of the Self;* Martin, "Contrasting Modernities."

90. See, eg., Ruth Prince with Phillipe Denis and Rijk van Dijk, "Engaging Christianities: Negotiating HIV/AIDS Health, and Social Relations in East and Southern Africa," *Africa Today,* special issue 56:1 (2009), especially editorial introduction, v–xviii.

91. Rijk van Dijk, "The Moral Life of the Gift in Ghanaian Pentecostal Churches in Diaspora: Questions of (In)dividuality and (In-)alienability in Transcultural Reciprocal Relations," in *Commodification: Things, Agency, Identities (The Social Life of things Revisited),* ed. W. M. J. van Binsbergen and P. L. Geschiere (Münster: Lit Verlag, 2005), 201–224; Richard Werbner, *Holy Hustlers, Schism and Prophecy: Apostolic Reformation in Botswana* (Berkeley: University of California Press, 2011).

92. McKim Marriott, "Interpreting Indian Society: A Monistic Alternative to Dumont's Dualism," *Journal of Asian Studies* 36:1 (1976): 189–195; Marilyn Strathern, *The Gender Gift* (Berkeley: University of California Press, 1988).

93. See also Jacqueline Ryle, "Laying our Sins and Sorrows on the Altar: Ritualizing Catholic Charismatic Reconciliation and Healing in Fiji," in Lindhardt, *Practicing the Faith,* 68–97.

94. Klaits, *Moral Passion.*

95. Rijk Van Dijk, personal communication on work in progress in Botswana, at the GloPent Conference on Pentecostalism and the Family, Uppsala, May 2011; Naar Mfundisi, personal communication on work in progress, and "From Stigmatization to Practical Intervention: Pentecostals in the Fight against HIV/AIDS in Zambia," paper presented at the GloPent Conference on Pentecostalism and the Family, Uppsala, May 2011; David Maxwell, personal communication on Zimbabwe and chapter in this volume.

96. Marshall, *Political Spiritualities.*

97. Ibid., 27.

98. Asonzeh F.-K. Ukah and Magnus Echtler, "Born-Again Witches and Videos in Nigeria," in Westerlund, *Global Pentecostalism,* 73–92.

99. Martin Lindhardt, "Ambivalence of Power: Charismatic Christianity and Occult Forces in Urban Tanzania," *Nordic Journal of Religion and Society* 22:1 (2009): 37–54.

100. Klaits, *Moral Passion.*

101. Ukah and Echtler, "Born-Again Witches."

102. Chen-Yang Kao, "The Cultural Revolution and the Post Missionary Trans-formation of Protestant China" (Ph.D. thesis, University of Lancaster, 2009).

103. Kristina Helgesson Kjellin, "The Servanthood of Men: The South African Congregation as an Arena for Challenging Masculinity Ideals," paper presented at the GloPent Conference on Pentecostalism and the Family, Uppsala, May 2011; Maria Frahm-Arp, "South African Pentecostalism" (Ph.D. thesis, University of Witwatersrand, 2008). The strength of expectations of male sexual license is illustrated in Anthony Simpson, *Boys to Men in the Shadow of AIDS: Masculinities and HIV Risk in Zambia* (New York: Palgrave/Macmillan, 2009).

104. Brusco, "Gender and Power."

105. Marcello Vargas, "A Pentecostal Experience of Aymara Culture" (draft Ph.D. thesis, University of Bangor/Oxford School of Mission, 2011). Vargas claims that Aymara gender roles were more equal before urbanization and capitalism affected them.

106. Jane Soothill found this claim in Ghana among charismatic women pastors but regards it as a myth; Soothill, *Gender, Social Change and Spiritual Power*.

107. David Maxwell, this volume.

108. Ben Jones, *Beyond the State in Rural Uganda* (Edinburgh: Edinburgh University Press, 2008).

109. Jones, *Beyond the State*.

110. Eric Strauss and Danielle Anastasion, director/producers, *The Redemption of General Butt Naked,* a documentary film about a Liberian war lord turned evangelical pastor; the film won the Sundance Film Festival Excellence in Cinematography award in 2011.

111. Smit, *More Than Conquerors.*

112. Personal communication from a Swedish woman Pentecostal missionary working with rape victims in Rwanda. A whole literature now exists on contested memory in post-Soviet society.

113. Juliette Koning and Heidi Dahles, "Spiritual Power: Ethnic Chinese Managers and the Rise of Charismatic Christianity in Southeast Asia," *Copenhagen Journal of Asian Studies* 27:1 (2009): 5–37.

114. Cao, *Building China's Jerusalem.*

115. "Healing and Redomestication: Reconstitution of the Feminine Self in South Korean Evangelical Cell Group Ritual Practices," in Lindhardt, *Practicing the Faith,* 98–128.

116. For example, Maxwell, *African Gifts.* The Greek Pentecostal Church, by con-trast, encourages, almost requires, marriage within the network of extended fam-ilies that make up the congregation in a country that discourages religious plural-ism among native Greeks: Evangelos Karagiannis, "More than a Metaphor: A Greek Pentecostal Church as a Family," paper presented at the GloPent Conference on Pentecostalism and the Family, Uppsala, May 2011.

117. Cao, *Building China's Jerusalem.*

118. Wanner, *Communities of the Converted.*

119. Smit, *More Than Conquerors.*

120. Leonardo Marcondes Alves, "*Pomba-Giras* and Created Queer by God: Neo-Pentecostal Perspectives on Homosexuality in Brazil," paper presented at the GloPent Conference on Pentecostalism and the Family, Uppsala, May 2011.

121. Anderson et al., eds., *Studying Global Pentecostalism,* part 3: "Theology," 223–308; Julie C. Ma and Wonsuk Ma, *Mission in the Spirit: Towards a Pentecostal/ Charismatic Missiology* (Oxford: Regnum, 2010), especially "Women in Mission," 194–208.

122. Anderson, *Introduction,* 273–276.

123. Miller and Yamamori, *Global Pentecostalism;* Ma and Ma, *Towards a Pentecostal Missiology;* Anderson, *Introduction* 243–270.

124. Claudia, interview. Interviews by Centro de Estudios Publicos in La Pintana, Chile (*Serie Antecedentes* 15, May 1994), include remarks by a schoolteacher that Pentecostals are unusually strict with their children.

125. Lindhardt, *Power in Powerlessness;* Martin Lindhardt found considerable evidence of third- and fourth-generation Pentecostals in his research in Valparaiso, Chile, and also reports the emergence of a generation of university-educated young people in a classical, ascetic Pentecostal church of the poor.

FIVE

Gender, Modernity, and Pentecostal Christianity in China

NANLAI CAO

China has experienced a strong revival of Christianity in the last few decades of economic reform. Recent estimates of the Chinese Christian population range from 23 million to 60 million.[1] Although the "Christianity fever" has swept across the country, there are clear regional variations in the pattern of church growth. These variations are further compounded by the differentiation between the official TSPM (Three-Self Patriotic Movement) churches and the so-called house church movement.[2] Generally, the many rural-based house churches feature a charismatic structure dominated by illiterate or semi-literate experientially inclined lay women, while the TSPM movement in urban areas has an institutionalized structure in which theologically trained male clergy assume leadership positions.[3] This experiential/theological or charismatic/bureaucratic split continues to be played out in the process of intensified urbanization and modernization. The Christian scene at the grassroots level is far more complex and varied.

Since the expulsion of foreign missionaries by the new Communist regime in the early 1950s, Christianity has been thoroughly indigenized through close contact with immediate local Chinese realities. The absence of an overarching central interpretative authority has contributed to the hybrid and fragmented nature of Chinese Christianity.[4] Pentecostalism appears to be the dominant form of Christian expression among organizationally independent church groups outside the officially controlled TSPM church system, mainly due to its ability to adapt to changing local circumstances and to address daily practical concerns.[5] This subject of this chapter is the Pentecostal/charismatic form of Christianity as it relates to the rise of a rationalized market modernity in the rapidly urbanizing and industrializing post-Mao period. Gendered charismatic authority and expression among prosperous Pentecostal-influenced communities in the coastal Wenzhou city serve as the focus of this discussion.

The Pentecostal sector of Christianity mainly appeals to socially marginalized groups in rural and newly urbanized areas. Faith healing, a technically illegal practice in the view of the authorities, has been cited as a major reason for the growth of the rural Chinese church by both researchers and converts.[6] Even though religious persecution is often harshest in the impoverished inland, the rural inland provinces such as Henan and Anhui have the fastest growth rates of Pentecostal-like house churches. The spectacular growth has to a large extent depended on a multitude of traveling revival preachers and fluid, horizontal Pentecostal church networks that the state cannot effectively control and monitor. Pentecostal leaders of the rural house church often draw on their experiences of suffering under oppression and hardship and embrace an identity of martyrdom. These church communities take a spiritual approach to social and political issues and are exclusivist in orientation. Low level of education, minimally trained clergy, lack of medical provision, and rural poverty all appear to have contributed to the Pentecostal tendency in the countryside.

This rural, anti-institutional, charismatic sentiment is not shared by the newly emerged house churches in major Chinese cities such as Beijing, where there are a great portion of university-educated intellectuals, academics, and other members of the urban middle class involved in church activities. These often Western-oriented or, more specifically, Anglo-American-oriented house churches focus on the study of Christian doctrines and actively engage in public discourse on human rights, with a focus on the religious rights of house Christians.[7] Led by some prominent liberal intellectuals and rights lawyers, with the ultimate vision of a Christian China, high-profile Beijing house churches represent the most organized and politically active sector of the Chinese house church community. It is not an exaggeration to say that a much politicized intellectual house church movement has taken shape in the capital city, under close monitoring and scrutiny by the central party-state.

The prosperous coastal city of Wenzhou in southeast China has produced another distinctive regional model of church development in the reform era in which the new rich businessmen, locally called "boss Christians," spearhead local church development.[8] Wenzhou's recent Christian revival has benefited from the city's political marginality and a mission-derived local faith tradition as well as a vibrant private household-based economy. It is now the most Christianized Chinese city, with a Christian population estimated to be as many as one million (15 percent of the local population). This upwardly mobile class of Christians, usually with rural origins, has a separate identity from either the official TSPM church, on the one hand, or inland rural house church groups or urban intellectual house churches on the other. Many Wenzhou churches are headed by boss Christians and are recognized by, but not officially registered with, the local state. This type of independent church is among the fastest growing of all newly founded Christian churches in the area, owing in large part to its flexibility. As this entrepreneurial city is in the midst of rapid rural industrialization and urbanization, most local churches have a recognizable rural Pentecostal origin, as shown in the emotional style of worship and the staging of spirit-filled revival meetings focused on faith healing.

Although urban-oriented modern Chinese Christians increasingly emphasize the systematic study of theology and a hierarchical, professionalized structure of church management, the established rural-based Pentecostal tradition continues to inform Chinese Christian development at the turn of the new century. This trend has been strengthened from the 1980s on by clandestine overseas Pentecostal missionaries in China, as well as by the introduction of Pentecostal teachings from Chinese-speaking East and Southeast Asia.[9] As China's pace of urbanization accelerates, some rural Pentecostal networks have also migrated to cities or been absorbed into newly urbanized areas. The Pentecostal energy has taken on new expressions in the evolving urban Chinese Christian community. For the most part, Pentecostalism as an imported concept has not become a conscious identity for the Chinese Christian community. Given the difficulty of defining a Chinese Pentecostal group, I follow David Martin in treating Pentecostalism not as a monolithic religious system but "a repertoire of recognizable spiritual affinities which constantly breaks out in new forms."[10]

Rapid urbanization of the countryside has blurred the line between the rural and the urban, the premodern and the modern, and has resulted in a new synthesis of the charismatic, experiential and the rational, theological forms of Christianity. This might best be seen in the boom city of Wenzhou, where a new wave of theology-minded entrepreneur church leaders and preachers interact with emotion-filled charismatic Christian women both within and outside the church. It will soon become clear that although a textually based, theology-driven Evangelical Christianity has developed in dynamic interaction with an emergent capitalist regional economy in China's advanced coastal regions, this elite mode of Christianity constantly manifests a Pentecostal sentiment, contributing to the growth of a neo-Pentecostal sector of post-Mao Chinese Christianity. In this chapter, I first discuss the social historical background of the Pentecostal growth in China. I then use the Wenzhou case to explore the multiple and conflicting dynamics of Chinese Pentecostal development in the context of a rationalized modernity.

While the recent Christian revival has evidently benefited from the relaxation of state control over religion as well as economic and social reforms in the post-Mao era, the exponential growth of Christianity most likely started

much earlier than is commonly believed. This is particularly true if we take
into account the fast-growing Pentecostal subcurrent. A closer examination
reveals historical links between post-Mao Christian revival and the development of an independent, Pentecostal sector of Chinese Christianity a century
ago.[11] The Pentecostal sector strengthened and expanded the appeal of the
imported Christian faith in the first half of the twentieth century, despite the
harsh conditions for the Chinese church brought by the Sino-Japanese war
(1937–1945) and the subsequent civil war (1946–1949). It might be argued
that early indigenous Pentecostal preachers and networks formed the prototype of Chinese Christianity that continues to inspire later generations of
Chinese believers.

The Historical and Social Context: Indigenization and the Pentecostal Undercurrent

In rural provinces such as Henan, Anhui, Shandong, and Hunan,
Pentecostal worship has been practiced in local congregations and homes
since the early twentieth century under the influence of some nationally
known Chinese evangelists (notable among them were Wang Mingdao, John
Song, and Watchman Nee).[12] Echoing anti-Western, anti-imperialist emotions prevalent at the time, these native evangelists were known for their
antagonism toward foreign mission churches and their strong determination
to build an independent Chinese church.[13] Paradoxically, they were often
brought up in the missionary context and had close contact with Western
Pentecostal missionaries who came to China in the wake of the Azusa Street
revival of 1906.

In an attempt to explain China's Pentecostal growth in the first half of
the twentieth century, church historians have observed the natural affinity
between Chinese sectarian religion and the Pentecostal emphasis on healing,
divine revelations, and millenarianism. For example, Daniel Bays has pointed
out some parallel themes between the True Jesus Church, a major indigenous Chinese Pentecostal group, and the sectarian White Lotus tradition.
He notes that when Pentecostal Christianity was first brought into China
by Western missionaries in the early twentieth century, "the new elements
of the Christian Pentecostal message may have been more effective bridges
to certain parts of traditional Chinese society than had been the nineteen-
century Christian message."[14] Gotthard Oblau went further to suggest that
contemporary Chinese Christianity bears inherent Pentecostal characteristics and can thus be viewed as "Pentecostal by default" (as he put it in the
title of his essay).[15] It seems that Pentecostalism furnished a flexible reli-

gious milieu in which indigenous Chinese preachers were able to creatively adapt Western-imported Christianity to the folk Chinese mode of religiosity. This Pentecostal paradigm provides a vantage point for understanding the dynamics of Christian growth in China today.

Reminiscent of "superstitious" elements that characterize Chinese folk religion, Pentecostal/charismatic Christian practices such as spiritual healing and performing miracles are subjected to negative labeling by both the state and the state-controlled churches in the reform era. Various antisuperstition campaigns and the recent crackdown against heretical sects (especially Falungong) have contributed to a serious stigma associated with charismatic phenomena in society.[16] State-approved clergy publicly disapprove of the miraculous mode of the religion, especially the Pentecostal style of healing meetings that continue to draw huge crowds in southeast China today.[17] For the TSPM and the larger Christian community, a by-product of such a dynamic and diverse Pentecostal revival is the emergence of various Christian-inspired heretical sects or new religious movements that often manifest a strong folk religious tendency.

As it often draws on popular cultural resources in local communities, Pentecostal-influenced Chinese Christianity has contributed to the spreading of indigenous church networks and become almost the ideal type of grassroots Christianity in rural China.[18] Even in the Mao-era harsh repression of religious activities was unable to eradicate this noninstitutional form of Christianity. In fact, political repression restructured Christianity from a nontraditional religion into a female-dominated Pentecostal-style religion thriving within the rural cultural framework of popular supernaturalism.[19] It is important to note that this indigenization has much to do with the charismatic power of many rural Christian women who actively engaged in the practices of healing and exorcism during and soon after the Maoist decades. This female-centered, individualized experiential religiosity was far more dynamic than the earlier mission-founded Christianity and greatly facilitated Christian breakthroughs during the Cultural Revolution. By the 1980s, Chinese Christianity had become largely a rural indigenous Pentecostal phenomenon and an overwhelmingly female institution. Given the serious shortage of trained clergy and the lack of institutionalized structures, the Pentecostal impulse in rural Christian communities can hardly be contained or tamed within the boundaries defined by officially approved TSPM churches.

Despite the popular image of Chinese Christianity as a disadvantaged female institution in the rural inland, more and more Chinese urban elites are turning to Christianity in recent decades because they identify it with the world's greatest modern industrial successes. While both intellectual house churchgoers in Beijing and Christian business elites in coastal areas consciously position Christianity as a civilizing and moralizing force in Chinese society, rural Christian women with their charismatic practices are often placed in a position antithetical to an Evangelical, textually oriented Christianity—the only correct faith in the eyes of many urban Christian elites. Rural, female-dominated Pentecostal/charismatic Christianity is deemed inferior for its tendency to develop highly syncretistic and communally embedded folk practices and for its lack of transnational religious connections, real or imagined. When charismatic-oriented rural women move into the city, they find themselves being placed on a continuum from backwardness to modernity and relegated to a stigmatized status in the symbolic universe of Chinese Christianity. This is in part due to the Chinese state discourse on modernity and science, in which folk Chinese religion is labeled "feudal superstition." Although their contribution to the church is publicly acknowledged, their Pentecostal energy is often scrutinized and controlled by the values of the new entrepreneurial and professional class of believers.

I will devote the remainder of the chapter to an ethnographic portrait of the gendered Pentecostal/charismatic development in the new entrepreneurial city of Wenzhou, to showcase what is unique about Pentecostal Christianity in China's post-Mao modernization and why it is so. In the last quarter-century Wenzhou has become the largest urban Chinese Christian center, known as China's Jerusalem. The reform-era revival of Wenzhou Christianity is led by a new entrepreneurial class of male believers and has accompanied the city's dynamic industrialization and modernization process. Although it is today a new regional center of the global market economy, producing and exporting small merchandise such as shoes, cloth, and cigarette lighters, two decades ago Wenzhou was an impoverished rural town that sent a great number of migrant workers and peddlers to the rural inland. Wenzhou churches used to be mostly charismatically oriented, as is the case in rural Henan and Anhui today.[20] There is still a strong charismatic tendency among Wenzhou Christian women today, but most local Christian men identify themselves as fundamentalists or Evangelicals and embrace textually centered church activities such as theology study—a very recent phenomenon, mainly owing to the rise of a rationalized modernity in industrialized coastal regions. A majority of Wenzhou Christian businessmen were born into a local faith tradition derived from early mission churches in the region. They were among the first to get rich after China's economic reforms began in the late 1970s. As many of these men hold a firm belief that their business success is due to God's blessing for Wenzhou's Christian tradition and their Christian family background, they began to develop strong attachment to the Christian community, which subsequently contributes to the elite male domination of the local church.

The Gendered Tension in Pentecostal Development

Holding a conservative theological orientation, the Wenzhou church forbids female pastors and discourages women to preach because, scripturally, women first committed sin and the head of the woman is the man.[21] The rise of the elite male sphere of Wenzhou Christianity is informed by and also reinforces a certain gender ideology in local society. Men are associated with qualities such as entrepreneurship, scholarship, and rationality in both Christian and non-Christian contexts. Christian men tend to engage in rational, textual, and mental forms of religiosity, while women are believed to be emotional, ritualistic, and bodily in religious practice. The unequal relationship between men and women in the church community is essentially one of interdependence, which resembles the urban-rural relationship in the uneven process of China's post-Mao modernization. However, the rationalization process associated with modernization has lent far more legitimacy to urban-oriented rationalistic Christianity than to the rural-based charismatic form of Christianity.

Today dominated by the male entrepreneurial class of believers, Wenzhou Christianity represents itself as rational, modern, and progressive. In the context of increased social mobility and general affluence, Wenzhou Christian men, like other Chinese men, are expected to be able to mobilize social resources and energies in a more public arena to support church work, especially in the form of church building and planting.[22]

However, most female church members visibly contribute to the church community by "sacrificing" their time and labor (rather than capital or intellect). They invest their energy in household duties such as cleaning and cooking before, during, and/or after church services. These practices in the "domestic realm" of the church embody a hierarchical and complementary gender order. It has been noted elsewhere in the world that Pentecostalism tends to support both men's monopoly on formal institutional positions and women's autonomy and equality in ritualistic and mythical contexts.[23] This is also true in Wenzhou, where women can play leadership roles in the church only on special occasions, particularly charismatic-oriented spiritual cultivation meetings (*peilinghui*). Such meetings are dominated by female participants who channel their emotional expressivity toward worshipping God through certain bodily practices and rituals.

The Emotional and Bodily Work of Lay Women

Spiritual cultivation meetings have roots in revival meetings (*fenxin-ghui*) conducted by traveling native Pentecostal evangelists early in the twentieth century. The two terms—spiritual cultivation (*peiling*) and revival (*fenxing*)—are sometimes interchangeable in Wenzhou today. They are not regular church services but take the form of special gatherings that can last several days, with the aim of deliberately achieving spiritual renewal. Such meetings feature prolonged prayer and worship sessions that are mixed with hymn singing throughout. Sermons and testimonies are kept short and are heavily focused on healing miracles. The healing of life-threatening diseases and injuries, as well as everyday illnesses, are always attributed to the active work of the Holy Spirit. Worshippers are encouraged to speak in tongues aloud during simultaneous individual prayers. This form of ecstatic prayer embodies female believers' affectionate piety and constitutes a Pentecostal habit that is common in other parts of the world.[24] Uncontrolled crying, laughing, singing, and dancing characterize the emotional intensity of such charismatic meetings. Spiritually experienced women, locally called "prayer-calling mothers" (*daogaopo*), play a "ritual master" role in this context of spiritual revival. They instruct the participants to sing, pray, cry, kneel down, stretch hands, admit sin, and repent in a such way as to suggest that God is speaking through them. Using a microphone, they can skillfully mobilize emotions and create a fervent atmosphere to induce people's "spirit-filled" experience. To seek emotional outbursts and the feelings of being filled by the Holy Spirit, many women attend spiritual cultivation meetings not only in their own churches but often in other churches and places. Unlike the hierarchical world of elite men, this female sphere of charismatic Christianity celebrates universal compassion, spontaneous feelings, and female solidarity cutting across class lines, particularistic ties, and congregational boundaries.

It is important to note that young and middle-aged men are ashamed of attending these female-dominated setting of spiritual cultivation. When asked why, some simply attributed this gendered practice of faith to men's rationality and women's emotionality. The stereotypical image is that women focus on prayer because they desire to live a pious life. I was told that some devout female believers (including almost all prayer-calling mothers) do not watch TV or read newspapers. This notion of women as emotionally expressive and bodily disciplined and men as rational and flexible reflects implicit elite male prestige in the church. Members of the younger generation of male believers, especially those university- or seminary-educated, take a critical stance on such charismatic meetings; they view charismatic women as "a product of the past," associated with the rural house church, and their emotional expressivity as a consequence of their "anti-intellectualism" or lack of necessary "theological equipment." One young man mocked the setting of spiritual cultivation as a "karaoke singing contest" in the church, saying in a derisive tone that these women need to "charge their batteries" (chongdian) periodically to sustain their passion.

Spiritual cultivation meetings have played an important part in the spread of Christianity in rural China, where pastoral care heavily relies on a small number of minimally trained itinerant preachers. Today, evangelism still takes the form of large-scale public meetings in many rural Chinese church communities, epitomizing the oral tradition of Chinese Christianity. But as textually based theological education and daily professional pastoral care are introduced to and become increasingly institutionalized in the local church community, the importance of spiritual cultivation meetings in the religious life of Chinese Christians has dramatically declined. This is especially the case in developed urban coastal areas where economic advancements and openness to overseas Christian development facilitate the professionalization of local clergy and the establishment of the Sunday school system. In Wenzhou city periodical renewal meetings are valued in the church, but not every church member is expected to attend. As Pentecostal worship produces loud sounds, large-scale Pentecostal meetings usually take place in carefully controlled settings (e.g., in rented church buildings in the suburb or nearby mountains) and are seen as an important complement rather than a core mechanism to the healthy development of the church.[25] Women can experience a sense of security, empowerment, and dignity in this female spiritual domain. But women's charismatic authority is also confined within this female-dominated context. Charismatic women are never invited to give prayers, speeches, sermons, or testimonies at high-profile evangelical lectures, banquets, and parties organized by the Christian businessmen.

For experientially inclined Christian women, bodily sensations are identified as proof of God's spiritual presence in life.[26] They take these unusual bodily experiences as their spiritual privilege even these experiences may not be replicable and are often ephemeral. However, elite Christian men have openly contested these charismatic women's claim of spiritual privilege. At a weekly Bible study meeting, one young church sister shared enthusiastically her experience of "being filled by the Holy Spirit" at a recent spiritual cultivation meeting she attended. According to her, continuous singing, jumping, and shouting "Hallelujah!" made her feel very excited. In fact she was too excited to remember what happened to her at the moment. She described her transient feeling at the meeting as completely "empty-minded." The

middle-aged male lay leader who organized the Bible study group immediately set out to correct her individualistic, experiential approach to faith,
saying that "it takes a learning process to experience God. It must involve
listening to sermons, bible study, and prayer, and this form of group meeting
is the key. You must have spiritual partners (*shuling de tongban*)."

The tension between evangelical scripturalism and experiential spirituality can also break out in open debate. During my fieldwork in Wenzhou in
2006, I observed a tense conversation over lunch between a male full-time
preacher and two middle-aged church sisters. Both church sisters argued that
being caught by the Holy Spirit is the ultimate spiritual experience, and that
loud crying and laughing are necessary signs of such. One woman insisted
that "only listening to the Word is not enough. One must be caught by the
Holy Spirit, and you can repent only after the Holy Spirit sheds light on you.
Without the Holy Spirit your sermon will become dry and you will be lacking in passion and oral skills. Without the Holy Spirit you can do nothing,
because there is spiritual warfare against demons." The male preacher, in his
early thirties, replied, "Different people have different forms of emotional
expression when they repent. Some shed more tears, others less. The Holy
Spirit leads us to the truth and uses the Word to remind us. God sheds light
on us, which is the motivation for us to follow the truth. The light is the Word.
One must be filled by the Holy Spirit constantly, not by momentarily attending a few [spiritual cultivation] meetings but without studying the Bible." The
debate shows the divergent understandings of the significance and manifestation of the Holy Spirit and speaks to the popular local Christian notion
that "sisters emphasize [spiritual] life, while brothers emphasize [Biblical]
truth." It also reveals the division of labor between men and women in the
church and the gendered construction of spiritual authority. In narratives of
spiritual experience, female believers frequently use the term "the Holy Spirit"
and highlight their emotional closeness to the Holy Spirit. They seek spiritual
empowerment through exhibiting dramatic emotionality, while men tend to
focus on textual study as the most important way to access God. Given the
subordinate and complementary position of women in the male-controlled
public sphere of the church, female religiosity constitutes a form of emotional
work in the eyes of elite men.

The practices of prayer-calling mothers illustrate how women's emotional work is employed and harnessed by elite male believers to their personal and familial advantages. Known for their enthusiasm for prayer and
the efficacy of their prayers, prayer-calling mothers are approached for help
with a wide range of practical issues, from mate selection, curing a disease,
or bearing a male heir, to whether one should emigrate, start a business,

or go to college. Some house churches even consult them to determine whether a particular man is suitable to be a church preacher or leader. Prayer-calling mothers in the same area are often familiar with one another and have formed informal networks to organize consecutive prayer sessions in their homes and perform requested prayers for church members. In many ways these women resemble female spiritual mediums in southeast China who actively engage in divination practices for clients seeking guidance and immediate miraculous responses.[27] Their popularity is due to their ability to address pragmatic concerns in local communities. However, institutionally, prayer-calling mothers are not considered formal church workers.

The narrative of a prayer-calling mother in an urban Wenzhou church highlights the locally perceived importance of moral lifestyle and feminine qualities such as purity, simplicity, and domesticity to the formation of charismatic authority among Christian women.

Sister Qinxiang is one of the most famous hosts of spiritual cultivation meetings in Wenzhou. She is in her late forties but has the appearance of someone in her sixties. This is mainly due to regular fasting (including not drinking water). Like other prayer-calling mothers, she is often seen in rustic, old-fashioned dress. She converted to Christianity at the age of seventeen after experiencing a healing miracle. Born with a congenital heart defect, she often showed symptoms of nausea and vomiting as a child. Qinxiang claimed that these symptoms have disappeared since an old woman prayed for her. With the woman she attended three consecutive large spiritual cultivation meetings at which she was repeatedly "filled by the Holy Spirit" (*bei shengling chongman*). In the same year, without any prior training or even preparation, she preached three sermons at spiritual cultivation meetings because she received "the gift from the Holy Spirit." She shared the details of her sermons with great joy. At that time it was still very rare for women to preach, as most churches did not allow female preachers. In the 1980s, as she recounted, she was "led by the Holy Spirit" to enter the business world with the hope of pulling her family out of poverty. She started first to make shoes, leather belts, and cases. Later on she switched to light industry to produce sewing machines and bill counters. Qinxiang even won a national gold medal award for her copyrighted bill counter production business. At the time, for her business achievement, she was often called "superwoman"(*nuqiangren*). She attributed her business success to God's blessing. In response to "God's calling," Qinxiang "sacrificed" herself at the age of thirty-three, quitting her business to serve the church full-time. Now she is frequently invited to lead spiritual cultivation meetings, not only in Wenzhou but among Wenzhou businesspeople's churches in other parts of the country. She expresses humility about her ability to speak in tongues and perform faith healing. For her, tongues-speaking is the smallest gift from the Holy Spirit. However, she is best known for the miraculous power of her prayers, which many come to her to request. Often overwhelmed by too many prayer requests at once following a church service, she will sometimes avoid going to church. In that case she has others tape-record the sermon so that she can listen to it at home. Occasionally she performs prayers for others, upon request, over the phone. When asked how she acquired the ability to pray, Sister Qinxiang attributes her ability to pray entirely to her sexual purity (*shengjie*)—in her words, "having no obscene ideas or thoughts since the Holy Spirit caught me when I was seventeen."

For Qinxiang, all personal, family, and business problems are results of "[spiritual] life with tears" (*shengming de pokou*); they need to be fixed through petitionary prayers. When choosing a mate, she kneeled down to pray to determine whom she should date. She declined to meet with several men because she learned through prayer that they were not appropriate for her. When dating a man from a Christian family, she took great caution in keeping sexual purity. According to her, whenever they met she would keep talking about the Bible with the man and avoid going to cinema with him. After they got married, the man badly wanted a son (due to the traditional Confucian desire to have a male heir). Trying to fulfill her husband's patri-archal, patrilineal ideal, she faithfully prayed for a son, and her prayer was miraculously answered.

The prayer-calling mother's asceticism, mysticism, and strong privatized piety point to a traditional Pentecostal tendency.[28] In stark contrast to male Christians' celebration of capitalist economic involvement, when women describe their determination to serve the church full-time, they often use such terms as "consecrate" (*fengxian*) and "let go of" (*fangxia*) to highlight their withdrawal from rational economic activities. Moreover, lay women repeatedly emphasize the importance of sexual purity in the construction of charismatic power, which is often in tension with the market economy. As Qinxiang's case shows, charismatic women are willing to celebrate their downward mobility or lack of mobility in a highly stratified economy. However, most male bosses preach on a part-time basis, and few would quit private business to become full-time church workers. Those who have made this shift face great pressure, and even stigma, both in and outside the church community. A fulltime male preacher and former boss, who used to own an enterprise in Wenzhou, is said to have to "feed on the church" (*chijiao*) for a living after suffering a ruinous business loss.

Male Christian bosses mostly avoid the strict bodily discipline and simple life advocated by charismatic-oriented lay women in order to participate in the morally decadent urban business world.[29] They stress the importance of "motivation" rather than the "form" to maintain their elite male prestige in a highly commercialized consumer-driven culture. This implies that one can still seek worldly wealth and pleasure as long as the ultimate life goal is to glorify Christ. They generally despise these middle-aged and elderly Christian women for their lack of rationality, low social standing, and earthy physical appearance. In a sermon, one Christian entrepreneur briefly commented in a regretful tone on a prayer-calling mother: "She lives in poverty and hardship. Her room is only eight square meters and is full of crosses. Her son is already thirty-three but has not yet married." In Wenzhou, as in coastal south China, it is a stigma for young men over thirty to remain unmarried, as this is often taken as a sign of the family's lack of ability to afford a bride price, and the poor can only wait till rich families have chosen their brides in this polarized socioeconomic context.[30] Despite an elite contempt for this simple lifestyle associated with prayer-calling mothers, the same Christian businessmen will go to them in private to request prayers when they want a male heir or to improve business results. Some turn to several different prayer-calling mothers for supernatural help. This is in line with the common business logic of contacting multiple clients at once, according to a fulltime young male preacher. Male bosses greatly value these women's sincerity (*kenqie*) and purity (*chun*) and take these feminine qualities as the key to one's ability to directly access the divine. Such ability often takes the form of spiritual gifts, such as speaking in tongues and prophesying. Although prayer-calling mothers do not have an active presence in mixed church settings, the efficacy of their prayers helps them reclaim feminine spiritual authority and establishes them as a type of religious specialist in the church community.

As the middle-aged businesspeople and the younger generation of college-educated Christian men increasingly associate Christianity with Western modernity, civility, and science, they see feminine spirituality as an obstacle to realizing this Christian modernity, due to its perceived link to superstition.[31] Prayer-calling mothers are sometimes under criticism for their shaman-like practices. When asked about the effectiveness of their interventions, they are reluctant to admit the pragmatic nature of their prayers. Instead, to avoid the allegation of engaging in superstition, they emphasize that they pray for people's better spiritual life and that that automatically leads to God's materialistic blessings. As a well-known prayer-calling mother in Wenzhou, sister Qinxiang recalled how a locally known boss preacher and his wife came to request her prayer for their shoe factory business. The boss Christian suffered a great business loss because of overstocking. Stressing the spiritual authenticity of her prayer, she said that it was unlike asking God to help make money directly. Instead, she tried to help them find out the (spiritual) cause of their business failure. It turned out that the boss had asked his mother (also a church worker) to help out with his shoe business, which kept her so busy that she had no time to conduct visitation ministry for her church. According to Qinxiang, after the couple realized this "weakness in their spiritual life" they cried, repented, and decided to listen to the Lord as they knew God must bless them. Two months later they managed to sell all surplus shoes and made a lot of money. The view of material benefits as mere by-products of the spiritual, along with the call for improving one's spirituality first before getting rich, allows charismatic women to both maintain their religious ideal and legitimize their disadvantaged social position. Such self-affirmation enlists devout female believers to continue being disadvantaged in order for the gendered division of labor in the church to be sustained.

By consuming the spiritual power and efficacy of the prayer-calling mothers, the bosses are often led to reflect on their own pragmatic belief and self-refashioning efforts. They have expressed frustration that "few bosses can both do good business and have good spirituality at once." This is because they are too busy and do not have personal spiritual experience. By implication, they often have to turn to or employ the work of spiritually experienced others. The male bosses perceive their economic rationality and self-control as the extreme opposite of spiritual efficacy. Paradoxically, the charismatic authority of prayer-calling mothers comes from their carefully maintained spiritual/secular binary and their marginalized position in the political economy. Although these women are marginalized by the male-centered discourse of Christianity, they play a vital role in the contradictory experiences and perceptions of the elite male believers. The Christian bosses' use of female religious service providers embodies both market and antimarket moralities, and this contradictory process speaks to what Robert Weller calls a "split market culture."[32]

Elite Male Spirituality and the Prosperity Gospel

The growth of Pentecostal/charismatic Christianity in the reform era helps reconcile the conservative spiritual tradition of the Chinese church formed in the early twentieth century with utopian dreams of capitalist success that are prevalent in China today. As members of the local business elite, the boss Christians often present themselves as God's steward and consider their financial contributions to the church as investment in God's miracles. Many hold a firm belief that "the more you give, the more God will give back."[33] They also stress that doing business is serving God and that without a private enterprise one would not be able to do good work in the church. As one influential boss preacher put it, straightforwardly, "Without money, no one would listen to you." Although this statement is perhaps a bit cynical, ordinary churchgoers are well aware that private bosses are resourceful and capable individuals who are in a better position than non-boss lay leaders to help develop the church, especially when facing state pressure. By channeling massive commercial wealth into various church projects, they manage to redefine what is acceptable and what is not in the church community. In sermons, local boss preachers often quote John Wesley, a key figure in the evangelical revival in eighteenth-century England, urging Christian entrepreneurs to "make all you can, save all you can, and give all you can." Such prosperity teachings place the most emphasis on one's entrepreneurial productivity and echo China's reformist leader Deng Xiaoping's slogans of "building socialist market economy with Chinese characteristics" and "poverty is not socialism" in their ideological effect of liberating and unleashing people's economic ambitions, which were severely suppressed in the Maoist era.

The rise of this entrepreneurial and professional class of Christians has largely moderated the power of charismatic women, as well as female-centered Pentecostal desire for emotion-filled meetings. As a volunteer reporter for a Wenzhou Christian entrepreneurs' fellowship between 2005 and 2006, I was able to observe the formation of male charismatic leadership from inside. I sat through many planning meetings and was able to witness various projects and activities from inception to completion. In the past two years I have made additional trips to Wenzhou and revisited several fellowship members there. These elite male Christians appreciate the spiritual help from the lay women but do not recognize their charismatic authority in the church. They strive to gain spiritual prestige and moral superiority through spiritualizing their economic success and elevating the status of Wenzhou as a local center of the world mission. As many Wenzhou bosses attribute their own economic success and Wenzhou's rapid development in the reform era to "the work of the Holy Spirit," they also express the hope of depending on the power of the Holy Spirit to "let China become the world's blessing." This is, in one boss Christian's words, to use an alternative force to help China rise. Prompted by their success in the new entrepreneurial world, some boss Christians have started to fashion themselves as part of a new generation of charismatic leaders in the Chinese church by articulating and spreading a new vision that they call "God's China vision" (*zhongguo yixiang*). Those who share the vision agree that China will rise not only in the economic sphere but also in the spiritual realm. As Brother Jian, a businessman in his thirties put it, characteristically,

> The international community is paying great attention to China. To look at the GDP, China is now the second-largest economy. In the spiritual field China will take the last relay baton in the global Evangelical movement. But China needs to be renewed and transformed first. Some individuals must rise to lead the revival. Based on my personal experience, I feel the most important thing is to have spiritual release and healing and to have a renewed purpose in life. To have [spiritual] influence on society one must pursue a business career.

The so-called China vision exemplifies these businessmen's attempt to discursively construct an elite mode of Chinese spirituality in tune with both state and capitalist modernities, as well as expressing their ambitions to reshape the global Christian landscape. This prophetic practice reveals a Pentecostal undercurrent behind the Christian resurgence in the era of post-Mao modernization and globalization. Being able to articulate prophetic visions is considered an important and valued spiritual gift in the church community. Like prayer-calling mothers, these elite male Christians make predictions that certain things will happen in the future. But unlike prayer-calling mothers, who are said to "have no big burden" in only praying for pragmatic benefits, the Christian bosses often show a strong sense of burden for the world mission. The "China vision" is embodied in the singing of a Chinese hymn titled "China's Mission" *(xuanjiao de zhongguo)*; Wenzhou Christian bosses are particularly fond of this hymn and like to sing it over and over again in various gatherings. The lyrics: "I walk forward with a mission, to wake up a sleeping China, we won't turn around even when shedding blood. I walk forward with a vision to see an evangelistic China and spread the Gospel to every corner of the world . . . one day China will rise, one day China will rise, break the closed door and the solid barracks, let the evangelical flag wave in China, let the church be united." A strong sense of mission permeates their narratives and forms their exclusive claim to leadership in world Christianity. There is an intense desire to compete with the West and to achieve elite status in global Christianity by exporting the Gospel from China to other parts of the world. For Chinese Christians the practice of public prophesying that China will one day take the lead in world mission helps overcome a sense of marginalization in the global Christian movement, in which they have been for the most part treated as agentless victims of the atheist Communist state.[34]

The fervent pursuit of market modernity in Chinese society has recon-figured the dynamics of Christian development that has Pentecostal origin. The charismatic insistence on spiritualizing economic modernization con-tributes to a strong impetus toward conducting evangelism in less devel-oped regions and among disadvantaged rural migrant workers. As a way of redeeming the divine blessing and showing the spiritual and moral signifi-cance of economic success, many businessmen-led Wenzhou churches have sent evangelical teams to the rural inland and impoverished ethnic minority regions in southwest China. There are also large-scale evangelical meetings regularly held in Wenzhou Christian–led factories nationwide. The Wenzhou church's linking of business with mission in both discourse and practice helps to build a bridge between the once-marginalized Chinese Christianity and the society at large, particularly in the context of the reformist state's formu-lation that "economic development is the fundamental principle."

Wenzhou Christians, both men and women, accept the spiritual signifi-cance of submitting to the Holy Spirit. But there seem to be significant gen-der differences in understanding the working of the Holy Spirit and how to realize the ideal of being guided and empowered by the Holy Spirit. Wenzhou men exercise spiritual authority by pursing a business-friendly prosperity theology along with an evangelical mission, while women search for charis-matic power by embracing asceticism, supernaturalism, and emotional reviv-alism, which underlay the development of early Chinese Pentecostalism in the midst of social and political chaos.

To counter the stereotype of Christianity as a disadvantaged female institution, and in order to raise the "quality of belief," successful Christian businessmen have taken the lead in the promotion and pursuit of formal religious education and a textually based faith in the church community.[35] Attending theology lectures and training sessions organized by local churches has become a fad among young and middle-aged male believers.[36] These lec-tures often feature invited outside speakers (usually Christian scholars) and take the form of classroom instruction, with written homework assignments given at the end of each class. These male-dominated settings of theological study privilege the textual knowledge of Christianity over the oral tradition of rural-based charismatic Christianity. Several lectures have even focused on explicitly critiquing the rural women-dominated charismatic movement. The introduction of scholarship contributes to establishing a binary opposition between charismatic Christianity and the modern among the local church community. Nowadays the rural charismatic movement has been objectified in the elite circle of male Christian professionals as a religious trend that sup-posedly appeals only to the underclass and marginalized social groups. In the local church community it is generally believed that only less educated and emotionally expressive rural women are inclined to charismatic Christianity, while urban men should be equipped with systematic theology and refrain from participating in charismatic activities.

However, in practice the highly emotional form of Christianity still has an appeal among elite men, especially if it is introduced from overseas and can evoke Chinese believers' imagination about the spiritual roots of modernity. The Wenzhou church's extensive transnational connections help introduce new religious concepts and authorities into the region. An elite masculine form of Pentecostalism, with a modern entrepreneurial outlook and less dramatic emotionality attached, has been a major religious import in recent years.

Sometimes, the anticharismatic sentiment can be part of the story of the rise of Pentecostal Christianity in post-Mao China. To rectify the oral charismatic tradition and enhance the "cultural quality" of the church, many churches and fellowship groups have started publishing their own magazines and newsletters and widely circulated them in the church circle and beyond. This church publication ministry has enabled local churches to network with overseas Christian communities, including the fastest-growing Pentecostal ones. A group of California-based Chinese American Christian entrepreneurs affiliated with the Full Gospel Businessmen's Fellowship International (FGBFI) found their way to Wenzhou during the Chinese New Year holiday of 2006 soon after they read the newsletter of Wenzhou's newly established professionals' fellowship. They said they were thrilled after reading what was going on in Wenzhou and could not wait to communicate with their Chinese counterparts on how to combine business investment with evangelization in China.

At a hotel's ballroom and banquet hall, three Chinese American members of FGBFI took turns to give testimonials and talks in front of an audience of mostly local businessmen, both Christian and potential converts. Besides taking great pains to emphasize the link between personal spirituality and business success, they stressed the important role businessmen can play in Christianizing China, repeatedly repudiating the old-fashioned notion that one has to give up his business career in order to serve God. One Chinese American brother said that he had nine years' experience working with the rural house church. Now he thinks that the city should be the priority of evangelism in China, and entrepreneurs should be the priority in the city. This is what he called a top-down approach to evangelism work, drawing on the resources and influence of the socioeconomic elites. The overseas and local entrepreneurs developed a shared vision that it is the entrepreneurs who should take the lead in transforming China into an Evangelical nation, and it is by influencing the economy first, then the culture, and finally politics that they can let China become the world's blessing and Wenzhou become China's blessing. Local Christian businessmen prefer such events to a regular church session, because their up-to-date theme and innovative modern style better fit the entrepreneurs' tastes and demands. The overly Pentecostal style of these events was also impressive. I heard several times that local Christian bosses commented in an envious tone on expressive worship performed by overseas Chinese Christians. Some realized that, compared with these overseas brothers, they were too restrained, while faith should enable them to be "released and natural." They also wanted to imitate these overseas brothers' Western manners by hugging one another. One local Christian boss even asked how to pronounce the word "hug" in English. Wenzhou Christian bosses speak highly of these overseas businessmen who are good at praying and shedding tears. Some have established a causal link between emotional release and success in modern business. Clearly, their initial attraction to Pentecostalism is due to the "modern" style of worship (rather than the ideology) and to their desire to tie themselves to a global network. Indeed, it is only in this elite male context (usually not in front of women) that these Christian businessmen find crying not just an acceptable but a desirable spiritual practice. Although these Christian businessmen find the fervent atmosphere of spirit-filled meetings appealing, most of them would resist the idea of Pentecostalizing the local church structure, as well as applying the Pentecostal label. This seems to be less a case of the globalization of neo-Pentecostal Christianity than an example of ambitious local Chinese believers seeking to go global by participating in a global diaspora of socially advantaged ethnic Chinese Christians.[37]

Male church leaders have expressed deep concern about the overrepresentation of women in the church because they associate women with emotionality and narrow-mindedness. Nevertheless, for many, the lack of emotional expressivity is perhaps an outward sign of their reluctance to submit to the Holy Spirit. Given that men are normatively expected to be more restrained and less emotionally exuberant in public, some have noticed that the practice of spiritual release needs to be directed by others, reporting charismatic encounters with overseas Pentecostal Christians as a significant factor in developing their experiential spirituality. For instance, a middle-aged local preacher shared in a Sunday sermon his memorable experience of attending a worship service in a Pentecostal church in Hong Kong. He was amazed by the worshippers' loud crying, shouting, and falling and felt embarrassed that he was only able to "fall to the ground" (*pudao*) with someone's assistance. Similarly, in testimony a young local businessmen and youth group leader traced his recent interest in Pentecostalism to his encounter with a visiting

Taiwanese preacher in Wenzhou four years ago. He admired the preacher not only for his emotionally charged sermon but also his childlike humble attitude. He learned the Pentecostal practice of laying on of hands from the Taiwanese preacher. Later, encountering a sudden microphone malfunction problem right before a fellowship meeting, he proclaimed to God the way the Taiwanese preacher taught him. He laid one of his hands on the microphone and miraculously fixed the problem. He has now switched from his home church, one that emphasizes reformed theology, to a new suburban church called the Bethlehem Harvest Church that was split from a local house church network and has ties with the City Harvest Church, a Pentecostal megachurch in Singapore.

The growing emphasis among Christian men on the written literacy of Christian orthodoxy does not conflict with their longing for direct supernatural experience, especially for those ambitious individuals seeking greater opportunities in the market. Brother Jian represents the younger generation of Chinese Pentecostals whose beliefs and practices have been shaped by the more recent global Pentecostal movement. He took pains to explain to me how his version of Pentecostal Christianity differs from that embodied by the practices of prayer-calling mothers, and how God's miraculous work follows a rationalized procedure and complies with market principles. For him, the key is the method of spiritual proclaiming (*lingli xuangao*). As he put it,

> Spiritual proclaiming is more fundamental than prayer-calling mothers' prolonged, superstition-like prayers, which involve neither spiritual warfare (*lingli zhengzhan*) nor biblical foundation but are a product of their own pride. Spiritual proclaiming is asking for the wealth that originally belonged to you to be released [from Satan]. It is for God to decide when this transfer of wealth happens. It is not that someone's billions of money suddenly gets transferred to your bank account by mistake. It is through providing you with managerial power and influence over others' wealth, or by making you a client of the wealth holder. It could also happen this way. An enterprise went bankrupt because of a policy change and is waiting to be incorporated and restructured. At this point you might be approached and presented this unprecedented opportunity by someone who is in your network of friends but whom you might not have met before. God will transfer wealth to the hands of those who follow His heart.

At first glance, there is no fundamental difference between "spiritual proclaiming" and "prayer calling"; both emphasizing supernatural power and God's blessings in physical and materialistic forms. However, such young male Pentecostals derive religious teachings and cultural resources from

Pentecostal churches overseas. They present themselves as more rational, sophisticated, and assertive in their materialistic requests, showing the profound influence of the global spread of the prosperity gospel.[38]

It almost goes without saying that overseas Chinese Christian preachers, with their Chinese fluency and elite masculine identity, have played a vital role in the transmission of Pentecostalism to the male segment of the local church community in Wenzhou. But there is little evidence that Pentecostal development in this overseas-oriented Chinese city has been synchronized with the global Pentecostal movement. The newly founded Bethlehem Harvest Church in suburban Wenzhou has received much criticism in local church communities for its splitting from the mother church and a heavy emphasis on the wealth and health gospel and speaking in tongues. Some local Christians attack the church's worship style as horribly heretical. Nevertheless, this newly imported Pentecostalism provides an alternative form of charismatic authority and a new transnational ideal of Christian masculinity that entrepreneurial church leaders can utilize to expand their religious structures in very creative, yet controversial, ways. Compared with women-dominated church networks in rural inland provinces and intellectual house churches in major Chinese metropolises, Christian communities in overseas-oriented trading centers in coastal China have a much greater propensity to be influenced by the global appeal of Pentecostal churches.

China's Global Rise and the Emergence of an Indigenous Discourse on Pentecostal Modernity

As an intense emotional form of religiosity and a model of spiritual renewal emphasizing miracles and wonders, Pentecostalism has been an integral and permanent feature of Chinese Christianity since the turn of the twentieth century. Early Chinese Pentecostal leaders, with their nationalistic feelings and their longing for direct, unmediated access to divine power, pushed Chinese Christianity to break away from foreign control and spread across the vast rural hinterland. Its noninstitutional character, millenarian belief, and ability to absorb folk religious and cultural elements enabled the Pentecostal-influenced rural church to survive persecution during the Maoist decades and flourish in the reform era. For some older Christians, their experiences of suffering furthered their dependence on God's supernatural power and their Pentecostal tendency.

The phenomenon of revivalism in the early twentieth century has continued relevance to today's Chinese Christian communities, which have developed largely in isolation from the global Christian movement. The Pentecostal spiritual tradition remains influential even among modern Chinese church groups that emphasize a rationalistic, systemized, theology-driven religion.[39] The state-controlled TSPM church is reluctant to deny its significance and value in the face of a new wave of Pentecostal and charismatic movement in economically advanced coastal regions. *Tianfeng,* the official Chinese Christian monthly, recently carried an article titled "Reflections on the Charismatic Phenomenon." While lamenting the disorder and emotionality of charismatic meetings and their emphasis on supernatural experience at expense of the biblical truth, it acknowledged that

> the pure pursuit of spiritual gifts can promote the development of evangelism and related ministries. On the one hand, spiritual gifts strengthen evangelists' proselytizing abilities and passion. On the other hand, under the influence of spiritual power, more and more nonbelievers have converted to Christianity and church member-ship continues to rise. Emphasis on prayer and worshiping the Lord can to some extent increase the vitality of the church and help to deal with the crisis that has resulted from the formalism and stiff-ness of the traditional church."[40]

This ambivalence toward grassroots Pentecostal/charismatic Christianity articulated by a member of the state-approved clergy highlights the divergent dynamics of Chinese Christian development that revolves around the themes of achieving spiritual power and engaging systematic theological reasoning.

In the reform era, Evangelical Christianity—especially its Pentecostal form—provides a complex response to both a common, individualistic pur-suit of market success in Chinese society and a deep-rooted rural supernatu-ralistic cultural tradition. Drawing on the Wenzhou case, I have identified two distinct but interrelated strands in the development of China's Pentecostal Christianity in interaction with a growing market economy, namely the female-centered experiential sector, emphasizing asceticism and mysticism, and the elite male-preached neo-Pentecostal-style prosperity gospel, which celebrates the competitive global market economy. However, the gendered pattern of charismatic activities and enthusiasm is undergoing transforma-tion in post-Mao modernization. As this study shows, the woman-dominated charismatic form of Chinese Christianity has gradually become subjugated to an elite male-centered spirituality in the context of marketization. The vitality of Pentecostal Christianity can be tied to the profound structuring forces of market modernity. It tends to lose dynamism as people increasingly embrace rationalization while participating in the market economy. At the same time, it can also gain new momentum in the current context of an increased individualization and privatization of spirituality that has been partly induced by the neoliberal marketization process. A notable illustration of this contradictory dynamic is the phenomenon of prayer-calling mothers, whose status is both sponsored and constrained by elite male boss Christians, and whose emotional practice of faith is taken as both a symptom of backwardness to be subdued and a symbol of piety to be emulated (depending on contexts).

Supernaturalism associated with Pentecostalism has at least temporarily survived socioeconomic mobility in the reform era. What is striking about Pentecostal development in an emerging Chinese entrepreneurial modernity is that elite men outsource the emotional and bodily work to economically powerless yet spiritually experienced women in a sociosymbolic universe in which emotionality and corporeality are relegated to a lower status. The two gender strands of Pentecostal development represent two conflicting models of constructing charismatic power in response to a rationalized modernity and the drastic transition from rural to urban life. The charismatic authority of lay women can be traced back to the early twentieth century, when spiritual revival meetings led by fundamentalist native evangelists swept across China. Later, this experiential type of spirituality fueled rural house church movements that continue till today. Dominated by charismatic women who celebrate their marginalized position, social immobility, and moral lifestyle, the rural Chinese church maintains a conservative spirituality that discourages social participation and avoids political activism. I would argue that as China's integration into the global capitalist economy intensifies, the upwardly mobile urban class of Chinese Christians will continue to be empowered to reconfigure the charismatic authority of the traditional rural-based Chinese church. This transformation has already been greatly facilitated through their contact with overseas Pentecostal missionaries, who are mostly male professionals. I would also predict that the future development of Chinese Pentecostalism will borrow heavily from overseas Chinese male spiritualism. Driven by a desire to belong to the international Christian community, the forward-looking male entrepreneurial class of believers is seeking resources, energy, and legitimacy from the emerging global Pentecostal and charismatic movement as they set up their own Pentecostal-like independent church groups and networks. This emerging urban elite sector of Pentecostal Christianity will increasingly place more emphasis on theology, in contrast to the female-dominated rural indigenous Pentecostal development, which has been driven primarily by oral testimonies and emotion-filled meetings. Its central concern with an individuated, autonomous spirituality also sets it apart from politicized urban intellectual house churches that advocate religious freedom in the public sphere. While independent congregations and house church movements provide a fertile ground for Pentecostal growth and formation of charismatic leadership, it remains to be seen whether urban-oriented Chinese Christian communities will undergo Pentecostalization, as has been the case in many other parts of the modern urban world. It is also too early to assess Pentecostalism's impact on economic morality and civic participation in Chinese society. We must bear in mind that these remarks draw mainly upon the Wenzhou case. Wenzhou is unique in the sense that it provides China's most commercialized economic milieu, in which Christians, both men and women, feel far more compelled to engage the market in secular and spiritual ways than do Chinese believers in other places.

Tensions abound between the experiential and the theological, the premodern and the modern, the rural and the urban, the local and the global, as well as between the rationalization and privatization of spirituality in the resurgence of China's Pentecostal-influenced Christian communities. These tensions exhibit a profoundly gendered nature and will continue to be played out in contemporary Chinese Christians' engagements with market modernity and the global world in which China has emerged as a powerful player. At the beginning of the twenty-first century, the Chinese church has become indigenized to such an extent that some ambitious lay leaders, backed by their recent experience of modernization, engage in the prophetic practice of formulating "God's China vision," participating in an elite nationalist discourse on Pentecostal modernity that increasingly excludes women's spiritual role. The rise of an indigenous Pentecostal modernity seems to be the early twentieth-century dream of native Pentecostal leaders coming true. While urban Chinese Christian men feel contempt for lay women's "only knowing how to kneel down to pray but without taking any action," their prophetic vision that China will rule the world not only in economic terms but in the spiritual realm equally comes from a Pentecostal origin. Imbued with elite nationalist emotions, the pronounced religious impulse has come full circle.

NOTES

When the term "Christianity" is used in this paper, it refers to Protestantism in particular. It is noteworthy that Chinese Pentecostalism may include a variety of spirit-focused forms of Christianity. Pentecostal Christians in China are mostly Evangelical in theological orientation and few accept the Pentecostal label, which seems to be a unique feature of Pentecostal development in Asia. See Allan Anderson and Edmond Tang, eds., *Asian and Pentecostal: The Charismatic Face of Christianity in Asia* (London: Regnum Books International, 2005). For an overview of the definitional problems regarding Pentecostalism, see Joel Robbins, "The Globalization of Pentecostal and Charismatic Christianity," *Annual Review of Anthropology* 33 (2004): 119–123.

1. David Aikman, *Jesus in Beijing* (Washington, DC: Regnery, 2003); Chinese Academy of Social Sciences, "An In-house Questionnaire Survey on Christianity in China," in *Annual Report on China's Religions,* ed. Jin Ze and Qiu Yonghui (Beijing: Social Sciences Academic Press, 2010): 190–212. I estimate that 60–80 percent of Chinese Christians can be considered Pentecostal or charismatic Christians.

2. "Three-Self" refers to self-administration, self-support, and self-propagation. Supported by the Chinese government, the Three-Self Patriotic Movement since its inception in the 1950s has sought to develop an independent Chinese church completely free from foreign control and influences. The churches registered with TSPM are known as (official) TSPM churches, while unregistered churches are often called (underground) house churches.

3. Despite this distinction the Pentecostal practice of faith healing can be found in both sectors of the Chinese church. Some church historians have argued that most Chinese Christians are Pentecostal in a broader theological sense. See, e.g., Gotthard Oblau, "Pentecostal by Default? Contemporary Christianity in China," in Anderson and Tang, *Asian and Pentecostal,* 411–436.

4. See Ryan Dunch, "Protestant Christianity in China Today: Fragile, Fragmented, Flourishing," in *China and Christianity: Burdened Past, Hopeful Future,* ed. S. Uhalley Jr. and X. Wu (Armonk, NY: M. E. Sharpe, 2001), 195–216.

5. Luke Wesley, "Is Chinese Church Predominately Pentecostal?" *Asian Journal of Pentecostal Studies* 7:2 (2004): 225–254.

6. Chinese Academy of Social Sciences, "An In-house Questionnaire Survey."

7. Gerda Wielander, "Bridging the Gap? An Investigation of Beijing Intellectual House Church Activities and Their Implications for China's Democratization," *Journal of Contemporary China* 18: 62 (2009): 849–864.

8. The discussion of Wenzhou Christianity in this chapter draws mainly on my ethnographic field research conducted in Wenzhou between 2005 and 2010. For a more complete picture of contemporary Wenzhou Christianity, see Nanlai Cao, *Constructing China's Jerusalem: Christians, Power, and Place in Contemporary Wenzhou* (Stanford, CA: Stanford University Press, 2011).

9. Hong Kong–based American Pentecostal missionary Dennis Balcombe had a profound impact on house church networks in Henan. See Aikman, *Jesus in Beijing,* 271–275.

10. David Martin, *Pentecostalism: The World Their Parish* (Oxford: Blackwell, 2002), 176.

11. See Daniel H. Bays, "Chinese Protestant Christianity Today," *The China Quarterly,* no. 174 (2003): 494–495, for a discussion of the Pentecostal legacy of Chinese independent churches early in the twentieth century.

12. Alan Hunter and Kim-Kwong Chan, *Protestantism in Contemporary China* (Cambridge: Cambridge University Press, 1993), 126–135.

13. Daniel H. Bays, "Christian Revival in China: 1900–1937," in *Modern Christian Revivals,* ed. Edith L. Blumhofer and Randall Balmer (Champaign: University of Illinois Press, 1993), 167–169; Deng Zhaoming, "Indigenous Chinese Pentecostal Denominations," in Anderson and Tang, *Asian and Pentecostal,* 439–440.

14. Daniel H. Bays, "Indigenous Protestant Churches in China, 1900–1937: A Pentecostal Case Study," in *Indigenous Responses to Western Christianity*, ed. Steven Kaplan (New York: New York University Press, 1995), 139.

15. Gotthard Oblau, "Pentecostal by Default?"

16. The official TSPM churches also organize spiritual cultivation meetings but hold highly ambivalent attitudes toward the truthfulness of healing miracles in the present-day world.

17. En Hui, "Comments on Spiritual Cultivation Meetings," *Tianfeng* 9 (2005): 18–19.

18. See Lian Xi, *Redeemed by Fire: The Rise of Popular Christianity in Modern China* (New Haven: Yale University Press, 2010).

19. Chen-Yang Kao, "The Cultural Revolution and the Emergence of Pentecostal-style Protestantism in China," *Journal of Contemporary Religion* 24:2 (2009): 171–188.

20. According to charismatically oriented older church leaders in Wenzhou, Calvinism-based reformed theology, which was introduced in the 1990s by an influential Chinese Indonesian pastor named Stephan Tong, was responsible for destroying the charismatic leadership structure of the Wenzhou house church. See also Aikman, *Jesus in Beijing*, 191.

21. See 1 Corinthians 11:3. As far as I know, only one TSPM church in Wenzhou has a female pastor.

22. Cf. P. Steven Sangren, *Chinese Sociologics: An Anthropological Account of the Role of Alienation in Social Reproduction* (London: Athlone Press, 2000), 179.

23. See, e.g., Diane J. Austin-Broos, *Jamaica Genesis: Religion and the Politics of Moral Orders* (Chicago: University Of Chicago Press, 1997), chapter 6; Bernice Martin, "The Pentecostal Gender Paradox: A Cautionary Tale for the Sociology of Religion," in *The Blackwell Companion to Sociology of Religion*, ed. R. K. Fenn (Oxford: Blackwell, 2002), 54; Robbins, "The Globalization of Pentecostal and Charismatic Christianity," 132.

24. Oblau, "Pentecostal by Default?" 425.

25. Holding renewal meetings has become local churches' spiritual solution to internal conflicts and perceived declining religious commitment among church members.

26. Tanya M. Luhrmann, "Metakinesis: How God Becomes Intimate in Contemporary U.S. Christianity," *American Anthropologist* 106:3 (2004), 518–528.

27. Erin M. Cline, "Female Spirit Mediums and Religious Authority in Contemporary Southeastern China," *Modern China* 36: 5 (2010), 520–555.

28. While some prayer-calling mothers can live a decent life by relying on rental income, they actively avoid talking about any involvement they may have in economic matters.

29. This is by no means to suggest that these Christian businessmen do not practice physical discipline. They do try to live up to Christian moral standards and represent themselves as more disciplined than non-Christian businessmen.

30. Cf. Helen Siu, "The Reconstitution of Brideprice and Dowry in South China," in *Chinese Families in the Post-Mao Era*, ed. Deborah Davis and Stevan Harrell (Berkeley: University of California Press, 1993), 165–188.

31. In Chinese history women's participation in folk religion has often been stigmatized as superstitious in nature. See Hill Gates, *China's Motor: A Thousand Years of Petty Capitalism* (Ithaca: Cornell University Press, 1996).

32. Robert P. Weller, *Alternate Civilities: Democracy and Culture in China and Taiwan* (Boulder, CO: Westview, 1999).

33. Tithing is always encouraged but not mandatory in Wenzhou churches, for it has been perceived as the elite responsibility of new rich Christian entrepreneurs.

34. Some elite-minded Christian entrepreneurs have wholeheartedly embraced the Back to Jerusalem Movement, a Chinese-led evangelistic campaign to send missionaries to countries between China and Jerusalem.

35. Nanlai Cao, "Raising the Quality of Belief: Suzhi and the Production of an Elite Protestantism," *China Perspectives* 4 (2009): 54–65.

36. To pursue advanced Christian studies, some male Wenzhou church preachers have even enrolled in part-time religious study programs at major Chinese universities.

37. A similar pattern in the globalization of local Chinese Christianity can be found among the Chinese Baptist church in the Philippines. See Brian Howell, *Christianity in the Local Context: Southern Baptists in the Philippines* (New York: Palgrave Macmillan, 2008), chapters 7 and 8.

38. See Simon Coleman, *The Globalisation of Charismatic Christianity: Spreading the Gospel of Prosperity* (Cambridge: Cambridge University Press, 2000).

39. For a discussion of native revivalism in the early twentieth century and its continued impact on contemporary Chinese Christianity, see Bays, "Christian Revival in China," 161–179.

40. Wang Lei, "Reflections on the Charismatic Phenomenon," *Tianfeng* 8 (2010): 14–16.

SIX

The Routinization of Soviet Pentecostalism and the Liberation of Charisma in Russia and Ukraine

CHRISTOPHER MARSH AND ARTYOM TONOYAN

The year 1989 was the first in which the promises of Gorbachev's perestroika were fulfilled. A mere year after the millennial celebration of the "Baptism of *Rus'*," as the conversion to Christianity by Kiev's Prince Vladimir is known, religious life in the Soviet Union had opened up in a way unseen since the Bolshevik Revolution of 1917, if even then. It was in this exhilarating environment that a young Pentecostal named Alexander gathered a few of his friends to go and sing hymns at a local cancer hospital in Zhitomir, Ukraine. Alexander's aunt was dying of cancer, and her condition made church attendance impossible. Why not bring the love of Christ to her and the other patients, Alexander thought. Their singing was most welcome by the patients, believers and nonbelievers alike, for obvious reasons. Similarly, Alexander and his friends also began singing around town and sharing the Gospel with passers-by, taking advantage of the new freedoms that perestroika had brought them.

Before long, however, Alexander was instructed to cease such acts of Christian compassion and evangelism. Neither was he an ordained minister in the Pentecostal church, he was told, nor was it appropriate to conduct such activities beyond the walls of the physical church to which they belonged. These instructions came not from Soviet authorities slow to respond to the liberalization of Soviet religion policy, but rather from Alexander's own Pentecostal church. He and his friends considered unsatisfactory the explanations he was given for this determination, and he discussed the issue with his older brother who had just finished his studies at the Pentecostal seminary in the neighboring province. Neither of the young men could see any theological reason to justify the church's decision. Rather, they felt that the church was stifled by traditions established during the Soviet era, when the survival strategy of the Pentecostals dictated that they lie low and refrain from public activities. Indeed, a reading of scripture led them to conclude that the church should not be limited in its evangelistic activities as they were being told. Feeling led by the Holy Spirit, the pair broke away from the church into which they had been baptized years before and started their own church, one that would not be constrained by any physical walls or Soviet-era traditions that were now outdated in the new sociopolitical environment.

That was nearly twenty-five years ago. Today, Pastor Alexander is the head of a large group of Pentecostal churches throughout Ukraine. His home church in Zhitomir, about an hour north of Kiev, is an active civic organization and enjoys warm relations with other churches of various denominations and runs numerous social activities, from summer camps to a basketball league. Pastor Alexander also enjoys excellent relations with the local mayor (who favors no single church, but rather meets regularly with leaders of all traditions). Beyond his hometown, Pastor Alexander serves informally as something of a "bishop" to other Pentecostal communities throughout Ukraine.

The story of Pastor Alexander and his vibrant charismatic church poignantly illustrates many of the characteristics of Pentecostal and charismatic churches in post-Soviet Russia and Ukraine. In particular, it exemplifies the routinization of charisma by Soviet Pentecostals, and the inability of most such churches to adapt to the freer environment ushered in by Gorbachev's reforms and indeed the collapse of Communist Party rule. On the other hand, the rapid spread of less routinized forms of Pentecostalism and more ambiguous forms of charismatic Christianity illustrated by the growth of his and other churches illustrates how, when given the opportunity, some groups were able to mobilize rapidly and respond to changed sociopolitical conditions. Finally, the evangelistic activities, mission work, and social programs of these churches testify to their commitment to the social and political progress of the nation and the prosperity of its citizens.

In the pages that follow, we offer a brief historical overview of the roots of Pentecostalism in the Soviet Union and the survival strategies employed during the period of persecution. Continuing, we discuss briefly the ways in which perestroika opened up the religious marketplace and how Pentecostalism and charismatic Christianity adapted to the drastically changed sociopolitical circumstances. We then discuss the variants of Pentecostalism and charismatic Christianity in Russia and Ukraine today, particularly the "old" and "new" variants and their sociopolitical implications. Finally, we consider how these post-Soviet examples relate to the other cases analyzed in this volume, and what the points of convergence and divergence may suggest about Pentecostalism globally.

Origins and Survival

The origins of Pentecostalism in the Russian Empire can be traced back to the beginning of the twentieth century to two distinct streams. The first was introduced in 1911, when the first Pentecostal missionary, a Mr. Urshan (possibly of Norway), began work in Helsinki, then part of the Tsarist empire. It was here that N. F. Smorodin and A. I. Ivanov, preachers from a sectarian group, joined the movement and rapidly became its indigenous leaders. The fledgling church promptly moved into the Vyborg region and established Russia's first Pentecostal congregation, which then quickly spread farther afield, first to St. Petersburg and then to Novgorod, followed by Moscow. By 1915 they had reached the Caucasus.[1]

The more significant stream, however, entered a few years later in Ukraine when Ivan Voronaev, a Russian Baptist who had converted to Pentecostalism while pastoring a congregation in New York, returned to the Russian Empire as a missionary in 1921 and settled in Odessa. By 1924 he had formed the Union of Christians of Evangelical Faith, and within another four years he was able to claim 350 assemblies with 17,000 members.[2] Pentecostals were not the only ones experiencing rapid growth at this time.

Pentecostals were able to spread rapidly during the advantageous political climate of the 1920s, when the Soviet authorities were less repressive toward religion in general, and even outright supportive of groups that could potentially attract members away from the powerful Russian Orthodox Church. The rapid rise of Voronaev's Pentecostals brought the attention of the Soviet authorities, and as the climate of religious tolerance changed under Stalin, Voronaev was imprisoned. He was released in 1935 but was shortly rearrested during the height of Stalin's purges, never to return. Thus began the Pentecostals' long period of persecution and their fight for religious freedom.

Despite persecution, purges, and war, by World War II the number of Pentecostals in the Soviet Union had reached 80,000.[3] It is also estimated that the movement was already 50 percent non-Russian, with strongholds in Belarus, Ukraine, and the newly incorporated territories along the post-war Soviet border, including the Baltics, eastern Poland, and Moldova.[4] Following the war and Stalin's liberalization on religion policy, they began to spread again, first throughout the black earth region and the Russian heartland, then moving east to Siberia and even to the Russian Pacific coast.

The end of the war led to a new Soviet strategy toward the Pentecostals, as well as the Baptists and other Evangelicals—to unite them into a single organization that could be used to monitor, co-opt, and infiltrate them, the All-Union Council of Evangelical Christians–Baptists. To the Soviets, the common theological belief in believer's baptism was apparently sufficient to warrant uniting these two groups who differ so much in theology and ritual.

While the Baptists emerged as the leaders of this group, the Pentecostals as a whole were unhappy with it, not only due to their disdain for centralized organization (which the Baptists favored), but due to the negative attitudes against them that they perceived from the Baptists and others in the union. Most of the Pentecostal congregations eventually joined the union, but only after an agreement that was supposed to be a concession to the Pentecostals by the Baptists. Instead, it was used to encourage them to preach against and eventually abandon practices such as foot-washing, glossolalia, and other "manifestations of the Holy Spirit that might destroy the decency and decorum" of Pentecostal religious services.[5] Essentially, the Baptists were trying to put an end to practices with which they were uncomfortable and disagreed theologically (for instance, the Baptists believed speaking in tongues was only a gift of the Holy Spirit to the Apostles themselves). Of course, this meant nothing short of eliminating the very practices that distinguished the Pentecostals from the Baptists.

In the end, Soviet authorities were able to force most Pentecostals to join the AUCECB. According to official figures, some 25,000 Pentecostals in more than 400 local congregations joined, with the majority coming from Ukraine, the Baltic republics, and Belorussia, while most Pentecostals in Russia preferred an illegal existence to AUCECB oversight. Those who were pushed into the AUCECB continually struggled with the Baptists who were its leaders. Even the Baptist journal *Bratskii Vestnik* (Brethren Herald) published articles critical of Pentecostals and their practices, singling them out for their unorthodox beliefs and rituals.

More than other religions, or even other Protestant denominations, the Pentecostals were "strange" to the Soviets—their speaking in tongues, love feasts, foot-washing, and "shaking" (as they would shake while speaking in tongues; they were even known colloquially as "shakers") all struck the average Soviet citizen as fanatical and bizarre. This was a fact the Soviet authorities played up; they made a short documentary on the Pentecostals, "In the World of a Nightmare," which was shown before full-length features in theaters, much like the "support the war" films shown in the United States during World War II. A photo-documentary was also produced in magazine form and made available, showing some excellent examples of antireligious propaganda (and some really bad examples of Soviet photo-doctoring).[6]

The Pentecostals behaved differently in more ways than just their rituals. Politically, Pentecostals were some of the first to engage in anti-Soviet political activities. As early as 1957, a full decade before the dissident movement in the

Soviet Union was to get under way, a pipe-fitter in the Kherson shipyards and his Pentecostal brethren "crashed" an atheism propaganda lecture.[7] After the young atheist lecturer (incidentally, a former Orthodox seminarian) finished his sermon on religion as a false doctrine, the Pentecostal elder responded that he did not believe only because he had never seen a genuine miracle, at which point he began trembling and speaking in tongues in front of the gathering. Behavior like this—coupled with Soviet propaganda efforts—did little to improve the image of Pentecostals among their fellow citizens.

Khrushchev's de-Stalinization and "thaw," while allowing greater freedoms in many areas, actually brought about an increased attack on religion, leading to the most severe persecution of religious belief during the Soviet era. In such a climate, the Pentecostals pursued a new strategy. Rather than face off with authorities, they migrated frequently, moving farther and farther east and eventually finding something of a refuge in Siberia. One account states that they moved as frequently as every two to three years, enjoying religious liberty upon settling in a new area unfamiliar with them and their practices, and then moving again as a group once local resentment and suppression became intolerable. This behavior must also be seen as part of their missionizing effort—if not as a strategy, then as an added benefit.

The Pentecostals understood the means of repression being used against them and tried to use that knowledge to thwart Soviet attempts to curb their activity. They were known to spend months planning clandestine meetings in the countryside, frustrating attempts to monitor and track them. To avoid the eye of the authorities, they would pass on information using only word of mouth, not phones or written announcements. Then, at the predetermined date and time, they would descend upon a river embankment or hillside in droves, sometimes ten to twenty thousand of them, with hundreds of candidates for baptism. As they conducted their service, they would ignore the police and KGB, who tried to disperse them but were unable to do so due to their large numbers and their lack of fear of Soviet authorities. Oftentimes, however, resistance was impossible, as the Soviet authorities would resort to harsher methods, such as water cannons and tear gas, tactics that proved more effective at breaking up the Pentecostal gatherings.

Perestroika and the Restructuring of Russian Pentecostalism

As Gorbachev launched his grand plan for restructuring economic, social, and political life in the Soviet Union in 1987, under the label of perestroika (restructuring), he initially showed little interest in liberalizing religion policy. His reforms, some thought, would perhaps differ little from those of Khrushchev, who liberalized much of Soviet life while simultaneously cracking down on religious belief. But the historical coincidence that 1988 would be the millennial anniversary of the baptism of Rus' excited many, both within the Orthodox fold and outside it—indeed even outside the Soviet Union itself.

Politburo member Konstantin Kharchev, who would be one of Gorbachev's strongest supporters, himself wrote an article in *Pravda* in January 1988 calling for a reconsideration of Soviet policies regarding religion: "We should ensure the correctness of our legislation on religious cults," he stated bluntly, and "the juridical principles of freedom of conscience," and bring them into line with contemporary circumstances.[8] Then in March Kharchev met with Orthodox religious leaders and informed them that perestroika was going to help find a solution to the problems concerning the activities of churches and religious associations in the Soviet Union.[9] Things on the church–state front were changing rapidly. As recently as 1986, the CPSU party program had listed religion among other "vices" such as corruption, alcoholism, and theft of state property. In Pospielovsky's phrase, "faith in God was still treated as a pathological deviation from the norm."[10] Though slow in addressing the issue of religion, in the first few months of 1988 Gorbachev quickly undid much of the restrictive Soviet policies toward religion from the previous seventy years.

While legislation and policy would take some time to be fleshed out, believers learned of these changes via the media and responded almost immediately. It was in this environment that all religious organizations began to experiment with the new-found freedoms of perestroika. Often this took place within the already established religious structures, while at other times and for other "groups" (sometimes these "groups" were very informal, even being referred to as *neformaly*) these experiments were simply spontaneous and sometimes fleeting attempts to practice beliefs and rituals that had been banned for so long. The case of Pastor Alexander discussed at the outset of this chapter is only one such example.

Although it would take until 1991 for the USSR to issue its new law on religion, the Russian Republic issued its own law in 1990, the Law on Freedom of Conscience and Religious Belief. This very liberal law introduced legal religious equality for the first time in Russian history, including the establishment of a secular state and a true separation of church and state. As with all new policies, however, its exact effects could not be determined in advance. One consequence of the law, which might have been predictable but was certainly unintended, was the flourishing of an open market of religious competition, one that prompted a dramatic increase in evangelism, proselytism, and the emergence of indigenous New Religious Movements (NRMs). This law then gave legal sanction to almost all of the activities that Pentecostals and others had been experimenting with over the preceding few years.

The 1990 law not only opened up Russia's domestic religious sphere, it also permitted Western religious organizations to began to operate in Russia, including established churches as well as new religious movements. Sometimes they did so in less than sensitive fashion, descending on a city and labeling their work a "crusade," and bombarding the local population with pamphlets asking them about their plans for the afterlife. It is no surprise that many were met with resistance not only by many of their intended converts, but also by government officials and the Russian Orthodox Church, as presenting a threat to Orthodoxy and even to Russian national identity. Before long, conspiracy theorists began to link these groups with the CIA— apparently their attack on Russian national identity was no coincidence, but part of a sinister plan to weaken Russian society so it could be more easily defeated. While the Orthodox Church quickly began to take a defensive position against Western religious organizations operating in Russia, many Pentecostals welcomed Western cooperation and, as they saw it, assistance. In fact, this further exacerbated a rift between those who welcomed their Western coreligionists and those who wanted nothing to do with them, and was a significant contributing factor to the division between the various forms of Pentecostals in Russia and Ukraine today.

The collapse of the Soviet Union opened up the religious marketplace, allowing religious groups of various persuasions, both previously established and newly introduced, to practice their faith and engage in evangelism. With nearly a century of persecution behind them, Pentecostals reinvented themselves in several ways; they began to experience significant growth among their congregations, often referred to as the "third wave" of Pentecostalism. Of course, most congregations experienced growth during this period of relative religious freedom, but Pentecostals perhaps experienced more than others. According to official statistics, the percentage share of Pentecostal/ charismatic churches in Russia, for example, almost quadrupled between 1985 and 2009, rising from 1.8 percent of total religious organizations to nearly 6 percent (calculations made by the authors).[11]

By rapidly adapting to the more accommodating sociopolitical environment, many new churches, attended primarily by the younger generation, began to emerge. The post-Soviet period has witnessed the mass registration of newly established Pentecostal churches of diverse persuasions under the legal protection of various "umbrella organizations." As a result, a particular Pentecostal union may include congregations with very different theological views. This spectrum of "new" and "old" churches characterizes the modern Pentecostal movement in Russia and Ukraine. What unites them is their common recognition of the baptism of the Holy Spirit as evidenced through speaking in tongues as an essential component of their Christian experience. They differ, however, over which gifts Christians may possess, their forms of worship, mission strategies, and what constitutes an appropriate relationship with secular culture.

Varieties of Pentecostalism

Though there is great solidarity among the different branches of Pentecostalism in Russia and Ukraine today, scholars have found it useful to categorize them into various groups. Lunkin developed the useful classification of Pentecostal congregations in Russia as traditional Pentecostals, moderate Pentecostals, and charismatics or "new" Pentecostals.[12] Traditional Pentecostals trace their lineage to the first wave of Pentecostalism in Russia during the 1910s and 1920s, and which established themselves during the Soviet period. They are traditional in both the liturgical and theological sense, and one could even refer to them as ultraconservative. They reject any attempt to modernize the liturgy or theology, and they condemn what they see as excessive emphases on spiritual gifts as carried out by other Pentecostals. Their conservatism also extends to social behavior, and they continue to adhere to a strict code of conduct (including a conservative dress code). In terms of church-state relations, they are staunchly separationist, and refuse to establish relations with the state. They survived underground during the Soviet era and today function as independently from the state as they can.

The moderate Pentecostals also trace their roots back to the first wave, but they have proved willing to establish relations with the state, leading to charges of having been co-opted/compromised. Like traditionals, they are also theologically conservative, but as their name implies, they constitute a more moderate wing of the first wave. Moderate Pentecostals are also less strict and accept more emotional forms of worship, though they generally reject overly emotional responses during liturgy, such as screaming, falling down, wailing, and they have a more relaxed attitude toward modernizing worship services (including using rock music).

Despite some disagreements between traditional and moderate Pentecostals over such questions as proper church administration and the role of women in the church, they still hold to similar theological principles. They consider themselves the spiritual children of Ivan Voronaev, and their foundational beliefs include the doctrines of conversion, holiness, sanctification, and baptism by the Holy Spirit as evidenced by glossolalia. They are known to eschew innovation in worship and to criticize extreme expressions of emotion and external signs, which are prevalent in charismatic churches. They have come to look with deep suspicion at the new Pentecostals, whose emphasis on worldly prosperity is looked upon by them as a deviation from the teachings of the humble carpenter from Palestine. Additionally, they advocate disengagement from modern secular and political concerns, which they consider as antithetical to their pacifism.

Moderate Pentecostals in Russia center around the Union of Christians of Faith–Evangelical-Pentecostal (UCFEP), while in Ukraine they simultaneously organized a similar organization, the All-Ukraine Union of Christians of the Evangelical Faith–Pentecostals (AUUCEFP). Both were founded in 1990, and consist primarily of loosely connected autonomous churches that had been incorporated into the AUCECB following World War II. By the end of the 1990s the Russian UCFEP numbered more than 1,500 churches which, according to some estimates, now have 100,000 or more members. Although data are not available on its membership, the Ukrainian AUUCEFP contains nearly as many churches, despite the fact that Ukraine's population is one-quarter that of Russia. Unlike their traditionalist counterparts, moderate Pentecostals have no problems with innovation in worship. At the same time both camps chide new Pentecostals for their insistence on prosperity, the manifestation of spiritual gifts, and the emotionalism that accompanies their services. For Pentecostals of both stripes, these excessive charismatic manifestations are signs of the abuse of the gifts of the Spirit rather than their genuine experience.

The new Pentecostals can be traced back to the early Gorbachev era, even predating perestroika, at which point they began to break away from the traditional and moderate Pentecostals and even to emerge spontaneously. Although Kuropatkina and others attribute their emergence to the third wave of Pentecostalism brought by American missionaries after the passing of the 1990 Russian religion law, in fact their roots are more squarely indigenous and can be traced back several years before.[13] Based upon our fieldwork and interviews with church leaders who emerged at this time, we argue that new Pentecostalism found expression in the third wave and embraced it, but they were responding to emerging social realities in their own way, without knowing of parallel developments taking place in the West, or indeed what had been going on for decades. The story of Pastor Alexander with which we opened this chapter is a prime example of how such new Pentecostals emerged from the other two Soviet-era variants.

Several characteristics distinguish the new Pentecostals from their traditional and moderate brethren. They are open to accepting new revelations from church leaders and have adopted more emotional forms of worship. They tolerate and even promote more active exercise of gifts of the spirit, including healings, prophecy, bursts of emotion during service. They support the use of popular culture in their services, such as rock music, references to contemporary trends and issues. Also of great significance is their very relaxed dress code. There are no requirements for wearing head coverings or against wearing makeup. Together, these things all give the service and the religious experience in general a sense of being modern and also helps appeal to the younger generation. In fact, this is part of what church leaders themselves have referred to as "image-maker," or the process of image-making for the church.

While all Russian Pentecostals practice the gifts of healing, prophecy, and revelation, the presence of these features in worship differs. For example, unlike traditional and moderate Pentecostals, new Pentecostals tend to organize grandiose "faith healing crusades" for stadium-sized audiences, not unlike their U.S. counterparts, with those seeking healing coming on stage. They also seek an outpouring of the gifts of prophecy and healing at every service. In addition, they typically embrace a more emotional, hard-edged style of preaching with full acceptance of a wide range of dramatic responses, including crying, laughing, and shouting. By contrast, traditional and moderate Pentecostal worship is more subdued, the emphasis being placed on inner spirituality rather than outward emotional outbursts, which they see as a sign of "carnality" rather than a genuine Christian experience.

Despite the relative distinctiveness of the various streams of Pentecostalism, in fact these groups are not always so easily distinguished from each other. As Kuropatkina points out, pastors and individual believers do not always easily fit into these interpretational frameworks, and there are even differences among members of a single church and different cliques within the church.[14] In general, however, these are useful categories and help explain the differences one observes. But collectively they do all share a larger Pentecostal identity.

New Pentecostals and Intra-Group Identities

The new Pentecostals themselves can be broken into several groups in terms of their relations to theology, culture, society, and the state. These groups can be described as intellectuals, fundamentalists, general masses, and official Pentecostals. The intellectual Pentecostals, given their unique embrace of the accoutrements of modernity, are of the most importance to us here, but let us first dispense with the other groups. The fundamentalists principally orient themselves toward the American model of Pentecostalism and/or the leadership of individual charismatic leaders. They fight against acculturation with larger society and adhere to strict internal discipline. They also maintain a sharp separation between church and state. In general, they stand in conflict with the wider culture, including state, society, and even other religious groups.

Less staunchly aligned against the state than the fundamentalists but still suspicious against power and wider society are what have been described by Kuropatkina as the general masses (*osnovnaya massa*), or they could perhaps be better described as mainline Pentecostals. They believe that "God's children" should be involved in politics, and they will fight for their rights when the need arises, though they are usually loyal subjects of the current regime. They try to be modern, and find value in modernity, but they do not go so far as attempt to articulate what that modernity might look like or to embrace the sort of Pentecostal modernity found among the intellectual Pentecostals.

Somewhat more outspoken about their rights, though still loyal to the new Russian state, are the official Pentecostals. This group includes the Pentecostal union headed by Sergei Ryakhovskii, the ROSKhVE. They are in solidarity with the general masses group on questions of prosperity and healing, though with greater emphasis on education and embracing the political process, which plays out in terms of their rights as a community of believers but also as regards the democratic process more broadly. This embrace of democracy, moreover, is not collective in terms of promoting a single political position among members, but rather simply encourages members to be engaged with the political process and larger society according to their own conscience.

Finally, there are the Pentecostal intellectuals, who are the most engaged with the state and who place the greatest amount of emphasis on education, knowledge, and modernity. Their emphasis on education includes liberal education and even the study of the theology of the Russian Orthodox Church. They strongly embrace democracy, including democratic methods within the church itself. In this regard they are very much concerned with the secular world, they are at the forefront of the new Pentecostals, and they constitute something of a vanguard that seeks to promote education and knowledge of both world culture and Russian culture more specifically.

We can see in almost all groups of the new Pentecostals a manifestation of the "middle-class" Pentecostalism we are interested in here. The one easy exception is the fundamentalists category, whose stance against culture and nonpolitical orientation makes it difficult to label them "middle-class." The other possible exception is the intellectuals, but we might exclude them for a different reason. They are *too positively* oriented to modernity, and are something of an elite that approximates what Timothy Shah has labeled an "Evangelical intelligentsia."[15]

The Consequences of Belief

Evidence from around the world suggests that the spread of Pentecostalism has consequences far beyond the church walls. A person's conversion to Pentecostalism not only results in different theological beliefs and religious practices, but seems to impact his or her economic, civic, and political values as well. The spread of Pentecostalism, therefore, may facilitate the spread of civic engagement and democracy, help generate strong bonds of social capital among members, and promote entrepreneurship. These "progressive Pentecostals,"[16] who are moved to address "the spiritual, physical, and social needs of people in their community," also behave differently themselves, and their forms of behavior may contribute to the spread of democracy and the development of a market economy.

Evidence from Russia and Ukraine seems to support much of this thesis, but not entirely and not without some important exceptions. Our research indicates that Pentecostals in Russia and Ukraine may not be any more politically efficacious than their Orthodox, Catholic, or agnostic countrymen. When it comes to joining boycotts, signing petitions, or joining in demonstrations, Pentecostals seem very much like their neighbors of other faiths (but more politically engaged than their nonbelieving neighbors). Membership in political parties is almost unheard of, though this is true for 99 percent of citizens in both countries. Democracy as an ideal, however, is embraced, with more than a quarter of Russian Pentecostals agreeing that "democracy may have problems, but it is better than the alternatives." Similarly, more than a quarter value having a democratic political system. These numbers actually fall short of devout Orthodox believers, of whom more than 40 percent agreed that democracy is the best political system and also valued living in a democracy.[17]

When it comes to their civic commitments, Pentecostals also trail Orthodox Christians. While more than 6 percent of Pentecostals say they have signed a petition, more than 10 percent of Orthodox responded similarly. Likewise with attendance at lawful demonstrations, with 18 percent of Pentecostals responding that they have, compared to more than 22 percent among Orthodox.

In terms of the much-touted consequences of Pentecostal belief for economic mobility, our available data have not yet provided clear evidence in support of this thesis, though there are some positive associations. As one of the authors here wrote back in 2006, Orthodoxy is not inconsistent with free-market economics, and there may be something of an "Orthodox ethic" that facilitates the "spirit of capitalism."[18] That piece also pointed out the positive association between valuing hard work and Orthodox Christianity, with 93 percent of Orthodox agreeing that children should be raised to value hard work. The good news is that there is no difference between Pentecostals and Orthodox in this regard, and both groups are more likely to agree with this statement than nonbelievers. But whereas only 55 percent of Orthodox agreed that work was important in their lives, an amazing 85 percent of Pentecostals feel that way—so much for the debunking of the Weberian Protestant ethic thesis.

When it comes to economics, we can begin to see the lingering effects of the Soviet period, and perhaps the Russian imperial system as well. While they may value hard work and be excellent entrepreneurs, Pentecostals in Russia and Ukraine are not Friedman neoliberals. Rather, they are significantly more Keynesian and support government intervention in the economy, both to provide a social safety net and to limit excessive wealth.

Finally, if their survival strategy during the Soviet era proves anything, it is that Pentecostals are able to use their social capital to carry out all sorts of activities, ranging from mercy ministries and relief efforts to dissident political activities and clandestine religious services. What is distinctive about them, however, is their strong in-group bonds of social capital. That is, the social capital that they are best at generating is more "bonding" as opposed to "bridging" social capital.[19] So while it may certainly facilitate a whole range of benefits for members of the group, it does not do so much to connect the group to the larger society, or to help achieve societal-level objectives. While this seems to be the case with Pentecostals, the charismatics discussed above seem much more agile and better able to connect with others in the community.

Russia and Ukraine are so diverse that even with our substantial research findings it is still too soon to reach any robust conclusions regarding the relationship between Pentecostal faith and its socioeconomic consequences. While more research into the topic is still needed, evidence collected thus far certainly seems to support the thesis that there are likely to be significant civic, economic, and political consequences to the embracing of Pentecostalism in Russia and Ukraine. The question is whether or not these consequences will all be positive.

Scholars of religion in Russia, such as Roman Lunkin, who studies sociological and political aspects of Pentecostalism in modern Russia, argue that Pentecostalism in its various forms has become in many respects a conduit of economic and cultural globalization, along with other Protestant sects and denominations. Pentecostals, much like many other Protestant Evangelical groups, have done their share to contribute to the modernization of social structures in the target country.[20] One such place where Protestants and, more specifically, Pentecostal, neo-Pentecostal, and charismatic churches have had visible and enduring success has been in the countries of the former Soviet Union, where economic dilapidation combined with the breakdown of law and order contributed to the inflow of great numbers of missionaries from the United States, Sweden, South Korea, and even Brazil, effectively redefining the field of religious competition or introducing one where none had existed before. According to Lunkin, more than any other Evangelical group in the former Soviet Union, Pentecostals have found a "common language with globalization."[21]

One of the greatest Pentecostal and neo-Pentecostal contributions to the post-Soviet religious landscape has been the creation and promulgation of novel social norms and claims. These are broadly defined Christian norms that, while drawing inspiration from historic Christian teachings, are nevertheless articulated in a new social idiom commensurate with the socioeconomic realities at hand. These also have certain normative dimensions that in the context of Russia and Ukraine and the predominance of Orthodox Christianity are considered foreign cultural imports, and therefore suspect. Despite the tacit hostility, however, neo-Pentecostal and charismatic churches have succeeded in attracting followers, not the least because of their attitudes toward financial responsibility and economic entrepreneurship in general. For many people, neo-Pentecostal and charismatic churches have become social and economic "micro-environments"[22] where their economic and financial ambitions are not only *not* frowned upon but are actively *encouraged*. What sets these sorts of micro-environments apart from others is that financial prosperity is not an end in itself, but is animated by a higher goal, the financing of God's work on earth, and more specifically contributing to the evangelization of their respective communities, cities, regions, and so on.

Financial prosperity can therefore bring about certain otherworldly commitments to the world of here and now. It is prosperity, but a burdensome one. It is a prosperity colored with Christian normative claims and the burden of social responsibility. Thus understood, the drive for prosperity and wealth is not animated by laissez-faire greed, but by the Great Commission of Christianity. With the influx of missionaries from the West, churches underwent gradual changes with regards to finances and economic success. If before it was inconceivable to reconcile a prosperous life with the Christian calling to a life of austerity and inner spiritual prosperity, following Jesus' injunction "For where your treasure is, there your heart will be also," extensive interaction with overseas missionaries tended to change the perceptions of local believers. Many of these missionaries came from churches that emphasized financial prosperity and their teachings regarding finances, tithing, and the like, were influenced by what they had been taught in their churches. With time these teachings were borrowed by local Russian and Ukrainian pastors in their own churches and sometimes bordered on obsession with wealth. Wealth became a sign of God's special grace, of election of the believer who had such wealth; consequently material poverty reflected the spiritual poverty of the believer. Thus the social and economic status of the believer was the best indication of the level and the quality of the believer's faith in God. Some of the most colorful proponents of this theologically dubious position were Ukraine's Nigerian-born charismatic pastor Sunday Adeladja and Riga's Aleksei Ledyaev, who nevertheless have extensive networks of churches throughout both Russia and Ukraine. Adeladja and Ledyaev also are close friends, exchanging visits to each other's churches quite frequently. Sunday Adeladja and his Embassy of God Church have been at the forefront of the "prosperity gospel" wishing for an "army of businessmen" throughout Ukraine and elsewhere to rise up and take back millions and billions of dollars that Satan has stolen from the church, and put it to work for God. As Lunkin has noted, market economics thus both contributes to and becomes necessary "for the realization of the ideals of Pentecostalism, in many ways defining the sociopolitical views of Pentecostal leaders."[23]

Although many of the proponents of prosperity gospel have since moderated their position, realizing the economic peculiarities of their countries and following the increasing unpopularity of the teaching among regular parishioners, in the late 1990s and early 2000s this teaching spread like wildfire —some would say like a virus—through neo-Pentecostal and charismatic churches throughout the former Soviet Union. Yet in a more balanced form, in countries such as Russia and Ukraine with transition economies, neo-Pentecostal and charismatic churches became social spaces where baptism in the Holy Spirit was taking place along with baptism in the Weberian "spirit of capitalism," educating parishioners in the importance of evangelism and of financial prosperity, emphasizing hard work and self-reliance but also community-conscious social programs, encouraging believers to achieve success in commercial, social, cultural, and increasingly political spheres.[24] In this moderate position money and wealth are perceived to be given not for enjoyment of earthly goods, which are here today and gone tomorrow, but in order for the faithful to invest it for the extension of the kingdom of God throughout the earth. This emphasis is indicative of a shift toward hard work and entrepreneurship, rather than financial blessing that comes regardless of the believer's business acumen or the quality of his or her faith.

Pentecostalism, Charisma, and Routinization

The resurgence of Christianity in Russia and Ukraine after seventy years of scientific atheism is possibly the great irony of the Communist experiment. Perhaps more than anything other than private property, the Communist Party sought to eradicate religion from the territory under its control. However, while it came perilously close, it ultimately failed to eradicate the desire for a spiritual life from people's hearts and minds. Not long after the suppression of religion began to relax, both formal and informal forms of religion began to emerge. In the end, the Soviet regime was effective only as long as it carried out repressive measures, and this success was limited to public displays of religion, not private belief. As soon as forced secularization ceased, desecularization began almost immediately. Religious belief did not simply return previous levels; in the case of religions such as Pentecostalism, it began to spread like never before.[25]

The story of the suppression, survival, and revival of religion has many amazing chapters, but the phenomenon of Pentecostalism stands out as one of the most harrowing. More than most other religious groups, Pentecostals survived under the most intense Soviet efforts to destroy them, and after the collapse of the Soviet Union they underwent one of the most dramatic revivals. Compared to some other religious groups who have an equally long history in the region, including Baptists, Lutherans, and Methodists, Pentecostalism and charismatic religion have experienced growth far outpacing these others. In Ukraine, Pentecostalism has grown so quickly and effectively that it is now a significant player in the country's religious economy. In Russia, on the other hand, it is still a minor player; but given its size and diversity it may only be a matter of time before Russia follows the Ukrainian model.

Whether or not Pentecostalism and charismatic Christianity will bring about democracy, vibrant civil societies, and free markets in Russia and Ukraine is still only a matter of speculation. It will take much more research and more time to pass before a clear path can be discerned and a trajectory mapped out. What can be concluded, however, is that Pentecostalism is proving itself a popular choice in the contemporary religious marketplace, and that that choice is not without significant civic, economic, and political consequences.

Finally, the case of Pentecostalism in Russia and Ukraine is a clear demonstration of the routinization of charisma. With Jesus, Muhammad, and Siddhartha Gautama, charisma was held by one person, and religious institutions emerged that sought to harness that charisma and wield its power after the charismatic figure left this world. Charisma then passed from a religious figure to a religious institution, and the teachings became routinized, formalized, dispersed, and ossified. Theologically, Pentecostalism has the potential to liberate charisma from this cycle, as it prevents charisma from becoming the sole property of the priestly class as the "gifts" can be possessed by all believers who manifest signs that they have received the gifts of the spirit, including glossolalia. Rather than an organization that can dictate what is right by reference to some special status or secret knowledge, Pentecostalism keeps charisma alive and tends to prevent its routinization.

In the Soviet Union, however, charisma became routinized as well. Perhaps this was because the Soviet persecution of religion forced Pentecostal leaders to develop a siege mentality, and to lie low and avoid attention. The fact that Soviet authorities also did their best to organize Pentecostals in a large, centralized religious body (one that was even antagonistic to its beliefs) also must have played a role in that process. Harnessed in this way, Pentecostal charisma became routinized as well, and the gifts of the Holy Spirit could only be used properly in certain contexts—not, for example, in a public place such as a hospital. These limitations were the result of political exigencies demanded by the survival strategy of the Pentecostals during the Soviet era, however, and not true components of the belief system. And once liberalization began, despite the fact that the institutions of the old Soviet-era Pentecostals were not prepared to liberalize, other less socialized members of their community fought the very routinization that had emerged. The result has been the emergence of a great diversity of "old" and "new" forms of Pentecostalism, representing a great wealth of theological and sociopolitical positions, but all sharing the belief in the transforming power of the Holy Spirit.

NOTES

1. William Fletcher, *Soviet Charismatics: The Pentecostals in the Soviet Union* (New York: Peter Lang, 1985), 28.

2. Walter Sawatsky, *Soviet Evangelicals Since World War II* (Scottsdale, PA: Herald Press, 1981), 43.

3. Steve Durasoff, *The Russian Protestants* (Teaneck, NJ: Fairleigh Dickinson University Press, 1969), 55.

4. Walter Kolarz, *Religion in the Soviet Union* (New York: Macmillan, 1961), 333–334.

5. Sawatsky, p. 93.

6. *V Mire Koshmara: Foto-ocherki* (In the World of a Nightmare: A Photo-study). Keston Archive and Library, Baylor University.

7. Sawatsky, 337.

8. Konstantin Kharchev, "Utverzhdaia svobodu sovesti" (Defending Freedom of Conscience), *Pravda* (27 January 1988), 3.

9. Moscow Patriarchate, "Celebration of the Millennium of the Baptism of Russ [*sic*]," Press Release, 11 May 1988: 2.

10. Dmitry Pospielovsky, *The Orthodox Church in the History of Russia* (Crestwood, NY: St. Vladimir's Seminary Press, 1998), 353.

11. *Religii Rossii: Uchebnoe, Spravochno-analiticheskoe Posobie Po Voprosam Gosudarstvenno-konfessional'nykh Otnoshenii i Religiovedeniiu* (Religions of Russia: Educational, Reference-analytical Aid on Questions of State-confessional Relations and Religious Studies) (Moscow: Russian Academy of State Service Publishers, 2009).

12. Roman Lunkin, "Traditional Pentecostals in Russia," *East-West Church & Ministry Report* 12:3, Summer 2004

13. Oksana V. Kuropatkina, *Religioznaia i Sotsiokult'urnaia Samoidentifikatsiia "Novykh" Piatidesiatnikov v Rossii* (Religious and Sociocultural Self-identification of "New" Pentecostals in Russia) (unpublished doctoral dissertation, Moscow State University of the Humanities, 2009), 15–18.

14. Ibid., 18.

15. Timothy Shah, "An Emerging Evangelical Intelligentsia? How the Evangelical Mind is Opening and Why it Matters." Conference program, Institute on Culture, Religion, and World Affairs, Boston University. Available at: http://www.bu.edu/cura/projects/evangelicalculture/

16. Donald Miller and Tetsunao Yamamori, *Global Pentecostalism: The New Face of Christian Social Engagement* (Berkeley: University of California Press, 2007).

17. Christopher Marsh, "Orthodox Christianity, Civil Society, and Russian Democracy," *Demokratizatsiia: The Journal of Post-Soviet Democratization* 13:3 (Summer 2005).

18. Christopher Marsh, "Orthodox Christianity and Market Transition in Russia," *Society* 44:1 (2006): 36–41.

19. Robert Putnam, *Bowling Alone: The Collapse and Revival of American Community* (New York: Simon and Schuster, 2001).

20. Roman Lunkin, "Protestantizm i globalizatsiia na prostorakh evrazii" (Protestantism and Globalization on the Expanses of Eurasia) in *Religii v evrazii* (Religion in Eurasia), ed. Aleksei Malashenko and Sergei Filatov (Moscow: Moscow Carnegie Center, 2008), 91.

21. Ibid., 93.

22. Ibid., 101.

23. Ibid., 104.

24. Ibid., 101.

25. Christopher Marsh, "Religion After Atheism," *Society* 48:3 (2010): 247–250. See also Christopher Marsh, *Religion and the State in Russia and China: Suppression, Survival, and Revival* (New York: Continuum, 2011).

SEVEN

Pentecost amid Pujas: Charismatic Christianity and Dalit Women in Twenty-First-Century India

REBECCA SAMUEL SHAH
AND TIMOTHY SAMUEL SHAH

Ernest George, pastor of the Garden City Assembly of God International Worship Centre, one of Bangalore's fastest growing and wealthiest Pentecostal churches, sat at a large oak desk when we visited him in August 2010, with his brass nameplate and two books prominently perched near him: one by Joel Osteen and the other by Rick Warren. Pastor George's church boasts a membership of over three thousand people, drawn mainly from Bangalore's growing middle class and the younger generation of Christians who grew up in the mainstream Church of South India or Mar Thoma Church. The Garden City AG church is entirely self-supporting. It has purchased a large building complex that houses its sanctuary, children's ministry buildings, and a state-of-the-art music school.

In the interview, Pastor George talked about his belief that India is a "rich country" and that Indian Christians should support themselves. He expressed his passionate eagerness to prove to Bangalore that Christians too can be "successful and important" members of society. During a recent visit by a missionary pastor from Durban, South Africa, George suggested an impromptu offering be taken. For their South African visitor, the congregation raised thousands of dollars—*dollars,* not rupees, Pastor George took pride in emphasizing—in a single collection at a single service. Indian Pentecostals, he wanted to underscore, are not lagging behind modernity but are surfing the wave of modernity to heights of success, status, and prosperity.

While million-dollar sanctuaries are being constructed to cater to one group of middle-class and upwardly mobile Pentecostals in Bangalore, another less well-known but equally dynamic track of Pentecostal growth winds its way through the slums and urban poor areas of the city. These are the ubiquitous "independent churches." These independent churches—reminiscent of "storefront" churches in urban America—are self-supporting microcommunities, separate from mainstream denominations. They unabashedly proclaim the full use and manifestation of the Pentecostal gifts of the Spirit. They are situated right in the middle of slum areas that are home largely to Dalits and poor members of the lower castes. Most of the congregants are Dalit (low caste, "untouchable") converts, and the Pentecostal pastors are often also Dalits.

Pentecostalism in India appears to be experiencing dramatic growth. But like everything in twenty-first century India, it is growing in a stratified way. We propose that Indian Pentecostalism will continue to progress in a two-tier way. The middle-class Indian Pentecostal movement, characterized by large megachurches such as the Garden City Church of God, led by Ernest George, and the Full Gospel Church of God in Bangalore, under the leadership of Paul Thangiah, draws its inspiration and in some cases its direction from American Pentecostalism. This movement will continue to serve urban middle-class young people who favor its Western-style worship and its understanding of the demands that modernity places on upwardly mobile people.

A very different form of Indian Pentecostalism is what may be called the "storefront Pentecostal movement." Our focus in this chapter is on this movement, and we suggest from a close examination of a small section of northern Bangalore that this movement, too—like its wealthy cousin—is in a high-growth mode. Beyond that, and more importantly, we propose to illuminate something of the inner life and culture of storefront Indian Pentecostalism by exploring how Dalit women participate in its distinctive congregations, cell groups, prayer meetings, and faith practices. Our goal here is not to explain what factors make Pentecostalism more appealing than Hinduism or Islam to the poor Dalit women we interviewed in the slums and shanty-towns of northern Bangalore. Our goal is to explore and elucidate how the Pentecostal religious faith of poor Dalit women functions in their lives—not only as instrumental in enabling them to achieve some modicum of social and economic freedom, but also as constitutive of their identities and sense of well-being. This paper explores how and why a poor Dalit woman, in the context of twenty-first-century Bangalore, could conceive of Pentecostal faith as valuable not just as a means of achieving extrinsic social and economic ends but as a worthwhile and constitutive end in itself. What we suggest is that it is not just that Pentecostalism in urban India is increasing its outreach *to* Dalit women—although that is happening. Rather, Dalit women are actively constructing their own Pentecostalism, and in the process Pentecostal Dalit women are defining and owning a distinct identity as independent and active Christians.

Where Is India on the Pentecostal Map?

There is a dearth of literature on Pentecostalism in India. Michael Bergunder's largely historical examination of Pentecostalism in southern India remains the only major monographic study of Indian Pentecostalism. Even so, it is essentially a catalogue of basic information—an impressively comprehensive catalogue, to be sure—concerning the early history of south Indian Pentecostalism, recounting the who, the what, the when, and the where.[1]

Why do scholars of Pentecostalism tend to neglect India? The lacuna is perplexing. Certainly with India's brimming spirituality and vibrant religious "marketplace," Pentecostalism's Indian forms and trajectory should have excited serious interest.

Scholars such as David Martin and Paul Freston have highlighted Pentecostalism's remarkable growth and impact on individuals, societies, and cultures in Latin America. Furthermore, Freston's work on Brazil raised important issues concerning the role of Pentecostalism in shaping the political landscape of the country.[2]

Alongside this continuing focus on Latin America, in the last twenty years, African Pentecostalism has gained prominence both in academic circles as well as in the public sphere. Through a wholehearted adoption and adaptation of the "prosperity gospel" in a wide variety of imported and indigenized forms, many African Pentecostals leaders—typified by Ezekiel Guti, founder of the Zimbabwe Assemblies of God Africa (ZAOGA), the subject of definitive scholarly treatment by David Maxwell, a contributor to this volume—became enormously influential in the religious and political fields.[3]

For most of the twentieth century, Pentecostalism has remained a powerful yet complex part of the religious landscape of India. The result is that at the time of this writing, in 2012, one can already speak of something like four generations of Indian Pentecostalism. In 1898, during the Keswick Convention in Keswick, U.K., Pandita Ramabai, a Marathi Brahmin convert to Christianity asked for prayer for a "missionary awakening" among Indians. Moved by what was happening in Wales and parts of Australia, Pandita Ramabai started a prayer circle in 1905 that led to a great revival in the Mukti Mission in Kedgaon, Maharashtra. The years that followed were accompanied by various manifestations of the Spirit and the use of tongues. Pandita Ramabai's Mukti Mission became a key link between the burgeoning Pentecostal movements in the West and in India.[4]

Encouraged by what was happening in places like the Mukti Mission, some Western Pentecostal missionaries went to India not long after the Azusa Street revival in Los Angeles that began in 1906. In 1908, an American,

George E. Berg, who was a participant in the Azusa Street revival, came to India and settled in Bangalore. Berg had already been to India as a missionary, and he used his relationship with the Brethren Christian community of Kerala, a state on the west coast of India, to spread the word about Pentecostalism. Robert Cumine, an Anglo-Indian Pentecostal worker, helped Berg to evangelize the people of Kerala, and by 1912 they had developed a fairly substantial Pentecostal congregation comprised mainly of converts from the Brethren movement in Kerala.

Already during World War I and the interwar period, indigenous Indian Pentecostal missionaries who had been trained under American Pentecostal missionary Robert Cook were given much freedom to evangelize and spread the word on their own, without the oversight of Western church leaders. The dispute between the Assemblies of God missionaries and the local Pentecostal leadership vis-à-vis the identity and title of the new church marked a new direction for the Pentecostal movement in Kerala. K. E. Abraham, one of the rising stars of Kerala's Pentecostal movement, broke completely with his missionary patrons and decided to build and register a new Pentecostal church in the name of the local congregation—against the express wishes of Mary Chapman, a British Assemblies of God missionary.[5]

Without a doubt, indigenous Pentecostal leaders such as K. E. Abraham were influenced by the parallel movement of the Ceylon Pentecostal Mission (CPM), which had originated in Ceylon in the middle of the 1920s and had successfully operated independently without any guidance or support from the West. Robert Cook continued to support Abraham, although he did not agree with the church's association with the CPM and in particular with their faith principles. Once Abraham was able to set up his own Indian Pentecostal Movement, which he fully controlled, he became the sole and powerful leader of one of the largest indigenous Pentecostal movements in India at the time.

As a result of the disruption and struggles in the Pentecostal movement, so-called "Thomas Christians"—the Syrian Malabar Nasrani, as they are commonly known in India—set themselves up as the leaders of the movement. Thomas Christians trace their origins to the missionary activity of St. Thomas the apostle in the first century CE and regard themselves as the oldest Christians after the Assyrians. Throughout the centuries Thomas Christians have maintained a strict adherence to caste and social structure and as such are regarded as "upper-caste" Christians who do not associate with "low-caste" or "untouchable" people, i.e., those who often call themselves Dalits (literally "broken people") today.

The upper-caste Thomas/Syrian Christian leadership that dominated the Pentecostal movement in Kerala in the early 1920s did little even to attempt to bring in the vast number of Dalit converts to Pentecostalism. This was despite the fact that Pentecostalism attracted numerous Dalit converts in Kerala and around south India. So great was, and is, the caste divide between Thomas Christians and Dalits in Kerala that it was not until the 1970s—with the support of K. P. Yohannan, an Indian pastor working the United States—that the Indian mission agency Gospel for Asia was formed to help develop indigenous Pentecostal missions to serve Dalits.

It is clear from the history of the Pentecostal movement in India, be it in Kerala, Tamil Nadu, or Andhra Pradesh, that the movements are marked by new and evolving challenges, such as the rapid growth of independent churches, as well as the lack of a cohesive Pentecostal identity to maintain spiritual and territorial unity in the vast religious marketplace of Indian Christianity. However, some modern charismatic Indian evangelists and revivalists have been an important resource for keeping the movement alive and consistently attracting large numbers of new members. During the 1980s and into the latter part of the twentieth century, one such Indian evangelist, D. G. S. Dhinakaran (1935–2008), became a key figure in raising the profile of Pentecostal faith principles, especially among the Tamil-speaking peoples of southern India. His personal warmth, combined with his dynamic sermons delivered to large audiences in an American evangelistic style, not only catapulted him into Pentecostal superstardom but made him one of India's most popular Christian leaders.[6]

Dhinakaran's "Jesus Calls" ministry, with pamphlets printed in all the South Indian languages, was particularly important because it reached large numbers of Tamil-speaking Christians and non-Christians throughout southern India, including Dalits in Tamil Nadu and those who had migrated to Karnataka and Andhra Pradesh. The popular evangelist's open-air meetings were for most Indians the first opportunity to witness an open and highly theatrical yet accessible demonstration of such gifts of the Spirit as healing, speaking in tongues, and prophecy. In Bangalore, one of the present authors, Rebecca Shah, personally attended Dhinakaran's meetings with her grandmother in the 1970s and 1980s and witnessed throngs of poor lower-caste and Dalit people—mainly from the nearby shantytowns and slums—making their way to the podium after the sermon to receive healing and special words of prophecy.

In the first one to two generations, then, Pentecostalism in India progressed at two levels. On one hand, there were mainstream indigenous Pentecostal churches, whose leadership was dominated by elite castes who did little to encourage the participation of Dalit members, much less Dalit leaders. On the other hand, a few Pentecostal evangelistic outreach activities, such as Jesus Calls or the All-Night Prayer meetings of N. Jeevanandam, presented Pentecostalism to the masses and kept the movement alive among Dalits and members of lower castes.

In Indian Pentecostalism's third and fourth generations, however, from the early 1970s to the present, there has been relatively little serious mapping or study of what has transpired. Yet we propose that it is only in the last decade and a half that Pentecostalism in India has taken off and come into its own as a distinct and sociologically significant phenomenon.

Pentecostalism in India: Christianity for the New Millennium?

To illustrate the growing influence of Pentecostalism among the urban poor, we conducted a mapping of a geographic area of northern Bangalore roughly equivalent to 1.5 square kilometers, or just under one square mile, in June 2010. This area included three of the oldest and best-known shanty-towns in Bangalore: Baglur, New Lingarajapuram, and Williams Town. Over the course of more than two months, we attempted to note every single prayer room and small independent church that dotted these slum areas.

Within this compact 1.5-square-kilometer area alone, we identified *no fewer than 117 Christian churches*. We found that 99 of these churches are identifiably Pentecostal or charismatic in some sense, based on interviews with church leaders and members, while only 18 are mainline Protestant or Roman Catholic churches or cell groups. Of the Pentecostal churches, however, only five belong to established Pentecostal denominations, such as the Assemblies of God or Ceylon Pentecostal Mission, while a full 87 are independent and mostly small storefront Pentecostal or charismatic churches.

These independent churches range from the Agape Church, which had an official membership of 3,000 people as of the summer of 2011, to the Gateway Hope Church, which had an official membership of 40, including the pastor and his family of four. By our reckoning, the average membership of the smaller churches ranged from around 40 to around 200 members.

All of the independent churches in our sample area were entirely self-supporting, sustained by the voluntary financial contributions of their members, not by external missions agencies. Worship was usually conducted in Tamil but in a few cases in English. In addition to the weekly Sunday services, a majority of these independent churches conducted weekly fasting and prayer meetings, which in some cases lasted all night, usually during the weekend. Only one church in our survey area had a female pastor, although there were many women evangelists who lived in the community and were actively involved in evangelism in the local slum areas. Many of the female evangelists were Dalit converts from Hinduism.

Beneath Bangalore's Flyovers: Understanding the Context of the Research

In the last twenty years, thanks to the generous support of the World Bank and a few wealthy private investors, the city of Bangalore has been crisscrossed with flyovers (overpasses, in U.S. English) and four-lane highways. Within a half hour one can be transported from Bangalore's new international airport into a designer-decorated office on Mahatma Gandhi Road, at the center of South Asia's technology mecca. Today, as they speed along the flyovers, few visitors even have the opportunity to see the underbelly of the city, with its still teeming slums and shantytowns. Strategically placed billboards advertising diamond necklaces or an upcoming concert by Elton John serve in effect as blinders as one zooms along the neon-lit pathway into Bangalore's information-technology metropolis.

Beneath one of the largest flyovers linking the airport to the main city lie the three large slums in northern Bangalore mentioned earlier. It is here, as noted, that we conducted our ethnographic survey of independent storefront Pentecostal churches.

Bangalore is divided into ninety-nine wards. Each ward has a controller responsible for the overall upkeep of the ward, as well as for securing grants from the state government to sustain various civic amenities and social services for the benefit of the ward's citizens. The composition of the wards is usually mixed, with some areas hosting large mansions and modern apartment buildings and others featuring slums and shantytowns.

Baglur slum is situated in Sagayapuram, which is coextensive with ward 60. The total area of the ward is just under a square kilometer, or less than half a mile. It contains over three thousand slum dwellings. In the last ten years, Baglur received a water connection, even though no home has a direct water line; water is available at certain times of the day at public taps situated within the settlement. Baglur has electricity and one tarred road. For over twenty years, the controller of this ward was Ms. Marimuttu, also known as the Hooch Queen, because twenty years ago her illegally brewed moonshine killed hundreds. Ms. Marimuttu was never arrested and continued to stand for election, which she won handily on four successive occasions.

Across the road from Baglur is the Lingarajapuram slum, based in ward 49. It measures about one square kilometer in area. In 1988, in order to woo

wealthy middle-class votes, Mr. Ramakrishna Hegde, who was then seeking
the office of chief minister of the state of Karnataka, promised to rid Bangalore
of the "terrible slums" in the center of the city. Many of the slum-dwellers
were migrant workers who were brought to the city in the 1950s to construct
Karnataka's massive legislative assembly building, the Vidhana Soudha. Once
elected, Mr. Hegde forcibly evacuated five thousand slum families from the
fashionable Queens Road and Millers Tank areas and placed them beyond
the city limits, in Lingarajapuram. Bereft of housing, employment, and access
to water and electricity, the residents of Lingarajapuram were left to fend
for themselves. Overnight, Lingarajapuram became one of Bangalore's most
notorious and dangerous slums. After dusk, few auto-rickshaw or taxi driv-
ers were willing to drive beyond the railway lines that divided respectable
Richards Town and Thomas Town from Baglur and Lingarajapuram.

The residents of these slums are primarily Dalits. The word literally means
"broken"; it is used to describe people traditionally regarded as "untouchable"
or "outcaste," according to the Hindu caste system.[7] An estimated 75 percent
of the slum population in Baglur and Lingarajapuram is Dalit Hindu, about
12 percent is Dalit Muslim, and about 12 percent is Dalit Christian, primarily
from a Roman Catholic background. The Dalits in the slum, whether they are
Hindu or Christian, mostly belong to the Adi Dravida group. This is a group
of Tamil-speaking Dalits who trace their origins to Tamil Nadu, although
the residents of Baglur and Lingarajapuram slums have by and large lived in
Bangalore for more than three generations.

One is born a Dalit and will die a Dalit—that is the way things have
been for centuries in India. Dalit status is a matter of irrevocable, hereditary
ascription, conferred by birth. Dalits are often employed in occupations that
befit their hereditary status—occupations that are seen as ritually polluted
and unclean—such as road sweepers, tanners, cleaners, and rag pickers.

While the caste system and the associated social status of Dalit are of
course derived from the indigenous collection of customs, traditions, and
rituals known conveniently though misleadingly under the umbrella of
"Hinduism," it is well known and firmly established that Muslim and Christian
Dalits are treated as socially distinct and utterly inferior communities by their
own coreligionists. "Upper-caste" Christians maintain their social distance
from Dalit Christians by prohibiting inter-caste marriages and imposing
severe sanctions on those who violate this prohibition. Segregation extends to
the religious sphere, in which upper-caste Christians tend to favor the mainstream churches such as the Church of South India, the Lutheran Church,
and the Mar Thoma Syrian Church. While the presence of a central hierarchy
in the Roman Catholic Church in India, which often deliberately flouts caste

prejudice in episcopal appointments, helps to reduce caste stratification in the church's leadership, Dalit Catholics are more like to attend Mass at different times than upper-caste and middle-class non-Dalit Catholics.

In a 2010 study that assesses the social and economic differentials between Dalits and non-Dalits of the same religion, Christians show greater *inter-caste* differentials and stratification than Muslim, Hindus, or Sikhs.[8] Dalits from all religious backgrounds earn similar amounts of money. The monthly per-capita consumption expenditure (MPCE) for the vast majority of Dalits—about 75 percent—regardless of religious background is less than 1,000 rupees per month ($22, or 75 cents a day). Yet the study reveals that the majority of upper-caste Christians (up to 75 percent) earn above $55 a month or $1.8 a day, and the top 25 percent of upper-caste Christians earn more than 4,050 rupees a month ($90 a month), which is four times greater than the amount earned by the average Dalit Christian. Upper-caste Christians are significantly better educated and are more likely to have occupations with regular wages, rather than serve as casual/landless laborers like their typical Dalit Christian counterparts. The inter-caste differentials between Dalits and upper-caste Christians are particularly marked in urban areas. Dalit Christians live in an entirely different socioeconomic world from that of their non-Dalit, upper-caste coreligionists, who dominate the leadership and membership of churches such as Ernest George's Garden City Assemblies of God Church.

The Microfinance Context:
Divya Shanthi Christian Association

Divya Shanthi Christian Association (DSCA) is one of the largest and most well-established community development organizations working in the three slums of northern Bangalore under discussion. Its microfinance program began in 1999 and has grown from about a hundred to some three thousand clients by 2010. Divya Shanthi is a confessedly Christian development organization, but one that nonetheless serves and employs people from all faith backgrounds. The basic DSCA microfinance product is a "canonical" group loan product. "Sangams" or self-help groups of ten to fifteen women are formed, and the women are jointly responsible for the loans of their group. Each group has a president who serves as the liaison with Divya Shanthi and who works with a Divya Shanthi social worker to organize group meetings and to collect the loan repayments. Loans to individual sangam members can range from 1,000 to 15,000 rupees. Loans must be repaid in fifty weeks, and DSCA charges an interest rate of 12 percent. If all the group members repay their loans on time, they are all—as a group—eligible for larger additional loans.

Given the circumstances in which most of the clients live, DSCA does not require that the loan be used primarily to start a business. The clients are given the freedom to determine how they wish to use their funds. Some women choose to use the money to fund their children's education, with some paying for their teenage children to attend college or to attend a better private school. Others choose to take a loan to help finance or purchase a vehicle for their husband's business.

Anyone who is at least eighteen years of age, who has been part of a sangam for more than a year, and who has some valid proof of address, such as a ration card, a voter card, or an electricity or hospital bill, is eligible for a loan. While the women are free to form their own sangams, DSCA ensures that sangams are not otherwise formed on the basis of ascriptive characteristics such as caste or creed. DSCA can thus prevent women from being excluded from sangams on the basis of caste or religion. However, some clients may be excluded if they fail to convince their fellow group members that they are able and likely to repay the loan. DSCA also provides monthly business training and guidance on preparing accounts and advises the women on how to set up savings accounts to save for contingencies and for upcoming family events and festivals.

We chose to interview a group of fifty women who were established clients of Divya Shanthi Christian Association's microfinance program. We interviewed women from Pentecostal, Hindu, and mainstream or "mainline" Protestant, Muslim, and Roman Catholic backgrounds. In order to gain a better understanding of the role of Pentecostalism in the lives of some of the women, we interviewed a larger number of Pentecostal women than other women. The women live in the three slum areas, Baglur, New Lingarajapuram, and Williams Town. The areas were selected because of the established presence of DSCA in these urban poor settlements for the past forty or so years. Because of the organization's long and trusted presence, we were confident that we could ask sensitive questions about earnings, family life, and especially about the client's faith and faith practices without raising eyebrows—something that is not necessarily easy or straightforward, since sectarian and communal tensions are common in Bangalore's slums. We selected these areas because—despite the fact that they are commonly called "slums"—they are not temporary dwellings but are permanent settlements with concrete houses and established water and electricity supplies.

All the women we interviewed had belonged to microcredit sangams for a minimum of two years. They were all established residents of the slum.

All the women were aged between 30 and 55, and they all had children and/or grandchildren living in the home. All the women had taken a loan from DSCA and had successfully repaid the loan in full.

Of the 50 women we interviewed, 27 identified themselves as members of independent Pentecostal churches. During our interviews, we discovered that 25 of the 27 Pentecostal clients were converts from Hinduism and 2 were converts from Roman Catholicism. There were no converts to Pentecostalism from Islam or mainstream Protestant denominations. Of the women interviewed, 7 were Muslim, 10 were Hindu, 4 were Roman Catholic, and 2 belonged to the local Anglican/Protestant community church.

The average Pentecostal family is a family of five, with a monthly expenditure of between 6,000 and 6,500 rupees ($130 to $150). Of the 27 Pentecostal women and their families, 11 lived in a house they owned and the rest of the Pentecostal women lived in a house they rented. All homes had cement floors, and all the homes had access to a common or a private latrine. The average rent for a one-room house with a common latrine and an electricity connection is between 3,000 and 3,500 rupees in the Baglur and Lingarajapuram areas. The value of land is between 1,000 and 1,500 rupees per square foot. The high cost of land is because the area has become prime real estate due the development of the nearby international airport and the burgeoning software industry in Bangalore. Almost all of the children between the ages of 6 and 16 go to school, and about 90 percent of the children aged 16 and above go to pre-university or college preparatory classes. A majority of the children from Pentecostal families (98 percent) go to private schools. These private schools include St. Nirmala Convent School, run by Roman Catholics; Divya Shanthi School, run by the Divya Shanthi Christian Association; or other private nursery schools in and around the slum area.

All Pentecostal women we interviewed had borrowed from the sangam. In addition, 7 of the 27 women had outstanding loans from moneylenders, friends, or neighbors and family members. Only 5 of the 27 Pentecostal clients had bank accounts, whether a current account or savings account. Apart from the regular saving and borrowing with the sangam, 80 percent of the Pentecostal clients had no strategies to help them cope with economic shocks such as a medical emergency.

Of the 27 Pentecostal clients, 10 either ran a small business or took out a loan to help their husband's business. The rest of the loans contributed to the down payment on or lease of a house, purchase of a consumer durable such as a refrigerator or washing machine, or payment toward the college education of their children. In almost all cases the husband was an auto-rickshaw driver. In cases where there was a business, it required low capital investment and had only one employee. The business assets usually included a wet grinder machine to grind grains such as rice, a sewing machine, a pushcart, candle-making equipment, and cheap plastic toys and utensils. When asked what would be the one item they wished to purchase if they had the money, 99 percent of Pentecostal clients said gold jewelry.

Yellama, Allah, and Yahweh: Understanding Worship and Faith in the Slums

Situated at the foot of the new Hennur Road flyover and immediately in front of the entrance to the Baglur slum stands a large, brightly decorated temple dedicated to Yellamma. Yellamma, sometimes known as Renuka, is commonly considered the incarnation of Kali, the goddess of death. Yellamma is the patron goddess of Dalit women, especially Dalit girls who are dedicated to serve the temple. These "devadasis" or "godly slave girls" are sold into prostitution and have become part of the growing sex trade in India. Shrines to Yellamma, Durga, Kali, Mariamma and the other incarnations of the goddess are found around the slum.

The attraction of the goddess Yellamma lies in her own sorry story. According to the myth, Yellamma was sentenced to death by her angry husband, the sage Jamagdani, for failing to return on time with water for him to drink. She was killed by one of her sons who did not wish to further infuriate his irate father. Feeling remorse for his mother's death, he asked his father to restore her life. No sooner did she return to life than she abandoned her life and family to live among the people of the lower castes, who vowed to worship and protect her. All the Dalit Hindu women in our sample were ardent followers of the goddess Yellama, and some of them had her name tattooed on their arm. The goddess Yellamma may be the only member of the whole pantheon of Hindu gods and goddesses who truly understands the ostracism and sense of abandonment of the outcaste, and especially of outcaste woman.

As for Muslim women in the Baglur and Lingarapuram slum areas, they do not go to the mosque to pray. If they do wish to pray outside the home, they will visit the tomb or *darga* of one of Bangalore's most famous female Sufi saints, Hazrath Bibi. Hazrath Bibi's darga is housed in a small building that is decorated in green silk cloth and red roses. People from all over the city stream through the darga to listen to the singing and chanting of the Sufi musicians.

During one of our interviews, Shanu, a thirty-year-old Muslim mother of five, told us that when she needs to pray for deliverance from illness or from financial problems she goes to the darga and brings home a rose. When asked why she likes to visit the darga instead of just staying at home to pray, she replied: "Just as the fragrance of the rose flower fills my small hut, that is how I know that God is with me and will deliver me from these problems." In the absence of regular opportunities to meet with the leaders or members of one's faith community, such as an imam, a darga such as that of Hazrath Bibi provides an important way for Muslim women to find religious community and a sense of concrete access to Allah.

Situated in the heart of Baglur slum and behind the local "arrack" (home-made liquor) distribution center stands a large hall with a corrugated iron roof. This is Agape Christian Fellowship, an independent Pentecostal church started by Pastor Reuben Satyaraj in 2006. Pastor Satyaraj comes from a respectable middle-class family; he used to be a heroin addict who attempted suicide more than once. He does little to hide his past. Indeed, he makes a special point of talking about his failures during the church services. This type of vulnerable Christian leadership may be familiar in some Christian circles in the West, but it is somewhat rare in Indian Christian communities, where the pastors are revered to such an extent that they are called "Iyer," a term used to describe a Hindu Brahmin priest who is often seen as a special emissary of the gods.

In 2006, Pastor Satyaraj welcomed twenty families every Sunday morning. Today Agape Christian Fellowship has over 3,000 members from both Baglur and New Lingarajapuram slums. In addition to the weekly church services, Agape holds daily prayer meetings and weekly fasting and prayer meetings. The church has a dedicated team of female evangelists who visit local women and serve to consolidate the membership of the fellowship. During our interviews, interestingly, Pastor Reuben Satyaraj refused to call his church a Pentecostal church, even though it clearly emphasizes the charismatic gifts of the Spirit, insisting instead that it is an "independent church that believes in sharing the gifts of the Spirit in all its manifestations." In his view, "Pentecostal" is a label that immediately places a church in the "mainstream" and makes it less accessible to those who live on the margins in the nearby slums.

Every evening at about six o'clock, Hindu families make their way to Yellamma's temple, while the lively worship songs of the Agape Independent Church remind nearby Pentecostal Christians of the evening prayer and worship meeting. On the other side of the street, Muslim women make their way to the darga of Hazarat Mastaani Ma, a female Sufi saint.

Most of the Muslim women we interviewed did not participate in joint worship and communal life. Uneducated Dalit Muslim women learn to recite the Koran from memory and pray alone or only with other female members of the family. When Haseena, a young single mother of four, was asked about whether she goes to the imam or to other senior Muslims to ask for prayer during times of crises, she replied, "Of course not, how can I ask them to pray for me? They are so busy talking to Allah." If they are in search of a faith community and an experience of common worship, Dalit Muslim women head to the darga of Hazarat Mastani Ma on Tannery Road, which is behind the slum and just beside the local abattoir.

In contrast to the austere and sparse whitewashed mosques of northern Bangalore, Hazarat Mastani Ma's darga is brightly decorated in green and gold silk. The tomb is covered in bright green silk cloth as well as jasmine flowers and rose petals. Musicians and singers fill the building and dance to celebrate the saint. Dalit Muslim women from all around the local Baglur area come to the Mastani Ma's shrine to join the dancing and singing of *ghazals,* and to enjoy spontaneous fellowship with other worshippers. At the darga, Muslim women can experience worship in an egalitarian community.

The experience of "spirit-filled" worship is not exclusive to Christian worship in Pentecostal churches, then, but is also seen in the trance-like worship practices at the goddess Yellamma's temple and at the darga. In India, a woman's receptivity to the gifts of the Spirit is regarded as impressive because she is able to worship in a unique way. During our conversations with Pentecostal clients, most of them were keen to mention their participation in the gifts of the Spirit, such as their ability to cast out demons, speak in tongues, and make prophesies about the future. For most of our Pentecostal clients, no conversion narrative was complete without a detailed description of the convert's prophetic dreams and visions about themselves and their families.

Reinventing Themselves: How the Pentecostal Poor Change Themselves and Claim the Future

In an interview, Joyce, a Pentecostal convert from Hinduism, described a "prophetic dream" in which her husband, Raja, an alcoholic and an adulterer, would be burned in a fire at work. She tried to warn him about her dream, but he ignored her. According to Joyce, a fortnight later, Raja suffered third degree burns from a kerosene oil stove at work and lost his job.

While a Pentecostal woman's charismatic gifts of prophecy and glosso-lalia are dramatic demonstrations of the power of her faith, it is her ability to explain and discuss the Bible that just as surely inspires the respect and deference of her community. Unlike their Muslim and Hindu neighbors, who participate in worship on the fringes of their faith community, Pentecostal

women such as Joyce operate as leaders in the church and are given responsibility to lead fasting and prayer meetings and healing services. Instead of
merely observing worship or participating in it as but one member of the
congregation, Joyce volunteers her home for weekly meeting and assumes
formal leadership to pray, read the Bible, and sing hymns and worship
songs. The pastors of the local Pentecostal churches in Baglur, like Agape
Independent Church, encourage the women to "experience" the Spirit and
to also delve deeply into the Bible. Women are asked to articulate their faith
and demonstrate the authenticity of their conversion experience through
oral testimonies. Many women, like Joyce, become motivated to attend adult
education programs to learn to read once they discover that they have access
to "knowledge" and the authority to participate in leadership and worship.

Pentecostalism's emphasis on the power of the spoken and written word
among the women in our study encourages verbal competence, an ability to argue, and the development of the fundamental skills necessary for
full-fledged involvement in the participatory politics of modern societies.
A majority of the women in our study did not attend school at all; those
that did attended elementary school for only two years. Yet a majority of the
Pentecostal clients mentioned that—second only to prayer—it was the ability
to read and understand the Bible that gave them the courage and strength to
cope with the numerous day-to-day challenges of their lives, such as domestic violence, abuse, unemployment, depression and poverty.

Furthermore, not only do the women begin to understand the value of
Bible reading and literacy for themselves, they also begin to value education
for their children. All the children of the Pentecostal clients in our study
attend school. Over 80 percent of the children of the Pentecostal microcredit
clients attend private or fee-paying schools. Private schools, unlike the local
government-run Kannada-medium schools, charge higher fees but tend to
provide a higher-quality education, with better teachers, lower dropout rates,
higher test scores, and a rigorous academic English-medium curriculum.

Sitting across from me in a neatly pressed blue sari and beside a shiny
burgundy LG refrigerator was Anthaz, mother of five, and successful busi-
nesswoman and owner of two small grocery stores in Baglur. Her walls are
pasted with Bible verses, and prominently displayed above the fish tank was a
calendar complete with the daily devotion and blessing from Pastor Satyaraj,
pastor of her independent church—which, as we saw earlier, is the luxuriantly
charismatic Agape Christian Fellowship that nonetheless makes a point of not
associating itself with the Pentecostal label. Anthaz excitedly recites all the
passages on the wall, complete with references and cross-references, and offers
to read us a passage from her well-worn Bible before we begin our interview.

For many of the women converts to Pentecostalism, the ability to understand and interpret the Bible figures prominently in their testimonies and has often contributed to their decision to become Pentecostals. Anthaz is a convert from Hinduism who became a Pentecostal after a brief interlude as a Roman Catholic. An active member of the Agape Independent Pentecostal Church, Anthaz speaks openly about the reasons she left the Catholic faith: "The sermons [in the Catholic church] were short and lasted for only seven or eight minutes. The priest did not talk from the Bible. And if he did read from the Bible, he didn't explain it to me. At Agape Church, Pastor Satyaraj explains the Bible and teaches me to use the Bible to deal with my everyday struggles at home. During problems at home I know what to do. I pray Psalm 121 to myself and I know that God is with me." Posted above her stainless steel cupboard in Anthaz's tiny living room is a list of Psalms and Bible passages that Pastor Satyaraj gives his church members to use during their daily meditation and prayer time. Such biblical education is an aid to propagation. Pentecostal clients are zealous evangelists; many women memorized passages or took adult literacy classes to read and explain the Bible to their non-Christian neighbors.

The confidence borne of literacy, leadership, and participation is exemplified in the way Pentecostals in Baglur relate to politicians, including representatives of the Hindu-nationalist Bharatiya Janata Party (BJP) and its militant wing, the Rashtriya Swayamsevak Sangh (RSS). The state of Karnataka has witnessed a marked BJP ascendancy since 2004 and has had a BJP-dominated government since 2008, and militant Hindu-nationalist groups are believed to have increasingly targeted and attacked Christians in various (especially rural) parts of the state during this period. A meeting with a group of Pentecostal microfinance clients who lived across the road from the local BJP/RSS headquarters in July 2010 revealed that the local Pentecostal church had—to our surprise—managed to befriend the local Hindu nationalist activists and remain a visible, yet unharmed, Christian minority in an increasingly anti-Christian environment. The Pentecostal women we interviewed seemed to harbor neither fear nor loathing of the BJP, RSS, or any other member of the Hindu-nationalist family of organizations. Indeed, when the subject of these Hindu-nationalist groups and their agenda was raised, the reaction of our Pentecostal respondents was serene and philosophical. According to several respondents, they knew the Hindu-nationalist leaders in their neighborhood so well that these leaders told them their militant religious rhetoric was only a tactic to attract votes at election time. Furthermore, many of these same Hindu-nationalist leaders confessed to their Pentecostal friends that they sent their children to Christian schools.

Many of the Pentecostal women such as Anthaz are converts from Hinduism and Roman Catholicism, as we have noted, and many of them report experiences of Hindu and Catholic priests that shaped their personal religious trajectories in important ways. Free education for the children of Roman Catholic parishioners is available only to those who have a family subscription book and who are full, paid-up members of the local Catholic church. If a family does not have a subscription book they cannot be baptized, married, or buried by any local Catholic priest. While not as strict as their Roman Catholic counterparts, Hindu priests are reluctant to perform Hindu rites for babies or conduct marriages and other religious ceremonies if they become convinced that a person has strayed from the Hindu flock. However, our Pentecostal respondents proudly reported to us that if a Pentecostal family in Baglur needs prayer, they simply call the pastor on his cell phone. Within a few hours, the pastor himself arrives or he dispatches one of the local evangelists to pray with the family in need.

Joel Robbins suggests that while Pentecostal converts will not admit the practice of routinized rituals, because they claim an unmediated and spontaneous relationship with the Spirit, they openly and routinely participate in spiritual practices that recognize and incorporate rituals borrowed from people of other faiths.[9] Our own research confirmed this pattern, as we found that the Pentecostal women in our study continued to place a high value on the role of traditional ritual practices such as fasting, all-night prayer, and healing services with the anointing of oil and water. In particular, the ritual of fasting, or *upavacum,* as it is called in Tamil, is the most frequent religious practice among the Pentecostal women in Baglur. Fasting is not restricted to any particular event, and the women fast at any time of the day, and on any day of the year. Hindus and Muslims both understand fasting as a means of obtaining the special favor of God or as a form of worship. So when Pentecostal women undertake to fast they observe a spiritual practice that is recognized by other faiths and also one that the women understand from their preconversion lives as an important means of accessing the power of God. Furthermore, for new Pentecostals the practice of fasting may in part serve as form of signaling that enables Dalit converts to demonstrate to their non-Christian neighbors their complete and wholehearted engagement in the life of their new Christian faith community in spiritual terms their neighbors can understand.

Writing about Pentecostals in Ghana, Birgit Meyer suggests that a primary concern of Pentecostals is making a complete break with the past. Pentecostal converts define their present ideas and values in terms of a radical rejection of their past ideas and values. A Pentecostal convert's life is marked by a tension between the life that existed before her conversion and the life that exists after her conversion. Indeed, ironically, Pentecostals are said to thrive simultaneously on distancing themselves from the past as well as on keeping the past alive by constantly defining themselves against it.[10]

Rather than defining their present by rejecting their past, the Dalit Pentecostal women in our study struck us as more forward-looking than backward-looking. They tended to frame their conversion in terms of opportunity—opportunity to realize their dreams and desires for the future. Both because they are Dalits and because they are women, Dalit women such as Joyce and Anthaz suffer a double subordination and a double marginalization to the shadows of family and public life. They describe their conversion to Pentecostalism as providing a connection between themselves and contexts and experiences that once were beyond their intellectual, physical, and spiritual reach. Conversion to Pentecostalism gives uneducated women such as Anthaz and Joyce an opportunity to use their minds, voices, and hands not in tasks relegated to shameful obscurity, but rather in "good works" with an honored public dimension. They exercise their minds in the reading, memorization, and exposition of scripture. They exercise their loosened tongues in spontaneous songs to God and in the instruction of their neighbors and peers. They use their hands to touch and help and heal people from all castes. For these women, Pentecostalism provides less a destructive hammer with which to smash the past than an aspirational bridge on which to cross over into a kind of dignified and public life they could not live—but desired—before their conversion.

There is another respect in which the familiar frame in Pentecostal studies of a radical break with the past does not work well with many Indian Pentecostals. The relationship of Dalit Pentecostal converts to their past is intertwined with their ongoing relationships with their extended families, many of whom are still Hindus or Roman Catholics, as well as with their neighbors and friends. In most cases, these relationships have by no means suffered a radical rupture. While most of the independent Dalit Pentecostal churches and cell groups formally teach the doctrine that individuals are "saved" one by one through a "born-again" conversion experience, Dalit Pentecostals themselves find it culturally difficult to reconcile this religious individualism with their family life and everyday existence in the slum community. In this, the experience of Dalit Pentecostals in Baglur's slums probably differs somewhat from that of the middle-class Pentecostal congregants in churches such as the Garden City Assembly of God Church. Members of Garden City are mainly young professionals who have moved to Bangalore to succeed in the emerging market economy. Garden City represents a

modern and successful church, which in turn appeals to a young professional's search for the success, emblems, goods, *as well as individuation* of
modernity. Cutting or at least attenuating ties with their mainstream home
church or with their parents and family networks—as in the case of converts
from Hinduism or Islam—makes good individualist sense for professionals seeking a self-affirming and self-liberating Pentecostalism. By contrast,
the Dalit relationships, communities, and networks one encounters in the
slum cut across religious lines and are strong and enduring, built on years of
shared struggles and sorrows. Many of the families in the slum have traveled
together from rural Tamil Nadu and Andhra Pradesh to the teeming unfa-
miliarity of Bangalore. If thriving as an upwardly mobile Pentecostal young
person in Bangalore requires or at least encourages individuation, surviving
as a Dalit Pentecostal in the city's slums requires or at least encourages strong
community within and across religious divides.

Women Reaching for Respect

Much has been written about why millions of women in Latin America
have turned to Pentecostalism over Catholicism in the last several decades. In
a series of studies, Elizabeth Brusco has demonstrated that Pentecostal conversion can be interpreted as a kind of strategy whereby women can sometimes subdue and domesticate male machismo.[11] In his 1997 study, Andrew
Chesnut argues that women in Brazil choose Pentecostalism because it is
a strategy for coping with sickness and suffering. Since women, he argues,
are the primary care givers, they are drawn to Pentecostalism because its
strict laws and moral codes discouraging excessive drinking and careless sex
lead to an overall healthier lifestyle and family environment.[12] Others, such
as David Martin, have suggested that Pentecostalism's attractiveness lies in
its many gatherings and meetings, and hence in its capacity to generate an
"autonomous social space" for women, and men, providing an opportunity
for friendship and a place to share their burdens.[13]

We suggest that for women we interviewed, such as Joyce and Anthaz,
Pentecostalism provides an opportunity to find respect and value within the
community. Many of these women have lived lives of profound and sustained
abuse and abandonment. As worshippers of Yellamma, they remained perpetually on the outside of the temple, and were never allowed inside. Indeed,
they revered a deity who was *herself*—literally—*an outcaste*. The independent
Pentecostal church community, with its openness and lack of upper-caste
pretensions, in contrast with mainstream and middle-class Pentecostalism,
provides an opportunity for Dalit women to find a community of people

among whom they can reclaim their dignity and begin to respect themselves again. For example, what drew Anthaz to Agape Christian Fellowship was the hope that at last she might have an opportunity to find "respect" and "value" through being a full-fledged participant in the activities of the church. Having stood outside the temple for years, she believed that now she could walk boldly into the presence of God at Agape Church and find "value," dignity, and freedom as a person. Not only was it important for women such as Anthaz to come into an active and vibrant faith community, it was also important for them to become agents of the church—legitimate and full-fledged performers of its central and defining rituals and activities. For many people in traditional religions, including in mainstream Christian churches such as the Church of South India or the Roman Catholic Church, the priest or presbyter is at least widely perceived as being solely or largely responsible for meeting and interceding with the transcendent or with the Divine. The congregants are expected to sit and receive his interpretation and blessing. In the independent churches, women such as Anthaz are not mere passive recipients of the church's benefits but are given freedom and encouragement to serve as agents and indeed embodiments of the church.

In the independent churches and ministries, illiterate women become self-assured experts in interpreting the Bible. Previous victims of domestic abuse on whom husbands and boyfriends laid one violent hand after another began to lay gentle hands on others to heal them and cast out the demons of violence and sickness. Fasting and prayer meetings become occasions when women who are unskilled in most things can meet with the transcendent and "hear God" speak to them—and transmit his words to others.

In her book *Valuing Freedoms,* Sabina Alkire recalls what happened when men's and women's groups in a remote desert area in Pakistan called Pan Hari were asked what changes—beneficial or harmful—had taken place as a result of their participating in a development project. Both men and women reported that "nonmaterial" goods, such as growth in their faith and devotion to God, and an increased level of unity and concern for one another, were as important as the accrued "material" goods of health, savings, and education. In other words, the material benefits of the program did not outrank the nonmaterial benefits of the program.[14]

A continuing challenge with the commonly held view that the goal of development is primarily to serve the autonomy or capabilities of the individual as an end in himself or herself is that the poor do not always agree. In her *Women and Human Development,* moral philosopher Martha Nussbaum insists on viewing individual persons as ends in themselves and not as agents or supporters of the ends of others. Each person "has just one life to live, not more than one," she argues, and "the food on A's plate does not magically nourish the stomach of B." Because poor women have been subjugated to violence, abuse, and terrible hardship, the overriding goal must be to give women the bargaining power they need to exercise greater influence on family outcomes, especially when it comes to their own health, safety, and protection.[15] But the objective that may be paramount for a philosopher or for a development organization—say, enhancing the autonomous bargaining power and material well-being of poor women—may not necessarily be the most important objective poor women have for themselves. In *Voices of the Poor: Can Anyone Hear Us?,* one of the most influential and largest cross-cultural poverty assessments ever conducted by the Word Bank, Deepa Narayan, the World Bank's principal social development specialist, discovered that the poor, including poor women, valued "harmony with the sacred" as much as they did being fed, kept warm, or being healthy. In addition, the poor valued relationships with family and with the wider community as much as they valued material well-being.[16]

In our own research, it was striking and significant that women such as Anthaz do not seek to redress the power imbalance in their position and improve their bargaining power at any cost, and particularly not at the cost of abandoning a serious yearning to achieve harmony with the sacred. They find Pentecostal faith attractive because it fulfills a deep yearning: a yearning for a spirituality that binds them to the transcendent as well as to a community that empathizes with their suffering and treats them as equals. These women seek access to the transcendent in a way that marks a radical shift—though not necessarily a violent rupture—from their birth religion, caste, and family traditions and toward a faith that confers dignity, equality, and respect. Armed with a new identity and with a new conception of themselves, they are better able to navigate their way through—and sometimes out of—indigence as well as to a better bargaining position within the family.

Given how much a religious tradition has validated their oppression and unequal status, both as women and as Dalits, it would be easy and understandable if they sought to abandon religion and the transcendent altogether, or were at least quietly or cynically diffident toward spiritual traditions and communities. For many secular feminists, religion is perceived as having a stranglehold on women from which they openly or secretly long to break free. However, for these women, an attractive or at least a possible avenue for redeeming their situation and improving their bargaining position remains the path of spirituality. Storefront Pentecostalism gives poor Dalit women an opportunity to be individuals, seeking the transcendent on their own terms and in their own time. It is within the independent Pentecostal church in the local slum that women come to realize and learn that they can voluntarily participate in a community of equals, and it is within this context of sharing and building an egalitarian community that the woman begins to see herself not merely as a passive recipient of concern but as an active agent of change not only for herself but also for the wider community.

When asked how their neighbors view them, all twenty-seven Pentecostal women said that they view them with "respect." In contrast, all ten Hindu women said that because of the success of their business or because of their new homes, their neighbors view them with jealousy. When asked why they think the community "respects" them, a majority of the Pentecostal women replied that it was because they had "made something of their life." Most of the Pentecostal women who belong to the sangams refuse to open a commercial bank account, explaining that if they do so they will lose the much-needed peer pressure of having to stay on a sound financial path in order to maintain face with their fellow sangam members. Furthermore, they said that they would miss the personal affirmation they receive from their fellow group members when they bring in their loan repayment. Being part of a commercial bank would also diminish their opportunities to help other women.

A majority of the Pentecostal clients were fortunate enough to have received a larger loan than the rest of the group. On average, the Pentecostal clients received a 15,000-rupee loan to begin a business, compared to other members who received 10,000-rupee loans. One reason that explains the tendency of Pentecostal clients to secure somewhat larger loans is that Divya Shanthi staff can verify the character and reliability of the client by consulting the network of independent churches and their pastors. In other words, insofar as they enjoy good reputations as respected members of close-knit independent church communities, the Pentecostal clients can be trusted as a "good risk," and the moral hazard of lending to them is reduced. Additionally, the overhead cost of administering loans to Pentecostal clients is lower. Because the women are well known and respected in the community, giving Divya Shanthi staff a lot of basic, baseline information about the clients, they are less likely to require frequent visits from Divya Shanthi staff to keep their loan repayments on track and are less likely to default on their loans.

In some ways, Pentecostalism provides a "third way" for Indian women. Secular feminism dismisses the role of the transcendent or suspects that faith is unlikely to play a positive role in the lives of these women. Traditionalist communitarians, or people who favor the religion of the group over the good of the individual, tend to dismiss the importance of the individual's own search for the transcendent and the voluntary nature of a person's relationship with the transcendent. Pentecostalism in some of the "storefront" forms we encountered has the potential to restore and secure and the identity and personhood of the individual woman, but not on her own or in isolation. It does so, rather, in community and among people who can identify with her past experience. Through storefront Pentecostalism, women such as Anthaz can sometimes become stronger and more confident precisely because they come to learn that being part of a faith community means that they will not always be the ones in need. In fact, they may be asked to help others and serve others who may never be able to return the favor. They find dignity and self-assurance not so much by acquiring greater power and a superior bargaining position but by expanding their capacity and opportunity for self-giving.

The most important measure of the impact of the independent Pentecostal church on the life of an individual may not be whether it has helped her to achieve a better business or better health at an individual and material level. Rather, it may be whether it has helped her to participate in a community and family in such a way that it uplifts the community and family and enriches rather than diminishes her own individual flourishing at the same time.

Reaching for the Future: Saving and Planning for a Better Life

Selvi sat across from us with her head in her hands, pondering her response to a question we had posed: *Some people believe their life is dominated by fate or some power beyond their control; some people believe their life is in the hands of God; and some people believe their life is in their own control. What do you believe?* She tapped her forehead and said, "Fate, number 1, that's my answer." The Tamil word for "fate" is "*Thalai Vidhi,*" which also means "to hit one's (fore)head." In contrast to Selvi, all our Pentecostal interviewees said that they were certain, adamant in fact, that their lives were in God's hands.

Selvi had taken a loan from the sangam to buy a vegetable push-cart for her husband. The business was struggling because of various family problems, including a serious illness that befell her husband. The family did not have any savings or additional funds to cover the costs of the repayment, and she was in the process of negotiating a repayment schedule with the sangam's president.

One of the biggest problems the poor face is the difficulty of saving money to purchase goods—including education and consumer durables—for which the returns are not immediate but can be realized only in the future (and perhaps only in the very long-term future). In addition, the poor (like everybody else) tend to be woefully economically myopic. They will spend today to win an immediate and relatively small payoff, when they could save today to gain far greater returns in the future.[17] But the poor struggle with the additional burden of having needs that are more dire and immediate and resources that are more meager and uncertain. Indeed, perversely, the very fact that the poor have so little now and are so uncertain about having anything later makes the temptation to spend what they have now for immediate gain even more powerful.

In an influential paper, Banerjee and Duflo conducted a study of the consumption and income generation patterns of the poor—those living on less than $1 a day—in thirteen countries.[18] For those living on $1 a day, spending 10 cents to purchase a cup of chai and a crispy samosa not only makes a disproportionate dent in their pay packet but also appears more tempting than for those who spend the same amount of money but may who earn $50 a day. This is because such "temptation" purchases are more tempting when they are less affordable and are less tempting when they are more affordable.

Among our very small (and admittedly unscientific) sample of women, Pentecostals seemed to operate on the basis of an economic time horizon that enabled them to resist somewhat the overwhelming temptation to sacrifice the future for the sake of the present. According to our group of women, 17 of 27 Pentecostal clients we visited had purchased a refrigerator and a washing machine, compared to 2 of the 10 Hindu clients and 1 of the 6 Muslim clients. When the Pentecostal clients were asked about how confident they were about providing for their family's needs over the next five years, the entire group of 27 Pentecostal women said that they were "*very* confident" about being able to provide for *all* of their family's needs. The majority of their Hindu counterparts—8 of 10 women—said they were "somewhat confident" about the future, while only 3 out of the 6 Muslim women expressed complete confidence in their ability to provide for all of their family members.

Anthaz was one of the Pentecostal women who told me that she is "very confident" that she can provide for her family. But she was not always so confident. Ten years ago Anthaz faced a stark choice: she could either live alone and raise her five children on her own, or permit her husband to bring his mistress to live with the family. It was not much of a choice. Eight years ago, when the drunken husband of Anthaz dragged her by the hair across the street because she refused to cook for him *and* his lover, a lady evangelist from the Agape Christian Fellowship offered to clean her wounds and pray with her. Sister Naomi continued to visit Anthaz and later invited her to church. Despite being beaten and abused by an even angrier husband, Anthaz continued to go to Agape Fellowship. A year later she enrolled in adult education classes with social workers from the Divya Shanthi Christian Association, the local community development organization. Two years later she joined the organization's microcredit sangam and was able to qualify for a 5,000-rupee loan (the equivalent of about $100). Anthaz bought a small shop and started her own business. She has taken four loans and has successfully repaid all of them. In 2010, Anthaz qualified for a 50,000-rupee small business loan from the local commercial bank. She plans to establish two more shops and also to employ some of the members of her sangam. Her husband does not abuse her anymore. But he does not attend church with Anthaz, and his extramarital affairs continue.

One of the features of microfinance credit is that a client is expected to begin repayments often within a week of receiving the loan. These repayments are to be made before any revenue has been earned. While some of the families own a small amount of working capital, such as a sewing machine or a wet grinder, in most cases they may have to use part of their loan to purchase the necessary equipment for the business. Because of these expenses, most clients experience a decline in income in the first few months of taking a loan. In addition, because of Indian affirmative action policies that benefit only members of "Scheduled Castes" or officially designated lower castes that are Hindus or Buddhists, most Christian Dalit and Muslim Dalit clients do not have the benefit of government-provided housing or employment benefits like their fellow Hindu sangam members of Dalit background. Dalit Christians and Muslims have to build or rent their own homes with little or no government assistance. The success of Pentecostal clients in being able to sustain and develop their own businesses is even more striking, then, because on average they have to cover a somewhat higher level of fixed costs in addition to making regular loan payments.

Perhaps more striking is the fact that, in addition to running a business and repaying their loans on time in order to be eligible for a larger loan, most Pentecostal clients reduced their nonessential spending—on movies, festivals, family events, and snacks—in favor of investing in durable goods for the business or the family or in the education of the family's children. The durable goods often included a sewing machine, a refrigerator, or a washing machine. The spending pattern of these clients is doubly beneficial: they not only refrain from spending their money on the temptations of the present, but they invest their money in the long-term welfare of their families and businesses. The results above may echo the finding that following a disciplined life and adhering to a Weberian other-worldly asceticism provides a person with the unintended consequences of economic prosperity and well-being. However, the difference is that these Pentecostal clients seek actively to name and claim a better economic future as a deliberate goal, not as an unintended consequence. In fact, they may well be what Peter Berger calls "intentional Weberians."[19] They seek success and intentionally claim the future because—unlike Selvi, our client who felt trapped by "fate"—the Pentecostal clients expressed a confidence that God has a special plan for them and that their life is in his hands. As such, it is their responsibility not only to live efficiently in the present but to shape and own a future they see as full of promise because it belongs to God.

When asked what was the one commodity they wished to purchase for themselves or their families, 90 percent of our Pentecostal respondents said "gold jewelry," compared to less than 50 percent for our non-Pentecostal respondents. While there may be cultural reasons for wanting to buy gold, most of the Pentecostal clients said they wanted to shore up security for their future and to ensure that their daughters had adequate gold jewelry when they got married. An important implication of this is that our Pentecostal clients wanted some insurance for the future and wedding jewelry for their daughters just as many Indian women do, but the Pentecostal women wanted to purchase gold jewelry now rather than borrow money from the local moneylender to buy their daughter's wedding jewelry later on. The women we interviewed talked about their hope for the future. The important point, though, is that the Pentecostal women we interviewed seemed to believe that the future is a tangible and somehow already present reality—a reality so tangible and so close that they can touch it and shape it and actively bring it into being for their own flourishing and for that of their families.

In the face of overwhelming exigencies, it is all too easy to look upon the future with dread. Consider Joyce, one of our Pentecostal respondents. In a way that dramatizes both the power as well as the limits of storefront Pentecostalism and its influence on poor Dalit women, we discovered that Joyce tried to kill herself three times. The most recent attempt was two days before we went to interview her. She walked to the railway lines with the intention of throwing herself in front of an express train from Hyderabad. After a few minutes, she turned around and made her way back home. Joyce lives with her two children and her husband, who also lives with his mistress down the road. She has been beaten, burned, and raped by her husband, but continues to live and work at home to protect and care for her teenage children.

As part of our interview, we asked Joyce the following question: *Do you believe that God dwells high up in heaven and very far away from you or here on earth and very close to you?* Her response was remarkable for its confidence and clarity. She turned to us, gesturing to her heart, and said, "My God is here within me."

In the course of our survey, we interviewed fifty women, and their responses to the question above were very striking indeed—striking because the Pentecostal clients consistently report a very intimate and intrinsically personal conception of God. This is all the more striking because these women are outcaste Hindu converts who spent their entire lives living on the periphery of family, community, and faith. Yet when asked about God's "location," as it were, a majority of Pentecostal clients replied that God is an intimate presence, residing deep within them or beside them. Most Hindu clients responded by saying that they are confident that God exists, and that he comes to them whenever they call upon him.

Most of our Pentecostal clients said that they prayed more than once a day, and that when they prayed they did so in their own words. Since many of them are illiterate, they recite verses and Bible passages from memory. Joyce was able to recite psalms and Bible passages, complete with references and cross-references, even though she could not read a single word. In other words, Pentecostal faith has not necessarily brought the Dalit women we interviewed peace, happiness, or success. There is little question, however, that Pentecostal faith has transformed Hindu Dalit women's notions of God. In their eyes, the transcendent had changed from being something out there and present only when called upon to being someone who was personally and intimately close all the time. This transformation of the way Dalit women view God is directly related to the way in which they now view themselves. These women now see themselves as respected members of a community and as having a personal relationship with a God who is present in their lives, so much so that they can speak to him in their own words, at any time and in any place. And from this reoriented theology and this self-assured identity comes a new relationship to the world. From having no experience in business, these outcaste women take loans to learn a new trade or build a new enterprise. Having never entered a school building, these illiterate women are saving money to send their children to college. Despite never uttering a word in public for most of their lives, these women go on to give their testimonies on the street and in crowded halls, in front of other women as well as men.

While Pentecostal faith seemed to encourage somewhat higher levels of economic self-sufficiency in the lives of the poor Dalit women we interviewed, the women themselves do not see their new faith as a mere means. We social-scientific observers may see the faith of these women as an imperfect instrument, but one whose imperfections we can forgive because the goals of empowerment, betterment, and self-assurance are so obviously worthwhile. However, it is probable that the women themselves see their new faith in their intimate God not as a mere means to some higher end but very much as the ultimate goal and orienting purpose of their life. And it is probable, too, that in the eyes of these women there is no merely instrumental, mechanistic relationship between their faith in God, on one hand, and the modest relational and economic betterment they have experienced, on the other. Instead, these women believe they are living a faith that intrinsically and organically yields a new identity, a new self-confidence, a new self-assurance, a better life, and the feeling of being respected and loved in a new way.

For these women and their families, it is good to have a refrigerator and a washing machine. But whatever material betterment faith might help bring, its deepest and most enduring value for Joyce is that it helps her live another day, believing that God walks with her, despite all the sadness and sorrow that surround her still.

NOTES

1. Michael Bergunder, *The South Indian Pentecostal Movement in the Twentieth Century* (Grand Rapids, MI: William B. Eerdmans, 2008).

2. David Martin, *Tongues of Fire: The Explosion of Protestantism in Latin America* (Oxford: Blackwell, 1990). For Freston's work on Pentecostalism in Latin America in general and Brazil in particular, see Paul Freston, *Evangelicals and Politics in Asia, Africa, and Latin America* (Cambridge: Cambridge University Press, 2001), and Paul Freston, ed., *Evangelical Christianity and Democracy in Latin America* (Oxford: Oxford University Press, 2008).

3. David Maxwell, *African Gifts of the Spirit: Pentecostalism and the Rise of a Zimbabwean Transnational Religious Movement* (Oxford: James Currey, 2006). See also Terence O. Ranger, ed., *Evangelical Christianity and Democracy in Africa* (Oxford: Oxford University Press, 2008).

4. Allan Anderson, *Spreading Fires: The Missionary Nature of Early Pentecostalism* (Maryknoll, NY: Orbis Books, 2007).

5. Bergunder, *South Indian Pentecostal Movement*.

6. Bergunder, *South Indian Pentecostal Movement*.

7. Chad M. Bauman, *Christian Identity and Dalit Religion in Hindu India, 1868–1947* (Grand Rapids, MI: William B. Eerdmans, 2008).

8. Satish Deshpande, "Dalits in the Muslim and Christian Communities: A Status Report on Current Social Scientific Knowledge," National Commission for Minorities, Government of India, 2008. Available at http://ncm.nic.in/pdf/report%20 dalit%20%20reservation.pdf; last accessed on 21 November 2011.

9. Joel Robbins, "Anthropology of Religion," in *Studying Global Pentecostalism: Theories + Methods,* ed. Allan Anderson, Michael Bergunder, Andre F. Droogers, and Cornelis Van der Laan (Berkeley: University of California Press, 2010), 156–178.

10. Birgit Meyer, "Pentecostalism and Globalization," in Anderson, Bergunder, Droogers, and Van der Laan, *Studying Global Pentecostalism,* 113–130.

11. Elizabeth E. Brusco, *The Reformation of Machismo: Evangelical Conversion and Gender in Colombia* (Austin: University of Texas Press, 1995); Elizabeth Brusco,

"Gender and Power," in Anderson, Bergunder, Droogers, and Van der Laan, *Studying Global Pentecostalism,* 74–92.

12. R. Andrew Chesnut, *Born Again in Brazil: The Pentecostal Boom and the Pathogens of Poverty* (New Brunswick, NJ: Rutgers University Press, 1997).

13. Martin, *Tongues of Fire.*

14. Sabina Alkire, *Valuing Freedoms: Sen's Capability Approach and Poverty Reduction* (Oxford: Oxford University Press, 2002).

15. Martha Craven Nussbaum, *Women and Human Development: The Capabilities Approach* (Cambridge: Cambridge University Press, 2000).

16. Deepa Narayan, *Voices of the Poor: Can Anyone Hear Us?* (Oxford: Oxford University Press, 2000).

17. Robert Strotz was the first economist to study what has come to be known as "dynamically inconsistent" consumption patterns—"inconsistent" because a person's behavior will most likely be at odds or inconsistent with what is his optimal behavior. Optimal behavior is choosing a plan of consumption or spending in the present that will maximize one's utility in the future. However, in most cases, instead of seeking to gain a greater reward for her future investment, she chooses instead to "precommit" her future to satisfy her desires at the present time. Those who continue to behave in such an "inconsistent" manner are often termed "spendthrifts," while others who recognize the errors of their ways and begin to change their consumption patterns are termed "thrifty."

18. Abhijit V. Banerjee and Esther Duflo, "The Economic Lives of the Poor," October 2006; unpublished paper. Available at http://econ-www.mit.edu/files/530; last accessed on 19 November 2012.

19. Peter Berger, "'You Can Do It!': Two Cheers for the Prosperity Gospel," *Books and Culture,* September/October 2008.

EIGHT

Politics, Education, and Civic Participation: Catholic Charismatic Modernities in the Philippines

KATHARINE L. WIEGELE

The Catholic charismatic group El Shaddai is among the most prominent of the renewalist movements in the Philippines, with followership estimates between 3 and 8 million worldwide, up to 7.5 percent of the domestic population.[1] It is likely the largest Catholic charismatic group worldwide with a well-developed prosperity gospel. In 2011 WikiLeaks released a 2005 cable from the U.S. embassy in Manila indicating that the embassy saw El Shaddai and the block-voting Iglesia ni Cristo (the country's largest independent indigenous Protestant church) as highly influential in national politics, a pattern they felt would continue for years.[2] Like other charismatic groups in Catholic majority countries, El Shaddai must contend with the Church hierarchy. However, it operates as an independent church, and this, combined with its prosperity gospel, means it shares much with its Pentecostal counterparts worldwide; members are "renewed" Catholics, therefore their Catholic identities and lifestyles are consciously chosen over other ascribed, mainstream, leftist-influenced, or secular-cultural forms of Filipino Catholicism.

Renewalism in the Philippines cuts across all sectors, though El Shaddai has been mostly a religion of the urban poor and overseas workers. In 2005 I documented the rise of El Shaddai among the marginalized urban poor in the Philippines.[3] I described how, through this new movement, Filipinos fashioned a renewed sense of socioeconomic self-determination, optimism, community, and national political relevance. Residents of the sprawling capital, Manila, created unique ritual forms using mass media and urban spaces that fostered a sense of social and spiritual connectedness. In this chapter, I describe how these ritual forms, along with the movement's prosperity gospel, have transformed not just popular Catholic practice but also understandings and practices of citizenship. Using 2010 fieldwork data, I then examine the developmental tensions that have arisen with the movement's recent investments in education, civic engagement, institutional growth, and national policy debates on population control and poverty. These developments impact attitudes toward gender roles and families, civic participation, and the Catholic hierarchy. They may also impinge on the sense of egalitarianism and spiritual animation that has characterized El Shaddai religious experience up to this point.

Charismatic and Pentecostal Christians in the Philippines

While the percentage of Catholics has remained largely stable at around 81 percent since the 1940s, charismatics (Pentecostals and charismatics in Catholic or mainline Protestant denominations) and Pentecostals (people belonging to Pentecostal churches) have accounted for an increasing segment of the Christian population since the 1970s. In the post-authoritarian era (post-1986) especially, the popularity of both Evangelical and renewalist groups has surged.[4] Around 19 percent of Christians are involved in the Pentecostal or charismatic renewal (15 percent of Catholics and 39 percent of non-Catholics).[5] Because of the Catholic majority, this means that the renewalist movement is largely a Catholic one, as 70 percent of Filipino renewalists are Catholic.[6] Charismatic Catholics are in general more religiously active than Catholics; therefore they may have a disproportionate impact on the Church.[7] Indeed, the charismatic movement is one of the main preoccupations of the Philippine Catholic Church at present, and El Shaddai is the largest of the charismatic groups.

Charismatics and Pentecostals share a distinctive religiosity that they practice diligently.[8] Socioeconomically and attitudinally they resemble the general population, with the educated slightly overrepresented.[9] However, different communities cater to different social classes. According to El Shaddai's social services department, the majority of their members are below the national poverty line, an observation confirmed by my own 1996 surveys. Other Catholic charismatic groups, such as Couples for Christ (CFC) and Loved Flock, cater to the middle class, while still others attract celebrities, businessmen, and other segments of the upper class.

El Shaddai began in 1984, while CFC, the second largest Catholic charismatic group, began in 1981, both in Manila. CFC has some 980,600 members in seventy-six countries.[10] They aim to renew and strengthen Christian family life and values, but they do not espouse the prosperity gospel. Classic Pentecostal churches like Assemblies of God and Church of the Foursquare Gospel began in the 1950s and 1960s.[11] Some of the big players among the independent "indigenous" Pentecostal churches are Jesus Is Lord (1978), the largest, and Bread of Life (1982).[12] In 1983, a network of independent neo-Pentecostal and charismatic churches formed the Philippines for Jesus Movement, headed by Eddie Villanueva, founder and head of Jesus Is Lord. Independent Pentecostal groups represent a highly dynamic sector of Philippine religious life.[13]

Nonetheless, the face of the Philippine renewal is still predominantly Catholic. Charismatic Catholic groups have varying degrees of independence from the Church hierarchy on issues such as style and place of worship, theology, and political engagement. Although the majority of charismatics have inherited their denomination, they arrive at their Catholic identity and values as a result of a conscious, deliberate choice, as "renewed Catholics," distinct from their mainstream counterparts.

El Shaddai Beginnings

El Shaddai began as a nondenominational radio program and within a few years described itself as a Catholic charismatic lay group. Within fifteen years, the group had millions of followers and chapters in nearly every province and in forty countries. Around 30 percent of the followers are overseas Filipinos. For most of its history, the group has been known for its weekly outdoor events in Manila, which each typically attract a half million to a million people. These "prayer and healing rallies" feature lively music and emotional preaching by "Brother Mike" Velarde, the group's founder, and are broadcast nationwide on television and radio. Tapes of Velarde's sermons and monthly magazines circulate widely among overseas workers. Neighborhood chapters hold barrio prayer meetings lead by rotating El Shaddai-trained preachers. The Pentecostal church Jesus Is Lord has a similar organizational pattern.

Brother Mike is a businessman turned preacher, with no formal religious training. His evocative and entertaining preaching style, his populist persona and message of prosperity, and the belief that he channels miracles, however, allow him to attract crowds and monetary collections that are the envy of Catholic clergymen.[14] During the 1990s, responding to criticisms that he was using tithes to enrich himself, he established social services for members, such as a cooperative store and a dental and a medical clinic. He has been influential in national politics to varying degrees, beginning with Fidel Ramos's presidency (1992–1998).

As in other renewalist movements worldwide, El Shaddai religiosity emphasizes the workings of the Holy Spirit (in faith healing, miracles, emotional worship experiences) over doctrine. As a Church-recognized Catholic lay movement, however, Catholic members need not opt out of Catholic cultural traditions like godparenthood and barrio fiestas, as Pentecostals often do. The group, however, downplays some mainstream traditions, such as All Soul's Day celebrations, rosaries, and Virgin Mary devotion. Although El Shaddai operates as if it were independent, chapters affiliate with local parishes, and a Catholic clergyman acts as spiritual advisor to the group. A portion of its collections go to the Church, and mass is said at rallies.

In 1996 I observed neighborhood chapters where El Shaddai healers merged prosperity teachings with shamanic, charismatic, and Roman Catholic style rituals. House calls by shaman-like home-grown "evangelists," for example, involved charismatic elements such as healing, exorcisms, spiritual counseling, speaking in tongues, "slaying in the spirit" (falling under the power of the Holy Spirit at religious services), praying-over, and "binding" through prayers and holy water. These were combined seamlessly with folk and Catholic ritual forms and addressed local social and cosmological concerns (engaging, for example, local spirits, the challenges of dislocation, changing family and gender roles). They also produced a revitalized spiritual arena in which so-called "authentic healing power," as opposed to learned priestly authority, gave credence to the prosperity message.

Socioeconomic Self-Determination: El Shaddai's Prosperity Gospel

El Shaddai is arguably the poster child of the prosperity approach in the Philippines. It shares with other prosperity groups an acceptance of material prosperity and an emphasis on healing and miracles.[15] Velarde teaches that "El Shaddai's Master Plan" for the faithful is prosperity, health, and success.[16] The approach was likely shaped by Pat Robertson's religious talk show/news program, the 700 Club, and Kenneth Hagin's "health and wealth" gospel. Hagin's booklet *El Shaddai* inspired the movement's name, which Velarde translates as "the God who is more than enough."[17] Hagin is the most senior of the "positive confession charismatics" and more generally of the contemporary "health and wealth movement."[18] Also called the "prosperity gospel," it has three distinctive features: a belief in spiritual healing of physical ailments; an emphasis on material prosperity; and positive confession.[19] Like Robertson, Velarde has always emphasized physical healing through positive confession, which is based on Mark 11:24: "Whatever you ask for in prayer, believe that you have received it and it will be yours."[20] In Velarde's words, "the word of faith is right in your tongue. [. . .] So whatever it is you would like to say or believe, truly those things will happen."[21]

Velarde uses the "miracle of seed-faith" principle to teach, as did Robertson, that tangible rewards are available to those who follow the principles of Yahweh El Shaddai: "you have heard the Good news of Salvation, healing and deliverance from sickness and afflictions, and the message of success and prosperity [. . .] to them who believe and serve!"[22] Eliciting blessings through tithes and offerings is central to Velarde's seed-faith principle.[23] Oral Roberts used the same concept, also calling it "seed-faith" in the 1970s.[24] For Robertson it was a "Kingdom Principle."[25] In a free pamphlet, Velarde explains that the miracle of seed-faith principle

> *is giving, not as an obligation we have to do, but as a miracle seed we sow.* It is an act of "faith expressing itself through love." The Lord in return, speaking through St. Paul, promised "to meet or supply all our needs according to His glorious riches in Christ Jesus." *And believe me, God's glorious source of miracle supply in Christ Jesus is not affected by recession, political unrest, inflation, strikes, fire, bankruptcies, earthquakes, and other calamities.* [. . .] *And as naturally as a seed of palay* [rice] *sown on fertile soil grows and multiplies, so does your seed-faith offering, given to the right mission or ministry, open God's source of miracle supply!* [emphasis in original].[26]

Thus, believers tithe not necessarily in gratitude or out of obligation, but to *elicit* miracles from God. Members should also follow lifestyle proscriptions, such as refraining from alcohol and drug abuse, smoking, gambling, borrowing, adultery, or maligning the El Shaddai ministry. Women should respect their husbands' authority and refrain from nagging. Furthermore, saving and desiring to improve one's lot are godly. Velarde writes, "Financial and material prosperity is not a sin nor a hindrance to spiritual maturity and well-being for as long as this is acquired and managed according to God's master plan. [. . .] Wealth and success, according to God's plan for you and me, include all our financial, material, physical, and spiritual needs."[27]

In 1995 Velarde encouraged every member to open a bank savings account. He suggested in a free booklet that 10 percent of one's income should go to tithes and the remainder should be allotted according to the accounting guide therein (savings, 10 percent, food, 20 percent; shelter, 30 percent; etc.).[28] My informants were very familiar with the allotment for tithing, while some knew of the allotment for savings. In a late 1990s survey, 73 percent of El Shaddai participants claimed they tithed regularly.[29] Though not a major preoccupation, Velarde also writes that borrowing goes against scripture and results in financial bondage.[30]

Aside from tithing, the faithful may also activate the seed-faith principle by donating to the ministry, blessing certain objects, and investing in El Shaddai's radio station, foundation, or programs. Objects associated with finances or career moves become catalysts for upward mobility, God's benevolence, or even profound life transformations if blessed by Brother Mike.

Money management teachings are relatively undeveloped compared to the direct entrepreneurial training of some other neo-Pentecostal churches (see David Maxwell's case study, this volume). However, members' public testimonies reveal positive changes in family life as a result of expectations of financial discipline and moral and lifestyle standards, a pattern discovered in my 1996 interviews as well, especially if the husband joins. Bernice Martin (this volume), Elizabeth Brusco and others describe a "gender bargain" among Pentecostals and Evangelicals in Latin America wherein women accept a gender ideology that entails subordination to their husbands' authority but demands that men meet their familial responsibilities as loyal husbands, heads of household, and stable providers.[31] The Philippine context resembles that of other former Iberian colonies in this regard, where normative masculinity is influenced to some extent by notions of *machismo*. Charismatic and prosperity teachings demand that men's time, money, and attention be devoted to children's education and other material and emotional needs within the family, not to vices.

Velarde points to a subtle but important attitudinal distinction when he says, "People call me a preacher of prosperity, but I would rather be called a preacher of generosity." He uses biblical support and his own life stories to validate the notion that charitable giving, above other calculated economic activities, results in material blessings. El Shaddai now teaches more self-consciously what it brands "El Shaddai spirituality," loosely defined by Velarde as "based on my own experience."[32] The power of his charitable giving features prominently in the nascent curriculum of his school, the College of Divine Wisdom, which I visited in 2010, the year it opened. Preachers-in-training study his 2009 autobiography, which describes how, for example, Velarde's large donations to the Catholic Church and sponsorship of charismatic and Pentecostal rallies miraculously lead to his profitable real estate sales, including land to the Manila Bay Casino developers and land sold to the state.[33] Even though some of these sales have been legally controversial, they are described in the book as harvests of the seed-faith.

By investing these profits fruitfully, in the early days of his ministry, it eventually became, in effect, a profit-generating enterprise itself. Although some aspects of his deals seem to be exempt from ethical oversight, they are described in the book within a neoliberal spiritual logic that seems to say that the ends justify the means—the money is put to the work of God. Velarde preaches that gambling is against the will of God, but he still profits by selling land to casino developers. Morality in politics is central to the group's political agenda, but it works largely from within the economic and political status quo. Similarly, Velarde's blessing of passports and overseas work applications does all but encourage Filipinos to leave home and family and take work abroad as they seek "prosperity" in the global market—but he does not question why the country cannot sustain its own population, nor express outrage at the toll that such heavy reliance on overseas contract work takes on families and communities.

These attitudes reflect Velarde's general lack of interest in the sorts of structural critique offered by leftist movements and liberation theology, as well as the unmet socioeconomic expectations following the 1986 revolution. The overwhelming message is that individual redemption, not structural change, will bring about national renewal. This message resonates with his followers, who see more transformative power in the prosperity teaching of self-determination and hope than in identification with any oppressed class.

The prosperity theology often figures substantially in members' sense of "renewal." It appeals in part because it rejects deterministic class labels, encourages self-reliance, and results in a life-changing sense of optimism. Kessler and Rüland note that the "practice and theology of tithing" (as they call the prosperity gospel) is widespread among charismatic and Pentecostal Filipinos and is independent of their level of active participation in renewal groups and churches. It is a specific mindset rather than a practice carried out in response to social pressure.

> Tithing is prescribed to practice giving instead of taking, of praising the Lord instead of praying for one's own well-being. This change of attitudes is seen as a basis for new strength, as liberation from the humiliating role of the beggar and the obsession with material gain. [. . .] if you let go of material things, if you stop holding on to money, if you stop striving for economic security, and if instead you trust the Lord to provide for you, He will.[34] [. . .] This basic conviction is shared by all Charismatics [renewalists], by those who tithe as well as by those who do not expect their members to tithe because they consider this an excessive burden on their poor members.[35]

Filomeno Aguilar analyzed members' narratives from the El Shaddai and Jesus Is Lord (JIL) groups. "A sense of efficacy and confidence in dealing with life's problems" was a recurring theme in both groups.[36] The prosperity gospel instigates changes in individuals' view of their personal histories, of their current life potential, and of their own place within society at large.

In addition to a sense of socioeconomic empowerment, El Shaddai teachings share an element of moral self-determination with other renewal groups. Aguilar's narratives revealed that in both El Shaddai and JIL, members describe a "palpable turn to moral responsibility."[37] One JIL member described, for example, a conscious decision to refrain from illegal activities; another, a former activist, made a conscious choice to forgive and let go of hatred for former president Marcos. The "ability to make deliberate moral choices" of self-control, personal accountability, and forgiveness was not automatic for the activist, but was an outcome of studying his situation.[38] Similarly, my El Shaddai informants articulated a heightened self-awareness, reflection, and effort in upholding family responsibilities and roles. One woman focused daily intentional effort on controlling feelings of anger toward her in-laws, while others described purposeful efforts in performing the roles of supportive husband or wife.

Of those individuals I interviewed in 1996, all had chosen El Shaddai; none had inherited the affiliation (now there are second generation members). That people can and should choose their religious commitments paralleled their embrace of moral and socioeconomic self-determination. Members described learning and deliberately choosing a different metaphysical view of their situations, as in the lyrics of this emblematic El Shaddai song: "Let the weak say 'I am strong,' let the poor say 'I am rich.'" Velarde explains to a rally congregation in February 1996 the transformation these words express:

> Many are coming to me saying, "Brother Mike, for four years my husband and I lost our jobs, and until now we cannot find jobs." And I ask her, "How many are your children?" She says four. "What are they doing?" "They are studying." Then praise God and be thankful to God because for four years you had no job, and yet your children are able to go to school and until now you are still alive [Applause.] [. . .] We cannot see the good news of the Lord to all of us because our mind and soul were blinded by the spirit of darkness [. . .]. Brothers and sisters, this is where new life begins, so that it will grow and be strong, so that the evil spirit will not defeat you anymore. . . . He can drive away the spirit of hunger, He can drive away the spirit that robs you of your work.

Velarde speaks here of defeating the spirit of darkness with a change in outlook. He tells the jobless woman to see blessings where before she saw hardship. El

Shaddai and other religious groups recast the 1986 People Power Revolution in renewalist language: it "was not the result of people's power, but of God's Power—the power of the Living God—Yahweh-El Shaddai."[39] Similarly, members' transformation stories reevaluate their lives using the newly acquired prosperity and charismatic language. As is true of many Christian conversion narratives, their testimonies are not primarily stories of things that occurred in the past, but are the reinvention of one's past and present.

"People are more receptive to God when they are weak," Velarde told me and a small group of friends while dining after a rally one Saturday in 1996. His followers, many of whom are economically, politically, or physically weak, are receptive to the message that faith and tithing will activate God's plan of miracles and prosperity, and that affirming one's aspirations ("I am rich!") will make them true. People whose lives have not improved materially in any obvious way remain convinced of the transformative power of these teachings, because now they indeed see prosperity and blessings where before they saw poverty or suffering. This change in outlook may positively affect other life areas, confirming the validity of the transformation. Vangie, a six-year El Shaddai member, compares El Shaddai to Bread of Life and other Pentecostal groups:

> Those in the other groups do not preach about prosperity, unlike Brother Mike. [. . .] But for me, I like that prosperity. At least I can see if I'm prospering, while instead they say, "I'm so poor." The Lord doesn't have children who are poor. You want to have it, but you just don't want to rise from poverty. The Lord has given you to rise, but you are the one who doesn't want to. You will not really prosper if you will not work. But in prosperity, I know the Lord is giving prosperity to us. He did not create a person to become very poor.

She affirms that hard work and grace are the ultimate source of prosperity. But the real focus is her new self-image. "At least I can see if I'm prospering, while instead they say, 'I'm so poor.'" The problem lies in the others' outlook.

Luz, another member and a fifty-two-year-old ambulant newspaper vendor, has a chronically ill husband and has at times been homeless. When asked, "What kind of people are drawn to El Shaddai?" she says, "The poor, because the poor don't know God. They think that because they are poor, they'll remain poor. But the Lord doesn't want you to always be poor. He wants you to progress." For Luz, seeing oneself as poor signifies a state of distance from God, "blinded by the spirit of darkness," as Velarde put it. But a person who "wants to rise from poverty" is closer to God. Luz says she tithes because "it is good to give to the poor." Although to her neighbors she is poor, she no longer identifies herself as poor. She embraces a religious language in which she can articulate her needs and desires, one that opens up a space for an alternative identification. Her poverty now represents potential, a miracle or blessing waiting to happen. As such it becomes temporary and personal, rather than determining.

Velarde's blinding "spirit of darkness" parallels liberation theology, developmental economics, and other discourses on culture in the Philippines that identify a so-called "culture of poverty"—an attitude of hopelessness and fatalism—that hinders organizing, economic striving, and mobility. The majority of El Shaddai members, like the Latin American Pentecostals observed by David Martin, "belong to groups which liberals cast in the role of victim, and in every way they refuse to play that role."[40] Far from facilitating a consciousness of collective oppression, the prosperity theology provides a language for casting off the "victim" or "beggar" identity. In a similar vein, Velarde and his followers emphasize a lack of class distinctions in their gatherings. "You can see an engineer standing next to a domestic [worker]," he says, and stories abound of illiterate preachers who can miraculously read the Bible. When asked about the composition of a huge rally, a woman in attendance told me, "[Here] we are all from different walks of life. No one is rich or poor in the eyes of God. But," she added ambivalently, "I see mostly the poor ones here." Others describe an atmosphere where social and class distinctions are irrelevant. "They don't mind who I am or what I am." While members recognize that the group attracts the "*masa*" (the masses) and "*mga mahirap*" (the poor), the group's demographics and class base are downplayed, as is an ideology or theology of class struggle.

Church of the Poor?

Some outsiders stress the movement's positive role in teaching the poor self-reliance, hope, and financial responsibility, which may serve larger national aspirations. Indeed, the aspirations expressed in Velarde's prosperity theology seem to parallel national development efforts, especially those in the decade following the 1986 revolution, when El Shaddai experienced its most rapid growth. In addition, the power vacuum created by the fall of Marcos in 1986, the disappointment with the subsequent leadership's failure to deal with poverty, corruption, land reform, and human rights abuses, and the weakening of the communist insurgency in the 1990s and 2000s provided the sociopolitical context for the emergence of Brother Mike and his populist message of prosperity and self-reliance.

However, many Filipinos on the street criticize a perceived capitalistic morality or a self-interested market approach to religion in El Shaddai that pollutes the authentic relationship with God. Said a former member, "The people are giving in order to receive. More capital, more return. . . . Does the Lord ask for payments?" Some Catholic clergy have faulted Velarde's teachings for ignoring "the wisdom of evangelical poverty"[41] and for their lack of a social justice concept. These Catholic leaders have an understanding of the Church that "embraces and practices the evangelical spirit of poverty, which combines detachment from possessions with a profound trust in the Lord as the sole source of salvation. While the Lord does not want anyone to be materially poor, he wants all of his followers to be 'poor in spirit.'"[42] This "Church of the Poor" approach, espoused within segments of the Philippine Church, recognizes that poverty has traditionally been a privileged site of God's grace and intervention, and reflects the dedication on the part of the mainstream Church to make more meaningful connections with the poor. Basic Ecclesiastic Communities (Basic Christian Communities–Community Organizing) have been part of this effort, but like liberation theology and similar efforts to construct more just societies in Latin America, these efforts have not necessarily sustained mass interest.[43] The mass appeal of religions that cater to private concerns over collective societal ones, especially in free religious markets (as opposed to religious monopolies), has been noted by Peter Berger and has been demonstrated in multiple contexts in Latin America.[44] The transition from a Catholic religious monopoly to an essentially open free religious economy in the twentieth century has produced similar trends in the Philippines.

Velarde offers a more triumphant image of Christ than the suffering, enduring one seen in mainstream Catholic contexts—Christ "taking up the cross." He abhors the notorious folk Catholic practices of self-flagellation and self-crucifixion performed by a few dedicated Filipinos (enthusiastically watched by many) in Pampanga Province during Holy Week. One Manilan priest articulated the attraction of his message thus:

> They're given hope, while if you go to the parish, the priest there is scolding you. And he's giving you hope. [The priests] tell you to "carry your cross daily," and here the man is suffering from cancer or TB or whatever. And Velarde says "We'll pray over you and you're going to get well." You see? And he gets well! Now, maybe it's from God, but he gets well. So he's for Mike Velarde now! He's not going back to his parish priest.[45]

El Shaddai's take on prosperity theology reflects the afflictions and aspirations of the *masa* (the masses, the lower classes) who apparently find more efficacy in belonging to a church of the self-proclaimed blessed than a "church of the poor."[46] El Shaddai's prosperity theology implies an apolitical and ahistorical view of inequality. It emphasizes personal action, self-reliance, and faith in divine action for overcoming desperate situations, as opposed to identifying structural, societal, or historical causes and solutions (or conversely, accepting one's "crosses" in life).

Mass Religious Rallies as Civic Activism

El Shaddai, Jesus Is Lord, and other groups participate in civic society through mass mobilization of members for rallies and public rituals. Partaking in such rallies, both religious and political, is a well-established tradition in the Philippines. El Shaddai in particular has mastered the art of organizing dramatic gatherings, where dedicated followers show up even during typhoons. Rallies typically begin after nightfall and feature a high level of crowd participation. Dramatic candlelight rituals and symbolic gestures like the blessing of eggs or water appeal to Filipino sensibilities. A rally can create a charged atmosphere and a strong sense of community, "a community outside of any community."[47] Vicente Rafael's description of political rallies in Manila illustrate the event-like quality of El Shaddai rallies as well: "The insistent and recurring proximity of anonymous others creates a current of expectation, of something that might arrive, of events that might happen. . . . Enmeshed in a crowd, one feels the potential for reaching across social, spatial, and temporal divides."[48] And Filomeno Aguilar writes, "For both El Shaddai and Jesus Is Lord adherents the nature of the religious assembly is perceived to be a space of radical difference from tradition and society. In it flourishes a subculture."[49]

In addition, participation in weekly El Shaddai prayer and healing rallies, which have drawn from a half million to one million participants each week, provides members with a sense of their own collective mass and power. People normally on the fringes of society and economy reach a national audience when these weekly rallies, called "Family Appointments," are broadcast live on radio and TV. Many politicians have shared the stage with Brother Mike to court favor with the huge congregation. Members hailing from dispersed and obscure squatter neighborhoods in Manila each week assert to outsiders the force of their own critical mass by disrupting the city through massive weekly traffic jams and the occupation of central public spaces for their rituals.[50] Rafael, writing about messianic politics in the Philippines, notes,

> The power of the crowd thus comes across in its capacity to overwhelm the physical constraints of urban planning and to blur social distinctions by provoking a sense of estrangement. Its authority rests on an ability to promote restlessness and movement, thereby undermining pressure from state technocrats, church authorities, and

corporate interests to regulate and contain such movements. In this sense, the crowd is a sort of *medium,* if by that word one means a way of gathering and transforming elements, objects, people, and things.[51]

Eva-Lotta Headman has analyzed participation in Philippine civil society as typified by performance and "specular" mobilization. She argues that mass performative displays such as candlelight vigils and citizen campaigns to safeguard the electoral process have taken on a "civil religion" quality. Monitoring ballot boxes in the notorious 1986 election became viewed as a Christian moral duty. Furthermore, she argues, "the very realization of 'civil society' itself rested on the performative display of such participation."[52] Civic participation hinges on the ability to reach a mass audience through newspapers, radio, and television; "over the years, the expanding audience for such performances greatly enhanced their dramatic import and thus the lived experience of participation."[53]

Religious groups have typically been part of mass political mobilizations in the Philippines. The role of the Catholic Church in the 1986 People Power Revolution is legendary: Church leaders had been publicly critical of the dictatorship, and in its final days, Archbishop Cardinal Jaime Sin and the Catholic Radio Veritas mobilized citizens for the peaceful demonstrations that led to the bloodless revolution. Miller and Yamamori write:

> Religious folks of every stripe gathered in the demonstrations against this corrupt government, including Evangelicals and Pentecostals. The head of a Christian research organization in Manila told us that this was the turning point for conservative Protestants. They started to see that it was not biblical to make a radical separation between the sacred and the profane, this world and the life hereafter. [. . .] They went searching in their Bibles for verses that justified their political activity.[54]

The Church has made a variety of decisive contributions to democracy building in the postauthoritarian era.[55] However, civic participation of many types in the Philippines—motivated by political as well as religious goals—often takes the form of massive public rallies. Such rallies display some form of "people power" that is then noticed by the press and mediated to a larger audience. El Shaddai, for instance, has organized or been visibly part of numerous secular rallies in Manila (a strategy also used by Jesus Is Lord and other groups). Members typically bring large signs proclaiming their El Shaddai membership, signs that can be seen from a distance in photos of the crowd. Pentecostals and charismatics were active in the 1992 and 1998 presidential elections, with media campaigns, prayer rallies, and voter education.

The Philippine Council of Evangelical Churches (PCEC) and the Philippines for Jesus Movement (an independent Pentecostal church network) held prayer rallies for honest elections. In 1997, when then president Ramos raised the possibility of changing term limits on the presidency, the Philippines for Jesus Movement lead supportive rallies, while other neo-Pentecostal groups like Bread of Life, in addition to the Catholic Church and El Shaddai, staged rallies opposing the constitutional changes.

El Shaddai's public positions have not always been in agreement with the Church's. In 1999, the Church lead nationwide protests against President Estrada's attempts to amend the constitution, while on the same day, El Shaddai's birthday party for Mike Velarde, attended by Estrada, turned into a prayer rally perceived as support for Estrada's position.[56] In 2000, corruption charges against Estrada led to a protest rally with a diverse crowd of over a million during the course of four days. Archbishop Cardinal Jaime Sin and some other Filipino bishops supported the crowd's action, and Couples for Christ (a middle-class Catholic charismatic group) was also a key actor.[57] Estrada was eventually ousted in "EDSA II," or "People Power II." El Shaddai's Velarde had been a strong supporter of the Estrada presidency.[58] A few months later a pro-Estrada rally, supported by some El Shaddai members, the Jesus Miracle Crusade, and Iglesia ni Cristo, was mobilized, dubbed "Poor People Power" in the press. Protestors, who were largely from the lower classes (Estrada's support base), demanded his release and reinstatement. Although unsuccessful, the action is indicative of a populist approach to politics on the part of Velarde, in which personal loyalty and friendship trump moral, ideological, and even religious commitments (Velarde was the spiritual advisor to President Estrada, a former actor renowned for his extramarital affairs and corruption). The action also demonstrated tensions between submission to Church hierarchy and the tendency toward populist antielitism. The protestors, Vicente Rafael writes, characterized in the press as a voiceless mass, "had been largely ignored by the elite politicians, the Catholic Church hierarchy, the middle-class-dominated left-wing groups, and the NGOs."[59] He continues, "The masses suddenly became visible in a country where the poor are often viewed by the middle class as literally unsightly, spoken about and spoken down to because they are deemed incapable of speaking up for themselves. They are acknowledged only in order to be dismissed. Marching to the palace, however, and chanting their slogans, they assumed an apocalyptic agency."[60] Antonio F. Moreno SJ observes, "The [Catholic] church, too, reflected on this event and realized the deep gulf that existed between them and the poor—a contradiction of the very vision they had opted for. . . ."[61]

Kessler and Rüland argue that renewalism in the Philippines, of which El Shaddai is their prime example, is a kind of religious populism analogous to political populism. The rally experience, for example, appeals to the emotions rather than the intellect; "the core of antielitism in populist religion is the emphasis of charismatic religion on the personal relationship with God, which does not need any religious elite. . . ."[62] Yet these collective assemblies require an acquiescence to the group leader's authority, typically depicted, as Velarde is, as "an ordinary believer qualified for leadership only by the grace of God."[63] Nonetheless El Shaddai's rallies, especially those held in large public spaces and televised, are crucial sites of engagement with larger society and can give the marginalized a sense of voice. This, along with its success as probably the largest voluntary organization of the poor and aspiring middle class, means that while the group espouses a classless, individualistic ideology, it ironically has become a movement with a collective voice that can carry considerable weight in the public forum.

Recent Investments and Developmental Tensions

El Shaddai celebrated its twenty-eighth anniversary in 2012 and Brother Mike his seventy-third birthday. As members continue to invest in miracles, its leadership has begun to hedge its bets by investing in institutional development and in a more direct approach to civic and political involvement. On 20 August 2009, Brother Mike opened the "El Shaddai International House of Prayer" (IHOP), a US$20 million worship structure. In 2010 he opened the College of Divine Wisdom in the same compound, which combines higher education and professional training with "El Shaddai spirituality." The college is also used for preacher training, which is more rigorous now with recent efforts to systematize the content and accreditation structure. In recent years they have begun to focus on national political engagement through representation in Congress and activism in support of Catholic hot-button issues such as birth control and reproductive health, and against political corruption—issues of intense national interest as of 2012. Efforts to define and control the "El Shaddai brand," engage directly in national politics, and invest in education must be balanced with the desire to maintain a sense of spiritual spontaneity and authenticity if El Shaddai wishes to remain relevant to its major constituency. At the same time, these efforts could result in establishing a larger following in the middle class, thereby consolidating El Shaddai's broader societal relevance and institutional longevity.

Spiritual Authenticity at a Crossroad

In the past, El Shaddai's creative use of mass media and gatherings in central public locations facilitated a sense not only of populist but of spiritual eventfulness.[64] In the mid-1990s, Brother Mike characterized the Catholic Church as bogged down with intellectualism and ritual, and told me he aimed to "free my people from the bondage of religion." El Shaddai preaching distinguished itself as unstudied but inspired, pristine, and emergent through experience, in contrast to the trained sermons of elite Catholic priests.[65] This era was characterized by a perceived sense of authentic and spontaneous spirituality for those involved.[66] The large weekly open air rallies were, for participants, enchanted with a sense of a Holy Spirit that moved freely in ritual space, within people, and often through passports, job applications, and prayer requests. *Communitas* often extended beyond the locale through radio and television. Neighborhood prayer meetings and home counseling sessions were often animated in unexpected ways, depending on the style and charismatic gifts of the evangelist, such as spirit exorcisms and mediation, speaking in tongues, healing, counseling, and slaying in the spirit. Standardizing minister training, codifying "El Shaddai spirituality," and shifting the weekly national-level prayer and healing rallies to the new IHOP may unintentionally mitigate this sense of spiritual spontaneity.

The new International House of Prayer (IHOP) has a seating capacity of 15,000, standing-room for 25,000, and overflow for 200,000. Then Philippine president Gloria Macapagal-Arroyo and other VIPs and clergymen attended its inauguration in the Velarde-owned "Amvel City" in Parañaque City, Metro Manila. In 2010, less than a year later, I attended weekly fellowships, preacher training sessions, and undergraduate classes at the College. Velarde describes the front area of the chapel as an ark-shaped "stage," and has decorated it with a large rainbow representing God's covenant with Noah.[67] The building also contains a baptismal healing pool, a second smaller, traditional-looking chapel with stained-glass windows, and a confessional area. The fellowships I attended felt like more like worship services and less like the theatrical rally-events of the past. What was before an outdoor stage now feels more like a grand altar. While beautifully crafted, it is nonetheless indoors, unchanging but for the banner decorations. The chapel is treated as a sanctified area where a gendered dress code is enforced, as was the case in previous outdoor venues (pre-IHOP) in the roped-off area near the stage. From outside the chapel there is no view of the altar, although the area outside is outfitted with a sophisticated sound system. During my visit, most congregants stayed outside, citing the heat and stuffiness inside, where many seats remained empty. Furthermore, a tangible feeling of formality in the chapel makes six hours on metal chairs seem less appealing despite their sturdy and comfortable construction. Informants reported that some prayer rallies bypass the chapel and use a temporary outdoor stage instead.

At previous venues, vending stalls at the crowd's edge contributed to the carnivalesque atmosphere, where one could not remain a spectator. Now, at a distant edge of the IHOP lawn, a building with permanent vendor stalls and a cooperative store deliberately separates market activity from worship. Closer to the church, Velarde has built two imposing luxury condominium buildings.[68] In the south part of metropolitan Manila, the new compound is not centrally located and is uncomfortably situated beneath the flight path of jets approaching the international airport. Unlike the rallies in central public spaces typical of El Shaddai's first twenty-five years, activity at the IHOP is relatively tucked away and unseen by the public, despite the soaring chapel structure visible from a distance.

My observations and interviews in 2010 suggest that the once emblematic spiritually charged festival atmosphere may be dampened at the IHOP. Some informants perceived diminished attendance and fewer appearances by the still energetic Brother Mike. Despite the pride in and convenience of the new structure, and the sustained affection for Brother Mike, the zeal of previous rally-goers in the mid-1990s (e.g., "I like it because it's live!") was lacking. Perhaps realizing this, Velarde has moved some major celebrations back to the centrally located Luneta Park.

The energy and openness to the spirit is still rigorous in smaller fellowships, however, and El Shaddai leaders still take pride in the gifted, often semi-literate preachers who seem to emerge divinely from the congregation's grassroots. But now these preachers must pass through the College of Divine Wisdom for accreditation. In 2008 El Shaddai began a major effort to systematize preacher formation through a year-long training program. Theology, spirituality, preaching style, and narrative structure are taught using Brother Mike's model. The fly-by-night "evangelist" category of untrained preachers I described in my earlier work no longer exists.[69] El Shaddai now has a system of ranking and advancement, through which it aims to create an elite group of experienced preachers well-enough versed in English and theology to minister to overseas congregations, congregations that might include other nationalities or more educated Filipinos. The new emphases on pastoral expertise and authority could abrade with the desire to nurture egalitarianism and openness to the spirit.[70] The head of preacher training and education, Rey Vargas, a former priest who converted to El Shaddai in California, affirms the importance of the gifts of the Spirit, the charisms, but notes that they are "gifts" and cannot be explicitly taught aside from their biblical background. He adds that the group now uses Catholic language to describe them, not the "Protestant" terms used previously, like "spiritual warfare." During one preacher formation I attended in 2010, scores of people were slain in the spirit by Vargas, who carefully described it later as being "overcome with emotion."

One of the main goals of preacher training, and indeed the college's undergraduate education, according to Vargas, "is to really soak them with El Shaddai spirituality." Brother Mike defines El Shaddai spirituality (a phrase not in use in the mid-1990s) as spirituality based on his own experiences and teachings.[71] A collection of his teachings and his self-authored autobiography[72] are used as not only as sources of stories and preaching topics, but as models for structure and style, too.[73]

Bernice Martin in this volume describes gendered dimensions to the tension between pastoral authority and openness to the spirit in Pentecostal communities. The expression of bodily ecstatic experiences, integral to women's participation, depends on the openness to the Spirit on the part of those in authority. An ethos of egalitarianism has allowed women to stand up and testify during prayer meetings and has been an attraction of El Shaddai experience. The college's dean and one of its instructors, retired Bishop Rev. Teodoro C. Bacani Jr., D.D., remarked that several girls in his class at the college showed talent and potential as preachers, and he encouraged Velarde to allow female preachers: "This is something he could do." But Velarde has not, and as a result women have virtually no leadership possibilities within El Shaddai, despite their numerous service roles in the organization.

Minor tensions remain with the Church clergy regarding the more charismatic aspects of El Shaddai's spirituality. Bishop Bacani asserts that the Catholic hierarchy has reined in the more spiritually wayward aspects of El Shaddai practice. For example, he says that at the Church's instruction, Brother Mike no longer claims direct divine contact (as in "God spoke to me") but rather speaks of biblical inspiration. And yet Brother Mike's new book is full of miracles and messages from God. El Shaddai's denominational identity, an early source of tension, has diminished over time as the Bishop's Conference has expressed confidence, at least officially, in Velarde's commitment to the church. I have argued previously that El Shaddai maintained an identity as a Catholic lay movement distinct from, but dependent on, the Church by congregating rallies in neutral public city spaces and over the airwaves. Through this delicately balanced identity, El Shaddai retains legitimacy among its Catholic members, and the Church retains its congregation despite the popularity of Pentecostal and charismatic groups. The Church does not, on the surface, seem threatened by the expression of independence that building IHOP could represent. Joro Archbishop Angel Lagdameo, the outgoing president of the Catholic Bishop's Conference of the Philippines (CBCP) said at the mass for the inauguration of IHOP, "This is my first time to address a people equivalent to six cathedrals."[74] El Shaddai has brought the Church into IHOP—priests celebrate mass at fellowships there, and Bishop Bacani even punches a time card when he arrives to teach. El Shaddai's increasing engagement in national politics, however, has been a greater source of tension with the Church.

Educating Christian Citizens

Brother Mike envisions College of Divine Wisdom graduates as professionals well versed in spiritual, moral, and biblical teachings, and deeply committed to evangelism and to a Christian lifestyle. Students and instructors alike must be Catholic, and students must be El Shaddai members; in fact, most were born into the community. Those receiving full scholarships, Brother Mike explains, "will be required to serve here [at the ministry], because that's what we need overseas. Because most of our preachers here are just high school graduates, and our chapters abroad—where there are other nationalities involved—now require more or less at least college graduates and those who can really deliver the Gospel in English."[75]

While the majority of the instructors are from outside the El Shaddai community, it is likely that the College will develop an educated professional segment from within; however, it is unclear if this is a conscious strategy. Rey Vargas (head of education and training) explained that at first Brother Mike envisioned building an evangelist training school, but eventually he decided on an undergraduate college where students learn "a way of life" that involves evangelism: "Brother Mike wants to see in you the real Christ in whatever profession you're in."[76] Vargas stressed that the College's emphasis on the internalization of El Shaddai spiritual and moral values through religiously oriented courses and strict monitoring of students' moral behavior was unique in the Philippines.[77] With the exception of a few Jesuit colleges, says Vargas, no other schools produce graduates with the "spiritual pride" they envision for theirs.

As of August 2010, the college offered an evangelism major, and was working toward degree programs in education, psychology, information technology, and accountancy. Brother Mike explained to me that his choice of majors was based on the current labor market. He reminds the youth in his congregation to maintain good grades so they can qualify for college scholarships. The instrumental value placed on education is consistent with mainstream values—education as a path to economic security. Education functions instrumentally in both professional and religious ways, however; it produces employed individuals who will spread the Word of God. The concern for the spiritual and moral life of the individual based on El Shaddai, Catholic, and biblical principles replaces the liberal humanistic model found in the best Catholic and public universities in the Philippines, whose perceived lower moral and spiritual expectations may undermine one's faith. Far from treating Catholicism as a cultural backdrop, this Catholic charismatic ministry comes to its Catholic identity and morality as a conscious, modern choice. This is especially apparent in El Shaddai's political involvement in recent years.

Modes of Political Engagement

Although El Shaddai has often been at loggerheads with the Catholic Church over various political issues, it has publically supported Church social policies against abortion, contraception, divorce, and homosexuality. Visible on the national political stage ever since he began to attract large crowds, Velarde is now toying with ways to "truly live the gospel" through more direct involvement in the political process and nurturing a more politically engaged flock. The extent to which these efforts remain responsive to the egalitarian and democratic allegiances of their members will likely have implications for their ability to retain mass appeal.

In 2004, for the first time, El Shaddai was represented with two seats in the house of representatives under the party-list system with its pro-life, anticontraceptive party, Buhay Hayaan Yumabong (Allow Life to Prosper). Commonly known as Buhay, meaning "life," it topped party-list polls in 2007 after using Brother Mike's face on campaign materials, winning three house seats that year. In 2010, with two seats, it was the third-highest vote-getter among party-list groups and the top performing religious group. Although party-list representation is restricted to marginalized sectors and religious groups are barred from it, in 2010 four other religious groups successfully sponsored parties including two indigenous Pentecostal groups. Other Catholic lay groups, including the pro-life Abay Pamilya, have not been successful in the system, nor as ambitious (the charismatic Couples for Christ has not formed a party). Velarde's son Rene represented Buhay for three terms ("the richest party-list congressman"). In 2010 his younger brother Michael, the future heir to the ministry, replaced him.[78]

Velarde's populist approach appears to be driven more by personal loyalties and less by ideology, exemplified by his support for his friend, President Joseph Estrada, a morally suspect center-left populist politician. In the 2010 presidential election, Velarde hinted to his flock his preference for Manny Villar, a neoliberal center-right candidate (who did not ultimately win).

Members do not block vote, and internal mock polls show that Velarde only exerts some influence over voting choices. However, local politicians at times instruct their followers to support the Velarde-endorsed candidate, multiplying members' influence beyond their own votes.[79] Velarde told me in 2010 of his plans to support district level congressional representatives. He even publically explored running for president in 2010, but eventually decided against it. His congregation generally did not support the idea, nor could he get an endorsement from the Catholic hierarchy. Eddie Villanueva, however, of Jesus Is Lord, ran for president in both 2004 and 2010, winning 3 percent of the vote.

The secretary general of Buhay, Willie Villarama, met Velarde in 2006 and has been his political strategist for several years, encouraging him toward more overt political engagement and more civic awareness amongst the flock. Villarama, a high-profile retired government veteran and self-described whistleblower, hopes to teach El Shaddai members to vote with their Christian conscience ("not tell them who to vote for"). He describes Velarde as a good listener, sensitive to Church hierarchy and his people, who only reluctantly enters the political limelight. But Villarama urges him to be more outspoken: "Brother Mike is not a priest, he's a charismatic leader. He has to lead the flock, speak out if there is something really wrong."[80] Villarama is exploring the idea of a "one-vote-movement," an ecumenical concept to unify Christian votes through internal primaries and a group of unified pastors. However, he expresses doubts about his overall mission. "I'm worried that I'll ruin the community," he said, perhaps recognizing the importance of egalitarianism to the life of this community.

The political activity of the group's leadership does not necessarily signal a desire on the part of ordinary members and rank-and-file preachers for more active civic participation. My 2010 interviews indicated members were mostly against Brother Mike running for president and "getting involved in politics," which they viewed as potentially corrupting and as contradicting the democratic principle of church-state separation. Yet they heartily supported the Buhay party and its pro-life, anticontraception, anti–Reproductive Heath Bill advocacy, which suggests some ambivalence about what citizenship, Christian/Catholic duty, and political engagement should mean for them as a religious group.[81]

Velarde has urged the Church to get more directly involved in the political process, asking clergy in 2007 to make a "short list" of senatorial candidates. "My position is the separation of Church and State does not apply to this process of selecting leaders because this is the time when leaders of the Church should have active participation not just in setting guidelines but also in guiding the flock on who the right candidates are," Velarde told the

Philippine Daily Inquirer.[82] He warned that public apathy invites abuse of power and urged the Church to be more like Iglesia ni Cristo, which, he said, really leads its people on such issues (indeed, they vote as one block). This was a surprising statement from one who has, over the years, taken pride in his more democratic approach, never explicitly directing votes. The president of the Catholic Bishop's Conference responded, "Dictating who to choose is as bad as buying votes." Velarde released his own list anyway.[83]

Pro-Family, Pro-Women?
The Moral and Political Platform

The fight against artificial contraception, abortion, and divorce (summa-rized by the phrase "pro-family") is at the center of El Shaddai's social and political engagement, and the central platform of Buhay. By law, party-list groups must represent marginalized sectors, and Buhay claims to represent unborn children. The fertility rate in the Philippines is 5.9 for poor women, 2.0 for wealthy, educated women. Poor women often cannot afford contra-ceptives and do not have the financial and legal resources for legal separa-tion and annulment in lieu of divorce (the country has no divorce law).[84] Reproductive Health legislation (known as the RH Bill) would, if passed, provide government subsidies for contraception for low-income families, family planning information, and sex education in public schools. Highly charged political and religious debates on the RH Bill have raged for years, as poverty alleviation and population control are intricately linked in this geographically small country of 97 million.

Seventy-one percent of the national population favor the RH bill, as do most women's organizations and many civic groups. The Church and the two largest Catholic charismatic groups, El Shaddai and Couples for Christ, are outspoken against it. In favor of the bill are nearly all other Christian groups and organizations and even some Catholic lay groups. As such, El Shaddai's position against the RH Bill is a decisive fault line aligning it with the Church hierarchy, even while El Shaddai's mode of engagement increasingly resembles the Pentecostal model. Despite its image of toeing the Catholic line, however, it is largely uninterested in other social issues to which the Church has long been dedicated, including democracy, human rights, and economic equality, cutting through the middle of the Church's social teachings.[85]

El Shaddai's "pro-family" stance responds to a number of modern pre-dicaments for Catholic charismatics, women, and the poor. It emerges as a conscious choice within a mainstream secular (and often nominal Catholic) context of human rights and gender equality where the Virgin Mary may be revered as feminist figure. While Catholic morality is still highly influential and the submissive, sacrificing image of the Virgin Mary (also cultivated by El Shaddai) is pervasive, the current trend is toward sexual permissiveness, decreased modesty, and increased use of family planning to limit family size, delay motherhood, or opt out of motherhood altogether (the quintessential modern woman's "choice"). The renewalist Catholic stance confronts these liberal tendencies with a more restrictive familial role for women, but it arrives there, as it does at its Catholic identity, by means of a conscious choice, too. Women's reproductive roles within the Catholic charismatic field are relatively over-valued in comparison with wider gender norms and, predictably, mothers are central to the focus on family renewal.

As the sites of both salvation and resubjugation, women's bodies are the locus of gendered tensions inherent in many Pentecostalisms, tensions that have religious dimensions as well.[86] Even as women are empowered in spiritual contexts to heal material conditions and the body and to receive the Holy Spirit, often in the unmediated, uncontrolled, bodily expressive ways typical of charismatic and Pentecostal worship, El Shaddai reasserts its control of women's bodies through imposed standards of female modesty, male pastoral authority, and a rejection of reproductive choice. The "gender bargain" reinforces conservative roles for both sexes that are rationalized in El Shaddai as essential for a strong and blessed family.[87] Similarly both sexes are encouraged to participate actively in the global economy, even if it means leaving their children in the care of other family members for years at a time because the work is understood as a sacrifice undertaken for the family. Likewise the message of healing, hope, and uplift through moral and economic self-determination is rationalized for women in relation to women's importance for the family, not as a function of women's emancipation or self-actualization (though other renewalist groups may cater to these concerns).

Yet women, who make up around 75 percent of the congregation, are more often the religious pioneers in their families, bringing the men along later. Men who join are encouraged to devote their resources to their families as "renewed" Catholics, and women who join choose a more family-centered role for themselves as well. On a national level, El Shaddai's and the Church's anti-RH Bill position make a significant contribution to the public debate over women's reproductive choices that could have far-reaching consequences for the nation's ability to deal with poverty.

Developmental Tensions

Through El Shaddai rituals and the prism of the prosperity gospel, Filipino Catholics have been able to reframe deterministic *socioeconomic* discourses that define them as victims, replacing them with more self-reliant and optimistic ones. These renewed Catholics share a sense of religious, moral, and socioeconomic self-determination with their Pentecostal counterparts, and respond to the group's emphasis on private concerns over collective ones. As a mass movement, El Shaddai does not hesitate to add its voice and the weight of its numbers to national debates. However, its social preoccupations reflect only a part of the mainstream Catholic Church's agenda, while ignoring other issues such as social justice and democracy. The movement's leadership buttresses a conservative and somewhat countercultural Catholic social platform against contraception and continues to exclude women from church leadership. Investment in education of its members may signal a desire for expanded influence in the middle class, but the question remains: Will the gender ideology seem regressive or outmoded to educated middle-class women, especially in overseas chapters?[88] Or will El Shaddai's focus on self-reliance and the family unit continue to strengthen the community? Velarde's recent shift toward more direct public engagement may increase the group's influence in civic life on a number of levels. But will that influence be mitigated if the approach alienates him from the group's egalitarian origins and sympathies?[89]

El Shaddai's current preoccupation with institutional expansion and the systematization of its "spirituality" may lead to developmental tensions within the movement if its leaders neglect the spiritual effervescence and egalitarianism that characterized the movement's first two decades. An unintended outcome of the increased control over minister training and the development of canonical texts may be that preachers begin to look more priest-like and less shaman-like. The sense of egalitarianism may have suffered another blow by Velarde's authoritarian decision to name his son as the group's future leader. A more spiritually inspired choice would have been in keeping with the group's antielitist roots, where even illiterate preachers gained legitimacy through displays of spiritual gifts and mediation. Similarly, building a worship center may secure the movement's longevity as an institution, but may also detract from the sense of spiritual animation, spontaneity, and demarginalization that previously appealed to rally-goers. In the meantime, charismatic expressions will likely continue to flourish in barrios and chapters small and large, even as the institution itself feels more staid and stolid.

NOTES

The Institute on Culture, Religion, and World Affairs at Boston University (CURA) supported the 2010 fieldwork for this chapter, and its director, Robert W. Hefner, provided insightful comments. El Shaddai ministries in Manila provided generous assistance, especially Mike Velarde, Willfredo Villarama, and Rey Vargas and family, as did Dr. Grace Gorospe-Jamon at the University of the Philippines–Diliman and Dr. Filomeno V. Aguilar Jr. of Ateneo de Manila University.

1. El Shaddai estimates its "followership" based on crowd estimates at mass rallies, prayer requests and tithes, prayer group attendance, chapter membership, radio listenership surveys, official membership, and election results. Many partici-pants are not registered members, resulting in lower official numbers: 252,463 as of 19 September 2005 (Mariano "Bro. Mike" Z. Velarde, personal interview, El Shaddai headquarters, Makati City, September 2005).

2. Jojo Malig, "WikiLeaks: US Sees El Shaddai, INC as 'Kingmakers,'" (abs-cbn-news.com, 8/26/11). See http://wikileaks.org/cable/2005/11/05MANILA5130.htm for the original 11/2/2005 U.S. Embassy cable.

3. Katharine L. Wiegele, *Investing in Miracles: El Shaddai and the Transformation of Popular Catholicism in the Philippines* (Honolulu: University of Hawai'i Press, 2005).

4. Antonio F. Moreno SJ, *Church, State, and Civil Society in Postauthoritarian Philippines: Narratives of Engaged Citizenship* (Quezon City: Ateneo de Manila Uni-versity Press, 2006), 75.

5. Christl Kessler and Jürgen Rüland, *Give Jesus a Hand! Charismatic Christians: Populist Religion and Politics in the Philippines* (Quezon City: Ateneo de Manila University Press, 2008). This rigorous 2006 survey included around 1,200 respondents nationwide. Another, "Spirit and Power: A 10-Country Survey of Pentecostals," by the Pew Forum on Religion and Public Life, the Pew Research Center (2006), found 40 percent of the population participated in the renewalist movement.

6. Kessler and Rüland, *Give Jesus a Hand!* 93.

7. Ibid., 96.

8. Ibid., 105.

9. Ibid., 104.

10. International Associations of the Faithful Directory, Pontifical Council for the Laity (www.vatican.va).

11. George W. Harper, "Philippine Tongues of Fire? Latin American Pentecostalism and the Future of Filipino Christianity," *Evangelical Review of Theology* 26:2 (2006): 153–180; citation from 169.

12. Jeong Jae Yong, "Filipino Independent Pentecostalism and Biblical Trans-formation," in *Asian and Pentecostal: The Charismatic Face of Christianity in Asia,* ed. Allen Anderson and Edmond Tang (Oxford: Regnum Books International, 2005), 391.

13. "Philippine Tongues of Fire?" 177.

14. Wiegele, *Investing in Miracles.*

15. Simon Coleman, *The Globalisation of Charismatic Christianity: Spreading the Gospel of Prosperity* (Cambridge: Cambridge University Press, 2000).

16. Brother Mariano "Mike" Z. Velarde, "El Shaddai's Master Plan for Real Success and Prosperity for You and Me," *El Shaddai God Almighty* 3:3 (Makati City: El Shaddai DWXI-PPFI, Inc., 1993): 3.

17. Kenneth E. Hagin, *El Shaddai: The God Who Is More Than Enough, the God Who Satisfies with Long Life* (Tulsa: Faith Library, 1980). While Velarde acknowledges Hagin's booklet in the naming of the El Shaddai group, I have not found direct references to Robertson in Velarde's preaching or published materials.

18. Nigel Scotland, *Charismatics and the Next Millennium* (London: Hodder and Stoughton, 1995), 14, and Steve Bruce, *Pray TV: Televangelism in America* (London: Routledge, 1990), 152.

19. Bruce, *Pray TV,* 153.

20. Scotland, *Charismatics and the Next Millennium,* 38.

21. Mike Velarde, live rally broadcast, PICC in Manila on DWXI, April 4, 1996, translated by Miren Sanchez.

22. Brother Mariano "Mike" Z. Velarde, *An Invitation to Store Riches in Heaven and Enjoy El Shaddai's Prosperity Plan on Earth Now* (Makati City: El Shaddai DWXI-PPFI, Inc., 1993).

23. Brother Mariano "Mike" Z. Velarde, *El Shaddai's Miracle Assurance Policy against Sickness, Famine, and Bankruptcy* (Makati City: El Shaddai DWXI-PPFI, Inc., 1993), 33.

24. Frances FitzGerald, "Reflections: Jim and Tammy," *The New Yorker* (April 23, 1990), 74.

25. Bruce, *Pray TV,* 150.

26. Brother Mariano "Mike" Z. Velarde, "The Miracles of Believing and Doing Likewise," *El Shaddai God Almighty* 4:1 (Makati City: El Shaddai DWXI-PPFI, Inc., 1994), 1.

27. Velarde, "El Shaddai's Master Plan for Real Success and Prosperity," 3.

28. Velarde, *El Shaddai's Miracle Assurance Policy,* 33.

29. Grace Gorospe-Jamon, "The El Shaddai Prayer Movement: Political Socialization in a Religious Context," *Philippine Political Science Journal* 20:43 (1999): 83–126; citation from 107.

30. Velarde, *El Shaddai's Miracle Assurance Policy,* 41–42.

31. Elizabeth E. Brusco, *The Reformation of Machismo: Evangelical Conversion and Gender in Colombia* (Austin: University of Texas Press, 1995, reprinted 2010).

32. Mariano "Bro. Mike" Z. Velarde, personal communication, August 2010.

33. Mariano "Bro. Mike" Z. Velarde, *With El Shaddai Miracles are Forever: 25 Years of Faith, Love and Unity* (Makati City: El Shaddai DWXI-PPFI, Inc. 2009), 56.

34. Kessler and Rüland, *Give Jesus a Hand!* 128.

35. Ibid., 129.

36. Filomeno V. Aguilar Jr., "Experiencing Transcendence: Filipino Conversion Narratives and the Localization of Pentecostal-Charismatic Christianity," *Philippine Studies* 54:4 (2006): 585–627; citation from 611.

37. Aguilar, "Experiencing Transcendence," 598.

38. Ibid., 599.

39. Brother Mariano "Mike" Z. Velarde, *El Shaddai God Almighty* 3:3 (Makati City: DWXI-PPFI, Inc., 1993): 16. The revolution, a popular uprising against Ferdinand Marcos, restored a democratic form of government. It was the culmination of many populace- and church-based efforts, though a military coup tipped the scales to topple the dictator.

40. David Martin, *Pentecostalism: The World Their Parish* (Oxford: Blackwell, 2002), 10.

41. Sheila A. Samonte, "As They Say, Religion is Good Business," *Business World*. 3 April 1996, p. 1.

42. Catholic Bishops Conference of the Philippines, "Acts and Decrees of the Second Plenary Council of the Philippines," 20 January–17 February 1991 (Manila: Secretariat, Second Plenary Council of the Philippines, 1992), 47–48.

43. R. Andrew Chesnut, *Competitive Spirits: Latin America's New Religious Economy* (Oxford: Oxford University Press, 2003), 12–13.

44. Peter Berger, *The Sacred Canopy* (Garden City, NY: Anchor Books, 1969), 147, cited in Chesnut, *Competitive Spirits,* 12. See *Competitive Spirits* for Latin American examples.

45. This priest requested anonymity.

46. See Katharine L. Wiegele, "Catholics Rich in Spirit: El Shaddai's Modern Engagements," in *The Charismatics,* ed. Filomeno V. Aguilar, special issue of *Philippine Studies* 54:4 (Quezon City, Philippines: Institute of Philippine Culture, Ateneo de Manila University, 2006): 495–520. Indeed, resisting class identification itself deploys the dominant class-based discourse.

47. Vicente L. Rafael, "The Cell Phone and the Crowd: Messianic Politics in the Contemporary Philippines" *Public Culture* 15:3 (2003): 399–425; citation from 416.

48. Rafael, "The Cell Phone and the Crowd," 415.

49. Aguilar, "Experiencing Transcendence," 601.

50. Wiegele, *Investing in Miracles,* 78–79.

51. Rafael, "The Cell Phone and the Crowd," 415.

52. Eva-Lotta Headman, "Watching the Watchers: The Spectacle of Civil Society in the Philippines," in *Staging Politics: Power and Performance in Asia and Africa,* ed. Julia C. Strauss and Donal B. Cruise O'Brien (London: I. B. Tauris, 2007), 215–242; citation from 216.

53. Headman, "Watching the Watchers," 238.

54. Donald E. Miller and Tetsunao Yamamori, *Global Pentecostalism: The New Face of Christian Social Engagement* (Berkeley: University of California Press, 2007), 126.

55. See Antonio F. Moreno SJ, *Church, State, and Civil Society in Postauthoritarian Philippines: Narratives of Engaged Citizenship* (Quezon City: Ateneo de Manila University Press, 2006).

56. Moreno, *Church, State, and Civil Society in Postauthoritarian Philippines,* 282, 121.

57. Ibid., 127

58. Gorospe-Jamon, "The El Shaddai Prayer Movement," 89.

59. Rafael, "The Cell Phone and the Crowd," 423.

60. Ibid., 424.

61. Moreno, *Church, State, and Civil Society in Postauthoritarian Philippines,* 131.

62. Kessler and Rüland, *Give Jesus a Hand!* 177.

63. Ibid.

64. See Wiegele, *Investing in Miracles.*

65. See David Martin, this volume.

66. See Wiegele, *Investing in Miracles.*

67. Niña Catherine Calleja, "P1B Church of El Shaddai Opens Thursday," *Philippine Daily Inquirer* (20 August 2009).

68. Most units are unsold; College of Divine Wisdom students occupy some units.

69. See Wiegele, *Investing in Miracles*. One might say the shamans have been replaced by priests.

70. See also Bernice Martin, this volume; these contradictions resonate in other charismatic groups.

71. Mike Velarde, personal interview, Manila, 2 August 2010; and Rey Vargas, personal interview, Manila, 22 July 2010.

72. Brother Mariano "Mike" Z. Velarde, *With El Shaddai, Miracles are Forever* (Makati City: El Shaddai Publishing, 2010).

73. Observations of preacher training, and interviews with College of Divine Wisdom students, instructors, and administrators, July–August, 2010.

74. Christian V. Esguerra, "Velarde Opens El Shaddai Church," *Philippine Daily Inquirer* (21 August 2009).

75. Mike Velarde, personal interview, 2 August 2010, El Shaddai Ministries, Makati City, Philippines.

76. Rey Vargas, personal interview, July 2010, College of Divine Wisdom, Parañaque City, Philippines.

77. The Pentecostal group, Jesus Is Lord, for example, started its own school in 1983.

78. Evelyn Macairan, "Bro. Mike names heir to El Shaddai Ministry," *Asian Journal* (28 Aug.–3 Sept. 2009).

79. Malig, "WikiLeaks: US Sees El Shaddai, INC as 'Kingmakers.'"

80. Willie Villarma, personal communication, July–August 2010, Manila.

81. Fieldnotes, July–August 2010, interviews of rally-goers, preachers, and preachers-in-training.

82. Juliet Labog-Javellana, "Catholic Church Urged to Name Bets," *Philippine Daily Inquirer* (13 March 2007).

83. Allison Lopez, "Bro. Mike Says Bishop Misunderstood Him," *Philippine Daily Inquirer* (20 March 2007).

84. Ninotchka Rosaka, "Filipinas Choose Choice," published on *Truthout* (http://www.truth-out.org) (7 March 2011) and Msmagazine.com (7 March 2011).

85. Moreno, *Church, State, and Civil Society in Postauthoritarian Philippines,* 73–78.

86. Bernice Martin, this volume. The re-moralization of body happens in other ways, too; for example, a Buhay-sponsored bill against the sale of sex toys, and Buhay support for increased film and billboard censorship.

87. On the gender bargain, see *The Reformation of Machismo* and Bernice Martin, this volume.

88. See David Maxwell's discussion in this volume of middle-class Pentecostals in Zimbabwe who seek an increasingly sophisticated theological presentation.

89. Other successful born-again leaders have made this mistake: see David Maxwell, this volume, and Paul Freston, *Evangelicals and Politics in Asia, Africa, and Latin America* (Cambridge: Cambridge University Press, 2001).

PETER L. BERGER

The completion of the project, the results of which are incorporated in this volume, gives me very great pleasure. I have been fascinated by Pentecostalism for many years (despite the fact that it has no personal attraction for me—it seems that I am incurably Lutheran). I first stumbled across the phenomenon when I was doing fieldwork for my master's thesis about religion among Puerto Rican migrants to New York City, and even then I was impressed by the dynamism of this religious movement. Since its founding in 1985, the Institute on Culture, Religion, and World Affairs (CURA), our research center at Boston University, has been engaged in studies of Pentecostalism in various countries, first in Latin America, then elsewhere. CURA supported David Martin's pioneering work, and both he and Bernice Martin have been valued interlocutors ever since. In the mid-1980s a research interest in Pentecostalism seemed somewhat odd in academic circles. The amazing global explosion of this religious movement has changed this, and in recent years a veritable cottage industry of Pentecostal scholarship has grown up. I believe that the present book constitutes a useful contribution to this body of knowledge: We now know a good deal about the roots of Pentecostalism among poor people in the throes of rapid social change, not to mention what happens when many Pentecostals are no longer poor, or when people who were never very poor at all join the movement. There still are marginal people clinging to their church as to a raft in a stormy sea, such as David Martin encountered when he began his research in Santiago de Chile. But now there are also the "boss Christians" in China described so vividly by Nanlai Cao, as there are the television-savvy entrepreneurs of the Universal Church of the Kingdom of God in Brazil. The chapters in this book provide instructive insights into the relatively new development of middle-class Pentecostalism.

Robert Hefner's introduction gives an excellent overview of the present state of Pentecostal scholarship. I fully agree with his analysis. I will only make some observations on currently debated issues.

Pentecostalism and the Protestant Ethic: Is Pentecostalism a new version of the Protestant ethic, which Max Weber saw as an important factor in the genesis of modern capitalism? David Martin first raised this issue, especially when he compared Pentecostalism today with the earlier role of Methodism and other free-church forms of Protestantism. Martin is a cautious scholar, and he never insisted on the parallel (I was less cautious). A number of the contributors here are skeptical about the Weberian analogy. I now think that the debate has been too narrowly concerned with economic production—that is, with the question of whether the Protestant morality of "inner-worldly asceticism" continues today to foster rational habits of work and eventual social mobility. There is also the question of a Protestant style of consumption. The two questions are related: If people behave in the way their preachers tell them to (obviously not all do), and if their social and economic environment provides opportunities, social mobility will indeed ensue—and with it an enhanced ability to consume. Martin early on discussed the Pentecostal domestication of men, moving them from the street to the kitchen, and thus into the bosom of nascent bourgeois family life. Bernice Martin has called this "the Pentecostal gender bargain": The women (graciously, and perhaps wisely) allow the men to strut around as preachers and public leaders, while the women take control of missionary work, healing ministries, and (most important) the household.

If one wants to ponder whether Pentecostalism is indeed (in Hefner's phrase) "the unexpected modern," it is equally important to look at its effect on the workplace and on private life. As Brigitte Berger has argued in a number of works, most fully in *The Family in the Modern Age* (2002), the bourgeois family is to be understood not just as an effect of modernization but as one of the latter's causal factors.[1] Thus it makes a great difference whether a breadwinner consumes his weekly earnings on getting drunk in a brothel or at home having dinner with his family. The affinity of Pentecostalism with the bourgeois family persists through social mobility, from the favela to the middle-class suburb. There is a distinctively bourgeois morality of consumption. Its original emergence in Europe has been documented by Colin Campbell in his *The Romantic Ethic and the Spirit of Modern Consumerism* (1987).[2] Thus I would answer in the affirmative whether Pentecostalism resembles the trajectory of the Protestant ethic in the earlier modern history of Europe and North America.

Pentecostalism and the Prosperity Gospel: As Hefner points out, a major alternative to a Weberian view of the empirical consequences of Pentecostalism is to see it as a replication of the so-called cargo cult that swept through South Pacific islands around the turn of the twentieth century: Charismatic preachers prophesized that ships (later it was airplanes) would soon come and bring to their faithful flocks all the good things of modernity. The prosperity gospel, which has become prominent not only among Pentecostals but in the broader Evangelical community, asserts that if you have faith and contribute financially to the church, God will make you rich. Critics of Pentecostalism have portrayed its preachers as corrupt exploiters of mostly poor people. Are there such Pentecostal preachers? I am sure there are. There are Catholic priests who engage in sexual abuse, which does not lead to a view of the Catholic Church as fostering lechery. The most reliable estimates of the worldwide number of Pentecostal or charismatic Christians (the two terms are essentially synonymous) hover around a figure of 600 million. I would take it for granted that both groups will be found in this huge population—let us call them neo-Puritans and quasi-Melanesians: Those who work hard for the modern "cargo," and those who sit back and wait for the goodies to fall from heaven. As an empirical social scientist, I will assume that the quasi-Melanesians will be disappointed. Not so the neo-Puritans—the prosperity gospel understood on their terms is not an empty promise, but a plausible prediction. It will not necessarily make them rich, but it will lead to what the Martins have called "betterment." Another point in this connection: It is not necessary that all Pentecostals act in a neo-Weberian fashion for their religion to have social and economic consequences—these will occur even if only a minority of Pentecostals so act. Vanguards have often brought about significant change.

Conversion as personal transformation: Hefner refers to David Maxwell and Frederick Klaits (who studied Pentecostalism in Botswana); he quotes an individual from Maxwell's study who describes the self-image resulting from his conversion in the following words—"I am not a nobody, but a somebody." Bernice Martin makes the same point with regard to Pentecostal women. Rebecca Shah (not in this volume but elsewhere) tells the touching story of a Dalit ("Untouchable") convert rebuked by an upper-caste shopkeeper for having put his unclean hands on some merchandise.[3] The convert replied: "I am not unclean. God has made me clean." A major result of a CURA study of Pentecostalism in South Africa was the surge of self-esteem and confidence about the future resulting from conversion. This transformation is significant in itself in empowering individuals to cope with the challenges of modernization. But it points to a more basic reason why Pentecostalism is a modernizing force: its relation to individuation.

In this connection it is useful to place Pentecostalism in the larger frame of Protestantism. The Protestant Reformation, in its theological legitimation of individual conscience, was an important factor (inadvertently, for sure) in the genesis of modern individualism: There is the icon of Luther standing before the Diet of Worms—"Here I stand, I can do no other" (never mind that he probably did not speak these exact words—the meaning was there). As is always the case with ideas, they interact with nonideational factors— technological, demographic, economic, political. Today individualism as an ideology has a strong affinity with all the nonideational forces of moderniza- tion, which serve to diminish the traditional embedment of the individual in stable collective identities. Inevitably, this throws the individual back on his own resources. I have described modernization as a gigantic transition from fate to choice in the human condition. Of course human beings, who are pro- foundly social by nature, will always need collectivities to sustain their iden- tity and worldview. But now these very collectivities are much less taken for granted; they too must be chosen. Thus the voluntary association becomes a primary modern institution (more so, of course, if freedom of association is legally protected).

Pentecostalism is an offspring of the particular variant of Protestantism commonly called Evangelical. Evangelicalism emerged historically from what David Martin has nicely called the "Amsterdam-London-Boston bourgeois axis." Its typical institutional form early on became the church as a volun- tary association. At the heart of its piety is an act of individual decision. All versions of Evangelicalism insist that one cannot be born as a Christian; one must be born again to be a Christian—in the words of American revivalism, one must come forward and "accept Jesus as one's personal lord and savior." As far as I know, Evangelical Protestantism is the only major religion which, at the core of its piety, insists on an act of personal decision. It is for this reason that I have proposed that Evangelicalism is the most modern faith in the world today. (Never mind that some Evangelicals have this or that prob- lem with biological or historical science). Pentecostalism is Evangelicalism with some add-ons—such as the gifts of the Spirit added to the born-again experience. It shares with its Evangelical parent the insistence on individ- ual choice. Accordingly I would assert that, well beyond any strictly neo- Weberian effects, Pentecostalism is a modernizing force. Most of Christianity in the global south is strongly charismatic, "Pentecostalizing" if not overtly Pentecostal (even among Filipino Catholics, as the chapter by Katharine Wiegele shows). Thus the modernizing significance of Pentecostalism cannot be emphasized enough. This also goes a long way to explain its great attrac- tion in developing societies. It provides a distinctive individualism, allowed to express itself while at the time it is supported by very strong communities. That is a very powerful package indeed.

The capacity to operate in multiple discourses: One of the important features of modernity is institutional differentiation—as between the family and education, the polity and the economy, the church from all of these. Each of these institutions engenders a specific discourse. One of the key insights of the sociology of knowledge is that every institution has its correlate in consciousness. For an individual to navigate effectively in a modern or modernizing environment, he must have the capacity to handle different discourses, not only in society but within his own mind. This is an important facet of the relation between Pentecostalism and modernity; it is commonly unperceived by those who see Pentecostalism as a counter-modern reaction, steeped in magic or superstition.

Can one simultaneously believe in healing miracles and in the efficacy of modern medicine? The empirical answer is an emphatic yes. Tanya Luhrmann's recent anthropological study of the Vineyard Fellowship, an American charismatic movement with its origins in the California counterculture, gives strong support to the above answer.[4] Presumably human beings have always been able to operate with different relevancies; for example, a physical object may be relevant as a weapon; it may also be perceived as beautiful. The mind can switch from a utilitarian to an aesthetic relevancy, and back again. Modernity builds on this capacity and greatly expands its range. There is no reason to think that religious relevancy is an exception to this. As Luhrmann nicely illustrates, one does not have to travel to Africa to see this phenomenon in full bloom: It is very instructive that the Sun Belt, an especially dynamic region of the U.S. economy, significantly overlaps with the Bible Belt. The gifts of the Spirit can be experienced in air-conditioned comfort.

Present and future importance: Matched only by resurgent Islam, Pentecostalism is one of the two most impressive religious phenomena in the contemporary world. Of course the two have different qualities and consequences, but both are important if we are to understand today's world. Their future is equally important. Social scientists have learned to shy away from predictions, as Paul Freston reminds us in his chapter. Yet when Freston (cautiously) suggests a future "historicity of Pentecostalism," he is probably on safe ground. This need not mean that a new generation of Pentecostals will become irreligious or move to other faiths. More likely is a move toward a more sedate Evangelicalism, which is exactly what has happened in the United States.

Some twenty years ago James Davison Hunter undertook the research among American Evangelicals that led to his book *Evangelicalism: The Coming Generation.*[5] He predicted a gradual secularization to take place within this community. He had good reasons for thinking this, as his data showed young Evangelicals moving away from some of the rigors of the "old-time religion."

What has happened since then is something rather complicated. Social mobility and higher education have modified the shape of Evangelical piety, generally in a more sedate direction. James Baldwin's first novel, *Go Tell it on the Mountain* (1953), provides a moving portrait of how an early move in this direction affected the life of a charismatic African American preacher.[6] However, American Evangelicalism has retained a robustly conservative piety, but in addition it has become more culturally sophisticated and politically assertive. A very interesting part of this has been the emergence of an increasingly self-confident Evangelical intelligentsia, not only in a network of Evangelical colleges, theological schools, and publications, but now visibly penetrating secular academia. (There is a curious similarity here with the way American Jews broke through the barriers that had previously kept them out of elite institutions.) The same development can now be observed among Pentecostals, both in America and in the global south. At this moment there are no indications that this development will be reversed.

Should this matter to anyone who is not personally or professionally interested in Pentecostalism? It should. One of the most important political questions in the world today is how a modern society can and should relate to religion. Shmuel Eisenstadt has coined the very helpful concept of "multiple modernities." Modernity does not come in one single package, originally put together in Europe. What could be an Islamic modernity? A modernity with Chinese characteristics? (Chinese intellectuals were fervently debating this in the late nineteenth century; the Japanese around the same time showed how something like this could be done.) What is the place of Hinduism in Indian democracy? Of Judaism in Israel? Can the Russian Orthodox Church adapt to religious pluralism? With the possible exception of Europe, all over the world today a secular discourse (Charles Taylor called it the "immanent frame") coexists with a variety of fervently held religious discourses.[7] Evangelicals in general and Pentecostals in particular show that such coexistence can be managed, personally as well as politically. This should also matter to those of us who have no inclination to speak in tongues.

NOTES

1. Brigitte Berger, *The Family in the Modern Age: More Than a Lifestyle Choice* (New Brunswick: Transaction, 2002).

2. Colin Campbell, *The Romantic Ethic and the Spirit of Modern Consumerism* (Oxford: Blackwell, 1987).

3. Rebecca Samuel Shah and Timothy Samuel Shah, "How Evangelicalism—Including Pentecostalism—Helps the Poor: The Role of Spiritual Capital," in *The*

Hidden Form of Capital: Spiritual Influences in Societal Progress, ed. Peter L. Berger and Gordon Redding (New York: Anthem Press, 2011), 61–90.

4. Tanya Luhrmann, *When God Talks Back* (New York: Alfred A. Knopf, 2012).

5. James Davison Hunter, *Evangelicalism: The Coming Generation* (Chicago: University of Chicago Press, 1987).

6. James Baldwin, *Go Tell It on the Mountain* (New York: Dell Publishing, 1981).

7. Charles Taylor, *A Secular Age* (Cambridge, MA: Harvard University Press, 2007).

CONTRIBUTORS

PETER L. BERGER is one of the twentieth century's most celebrated sociologists of religion; he is Professor of Sociology and Theology Emeritus at Boston University; the founding director of the Institute on Culture, Religion, and World Affairs; and the author of more than twenty books on religion, society, and modernity.

NANLAI CAO is Associate Professor of Anthropology at the Hong Kong Institute for Humanities and Social Sciences at the University of Hong Kong and the author of the first in-depth ethnography of Protestant Christians in China, *Constructing China's Jerusalem: Christians, Power, and Place in Contemporary Wenzhou.*

PAUL FRESTON is Professor and CIGI Chair in Religion and Politics in Global Context, Balsillie School of International Affairs, Wilfrid Laurier University, and the author of numerous books on Pentecostalism and Evangelicalism, including *Evangelicals and Politics in Asia, Africa and Latin America* and *Evangelical Christianity and Democracy in Latin America.*

ROBERT W. HEFNER is Director of the Institute on Culture, Religion, and World Affairs at Boston University and the author or editor of eighteen books on religion and politics, including *Shari'a Politics: Islamic Law and Society in the Modern World* (Indiana University Press, 2011) and *Muslims and Modernity: Society and Culture Since 1800.*

CHRISTOPHER MARSH is Professor of Russian and Eurasian Affairs at the U.S. Air Force Special Operations School and the author of several books on religion in Russia, including, *Religion and the State in Russia and China: Repression, Survival, and Revival.*

BERNICE MARTIN is Emeritus Reader in Sociology at London University and the author of numerous works on religion, gender, and modernity, including the now classic "The Pentecostal Gender Paradox: A Cautionary Tale for the Sociology of Religion."

DAVID MARTIN is Emeritus Professor of Sociology at the London School of Economics and the author of numerous books, including *Pentecostalism: The World Their Parish* and *The Future of Christianity*.

DAVID MAXWELL is Dixie Professor of Ecclesiastical History at Cambridge University and the author of many works on African Pentecostalism, including *African Gifts of the Spirit: Pentecostalism and the Rise of a Zimbabwean Transnational Religious Movement*.

REBECCA SAMUEL SHAH is a Fellow with the Oxford Centre for Religion and Public Life, a Research Associate with the Belief in Enterprise Project at Cambridge University, and the Principal Investigator for a Templeton Foundation project, "Tithing and Thrift among the Enterprising Poor in India."

TIMOTHY SAMUEL SHAH is Associate Director and Scholar in Residence at the Religious Freedom Project, Berkley Center for Religion, Peace, and World Affairs at Georgetown University, and the author or editor of several books on religion and world affairs, including *God's Century: Resurgent Religion and Global Politics* (with Monica Duffy Toft and Daniel Philpott).

ARTYOM TONOYAN is a Ph.D. candidate in the Program in Religion, Politics, and Society at Baylor University, where he is finishing a dissertation on religion, nationalism, and violence in the South Caucasus.

KATHARINE L. WIEGELE is Adjunct Assistant Professor of Anthropology at Northern Illinois University and the author of *Investing in Miracles: El Shaddai and the Transformation of Popular Catholicism in the Philippines*.

INDEX

Crumbley, Deirdre, 130
Csordas, Thomas, 145n82
Cucchiari, Salvatore, 11, 125, 129
Cultural Revolution (China), 47, 51, 57, 135, 153
culture wars, 122, 125, 128

Dalit ("untouchable" caste, India), 11, 25, 47, 124, 131, 195, 197, 201–202, 218, 220, 253; government aid programs to, 218; patron goddess of, 205, 212. *See also* India; women
Davis, Mike, 109–110
decommitment, religious, 28, 65, 72. *See also* secularism
democratization, 59, 106, 186; Pentecostalism as school for, 91. *See also* civil society; Pentecostalism; politics, state-centered
D'Épinay, Lalive, 20, 32n51, 68–69
developmental tensions, viii, 3, 4, 5, 9, 11, 17, 29n6, 223, 237, 245–246; Pentecostal growth and, viii, 3, 9, 63–64, 141n2; subjective piety vs. mass politics, 17
Dhinakaran, D. G. S. (Tamil mission leader), 198
dividuality, 132–133, 139. *See also* individuation
Divya Shanthi Christian Association (India), 202–203, 215, 218
domininionist theology, 26
Duflo, Esther, 217

Edinburgh Missionary conference, 40
education, 8, 12, 27, 99, 101, 150, 210, 228; class and, 80, 81, 165, 203; Islamic, 36n121
education, higher: correlation with Pentecostal affiliation, 80–81, 186; impact on religious conviction, 27, 74, 78–79, 81, 256; Pentecostal and charismatic attitudes toward, 10, 41–42, 81–82, 95, 101, 102, 203, 204, 208, 241
Eisenstadt, Shmuel, 120, 122, 142n24, 256. *See also* modernity

El Shaddai (Philippines), 8, 16–17, 23, 39, 56–57, 130; apolitical view of inequality, 223, 233; class composition, 224; doctrines, 225–226, 232–233; educational programs, 237, 238, 239, 241–242; mass rallies, 234–235, 237; membership, 223, 247n1; new pastoral programs, 239–240; opposition to contraception and abortion, 244–245; organizational ties to Catholic Church, 240–241; origins, 224–226; patriarchal gender bargain, 245; political differences with Catholic Church, 236, 241–243; political involvements, 17, 225, 234, 235, 242–243; prohibition of female preachers, 240; prosperity ethic, 23, 223, 226–227; women, as proportion of membership, 245
Elish, Omri, 36n119
Engelke, Matthew, 10, 31n27, 44
Enlightenment, 58, 124, 132, 256
Estrada, Joseph, 17, 236, 242
ethical subject formation: centrality in Pentecostalism, 9, 110; implications for state-oriented politics, 15, 19, 86–87; for men, 10. *See also* individuation; masculinity; women
Europe, 44, 52, 67, 69, 107, 252; modernity and, 44, 58, 120, 256; Pentecostal weakness in, 6, 52, 116; as religiously "backslidden," 107. *See also* individuation; modernity; secularization
Evangelicalism: in China, 151, 154; contrast with Pentecostalism, 66, 151, 254; development of a self-confident intelligentsia, 256; fuzzy borders with Pentecostalism, 33n68; gender dynamics, 126; mission dynamics, 51, 55; Moral Majority (U.S.), 53; as most modern religion, 91, 254; Pentecostal origins in, 254; Pentecostal shift

www.ingramcontent.com/pod-product-compliance
Lightning Source LLC
Chambersburg PA
CBHW020843270326
41928CB00006B/525